A Commentary on the Book of Hebrews

ANDREW
MURRAY

Holiest of All

WHITAKER
HOUSE

Publisher's note:
Andrew Murray's selection of Bible versions has been retained whenever possible, including the Revised Version, as he originally cited it. However, the text of this new edition from Whitaker House has been updated for the modern reader. Words, expressions, and sentence structure have been revised for clarity and readability.

Unless otherwise indicated, all Scripture quotations are taken from the Revised Version of the Holy Bible. Scripture quotations marked (KJV) are taken from the King James Version of the Holy Bible.

THE HOLIEST OF ALL

ISBN: 978-0-88368-523-5 • eBook ISBN: 978-1-60374-817-9
Printed in the United States of America
© 1996, 2004 by Whitaker House

Whitaker House
1030 Hunt Valley Circle
New Kensington, PA 15068
www.whitakerhouse.com

Library of Congress Cataloging-in-Publication Data

Murray, Andrew, 1828–1917.
The holiest of all / Andrew Murray.—Updated ed.
   p.   cm.
ISBN 0-88368-523-X (trade pbk.: alk. paper)
1. Bible. N.T. Hebrews—Commentaries. I. Title.
BS2775.53.M87 2004
227'.87077—dc22
                                    2004006635

5 6 7 8 9 10 11 12 13 14 15 **ω** 24 23 22 21 20 19 18 17 16

Holiest
of All

Contents

FIRST HALF—DOCTRINAL—HEBREWS 1:1–10:18
THE SON OF GOD: THE MEDIATOR *Intercessor*
OF THE BETTER COVENANT *Go Between*
Peace maker

The Theme—Hebrews 1:1–3
The Glory of the Son in His Person and Work

First Section—Hebrews 1:4–14
The Son of God More than the Angels

The First Warning—Hebrews 2:1–4
To Take Heed to What the Son Speaks *It's Better speaking!!!*

Second Section—Hebrews 2:5–18
Jesus as Man More than the Angels:
The Reasons of His Humiliation

go to the aid of relieve

Third Section—Hebrews 3:1–6
Christ Jesus More than Moses

The Second Warning—Hebrews 3:7–4:13
Not to Come Short of the Promised Rest

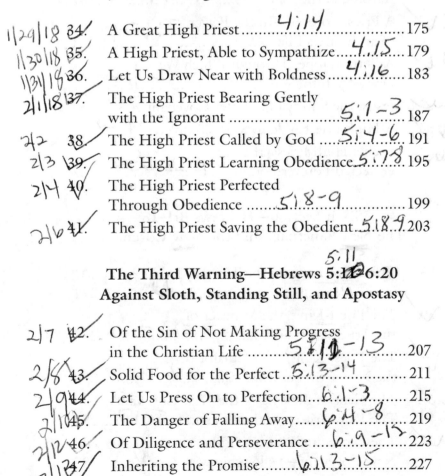

Fourth Section—Hebrews 4:14–5:10 *9*
Jesus Our High Priest More than Aaron

The Third Warning—Hebrews 5:11 *5:11* 6:20
Against Sloth, Standing Still, and Apostasy

Fifth Section—Hebrews 7:1-28
The New Priesthood After the Order of Melchizedek

Sixth Section—Hebrews 8:1-13
The New Sanctuary and the New Covenant

Father
Son
Spirit

SECOND HALF—PRACTICAL
HEBREWS 10:19–13:25
THE CALL TO A LIFE IN HARMONY WITH THE GLORY OF GOD'S REVELATION OF HIMSELF IN THE SON

Ninth Section—10:19–25
Of Life in the Holiest of All

First Fruits! O Happy Day!

The Fourth Warning—Hebrews 10:26–39
Of Those Who Sin Willfully and Draw Back

KT+w coming!

The Fifth Warning—Hebrews 12:14–29
Against the Rejection of God's Son

Twelfth Section—Hebrews 13:1–25
Love and Good Works

LOVE

10/23/17

10/27/17

Preface

When I first undertook the preparation of this exposition in Dutch for the Christian people I labor among, it was under a deep conviction that the epistle of Hebrews contained just the instruction they needed. In reproducing it in English, this impression has been confirmed, and it is as if nothing could be written more exactly suited to the state of the whole church of Christ in the present day. The great complaint of all who have the care of souls is the lack of wholeheartedness, of steadfastness, of perseverance, and of progress in the Christian life. Many—of whom one cannot but hope that they are true Christians—come to a standstill and do not advance beyond the rudiments of Christian life and practice. And many more do not even remain stationary but rather turn back to a life of worldliness, formality, and indifference. And the question is continually being asked, "What is the need in our religion so that, in so many cases, it gives no power to stand, to advance, and to press on to perfection?" And what teaching is needed to give that health and vigor to the Christian life in order that, through all adverse circumstances, it may hold fast from the beginning, firm until the end?

The teaching of the epistle of Hebrews is the divine answer to these questions. In every possible way, it sets before us the truth that only the full and perfect knowledge of who Christ is and what He does for us can bring us to a full and perfect Christian life. The knowledge of Christ Jesus that we need for conversion does not suffice for growth, for progress, for sanctification, and for maturity. Just as there are two dispensations—the Old Testament and the New—and just as the saints of the Old, with all their faith and fear of God, could not obtain the more perfect life of the New, so it is with the two stages in the Christian life of which this epistle speaks. Those who, through sloth, remain babes in Christ and do not press on to maturity are ever in danger of hardening their hearts, of coming short, and of falling away. Only those who hold fast from the beginning, firm until the end; who give diligence to enter the rest of Christ; and who press on to perfection do, in very deed, inherit and enjoy the wonderful new covenant blessings secured for us in Christ. And the great objective of the epistle is to show us that if we will only follow the Lord fully and yield ourselves wholly to what God, in Christ, is ready to do, we will find, in the Gospel and in Christ, everything we need for a life of joy, strength, and final victory.

The cure the epistle has for all our failures and feebleness— the one preservative from all danger and disease—is the knowledge of the higher truth concerning Jesus, the knowledge of Him in His heavenly priesthood. In connection with this truth, the writer has three great mysteries he seeks to unfold. The first is that the heavenly sanctuary has been opened to us so that we may now come and take our place there, with Jesus, in the very presence of God. The second mystery is that the new and living way by which Jesus has entered—the way of self-sacrifice and perfect obedience to God—is now the way in which we may and must draw near. The third mystery is that Jesus, as our heavenly High Priest, is the Minister of the heavenly sanctuary and dispenses to us its blessings—the spirit and the power of the heavenly life—in such a way that we can live in the world as those who are come to the heavenly Jerusalem and as those in whom the spirit of heaven is the spirit of all life and conduct. In this heavenly priesthood of Jesus, heaven is opened to us day by day, we enter it by the new and living way, and heaven enters by the Holy Spirit. Such is the Gospel to the Hebrews that this epistle brings. Such is the life to which it reveals the way and the strength. The knowledge of the heavenly character of Christ's person and work is what alone can make heavenly

Christians, who, amid all the difficulties and temptations of life on earth, can live as those whom the superior power of the upper world has possessed, and in whom it can always give the victory.

In offering these meditations now to a wider circle of readers, I do so with the prayer that it may please God to use them to inspire some of His children with new confidence in their blessed Lord, as they learn to know Him better and give themselves up to expect and experience all that He is able to do for them. I have not been afraid of continually repeating this one thought: Our one need is to know Jesus better, and the one cure for all our feebleness is to look to Him on the throne of heaven and really claim the heavenly life He waits to impart.

Just as I was about to write the preface to the Dutch issue during the first week of last year, I received from my beloved colleague as a New Year's text—with the wish that it might be my experience—these words: *"Jesus taketh with him Peter, and James, and John, and bringeth them up into an high mountain apart by themselves: and he was transfigured before them"* (Mark 9:2). I at once passed the word on to my readers, and I do so again. May the blessed Master take us "with Himself" into the *"mountain,"* even the Mount Zion, where He sits as Priest King upon the throne in power, each of us "apart by himself." And may He prepare us for the blessed vision of seeing Him "transfigured before us," seeing Him in His heavenly glory. He will then still be to us the same Jesus we know now—and yet, not the same, but rather His whole Being, bright with the glory and the power of the heavenly life that He holds for us and waits to impart day by day to them who forsake all to follow Him.

In humble trust and prayer that it may be so, I commend all my readers to His blessed teaching and guidance.

—Andrew Murray

THE EPISTLE TO
THE HEBREWS

The Epistle to the Hebrews

(Revised Version)

The Knowledge of the Son of God, the Secret of the True Christian Life

[handwritten: the strength]

[handwritten: The Theme: 1:1-3 THE GLORY of the SON (in) HIS PERSON + WORK]

Chapter 1

[handwritten left margin: First section]

[handwritten left margin: 4-14 THE SON OF GOD MORE THAN THE ANGELS]

¹God, having of old time spoken unto the fathers in the prophets by divers portions and in divers manners,

²Hath at the end of these days spoken unto us in his Son, whom he appointed heir of all things, through whom also he made the worlds;

³Who being the effulgence of his glory, and the very image of his substance, and upholding all things by the word of his power, when he had made purification of sins, sat down on the right hand of the Majesty on high;

⁴Having become by so much better than the angels, as he hath inherited a more excellent name than they.

⁵For unto which of the angels said he at any time,

Thou art my Son,
This day have I begotten thee?

and again,

I will be to him a Father,
And he shall be to me a Son?

⁶And when he again bringeth in the firstborn into the world he saith,

And let all the angels of God worship him.

⁷And of the angels he saith,

Who maketh his angels winds,
And his ministers a flame of fire:

⁸But of the Son he saith,

Thy throne, O God, is for ever and ever;
And the sceptre of uprightness is the sceptre of thy kingdom.

⁹Thou hast loved righteousness, and hated iniquity;
Therefore God, thy God, hath anointed thee
With the oil of gladness above thy fellows.

¹⁰And,

Thou, Lord, in the beginning hast laid the foundation of the earth,
And the heavens are the works of thy hands:

¹¹They shall perish; but thou continuest:
And they all shall wax old as doth a garment;

¹²And as a mantle shalt thou roll them up,
As a garment, and they shall be changed:
But thou art the same,
And thy years shall not fail.

¹³But of which of the angels hath he said at any time,

Sit thou on my right hand,
Till I make thine enemies the footstool of thy feet?

¹⁴Are they not all ministering spirits, sent forth to do service for the sake of them that shall inherit salvation?

To Take Heed to what the Son speaks

THE FIRST WARNING

Chapter 2

[1]Therefore we ought to give the more earnest heed to the things that were heard, lest haply we drift away from them.

[2]For if the word spoken through angels proved stedfast, and every transgression and disobedience received a just recompense of reward;

[3]How shall we escape, if we neglect so great salvation? which having at the first been spoken through the Lord, was confirmed unto us by them that heard;

[4]God also bearing witness with them, both by signs and wonders, and by manifold powers, and by gifts of the Holy Ghost, according to his own will.

Second section. 5-18

[5]For not unto angels did he subject the world to come, whereof we speak.

[6]But one hath somewhere testified, saying,

Jesus as Man more than the angels.

What is man, that thou art mindful of him?
Or the son of man, that thou visitest him?

The Reason of His Humiliation

[7]Thou madest him a little lower than the angels;
Thou crownedst him with glory and honour,
And didst set him over the works of thy hands:

5-8 all things made subject to man, not to angels

[8]Thou didst put all things in subjection under his feet.

For in that he subjected all things unto him, he left nothing that is not subject to him. But now we see not yet all things subjected to him.

man's destiny fulfilled in Jesus

[9]But we behold Him who hath been made a little lower than the angels, even Jesus, because of the suffering of death crowned with glory and honour, that by the grace of God He should taste death for every man.

[10]For it became him, for whom are all things, and through whom are all things, in bringing many sons unto glory, to make the author of their salvation perfect through sufferings.

[11]For both he that sanctifieth and they that are sanctified are all of one: for which cause he is not ashamed to call them brethren,

[12]Saying,

I will declare thy name unto my brethren,
In the midst of the congregation will I sing thy praise.

[13]And again, I will put my trust in him. And again, Behold, I and the children which God hath given me.

[14]Since then the children are sharers in flesh and blood, he also himself in like manner partook of the same; that through death he might bring to nought him that had the power of death, that is, the devil;

[15]And might deliver all them who through fear of death were all their lifetime subject to bondage.

[16]For verily not of angels doth he take hold, but he taketh hold of the seed of Abraham.

[17]Wherefore it behoved him in all things to be made like unto his brethren, that he might be a merciful and faithful high priest in things pertaining to God, to make propitiation for the sins of the people.

[18]For in that he himself hath suffered being tempted, he is able to succour them that are tempted.

Chapter 3

[1]Wherefore, holy brethren, partakers of a heavenly calling, consider the Apostle and High Priest of our confession, even Jesus;

19

²Who was faithful to him that appointed him, as also was Moses in all his house.

³For he hath been counted worthy of more glory than Moses, by so much as he that built the house hath more honour than the house.

⁴For every house is builded by some one; but he that built all things is God.

⁵And Moses indeed was faithful in all his house as a servant, for a testimony of those things which were afterward to be spoken;

⁶But Christ as a son, over his house; whose house are we, if we hold fast our boldness and the glorying of our hope firm unto the end.

⁷Wherefore, even as the Holy Ghost saith,

To-day if ye shall hear his voice,
⁸Harden not your hearts, as in the provocation,
Like as in the day of the temptation in the wilderness,
⁹Wherewith your fathers tempted me by proving me,
And saw my works forty years.
¹⁰Wherefore I was displeased with this generation,
And said, They do alway err in their heart:
But they did not know my ways;
¹¹As I sware in my wrath,
They shall not enter into my rest.

¹²Take heed, brethren, lest haply there shall be in any one of you an evil heart of unbelief, in falling away from the living God:

¹³But exhort one another day by day, so long as it is called To-day; lest any one of you be hardened by the deceitfulness of sin:

¹⁴For we are become partakers of Christ, if we hold fast the beginning of our confidence firm unto the end:

¹⁵While it is said,

To-day if ye shall hear his voice,
Harden not your hearts, as in the provocation.

¹⁶For who, when they heard, did provoke? nay, did not all they that came out of Egypt by Moses?

¹⁷And with whom was he displeased forty years? was it not with them that sinned, whose carcases fell in the wilderness?

¹⁸And to whom sware he that they should not enter into his rest, but to them that were disobedient?

¹⁹And we see that they were not able to enter in because of unbelief.

Chapter 4

¹Let us fear therefore, lest haply, a promise being left of entering into his rest, any one of you should seem to have come short of it.

²For indeed we have had good tidings preached unto us, even as also they: but the word of hearing did not profit them, because they were not united by faith with them that heard.

³For we which have believed do enter into that rest; even as he hath said,

As I sware in my wrath,
They shall not enter into my rest:

although the works were finished from the foundation of the world.

⁴For he hath said somewhere of the seventh day on this wise, And God rested on the seventh day from all his works;

⁵And in this place again,

They shall not enter into my rest.

⁶Seeing therefore it remaineth that some should enter thereinto, and they to whom the good tidings were before preached failed to enter in because of disobedience,

⁷He again defineth a certain day, saying in David, after so long a time, To-day, as it hath been before said,

To-day if ye shall hear his voice,
Harden not your hearts.

⁸For if Joshua had given them rest, he would not have spoken afterward of another day.

⁹There remaineth therefore a sabbath rest for the people of God.

¹⁰For he that is entered into his rest hath himself also rested from his works, as God did from his.

¹¹Let us therefore give diligence to enter into that rest, that no man fall after the same example of disobedience.

¹²For the word of God is living, and active, and sharper than any two edged sword, and piercing even to the dividing of soul and spirit, of both joints and marrow, and quick to discern the thoughts and intents of the heart.

¹³And there is no creature that is not manifest in his sight: but all things are naked and laid open before the eyes of him with whom we have to do.

¹⁴Having then a great high priest, who hath passed through the heavens, Jesus the Son of God, let us hold fast our confession.

¹⁵For we have not a high priest that cannot be touched with the feeling of our infirmities; but one that hath been in all points tempted like as we are, yet without sin.

¹⁶Let us therefore draw near with boldness unto the throne of grace, that we may receive mercy, and may find grace to help us in time of need.

Chapter 5

¹For every high priest, being taken from among men, is appointed for men in things pertaining to God, that he may offer both gifts and sacrifices for sins:

²Who can bear gently with the ignorant and erring, for that he himself also is compassed with infirmity;

³And by reason thereof is bound, as for the people, so also for himself, to offer for sins.

⁴And no man taketh the honour unto himself, but when he is called of God, even as was Aaron.

⁵So Christ also glorified not himself to be made a high priest, but he that spake unto him,

Thou art my Son,
This day have I begotten thee:

⁶As he saith also in another place,

Thou art a priest for ever
After the order of Melchizedek.

⁷Who in the days of his flesh, having offered up prayers and supplications with strong crying and tears unto him that was able to save him from death, and having been heard for his godly fear,

⁸Though he was a Son, yet learned obedience by the things which he suffered;

⁹And having been made perfect, he became unto all them that obey him the author of eternal salvation;

¹⁰Named of God a high priest after the order of Melchizedek.

¹¹Of whom we have many things to say, and hard of interpretation,

seeing ye are become dull of hearing.

¹²For when by reason of the time ye ought to be teachers, ye have need again that some one teach you the rudiments of the first principles of the oracles of God; and are become such as have need of milk, and not of solid food.

¹³For every one that partaketh of milk is without experience of the word of righteousness; for he is a babe.

¹⁴But solid food is for full-grown men, even those who by reason of use have their senses exercised to discern good and evil.

Chapter 6

¹Wherefore let us cease to speak of the first principles of Christ, and press on unto perfection; not laying again a foundation of repentance from dead works, and of faith toward God,

²Of the teaching of baptisms, and of laying on of hands, and of resurrection of the dead, and of eternal judgement.

³And this will we do, if God permit.

⁴For as touching those who were once enlightened and tasted of the heavenly gift, and were made partakers of the Holy Ghost,

⁵And tasted the good word of God, and the powers of the age to come,

⁶And then fell away, it is impossible to renew them again unto repentance; seeing they crucify to themselves the Son of God afresh, and put him to an open shame.

⁷For the land which hath drunk the rain that cometh oft upon it, and bringeth forth herbs meet for them for whose sake it is also tilled, receiveth blessing from God:

⁸But if it beareth thorns and thistles, it is rejected and nigh unto a curse; whose end is to be burned.

⁹But, beloved, we are persuaded better things of you, and things that accompany salvation, though we thus speak:

¹⁰For God is not unrighteous to forget your work and the love which ye shewed toward his name, in that ye ministered unto the saints, and still do minister.

¹¹And we desire that each one of you may shew the same diligence unto the fulness of hope even to the end:

¹²That ye be not sluggish, but imitators of them who through faith and patience inherit the promises.

¹³For when God made promise to Abraham, since he could swear by none greater, he sware by himself,

¹⁴Saying, Surely blessing I will bless thee, and multiplying I will multiply thee.

¹⁵And thus, having patiently endured, he obtained the promise.

¹⁶For men swear by the greater: and in every dispute of theirs the oath is final for confirmation.

¹⁷Wherein God, being minded to shew more abundantly unto the heirs of the promise the immutability of his counsel, interposed with an oath:

¹⁸That by two immuatable things, in which it is impossible for God to lie, we may have a strong encouragement, who have fled for refuge to lay hold of the hope set before us;

¹⁹Which we have as an anchor of the soul, a hope both sure and stedfast and entering into that which is within the veil;

²⁰Whither as a forerunner Jesus entered for us, having become a high priest for ever after the order of Melchizedek.

Chapter 7

¹For this Melchizedek, king of Salem, priest of God Most High, who met Abraham returning from the slaughter of the kings, and blessed him,

²To whom also Abraham divided a tenth part of all (being first, by interpretation, King of righteousness, and then also King of Salem, which is, King of peace;

³Without father, without mother, without genealogy, having neither beginning of days nor end of life, but made like unto the Son of God), abideth a priest continually.

⁴Now consider how great this man was, unto whom Abraham, the patriarch, gave a tenth out of the chief spoils.

⁵And they indeed of the sons of Levi that receive the priest's office have commandment to take tithes of the people according to the law, that is, of their brethren, though these have come out of the loins of Abraham:

⁶But he whose genealogy is not counted from them hath taken tithes of Abraham, and hath blessed him that hath the promises.

⁷But without any dispute the less is blessed of the better.

⁸And here men that die receive tithes; but there one, of whom it is witnessed that he liveth.

⁹And, so to say, through Abraham even Levi, who received tithes, hath paid tithes;

¹⁰For he was yet in the loins of his father, when Melchizedek met him.

¹¹Now if there was perfection through the Levitical priesthood (for under it hath the people received the law), what further need was there that another priest should arise after the order of Melchizedek, and not be reckoned after the order of Aaron?

¹²For the priesthood being changed, there is made of necessity a change also of the law.

¹³For he of whom these things are said belongeth to another tribe, from which no man hath given attendance at the altar.

¹⁴For it is evident that our Lord hath sprung out of Judah; as to which tribe Moses spake nothing concerning priests.

¹⁵And what we say is yet more abundantly evident, if after the likeness of Melchizedek there ariseth another priest,

¹⁶Who hath been made, not after the law of a carnal commandment, but after the power of an endless life:

¹⁷For it is witnessed of him,

Thou art a priest for ever
After the order of Melchizedek.

¹⁸For there is a disannulling of a foregoing commandment because of its weakness and unprofitableness

¹⁹(For the law made nothing perfect), and a bringing in thereupon of a better hope, through which we draw nigh unto God.

²⁰And inasmuch as it is not without the taking of an oath

²¹(For they indeed have been made priests without an oath; but he with an oath by him that saith of him,

The Lord sware and will not repent himself,
Thou art a priest for ever);

²²By so much also hath Jesus become the surety of a better covenant.

²³And they indeed have been made priests many in number, because that by death they are hindered from continuing:

²⁴But he, because he abideth for ever, hath his priesthood unchangeable.

²⁵Wherefore also he is able to save to the uttermost them that draw near unto God through him, seeing he ever liveth to make intercession for them.

²⁶For such a high priest became us, holy, guileless, undefiled, separated from sinners, and made higher than the heavens;

²⁷Who needeth not daily, like those high priests, to offer up sacrifices, first for his own sins, and then for the sins of the people: for this he did once for all, when he offered up himself.

²⁸For the law appointeth men high priests, having infirmity; but the word of the oath, which was after the law, appointeth a Son, perfected for evermore.

Chapter 8

¹Now in the things which we are saying the chief point is this: We have such a high priest, who sat down on the right hand of the throne of the Majesty in the heavens,

²A minister of the sanctuary, and of the true tabernacle, which the Lord pitched, not man.

³For every high priest is appointed to offer both gifts and sacrifices: wherefore it is necessary that this high priest also have somewhat to offer.

⁴Now if he were on earth, he would not be a priest at all, seeing there are those who offer the gifts according to the law;

⁵Who serve that which is a copy and shadow of the heavenly things, even as Moses is warned of God when he is about to make the tabernacle: for, See, saith he, that thou make all things according to the pattern that was shewed thee in the mount.

⁶But now hath he obtained a ministry the more excellent, by how much also he is the mediator of a better covenant, which hath been enacted upon better promises.

⁷For if that first covenant had been faultless, then would no place have been sought for a second.

⁸For finding fault with them, he saith,

Behold, the days come, saith the Lord,
That I will make a new covenant with the house of Israel and with the house of Judah;
⁹Not according to the covenant that I made with their fathers
In the day that I took them by the hand to lead them forth out of the land of Egypt;
For they continued not in my covenant,
And I regarded them not, saith the Lord.
¹⁰For this is the covenant that I will make with the house of Israel
After those days, saith the Lord;
I will put my laws into their mind,
And on their heart also will I write them:
And I will be to them a God,

And they shall be to me a people:

[11]And they shall not teach every man his fellow-citizen, And every man his brother, saying, Know the Lord: For all shall know me, From the least to the greatest of them.

[12]For I will be merciful to their iniquities.

And their sins will I remember no more.

[13]In that he saith, A new covenant, he hath made the first old. But that which is becoming old and waxeth aged is nigh unto vanishing away.

Chapter 9

[1]Now even the first covenant had ordinances of divine service, and its sanctuary, a sanctuary of this world.

[2]For there was a tabernacle prepared, the first, wherein were the candlestick, and the table, and the shewbread; which is called the Holy place.

[3]And after the second veil, the tabernacle which is called the Holy of the holies;

[4]Having a golden censer, and the ark of the covenant overlaid round about with gold, wherein was a golden pot holding the manna, and Aaron's rod that budded, and the tables of the covenant;

[5]And above it cherubim of glory overshadowing the mercy-seat; of which things we cannot now speak severally.

[6]Now these things having been thus prepared, the priests go in continually into the first tabernacle, accomplishing the services;

[7]But into the second the high priest alone, once in the year, not without blood, which he offereth for himself, and for the errors of the people:

[8]The Holy Ghost this signifying, that the way into the holy place hath not yet been made manifest, while as the first tabernacle is yet standing;

[9]Which is a parable for the time now present; according to which are offered both gifts and sacrifices that cannot, as touching the conscience, make the worshipper perfect,

[10]Being only (with meats and drinks and divers washings) carnal ordinances, imposed until a time of reformation.

[11]But Christ having come a high priest of the good things to come, through the greater and more perfect tabernacle, not made with hands, that is to say, not of this creation,

[12]Nor yet through the blood of goats and calves, but through his own blood, entered in once for all into the holy place, having obtained eternal redemption.

[13]For if the blood of goats and bulls, and the ashes of a heifer sprinkling them that have been defiled, sanctify unto the cleanness of the flesh:

[14]How much more shall the blood of Christ, who through the eternal Spirit offered himself without blemish unto God, cleanse your conscience from dead works to serve the living God?

[15]And for this cause he is the mediator of a new covenant, that a death having taken place for the redemption of the transgressions

that were under the first covenant, they that have been called may receive the promise of the eternal inheritance.

¹⁶For where a testament is, there must of necessity be the death of him that made it.

¹⁷For a testament is of force where there hath been death: for doth it ever avail while he that made it liveth?

¹⁸Wherefore even the first covenant hath not been dedicated without blood.

¹⁹For when every commandment had been spoken by Moses unto all the people according to the law, he took the blood of the calves and the goats, with water and scarlet wool and hyssop, and sprinkled both the book itself, and all the people,

²⁰Saying, This is the blood of the covenant which God commanded to you-ward.

²¹Moreover the tabernacle and all the vessels of the ministry he sprinkled in like manner with the blood.

²²And according to the law, I may almost say, all things are cleansed with blood, and apart from shedding of blood there is no remission.

²³It was necessary therefore that the copies of the things in the heavens should be cleansed with these; but the heavenly things themselves with better sacrifices than these.

²⁴For Christ entered not into a holy place made with hands, like in pattern to the true; but into heaven itself, now to appear before the face of God for us:

²⁵Nor yet that he should offer himself often; as the high priest entereth into the holy place year by year with blood not his own;

²⁶Else must he often have suffered since the foundation of the world: but now once at the end of the ages hath he been manifested to put away sin by the sacrifice of himself.

²⁷And inasmuch as it is appointed unto men once to die, and after this cometh judgement;

²⁸So Christ also, having been once offered to bear the sins of many, shall appear a second time, apart from sin, to them that wait for him, unto salvation.

Chapter 10

¹For the law having a shadow of the good things to come, not the very image of the things, they can never with the same sacrifices year by year, which they offer continually, make perfect them that draw nigh.

²Else would they not have ceased to be offered, because the worshippers, having been once cleansed, would have had no more conscience of sins?

³But in those sacrifices there is a remembrance made of sins year by year.

⁴For it is impossible that the blood of bulls and goats should take away sins.

⁵Wherefore when he cometh into the world, he saith,

Sacrifice and offering thou wouldest not,
but a body didst thou prepare for me;
⁶In whole burnt offerings and sacrifices for sin thou hadst no pleasure:
⁷Then said I, Lo, I am come
(In the roll of the book it is written of me)
To do thy will, O God.

[8]Saying above, Sacrifices and offerings and whole burnt offerings and sacrifices for sin thou wouldest not, neither hadst pleasure therein (the which are offered according to the law),

[9]Then hath he said, Lo, I am come to do thy will. He taketh away the first, that he may establish the second.

[10]By which will we have been sanctified through the offering of the body of Jesus Christ once for all.

[11]And every priest indeed standeth day by day ministering and offering oftentimes the same sacrifices, the which can never take away sins:

[12]But he, when he had offered one sacrifice for sins for ever, sat down on the right hand of God;

[13]From henceforth expecting till his enemies be made the footstool of his feet.

[14]For by one offering he hath perfected for ever them that are sanctified.

[15]And the Holy Ghost also beareth witness to us. for after he hath said,

[16]This is the covenant that I will make with them
After those days, saith the Lord;
I will put my laws on their heart,
And upon their mind also will I write them;
then saith he,

[17]And their sins and their iniquities will I remember no more.

[18]Now where remission of these is, there is no more offering for sin.

[19]Having therefore, brethren, boldness to enter into the holy place by the blood of Jesus,

[20]By the way which he dedicated for us, a new and living way, through the veil, that is to say, his flesh;

[21]And having a great priest over the house of God;

[22]Let us draw near with a true heart in fulness of faith, having our hearts sprinkled from an evil conscience, and our body washed with pure water:

[23]Let us hold fast the confession of our hope that it waver not; for he is faithful that promised:

[24]And let us consider one another to provoke unto love and good works;

[25]Not forsaking the assembling of ourselves together, as the custom of some is, but exhorting one another; and so much the more, as ye see the day drawing nigh.

[26]For if we sin wilfully after that we have received the knowledge of the truth, there remaineth no more a sacrifice for sins,

[27]But a certain fearful expectation of judgement, and a fierceness of fire which shall devour the adversaries.

[28]A man that hath set at nought Moses' law dieth without compassion on the word of two or three witnesses:

[29]Of how much sorer punishment, think ye, shall he be judged worthy, who hath trodden under foot the Son of God, and hath counted the blood of the covenant, wherewith he was sanctified, an unholy thing, and hath done despite unto the Spirit of grace?

[30]For we know him that said, Vengeance belongeth unto me, I will recompense. And again, The Lord shall judge his people.

4th warning continued

³¹It is a fearful thing to fall into the hands of the living God.

³²But call to remembrance the former days, in which, after ye were enlightened, ye endured a great conflict of sufferings;

³³Partly, being made a gazing-stock both by reproaches and afflictions; and partly, becoming partakers with them that were so used.

³⁴For ye both had compassion on them that were in bonds, and took joyfully the spoiling of your possessions, knowing that ye yourselves have a better possession and an abiding one.

³⁵Cast not away therefore your boldness, which hath great recompense of reward.

³⁶For ye have need of patience, that, having done the will of God, ye may receive the promise.

³⁷For yet a very little while,
He that cometh shall come, and shall not tarry.

³⁸But my righteous one shall live by faith:
And if he shrink back, my soul hath no pleasure in him.

³⁹But we are not of them that shrink back unto perdition; but of them that have faith unto the saving of the soul.

Chapter 11

¹Now faith is the assurance of things hoped for, the proving of things not seen.

²For therein the elders had witness borne to them.

³By faith we understand that the worlds have been framed by the word of God, so that what is seen hath not been made out of things which do appear.

⁴By faith Abel offered unto God a more excellent sacrifice than Cain, through which he had witness borne to him that he was righteous, God bearing witness in respect of his gifts: and through it he being dead yet speaketh.

⁵By faith Enoch was translated that he should not see death; and he was not found, because God translated him: for before his translation he hath had witness borne to him that he had been well-pleasing unto God:

⁶And without faith it is impossible to be well-pleasing unto him: for he that cometh to God must believe that he is, and that he is a rewarder of them that seek after him.

⁷By faith Noah, being warned of God concerning things not seen as yet, moved with godly fear, prepared an ark to the saving of his house; through which he condemned the world, and became heir of the righteousness which is according to faith.

⁸By faith Abraham, when he was called, obeyed to go out unto a place which he was to receive for an inheritance; and he went out, not knowing whither he went.

⁹By faith he became a sojourner in the land of promise, as in a land not his own, dwelling in tents, with Isaac and Jacob, the heirs with him of the same promise:

¹⁰For he looked for the city which hath the foundations, whose builder and maker is God.

¹¹By faith even Sarah herself received power to conceive seed when she was past age, since she counted him faithful who had promised:

¹²Wherefore also there sprang of one, and him as good as dead, so many as the stars of heaven in multitude, and as the sand, which is by the sea shore, innumerable.

¹³These all died in faith, not having received the promises, but having seen them and greeted them from afar, and having confessed that they were strangers and pilgrims on the earth.

¹⁴For they that say such things make it manifest that they are seeking after a country of their own.

¹⁵And if indeed they had been mindful of that country from which they went out, they would have had opportunity to return.

¹⁶But now they desire a better country, that is, a heavenly: wherefore God is not ashamed of them, to be called their God: for he hath prepared for them a city.

¹⁷By faith Abraham, being tried, offered up Isaac: yea, he that had gladly received the promises was offering up his only begotten son;

¹⁸Even he to whom it was said, In Isaac shall thy seed be called:

¹⁹Accounting that God is able to raise up, even from the dead; from whence he did also in a parable receive him back.

²⁰By faith Isaac blessed Jacob and Esau, even concerning things to come.

²¹By faith Jacob, when he was a dying, blessed each of the sons of Joseph; and worshipped, leaning upon the top of his staff.

²²By faith Joseph, when his end was nigh, made mention of the departure of the children of Israel; and gave commandment concerning his bones.

²³By faith Moses, when he was born, was hid three months by his parents, because they saw he was a goodly child; and they were not afraid of the king's commandment.

²⁴By faith Moses, when he was grown up, refused to be called the son of Pharaoh's daughter;

²⁵Choosing rather to be evil entreated with the people of God, than to enjoy the pleasures of sin for a season;

²⁶Accounting the reproach of Christ greater riches than the treasures of Egypt: for he looked unto the recompense of reward.

²⁷By faith he forsook Egypt, not fearing the wrath of the king: for he endured, as seeing him who is invisible.

²⁸By faith he kept the passover, and the sprinkling of the blood, that the destroyer of the firstborn should not touch them.

²⁹By faith they passed through the Red sea as by dry land: which the Egyptians assaying to do were swallowed up.

³⁰By faith the walls of Jericho fell down, after they had been compassed about for seven days.

³¹By faith Rahab the harlot perished not with them that were disobedient, having received the spies with peace.

³²And what shall I more say? for the time will fail me if I tell of Gideon, Barak, Samson, Jephthah; of David and Samuel and the prophets:

³³Who through faith subdued kingdoms, wrought righteousness, obtained promises, stopped the mouths of lions,

³⁴Quenched the power of fire, escaped the edge of the sword, from weakness were made strong, waxed mighty in war, turned to flight armies of aliens.

³⁵Women received their dead by a resurrection: and others were tortured, not accepting their deliverance; that they might obtain a better resurrection:

³⁶And others had trial of mockings and scourgings, yea, moreover of bonds and imprisonment:

³⁷They were stoned, they were sawn asunder, they were tempted, they were slain with the sword: they went about in sheepskins, in goatskins; being destitute, afflicted, evil entreated

³⁸(Of whom the world was not worthy), wandering in deserts and mountains and caves, and the holes of the earth.

³⁹And these all, having had witness borne to them through their faith, received not the promise,

⁴⁰God having provided some better thing concerning us, that apart from us they should not be made perfect.

Chapter 12

¹Therefore let us also, seeing we are compassed about with so great a cloud of witnesses, lay aside every weight, and the sin which doth so easily beset us, and let us run with patience the race that is set before us,

²Looking unto Jesus the author and perfecter of our faith, who for the joy that was set before him endured the cross, despising shame, and hath sat down at the right hand of the throne of God.

³For consider him that hath endured such gainsaying of sinners against themselves, that ye wax not weary, fainting in your souls.

⁴Ye have not yet resisted unto blood, striving against sin:

⁵And ye have forgotten the exhortation, which reasoneth with you as with sons,

My son, regard not lightly the chastening of the Lord,

Nor faint when thou art reproved of him;

⁶For whom the Lord loveth he chasteneth,

And scourgeth every son whom he receiveth.

⁷It is for chastening that ye endure; God dealeth with you as with sons; for what son is there whom his father chasteneth not?

⁸But if ye are without chastening, whereof all have been made partakers, then are ye bastards, and not sons.

⁹Furthermore, we had the fathers of our flesh to chasten us, and we gave them reverence: shall we not much rather be in subjection unto the Father of spirits, and live?

¹⁰For they verily for a few days chastened us as seemed good to them; but he for our profit, that we may be partakers of his holiness.

¹¹All chastening seemeth for the present to be not joyous, but grievous: yet afterward it yieldeth peaceable fruit unto them that have been exercised thereby, even the fruit of righteousness.

¹²Wherefore lift up the hands that hang down, and the palsied knees;

¹³And make straight paths for your feet, that that which is lame be not turned out of the way, but rather be healed.

¹⁴Follow after peace with all men, and the sanctification without which no man shall see the Lord:

¹⁵Looking carefully lest there be any man that falleth short of the grace of God; lest any root of bitterness springing up trouble you, and thereby the many be defiled;

¹⁶Lest there be any fornicator, or profane person, as Esau, who

for one mess of meat sold his own birthright.

¹⁷For ye know that even when he afterward desired to inherit the blessing, he was rejected (for he found no place of repentance), though he sought it diligently with tears.

¹⁸For ye are not come unto a mount that might be touched, and that burned with fire, and unto blackness, and darkness, and tempest,

¹⁹And the sound of a trumpet, and the voice of words; which voice they that heard intreated that no word more should be spoken unto them:

²⁰For they could not endure that which was enjoined, If even a beast touch the mountain, it shall be stoned;

²¹And so fearful was the appearance, that Moses said, I exceedingly fear and quake:

²²But ye are come unto mount Zion, and unto the city of the living God, the heavenly Jerusalem, and to innumerable hosts of angels,

²³To the general assembly and church of the firstborn who are enrolled in heaven, and to God the Judge of all, and to the spirits of just men made perfect,

²⁴And to Jesus the mediator of a new covenant, and to the blood of sprinkling that speaketh better than that of Abel.

²⁵See that ye refuse not him that speaketh. For if they escaped not, when they refused him that warned them on earth, much more shall not we escape, who turn away from him that warneth from heaven:

²⁶Whose voice then shook the earth: but now he hath promised, saying, Yet once more will I make to tremble not the earth only, but also the heaven.

²⁷And this word, Yet once more, signifieth the removing of those things that are shaken, as of things that have been made, that those things which are not shaken may remain.

²⁸Wherefore, receiving a kingdom that cannot be shaken, let us have grace, whereby we may offer service well-pleasing to God with reverence and awe:

²⁹For our God is a consuming fire.

Chapter 13

¹Let love of the brethren continue.

²Forget not to shew love unto strangers: for thereby some have entertained angels unawares.

³Remember them that are in bonds, as bound with them; them that are evil entreated, as being yourselves also in the body.

⁴Let marriage be had in honour among all, and let the bed be undefiled: for fornicators and adulterers God will judge.

⁵Be ye free from the love of money; content with such things as ye have: for himself hath said, I will in no wise fail thee, neither will I in any wise forsake thee.

⁶So that with good courage we say,

The Lord is my helper; I will not fear:

What shall man do unto me?

⁷Remember them that had the rule over you, which spake unto you the word of God; and considering the issue of their life, imitate their faith.

⁸Jesus Christ is the same yesterday and to-day, yea and for ever.

⁹Be not carried away by divers and strange teachings: for it is good that the heart be stablished by grace; not by meats, wherein they that occupied themselves were not profited.

¹⁰We have an altar, whereof they have no right to eat which serve the tabernacle.

¹¹For the bodies of those beasts, whose blood is brought into the holy place by the high priest as an offering for sin, are burned without the camp.

¹²Wherefore Jesus also, that he might sanctify the people through his own blood, suffered without the gate.

¹³Let us therefore go forth unto him without the camp, bearing his reproach.

¹⁴For we have not here an abiding city, but we seek after the city which is to come.

¹⁵Through him then let us offer up a sacrifice of praise to God continually, that is, the fruit of lips which make confession to his name.

¹⁶But to do good and to communicate forget not: for with such sacrifices God is well pleased.

¹⁷Obey them that have the rule over you, and submit to them: for they watch in behalf of your souls, as they that shall give account; that they may do this with joy, and not with grief: for this were unprofitable for you.

¹⁸Pray for us: for we are persuaded that we have a good conscience, desiring to live honestly in all things.

¹⁹And I exhort you the more exceedingly to do this, that I may be restored to you the sooner.

²⁰Now the God of peace, who brought again from the dead the great shepherd of the sheep with the blood of the eternal covenant, even our Lord Jesus,

²¹Make you perfect in every good thing to do his will, working in us that which is well-pleasing in his sight, through Jesus Christ; to whom be the glory for ever and ever. Amen.

²²But I exhort you, brethren, bear with the word of exhortation: for I have written unto you in few words.

²³Know ye that our brother Timothy hath been set at liberty; with whom, if he come shortly, I will see you.

²⁴Salute all them that have the rule over you, and all the saints. They of Italy salute you.

²⁵Grace be with you all. Amen.

Introduction

Before we enter upon the study of our epistle, there are some questions on which it is desirable to shed some light. It is good to know what can be told as to its author, the church to which it was addressed, the object the author had in view, and the plan he adopted to attain that object. The reader then knows something of what he is to expect and has a point of view suggested from which to overlook the whole.

The Author of the Epistle

[handwritten: David Pawson does not believe Paul wrote it, we do know, God wrote it.]

From the very earliest times there have been some among the church fathers who maintained that the epistle was written by Paul, while those who held another view admitted that they had no decisive evidence to offer to disprove his authorship. All admit that the literary style is not found in Paul's writings. Some say that the substance of the teaching differs, too, and that the great truth that he had been set apart to announce—that the Gentiles are fellow heirs of the same body—is entirely missing from the text. The epistle speaks as if salvation was for the Jew only; it is absolutely silent as to the existence of a heathen or Christian world outside the church it addresses.

On the other hand, it may be said that the epistle contains so much of what had been specially revealed to Paul more than to others concerning the fulfillment of the Law in Christ and its passing away,

[handwritten notes at bottom: "bath in front of fire or running hot water in a stony tub"; "washing clothes by hand or clothes washing machine"]

concerning the glory of Christ seated on the throne of heaven, and concerning the power of faith alone, that it is almost impossible not to recognize Paul's spirit in its teaching. What adds special weight to this view is that, while from the style it is certain that it cannot be the work of any other of our Bible writers, it appears strange that the history of the church does not even mention the name of a man who had been favored with such special revelations from God as the epistle bears witness to.

The difficulty has led from the earliest times to the supposition that either Paul wrote the letter to the Hebrews in their tongue and that we only have it in the Greek translation, or that he gave the substance of its contents to someone who gave expression to them in his own praticular style. The names of Barnabas, Luke (to whose style in the Acts there is considerable resemblance), Aquila, Apollos the Alexandrian (eloquent and mighty in the Scriptures), and Clement of Rome have all been suggested. There is such an entire absence of material for forming a decision that we are compelled to rest in the certainty that the name of the author cannot be known. All the more, we praise God that we know for certain that the Holy Spirit spoke in him who wrote and that it is He who has given us, through the epistle, one of the deepest and fullest revelations that the Bible contains of the counsel of redemption and the glory of the Son who makes us partakers of it.

To Whom the Epistle Was Written

The Jews had the name of *Hebrews* from Abraham, who, in Genesis 14:13, is spoken of as *"the Hebrew."* It was counted a title of honor, as we see in Paul's, *"a Hebrew of the Hebrews"* (Philippians 3:5). Some have thought that, because no special place or church is mentioned, it was meant for all Christians among the Jews. But expressions such as "Pray that I may be restored to you the sooner" and "With Timothy, if he come shortly, I will see you" (see Hebrews 13:19, 23), compel us to think of some special community. The most probable view is that it was addressed, in the first place, to the Christians in Jerusalem. From Acts 21:20, we know that there were many thousands of them. These Christians, while believing in Christ, yet clung to the temple and its worship. Nowhere were they in greater danger of yielding to the temptation of conformity to the spirit of the world around them and losing the boldness and bright ness of their Christian life. And nowhere would there be better opportunity of securing the widest possible circulation of the letter through all the scattered Christian churches among the Jews.

The Object of the Epistle

What was it that led the writer to take his pen? The epistle itself gives us the answer. The religious state of those to whom it was addressed was far from right or satisfactory. Some had grown *"slothful"* (Hebrews 6:12 KJV), were not giving *"earnest heed"* (2:1), and were *"neglect*[ing] [the] *great salvation"* (2:3). They were no longer *"hold*[ing] *fast* [their] *profession"* (4:14; 10:23 KJV) or *"confidence"* (3:6 KJV). The Christian life was feeble and ready to die. Others had gone back, were in danger of coming short of the promises (4:1), and, yielding to willful sin, *"draw*[ing] *back unto perdition"* (10:39 KJV). Still others were in danger of refusing Him who speaks from heaven (10:25) and giving up their faith in Jesus. Expressions such as we have quoted, and others, clearly indicate that there had been much backsliding and that the church was in a state that needed a most solemn and pointed warning.

Great stress, or emphasis, has been laid upon the difficulties that arose in the mind of the Hebrews from the circumstances in which they were placed. They had hoped that their countrymen would speedily accept the Messiah, but they had been disappointed in this matter. They still clung to the old worship but, more and more, felt that, as suspected and despised as they were, they could no longer be at home there. The prophecies appeared to fail them, both in regard to the power with which Christ should reign and the blessing He would bestow. To meet these difficulties, it is said, the epistle seeks to open up the true glory of the religion of Christ and to show that all that they lost in the old worship was a hundredfold restored in the *"something better"* (11:40), God had now provided. It seeks to solve the problem that troubled them in the light of the Gospel.

There is doubtless a measure of truth in this view, and yet, the more I study the epistle, the more confident I feel that this was not the chief trouble. I believe the main difficulty lay in the want of religious earnestness. Their case was very much what has been the story of almost every church and what marks the state of the greater part of Christendom in the present day.

Our author took up his pen to meet this spirit of backsliding, to warn against the disease and its danger, and to make known the infallible cure. He saw that the one cause of all feebleness and faithlessness was this: the want of knowledge and faith of what Christ and His salvation truly are. He set himself to show them how wonderfully, and how divinely, all the prophecies and types of the Old Testament have their fulfillment in the salvation that the Son of God has wrought for us. He unceasingly placed their weakness and Christ's person side by side: He was sure that, if they only knew Christ, all would be well.

The Plan of the Epistle

In what way did the writer propose to attain his object? In the opening verses we find the substance of his whole argument. God, who spoke to the fathers through the prophets, has now spoken to us through the Son. There have been two revelations of God to man. The first was through men; the second, through the Son. As much more glorious as God's Son is than His servants, the new revelation has as much more of life and of glory than the old. The writer not only wrote to prove the superiority of the new above the old but also to show specially what intrinsic excellence gives it that superiority. Both faith and experience will find their strength in the knowledge of its excellence. The contents of the epistle, taking its doctrinal and practical aspect together, may be summarized as follows: the knowledge of the Son of God and the power of the Christian life.

The epistle is divided into two parts. In the first part, the doctrinal half (1:1–10:18), we have the glory of the person and work of Christ set forth. In the second part, or practical half (10:19–13:25), the life that the knowledge of Christ and His salvation will enable us to live is described.

I have had the epistle printed at the beginning of the book, with the view of inviting and helping the reader to make himself master of the writing as a whole. It is of great consequence that the student of God's word should not only seek his edification from individual texts or passages but that each book should be to him a living and connected organism, all alive with the Spirit that dwells in it. The more we thus take time and trouble to accept the great thoughts of God, the more our lives will be brought to that unity and breadth, in which the purpose of God will be perfectly fulfilled.

The first three verses give us the summary of the doctrinal part.

Then follow twelve sections.

1. Christ, as Son of God, is more than the angels (1:4–14).

2. Jesus, as Son of Man, is more than the angels, too. Reasons for His being made lower than the angels are given (2:5–18).

3. Christ Jesus is more than Moses (3:1–6).

4. Jesus, our High Priest, is more than Aaron (4:14–5:10).

5. The new priesthood after the order of Melchizedek is described (chapter 7).

6. The new sanctuary and the new covenant are explained (chapter 8).

7.   The power of Christ's blood to inaugurate the new sanctuary and the new covenant are set forth (chapter 9).

8.   The new way into the Holiest is shown (10:1–18).

Here commences the second section, the practical half, with
its call to a life corresponding to our privileges.

9.   Of entering the Holiest and dwelling there (10:19–25).

10.   Of the fullness of faith (11:1–40).

11.   Of the patience of hope (12:1–13).

12.   Of love and good works (13:1–25).

In this summary of contents, I have not taken up the passages
containing the solemn warnings by which the epistle is characterized. They are so inserted that they could in each case be left out,
without the argument suffering. In some cases, the connection
would in fact be clearer. I have had this indicated in the printing
because I am sure that it is of importance, if we are to thoroughly
master the lesson given us, that we fully apprehend the danger that
threatened and, in some right measure, see how the only deliverance for Christians from all that weakens and hinders them is the
full knowledge of the person and work of Jesus.

The Warnings

1.   After the proof of Christ being more than the angels,
the writer reminds us not to *"neglect so great salvation"*
(2:1–4).

2.   After the proof of Christ being more than Moses, the
writer reminds us not to come short of the promised
rest, like Israel did in the wilderness (3:7–4:13).

3.   After the mention of Christ being more than Aaron,
the writer warns us against the danger of sloth, standing still, and falling away (5:11–6:20).

4.   After the call to enter the opened Holiest, the writer
warns us against sinning willfully and drawing back to
perdition (10:26–39).

5. After the exhortation to patience, the writer warns us against falling short of the grace of God and refusing Him who speaks (12:14–29).

The deeper our impression is of the danger that existed, the clearer will be our insight into the truth that the only source of health and strength to the church is the knowledge of Christ Jesus.

The Epistles and the Church of Our Days

There is one more point in which an introduction can help the reader. It is to suggest the way in which a book addresses the special needs of our present times.

In the Christian church of our day, the number of members whose experience corresponds exactly to what the epistle pictures and seeks to meet is very large. How many Christians are there yet who, after the profession of faith in Christ, come to a standstill? "Taking more abundant heed to what they hear" (2:1); "giving diligence to enter into the rest of God"; *"pressing on unto perfection"* (6:1); *"run*[ning] *with patience the race"* (12:1)—these are the things that are so little found. So many rest contented with the thought that their sins are pardoned and that they are in the path of life. However, they know nothing of a personal attachment to Christ as their leader or of a faith that lives in the invisible and walks with God.

With many, this is the consequence of hopelessness that came from failure of their utmost efforts to live as they desired. They struggled in their own strength, they did not know Christ as the secret of strength, and then they lost heart and went back. The profession of faith is not cast away and religious habits are kept up, but there is nothing to show that these men and women have entered or are seeking to enter the Holiest to dwell there. The power of the world, the spirit of its literature, the temptations of business and pleasure—all of these unite to make up a religion in which it is sought to combine a comfortable hope for the future with the least possible amount of sacrifice in the present. The epistle, with its warnings, is indeed a mirror in which the church of the present day may see itself.

But it is a mirror, too, thank God, in which we can see the glory of Jesus on the throne of heaven, in the power that can make our heart and life heavenly, too. What the Hebrews needed is what we need today. Salvation is not in ourselves or in our efforts but only in Christ Jesus. To see Him, to consider Him, and to look to Him as He lives in heaven—these will bring healing. As little as the Hebrews—with the Old Testament, its God-given law, its temple service, and its prophecy—could withstand the temptation to wax weary and grow faint can the New Testament—with a sound church and church doctrine, and its religious services—give us the true life and power of godliness. It is Jesus Christ alone whom we must know better. It is He who lives today in heaven; who can lead us into the heavenly sanctuary and keep us there; and who can give heaven into our heart and life. The knowledge of Jesus in His heavenly glory and His saving power—it is this that our churches and our Christians need. It is this that the epistle will bring us, if we yield to that Spirit who speaks in it to reveal it in us.

It is, therefore, with great confidence that I invite all who long for the rest of God, for a life in the holiest of God's love, for the fullness of faith and hope and love to take up the study of the epistle with the confident assurance of finding, in its revelation of what Christ and His salvation are, the deliverance from sin and sloth and the joy and the strength of a new life.

FIRST HALF—DOCTRINAL
HEBREWS 1:1–10:18

The Son of God:
The Mediator of the
Better Covenant

The Theme—Hebrews 1:1–3
THE GLORY OF THE SON IN HIS PERSON AND WORK

One

The Son—In Whom God Has Spoken

*God, having of old time spoken unto the fathers in the
prophets by divers portions and in divers manners, hath at
the end of these days spoken unto us in his Son.*
—Hebrews 1:1–2

God has spoken! This is the magnificent portal by which we enter the temple where God is to reveal His glory to us! We are at once brought into the presence of God Himself. The one object of the epistle is to lead us to God, to reveal God, to bring us into contact with Himself. Man was created for God. Sin separated us from God. Man feels his need and seeks for God. This epistle comes with the gospel message of redemption, to teach us where and how to find God. Let all who thirst for God, for the living God, draw nigh and listen.

God has spoken! Speaking is the vehicle of fellowship. It is a proof that the speaker considers the one he addresses as capable of fellowship with himself, a token that he longs for that fellowship. Man was created for fellowship with God; sin interrupted it.

Andrew Murray

Nature speaks of God and His work; but of Himself, His heart, and His thoughts of love toward us as sinners, nature cannot tell. In his deepest misery, man seeks for God—but how often, to all appearance, in vain. But, God be praised, this seeking in vain is not for always. The silence has been broken. God calls man back to fellowship with Himself. God has spoken! *Hallelujah*

God has spoken! For a time, He spoke imperfectly and provisionally in the prophets, in preparation for the more perfect revelation of Himself. But now, at length, the joyful tidings are heard—God has spoken in His Son! God—the infinite, incomprehensible, unseen One—has spoken! And that, in His Son! Oh, the joy and the glory! Who can measure it? *"Hear, O heavens, and give ear, O earth, for the LORD hath spoken"* (Isaiah 1:2).

God has spoken! When man speaks, it is the revelation of himself, to make known the otherwise hidden thoughts and dispositions of his heart. When God—who dwells in light that is inaccessible—speaks out of the heights of His glory, it is so that He may reveal Himself. He would have us know how He loves us and longs for us, how He wants to save and to bless, how He would have us draw nigh and live in fellowship with Himself.

God has spoken in His Son! The ministry of angels and prophets were only to prepare the way. These never could satisfy the heart either of God or man. The real power of the life of God, the full experience of His nearness, the true deliverance from sin, the shedding abroad of the love in the heart—these could not be communicated by the ministry of creatures. The Son Himself had to come as the Word of God to us, the bearer of the life and love of the Father. The Son Himself had to come to bring us into living contact with the Divine Being; to dwell in our hearts, as He dwells in God's heart; to be God's Word in us as He is in God; and so to give us the living experience of what it means that God speaks to us.

God has spoken! The words of a man carry weight according to the idea I have of his wisdom, his veracity, his power, and his love. The words of God! Oh, who can express what they ought to be worth to us! Each word carries with it all the life of God, all His saving power and love. God speaking in His Son! Surely they who have begun to know Him will be ready to cast aside everything for the sake of hearing Him.

God has spoken! The words of men have often exerted a wonderful and mighty influence. But the words of God—they are creative deeds, they give what they speak. *"For he spake, and it was done"* (Psalm 33:9). When God speaks in His Son, He gives Him to us—not only for us and with us but also in us. He speaks the Son out of the depth of His heart into the depths of our hearts. Men's words appeal to the mind or the will, the feelings or the passions. God speaks to what is deeper than all: the heart, that central depth within us where dwell the issues of life. Let us believe the mighty, quickening power that God's word will have.

God has spoken! Speaking claims hearing. God asks but one thing—it is so simple and right—and that is that we would listen. Will we not hearken, in holy reverence and worship, with wholehearted attention and surrender to what He would say to us in this epistle, too? We, too, will know the power and the joy of God speaking to us in His Son. God is a Spirit. As such, He has no other way of communicating to us His life or His love except by entering our spirit and dwelling and working there. There, He causes Christ to dwell. And there, He speaks to us, in Christ, these words of redeeming love and power, which bring life to us. The words of Christ can bring us no profit, except as they unfold to us what God is working in us and as they direct us to what is to be revealed in our hearts. It is the heart that God wants. Let us open the whole heart to listen and to long.

God has spoken in His Son! The living Jesus—come forth from the fiery furnace of God's holiness, from the burning glow of everlasting love—He Himself is the living Word. Let us seek in the study of this epistle, in which His glory is so wondrously revealed, to come into contact with Him, to receive Him into our hearts, and to take Him as our life, that He may bring us to the Father. In the beginning, God spoke, *"Let there be light: and there was light"* (Genesis 1:3). Even so, now He speaks with creative power in His Son, and the presence and the light of Christ become the life and the light of the soul. *yes.*

Chapter Notes...

1. What trouble people take to learn a foreign language, to have access to its writers. Let no trouble be too great to understand the language of God, His Word, and His Son. To learn a foreign language, I get someone who knows it to teach me. The language of God is heavenly, spiritual, supernatural—altogether divine; only the Holy Spirit can teach me to understand it and to think God's own thoughts. Let me take Him as my teacher. *yes 10/17/17*

2. *"And Abram fell on his face: and God talked with him"* (Genesis 17:3). As personally and directly, even more wonderfully and effectually, will God speak to me in His Son; but deep, holy reverence, and an intense desire to know what God says, must be the spirit in which I study the epistle and hearken to the blessed Son.

3. "Heavenly truth is nowhere spoken but by the voice of Christ, nor heard but by the power of Christ, living in the hearer."* *"He that is of God heareth God's words"* (John 8:47 KJV). Only he who yields himself to the new nature can truly know what God's speaking in Christ is.

4. During Christ's life, the word of God was thrice heard. Each time, it was *"This is my beloved Son: hear him"* (Luke 9:35 KJV) and *"I have glorified thee"* (John 17:4 KJV). Let us allow God to speak this one word into our hearts—*"My beloved Son."* O my God! Speak to me in Thy Son. Oh, speak that one word out of the depth of Thy heart into the depth of my heart. *Amen. So be it. yes come Lord Jesus*

---

* William Law, M.A., *A Collection of Letters on the Most Interesting and Important Subjects, and on Several Occasions* (London: J. Richardson, Pater-Noster Row, 1760). <http://www.ccel.org/l/law/letters/let.RTF>

God, after He spoke long ago to the fathers in the prophets in many portions and in many ways, in these last days has spoken to us in His Son
Heb 1:1-2

Two

The Son—<u>More</u> than the Prophets

God, having of old time spoken unto the fathers in the prophets by divers portions and in divers manners, hath at the end of these days spoken unto us in his Son.
—Hebrews 1:1–2

We all know that there are two testaments—the Old and the New. These represent two dispensations, two modes of worship, two sorts of religions, two ways in which God has communion with man and man draws nigh to God. The one was provisional, preparatory, and intended to pass away. What it gave and wrought was not meant to satisfy, but only to awaken the expectation of something better that was to come. The other was the fulfillment of what had been promised, and it was destined to last forever because it was itself a complete revelation of an everlasting redemption, of a salvation in the power of an endless life.

In both the Old and New Testament, it was God who spoke. The prophets in the Old, and the Son in the New, were equally God's messengers. God spoke in the prophets no less truly than in the Son. But in the Old, everything was external and through the mediation of men. God Himself could not yet enter and take possession of man and dwell in him. In the New, all is more directly and immediately divine—in an inward power and reality and life, of which the Old had only the shadow and hope. The Son, who is God, brings us into the very presence of God.

And why was it that God did not—in fact, could not—from the very beginning reveal Himself in the Son? What need was there of these two ways of worshiping and serving Him? The answer is twofold—if man were indeed to appropriate God's love and redemption intelligently and voluntarily, he needed to be prepared for it. He needed first of all to know his own utter helplessness and hopeless wretchedness. And so, his heart had to be wakened in true desire and expectancy to welcome and value what God had to give.

When God speaks to us in Christ, it is as the Father dwelling in the Son. *"The words that I say unto you I speak not from myself: but the Father abiding in me doeth his works"* (John 14:10). Just as God's speaking in Christ was an inward thing, so God can still speak to us in no other way. The external words of Christ, just like the words of the prophets, are to prepare us for and point us to that inner speaking in the heart by the Holy Spirit, which alone is life and power. This is God's true speaking in His Son.

It is of the utmost consequence for our spiritual life that we rightly understand these two stages in God's dealing with man. In two ways—not in one and not in more than two—in two ways has God spoken.

They indicate, in substance, God's way with every Christian.* There is, after his conversion, a time of preparation and testing, to see whether he willingly and heartily sacrifices all for the full blessing. If, in this stage, he perseveres in earnest effort and striving, he will be brought to learn the two lessons the Old Testament was

* "The characteristics, which before marked the revelation itself, now mark the human apprehension of the final revelation." —Westcott

meant to teach. He will become more deeply conscious of his own helplessness, and the strong desire for a better life will be wakened; and this will be found in the full revelation of Christ, who alone is able to save completely. When these two lessons are learned—the lesson of self-despair and of hope in God alone—the soul is prepared, if it will yield itself in faith to the leading of the Holy Spirit, to enter truly into the New Testament life within the veil, in the very Holiest of all (Hebrews 9:3), as it is set forth in this epistle.

Where Christians—through defective instruction or through neglect and sloth—do not understand God's way for leading them on to perfection, the Christian life will always remain full of feebleness and failure. It was thus with the Hebrew Christians. They belonged to the New Testament, but their life was anything but the exhibition of the power and joy Christ came to reveal. They were far behind what many of the Old Testament saints had been, and the reason was this: They did not know the heavenly character of the redemption Christ had brought. They did not know the heavenly place in which He ministers nor the heavenly blessings He dispenses nor the heavenly power in which He secures our enjoyment of these blessings. They did not know the difference between the prophets and the Son nor what it means that God has now spoken to us in His Son. The one object of the epistle is to set before us the heavenly priesthood of Christ and the heavenly life to which He, in His divine power, gives us access. This gives the epistle its inestimable value for all time—that it teaches us the way out of the elementary stage of the Christian life to that of full and perfect access to God. *wow!*

Let us grasp and hold firmly to the difference between the two stages. In the one, the action of man is more prominent: God speaks in the prophets. In the other, the divine presence and power are more fully revealed: God speaks in the Son, who bears and brings the very life of God, and brings us into living contact with God Himself. In the one, it is the human words that occupy and influence and help us to seek God; in the other, the divine indwelling Word reveals its power within. In the one, it is multiplicity of thoughts and truths, of ordinances and efforts; in the other, the simplicity and the unity of the one Son of God, and faith in Him alone.

How many have sought—by study and meditation and acceptance of the words of the Bible—to find God, and yet have failed. They did not know that these were but the fingerposts pointing to the living Son—words coming indeed from God, most needful and profitable, and yet not sufficient, only yielding us their true blessing when they have brought us to hear God Himself speaking in His Son.

Chapter Notes...

1. Let none of us rest content with the lower stage. Personal fellowship with God, through the Holy Spirit, is what Christ gives. God calls us to it: Christ lives in heaven to work it through the Spirit He gives from heaven.

2. One may know much of the Bible and the words of God and yet remain feeble. What one needs is to know the living Word, through whom God speaks, in life and power.

3. All the prophets point to the Son as the true Prophet. Let us take them very definitely as our teachers, to reveal God in us.

4. When I speak a word, I desire all its meaning and force to enter into the one I address. In these last days, God has but one Word. He desires to have all that that Word is and means to enter and live in us. Let us open our hearts, and God will speak into us that one Word, "This is my Son" (Luke 9:35), in such a way that He will indeed be all our own.

Whom He appointed heir of all things, through Whom also He made the world. And He is the radiance of His glory & the exact representation of His nature, & upholds all things by the word of His power. Heb 1:2-3

Three

The Son—The Glory of His Person

[God] *hath at the end of these days spoken unto us in his Son, whom he appointed heir of all things, through whom also he made the worlds; who being the effulgence* of his glory, and the very image of his substance, and upholding all things by the word of his power.*
—Hebrews 1:2-3

We know that whatever a man sets his heart on exercises a mighty influence on his life and leaves its stamp upon his character. He who follows after vanity becomes vain. He who trusts in a god of his own fancy will find his religion an illusion. He who sets his heart upon the living God will find the living God taking possession of and filling his heart. This makes it of such infinite consequence that we should not only have a general idea of the Christ through whom God speaks to us but should also know Him aright and have our hearts filled with all that God has revealed of Him. Our knowledge of Him will be the food of our faith. And

* Outshining.

50

as our faith is so, too, will be our experience of His saving power and of the fellowship with God to which He leads. Let us listen to what we are taught of the Son in whom God speaks to us.

"Whom He appointed heir of all things." The great object and aim of God in creation was to have an inheritance for His Son, in which He might show forth His glory and find His blessedness. The Son is the Final Cause, the End of all things.

He is the Beginning, too. *"Through whom also He made the worlds."* He is the Origin and Efficient Cause of all that exists. *"Without him was not anything made that hath been made"* (John 1:3). The place the Son had in the Divine Being was such that God's relation to all that was outside of Himself was only through the Son. Of all that exists, the end and the beginning meet in Him.

And He is the Middle, too. *"Upholding all things by the word of his power."* He bears all things. *"In him all things consist"* (Colossians 1:17). Since they were not created without Him, can they exist without Him? He upholds them *every moment* by the word of His power, even as by His word they were created. This is the Son through whom God speaks to us.

And what is it that makes Him worthy of taking this high place between the Creator and the creature? Because, as the Son, it is He alone in whom the unapproachable and utterly incomprehensible glory of God is made manifest. It is through Him, as Mediator, that the uncreated God and the works of His hand can come into contact and fellowship with each other. His relation to creation rests on His relation to the Father. He is *"the effulgence of his glory, and the very image of his substance."* As we only know the sun by the light that shines from it, so is Christ *"the effulgence,"* or outshining, the revelation of God's glory. As the light that shines from the sun is of the same nature with it, so the Son is of one nature with the Father—God of God. And as a son bears the likeness of his father because he has his life and nature from him, so the Son of God is *"the very image of his substance."* He is of one substance with the

Father—its express image—and has therefore life in Himself, even as the Father has life in Himself

Someone may be tempted to think that these are theological mysteries too deep for the ordinary Christian and not needful for our Christian faith and life. And he may be inclined to ask, "Of what importance can it be to a simple believer to know all this?" My brother, think not thus. It is all-important that we know the glory of Jesus. The more the soul is filled with that glory and worships Him in it, the more it will see with what confidence it can count upon Him to do a divine and supernatural work in us and to lead us to an actual living fellowship with God as our Father. Oh, let us not be so selfish and mean as to be content with the hope that Jesus saves us while we are careless of having intimate personal acquaintance with Him. If not for our sake, then for God's sake—for the sake of His infinite love and grace—let us seek to know aright this blessed Son whom the Father has given us. Let us turn away from earth—let us meditate and gaze and worship—until He, who is the outshining of the divine glory, *shines into* our very hearts. Let us worship until He, to whom the Father has given such a place as Creator and Upholder and Heir of all, takes that place in our hearts, too, and is to us the Beginning and the Center and the End of all.

God speaks to us through this Son. Not through the words of the Son only, for they, too, are human words and may, just like the inspired words of the prophets, bring in but little profit. It is directly through the Son—the living, mighty, divine Son—that God speaks: Only in direct living contact with the Son can the words profit. And the Son—not as we superficially think of Him, but the real divine Son, as God has revealed Him, known and worshiped and waited on as the outshining of the divine glory—it is this Son of God, entering into our hearts and dwelling there, in whom God will speak to us and in whom we will be brought near to God. When Christ reveals the Father, it is not in the mind, to give us new thoughts about Him, but rather in the heart and life, so that we know and experience the power in which God can dwell and work in man, restoring him to the enjoyment of that blessed fellowship for which he was created and that he lost by the Fall.

The great work of God in heaven—the chief thought and longing of His heart—is to reach your heart and speak to you through His Son. Oh, let it be the great work of your life, and the great longing of your heart, to know this Jesus. As a humble, meek disciple, may you bow at His feet and let Him teach you of God and eternal life. Yes, even now, let us bow before Him in the fourfold glory in which the Word has set Him before us. He is the Heir of all that God has. He is its Creator. He is the Upholder, too. And He is the outshining of God's glory, the perfect Image of His substance. O my Savior! anything to know Thee better and, in Thee, to have my God speak to me!

Chapter Notes...

1. *"No one knoweth the Son, save the Father; neither doth any know the Father, save the Son, and he to whomsoever the Son willeth to reveal Him"* (Matthew 11:27). How dependent we are on the Father to know the Son and on the Son to know the Father. Let us acknowledge this dependence in deep humility. Let us believe and wait in meekness of soul for the divine revealing.

2. There are times when a deep longing to know God arises in the soul. External teaching does not satisfy. Treasure such longing as God's loving drawing. Turn from the world in stillness of soul, and exercise faith in the secret power that Jesus can exert in the heart. Become a disciple of Jesus, one who follows Him and learns of Him.

3. O Thou, who art Heir, Creator, Upholder of all, the Brightness of the Father's glory, the express Image of His substance—O my Lord Jesus, reveal the Father to me, that I may know that God speaks to me.

When He had made purification of sins He sat down at the right hand of the majesty on high,

Heb 1:3

Four
The Son—The Glory of His Work

Who...when he had made purification* of sins, sat down on the right hand of the Majesty on high.
—Hebrews 1:3

The description of the glory of Christ's person is followed by that of the work of this Son in whom God speaks to us. God's words are deeds. It is in what Christ is and works that God speaks to us. In His divinity and incarnation we see what God has given us. In His life, death, and ascension we see how the gift of God enters and acts in all our human life, how complete our salvation is, and what God now asks of us. All Christ's work is God's word to us.

That work consists in two parts: the one on earth, the other in heaven. Of the former, it is said, "When he had effected the cleansing of our sins"; of the latter, it is said, *"He...sat down on the right hand of the Majesty on high."* In a healthy Christian life, we must

---

* Effected the cleansing.

accomplishment
fulfillment

54

know and hold fast to both parts of Christ's work. The work He did upon earth was but the beginning of the work He was to do in heaven; in the latter, the work on earth finds its perfection and its glory. As Priest, He effected the cleansing of sins here below; as Priest-King, He sits on the right hand of the throne to apply His work, to dispense its blessings in heavenly power, and to maintain within us the heavenly life. *Yes Ty Lord!*

incarnation 1st

"*When he had made purification of sins.*" The cleansing of sins, as something effected by Christ before He went to heaven, is the foundation of all His work. Let us learn, at the very start, that what God has to speak to us in Christ begins here: Sin must be cleansed away. This is the root-thought of redemption. As long as we seek salvation chiefly from the desire of personal safety, or as long as we approach the study of Christ's person and work as the revelation of what is true and beautiful and good, we cannot enter fully into its power. It is the cleansing of *sin* God insists on—and with a desire so intense that He gave *sent* His Son to die for it! It is in the intense desire for the cleansing of sins that, all the way through the Christian life, our spiritual capacity to approach and enter into the salvation of Christ will be found. This desire of God's heart *His love for us!* lies at the root of all. It is the secret of Christian perfection. It was only when Christ had effected this cleansing that heaven opened to *true* Him. The full acceptance of the cleansing of sins—as the meaning of the word *cleansing* will be unfolded later on—will be to us, too, the entrance into the heavenly life.

When He had effected the cleansing of sins, he "*sat down on the right hand of the Majesty on high.*" There He lives! opening up and keeping open the blessed access to God's presence and fellowship for us while lifting us up into and maintaining us in its enjoyment. And in the power that prevails there, He makes the kingdom of heaven a reality within the heart. It is the great object of the epistle to bring home to us the heavenly glory of Christ as the ground of our confidence, the measure of our expectation, and the character of that inward salvation He imparts. That Christ, as our Leader and Forerunner, has rent asunder the veil and, in the power of His blood, has taken possession of and secured access into the Holiest of All does not mean that we are to enter heaven only when we die. The whole practical teaching of the epistle is summed up and applied in the one word: "We have boldness for entering in. Let us draw near. Let us enter in." (See Hebrews 10:19–22.) The fact of Christ being seated on the throne in heaven means we can actually be brought—through the supernatural power that the Holy Spirit supplies—into God's holy presence, living there our daily life. It was because the Hebrews did not know this—because they had rested content with elementary truths about faith and conversion and the life in heaven after death—that they had so notably failed. Truly, to know Jesus at the right hand of God would be the healing of diseases and their restoration to the joy and strength of a life carried out in accordance with their heavenly calling.

The church of our days is suffering from the same cause, and needs the same cure. It is so much easier to understand the work of Christ on earth than His work in heaven. It is so much easier to take in the doctrine of a Substitute and an atonement, of repentance and pardon, than the doctrine of a High Priest bringing us into God's presence and keeping us in loving communion with Him. It is not the blood-shedding upon earth only; it is the blood-sprinkling in heaven and the blood-sprinkling from heaven on our hearts and consciences that bring the power of the heavenly life unto us. And it is this alone that makes us Christians who not only seek to enter the gate but who daily press on in the living way that leads ever deeper into the Holiest.

Let no one think that I speak of what is too high. I speak of what is your heritage and destiny. The same share that you have in Jesus on the cross, you also have in Jesus on the throne. Be ready to sacrifice the earthly life for the heavenly; to follow Christ fully in His separation from the world and His surrender to God's will. Christ in heaven will then prove in you the reality and the power of His heavenly priesthood. Let the cleansing of sins be to you, as it

Andrew Murray

was to Christ, the entrance into the Holiest. He who effected the *(accomplished/fulfilled)* cleansing on earth and applies it in person from heaven will assuredly lead you into all the fullness of blessing it has opened up for Him and for you. *Dear.*

Chapter Notes...

1. Faith has in its foundation four great cornerstones on which the building rests—① the divinity of Christ, ③ the Incarnation, the ② atonement on the cross, and ④ the ascension to the throne. The last in this list is the most wonderful—the crown of all the rest and the perfect revelation of why God has made Christ for us. And so, in the Christian life, Christ's ascension to the throne is the most important. It is the glorious fruit of all that goes *my desperately needed Helper* before.

2. The Holy Spirit was sent down after the ascension. Why? *"I will not leave you as orphans;* That He might witness to us of a heavenly Christ and bring *I will come to you, dear.* the kingdom of heaven into our hearts and lives. *wow!* *John 14:18*

3. Regarding the cleansing of sins, someone may say, "At this time, I saw plainly that whatever the Lord would communicate and make known of Himself and the mystery of His kingdom, He would do so in a way of purity and holiness." There are two sides from which we can approach the higher truth of God's Word regarding holiness and likeness to Jesus. The one is the desire to know all Scripture truthfully and to have our system of doctrine complete and perfect. The other is the deep, intense longing to be made free from sin, as free as God can make us in this life. It is only from this side that real access will be given into the heavenly life of Christ.

The same share that you Dear have in Jesus on the cross, you also have in Jesus on the throne. Wow! 10/21/17

[handwritten at top: having become as much better than the angels, as He has inherited a more excellent name than they. For which of]

First Section—Hebrews 1:4–14
THE SON OF GOD
MORE THAN THE ANGELS

[handwritten: the angels did He ever say,] *[circled: Ps 2:7]*

[handwritten boxed: "YOU ARE MY SON, TODAY I HAVE BEGOTTEN YOU"?]

[handwritten: and again]

Five

[handwritten: "I WILL BE A FATHER TO HIM AND HE SHALL BE A SON TO ME"] *[circled: 2 Sam 7:14]*

The Son—A More Excellent Name → *[handwritten: SON!!!! Heb 1:4-5]*

[handwritten: Thus he became / for]
[handwritten left margin: more superior]

Having become by so ~~much~~ better than the angels, as he hath inherited a more excellent name than they. For unto which of the angels said he at any time, Thou art my Son, this day have I begotten thee? and again, I will be to him a Father, *[handwritten: fathered]* And he shall be to me a Son?
—Hebrews 1:4–5

[handwritten circled: First Section]

The superior excellence of the New Testament above the Old consists in this: that God *[handwritten: Father]* has spoken to us and wrought salvation for us in His Son. The whole epistle of Hebrews is the unfolding of the glory of the person and work of the Son. *[handwritten: Father, Father's]* The more completely we understand this and have our hearts permeated by it, the better we will understand the completeness of the salvation God *[handwritten: Father]* has now provided for us. To know Jesus Christ in His *[handwritten: Father's]* glory is the great need. It is the only safeguard and the sure growth of the Christian life.

There is often no better way of knowing a thing than by placing it in contrast with something that is less perfect. Our epistle would

[handwritten at bottom: Father + Son are inseparable!]

58

teach us the glory of the New Testament by placing it in contrast with the Old, especially with those who were its great mediators and representatives. It shows us the superiority of Christ over the angels and over Moses, Joshua, Abraham, Levi, and Aaron.

It begins with the angels. *"Having become by so much better* than the angels, as he hath inherited a more excellent name than they."* Though these words belong grammatically to the preceding verses, they are in reality the heading of what follows. They form the transition from the theme to the first part of the argument— the excellence of Christ as Son of God above the angels. The Jews counted it one of their great privileges that the Law was given by the ministration of angels (Hebrews 2:2; Acts 7:38, 53; Galatians 3:19), heavenly spirits who came directly from the throne of God. The manifestation of God had frequently been in the form of an angel. *"The angel of God"* (Exodus 14:19), for instance, had been Israel's leader.

And yet, as great as the privilege to hear from angels was, it was nothing compared to the new revelation. Angels were but creatures. They might show signs of heavenly power and speak words of heavenly truth. As creatures, however, they could not bring down the life of God itself nor truly reach into the life of man. They had, indeed, been called *"sons of God"* (Job 38:7) as a title of honor. There is but One, however, to whom it was said, *"Thou art my Son, this day have I begotten thee."* Christ alone, making us partakers of the very life of God, could indeed bring God near to us and bring us near to God.

It is the superiority of the Son to the angels that the writer is going to prove in this first chapter by a series of quotations from Old Testament Scripture. We must not, however, only regard these as so many proof-texts for the divinity of our Savior. We must see them as divine revelation of the glory of that divinity in its various

---

* The word *better* is one of the key words of the epistle. It occurs thirteen times. See notes at end of chapter.

aspects. At the very commencement of his argument, the writer will prove how the Old Testament had all along borne witness to the glory of God's Son—God's Son who, as the great thought in God's revelation to man, always had the first place in God's heart.

Before we proceed to study the texts themselves, it is of importance that we notice how the writer uses them. When our Lord on earth, or Paul, cited the Old Testament, they would say, "Moses says," or "David says," or "the prophets say." Our epistle, however, mostly quotes the words as coming from the lips of God Himself. In the quotations in our chapter, it is often, *"He saith."* Further on we find, *"The Holy Ghost saith"* (3:7). Scripture has two sides: the human and the divine. The knowledge of all that can illustrate the Scriptures as human compositions has very great value. But it is of still more importance never to forget the divine side, and to be full of the conviction that Scripture is indeed God's word—that God Himself, through His Spirit, spoke in the prophets, and that it has the power of God dwelling in it.

This conviction will teach us two things that are absolutely necessary to the profitable study of our epistle. The one is that we must recognize that these words of God contain a divine depth of meaning that the human mind can never grasp or expound. The wonderful exposition of Psalm 2 and the Son of God; Psalm 8 and the human nature of Jesus; Psalm 95 and the rest of God; and Psalm 110 and the priesthood of Melchizedek—all of these prove to us how they were inbreathed by that Spirit of Christ who knew what was to come, and how it was that same Spirit alone who could have taught our writer to apprehend and unfold their divine meaning.

The other lesson is this: that the divine thoughts deposited in the Old Testament as a seed by the Holy Spirit and unfolded by that same Spirit in the New still need the teaching of the Spirit to make them life and truth to us. God must shine in our hearts to give the knowledge of His glory in the face of Jesus Christ. Christ

Andrew Murray

is the Word that *"was God"* (John 1:1) and who speaks to us as coming out of the depth of God's heart; He is a living person. It is only the heart that yields to be led by the Holy Spirit that can expect to profit by the teaching of the Word and truly to know Christ in His divine saving power. The truths of Christ's sonship and divinity and priesthood and redemption were given in charge to the Holy Spirit; He revealed them from time to time; He alone can reveal them to us. To the written words all have free access; our minds can see their purport; but their life and power and blessing, the glory of the Son of God as a power of salvation—this is given to none but those who wait humbly on God's Spirit to teach them.

Chapter Notes...

1. The angels brought wonderful messages from God of old, but God is now drawing far nearer to you and waiting to speak in a far more wonderful and blessed way: by revealing the eternal Word in your heart.

2. Words and wonders—these, angels could bring. But to bring the life and the love of God and to give it in the heart—this the Son alone can do. But He does it. Christ is the divine nature manifesting and communicating itself. I have no contact with Christ, or God in Him; but as I receive Him, the divine nature imparts itself, as manifested in His human life, will, and character.

3. If I were favored this day with the visit of an angel—what a privilege I would count it. But Christ, the Son at the right hand, will not only visit but also dwell in me. O my soul, rise to your privileges: God speaks to you in His Son.

For to which of the angels did He ever say, "YOU ARE MY SON, TODAY I HAVE BEGOTTEN"? Ps 2:7 And again, "I WILL BE A FATHER TO HIM AND HE SHALL BE MY SON." 1 Sam 7:14 And when He again brings the firstborn into the world, He says, "AND LET ALL THE ANGELS OF GOD WORSHIP HIM." Ps 97:7

Heb 1:5-6

Six

The Son—
The Only Begotten

For unto which of the angels said he at any time, Thou art my Son, this day have I begotten thee (see Psalm 2:7)? and again, I will be to him a Father, and he shall be to me a Son (see 2 Samuel 7:14)? And when he again bringeth in the firstborn into the world he saith, And let all the angels of God worship him (see Psalm 97:7).
—Hebrews 1:5–6

It is because Christ is the Son of God that He is higher than the angels, and that the New Testament is so much higher than the Old. If we would grasp the teaching and get the blessing of our epistle—and indeed become partakers of the inner power and glory of the redemption Christ has brought—we must tarry here in deep humility until God reveals to us what it means. And this is what it means: that *His only Son* has become our Savior. The infinite excellence of the Son above the angels is the measure of the excellence of the heavenly life that He brings and gives within us. The angels could tell of God and of life; the Son, however, has and is the life of God. And the Son gives that life. He that has the Son, has life.

1 John 5:12

*Paul stood up 13:16, "Men of Israel..." (33) God has fulfilled this
for us their children in that He raised up Jesus, as it is also
written in Ps 2: "you are My Son (today) I have begotten You,"*

Andrew Murray

"Thou art my Son, this day have I begotten thee." These words
are also used in Acts 13:33, referring to the resurrection of Christ.
So, the word **"firstborn"** in the next verse also has reference to the
Resurrection (Colossians 1:18; Revelation 1:5). The Son was not
only begotten of the Father in eternity but also begotten again
in the Resurrection. In the Incarnation, the union between the
divine and the human nature was only begun. This union had to
be perfected by Christ, through His human will yielding Himself *(overcome)*
to God's will even unto the death. In the Resurrection, He was *(Baxter)*
"declared to be the Son of God with power" (Romans 1:4). Here, the
full new birth of humanity into the perfected fellowship and equality with Deity was completed and the Son of Man was begotten
into all the likeness and glory of the Son of God. This is how Paul
applied it: *"God...raised up Jesus; as also it is written in the second
psalm, Thou art my Son, this day have I begotten thee"* (Acts 13:33).
He then became the first begotten from the dead.

"And again, I will be to him a Father, and he shall be to me a *2 Sam*
Son." The words were spoken to David of a son that God would give *7:14*
to him, but with the clear indication that their meaning reached far
beyond what any mere man could be. In the Son of Man, who in
the Resurrection was raised up in power and declared to be the Son *The*
of God, they find their complete fulfillment. *Great*

"And when he again bringeth in the firstborn into the world he *Mystery =*
saith, And let all the angels of God worship him." The psalm speaks *God*
of Jehovah coming to redeem His people. The Son is one with the *has*
Father so that just as the Father works only through the Son and *a*
can only be known in Him, worship can only arise to God through *Son!*
the Son. The angels worship the deliverer as Jehovah. ?

Christ is the Son of God! What does this mean to us, and
what is the blessing it brings our faith? It points us first to the great
mystery that God has a Son! This is the mystery of divine love, and
that in a double sense. Because God is love, He begets a Son to
whom He gives all He is and has Himself; in whose fellowship He

*NKJV Col 1:18 and He is the head of the body, the church, who
is the beginning, the first born from the dead (Isa)
that in all things He may have the preeminence, (arr)
also Rev 1:5*

finds His life and delight; through whom He can reveal Himself; and with whom He shares the worship of all His creatures. And because God is love, this Son of God becomes the Son of Man; and the Son of Man, having been perfected forevermore, enters through death and resurrection into all the glory that belonged to the Son of God. And now this Son of God is to us the revelation and bearer of love from the Divine Being. In Him, the love of God dwells in us. In Him, we enter and rest in this love. When God speaks to us through His Son, it is the infinite love imparting itself to us, becoming the inward life of our life.

And if we ask how this can be done, our answer is the second great lesson taught to us by the truth that Christ is the Son of God. It was by being begotten of God, by a divine birth, that Christ became the Son. In eternity, it was a birth; in the Resurrection, it was a birth from the dead. And so it is only by a divine birth that the Son, the Love of God, can enter and possess us. It is by an eternal generation that the Son is God. In eternity there is no past. What God is and does is all in the infinite power of an ever-present now. And so it is in the power of that eternal generation that the Father begets us in His Son (1 John 5:1–18) while also begetting His Son in us. It is in the power of that eternal generation that the Father speaks the eternal Word to us and in us. The Word of God is the Son, coming from the heart of the Father, spoken into our hearts, and dwelling there (John 1:1). The Son is the Love of God. And as the Son is begotten within us, so is the Love of God born in us, making us, by a new birth, partakers of its own nature and blessedness.

If we would learn the lesson of the epistle and experience in our Christian life the full power of the everlasting redemption, we must above all learn to know Jesus better. The general knowledge we had of Him before and at conversion is not enough for a strong and healthy growth. God desires that we come to a close friendship and into an intimate acquaintance with His beloved Son, and that we should be the loving, happy witnesses of how completely

Andrew Murray

He can save. Let us do so. Remembering that angels and prophets could only point to Him who was to come and that the words of Scripture, and even of Christ Himself, only profit as they waken the expectancy of something higher, let us wait on God to speak in His Son to us. God's speaking to us will be a mighty act of creative power, a birth of His love within us.

O God, teach us that the blessed secret of a full salvation is this—Christ, our Savior, is the Son of God.

Chapter Notes...

1. Christ, the Son of God's love; He is in God's heart and in mine.

2. *"Let all the angels of God worship him."* All the servants around His throne point to Him. We must look to Him. And we must look in worship. It is worship, worship, worship that the Son must have. To the heart that worships Him, He will make Himself known. Let our study of the glory of Christ in the epistle be all in the spirit of worship, all tending to make us fall down in adoring worship.

3. The Son is a Son only in the power of a divine birth. And this is not only in eternity and the Resurrection, but also in our hearts. This is the mystery of the divine life. Let us bow in deep impotence and ignorance, waiting on God Almighty to reveal the Son to us.

4. The Son is the Word, because the divine speaking is but another aspect of the divine begetting. Speaking to us in His Son is all in the power of a divine life. The speaking, just as the begetting, is love imparting and communicating itself in divine power as an inward life. It is by God speaking to us in the First Begotten that we are begotten of God.

Handwritten annotation at top of page:

And of the angels He says
"WHO MAKES HIS ANGELS WINDS
AND HIS MINISTERS A FLAME OF FIRE."
Ps 104:4

But
of the Son He says,
YOUR THRONE, O GOD, IS FOREVER + EVER
AND THE RIGHTEOUS SCEPTER IS THE SCEPTER OF
HIS KINGDOM, YOU HAVE LOVED RIGHTEOUSNESS
+ HATED LAWLESSNESS, THEREFORE GOD, YOUR
GOD HAS ANOINTED YOU WITH THE OIL OF GLAD-
NESS ABOVE YOUR COMPANIONS. Ps 45:7-8

Seven

The Son—Himself God

*And of the angels he saith, Who maketh his angels winds,
and his ministers a flame of fire (see Psalm 104:4): But of
the Son he saith, Thy throne, O God, is for ever and ever;
and the sceptre of uprightness is the sceptre of thy kingdom.
Thou hast loved righteousness, and hated iniquity;
therefore God, thy God, hath anointed thee with the oil of
gladness
above thy fellows (see Psalm 45:7–8).*
—Hebrews 1:7–9

In contrast to what is said of the angels as servants, the Holy
Spirit said of the Son, *"Thy throne, O God, is for ever and ever."*
Christ is not only the Son but is also God. He is one with the
Father. As Son, He is partaker of the Father's own nature and being. *essence*
person
Christ is God! To many Christians this has been a dead article of
faith: It has been held fast to and proven from Scripture, but it does not
have any living influence on the soul. To the true believer, however, it
is one of the deepest and most precious truths for the nourishment of
the inner life. Christ is God: The soul worships Him as the almighty
One, able to do a divine work in the power of divine omnipotence.
Christ is God: Even as God works in all nature from within, and in

Andrew Murray

secret, so the soul trusts Christ as the always present Indwelling One, doing His saving work in the hidden depths of its being. Christ is God: In Him we come into living contact with the person and life of God Himself. This truth lies at the foundation of our epistle and the Christian life that it would build up: Christ is God.

"Thy throne, O God, is for ever and ever." As God, Christ is King: The throne of heaven belongs to Him. When an earthly father has begotten a son, they may be separated from each other by great distance, both in place and character, and know each other no more. In the Divine Being, however, it is not so. The Father and the Son are inseparable, one in life and love; all that the Father is and has, the Son is and has, too. The Father is ever in the Son, and the Son is in the Father. God is on the throne, and Christ is in Him: The throne and the kingdom are Christ's, too.

"For ever and ever." Christ is the King eternal. His dominion is an everlasting dominion. The full meaning of the word *eternal* will become clear to us later on. Eternal is that in which each moment always exists in its full strength—immovable and unchangeable. We receive a kingdom that cannot be moved, because our King is God and His kingdom is *"for ever and ever."* The rule of Christ, our Priest-King, even now in our souls, is in the power of an endless and imperishable life. The faith that receives this will experience it.

"And the sceptre of uprightness is the sceptre of thy kingdom." Christ is a righteous King. He is Melchizedek, the King of Righteousness. In His kingdom, all is righteousness and holiness. It is in His kingdom that grace reigns through righteousness. It is the kingdom of heaven: In his kingdom, the will of God is done on earth as in heaven. And when it is further said, *"Thou hast loved righteousness, and hated iniquity,"* we are reminded that the righteousness is not only His as a divine attribute but His, too, as the fruit of His life on earth. Here, on earth, He was tested, tried, perfected, and found worthy as Man to sit upon the throne of God. The throne that belonged to Him, as Son of God and heir of all

things, He had to win as Son of Man, as well. And now He reigns over His people, teaching them by His own example and enabling them by His own Spirit to fulfill all righteousness. As the King of Righteousness, He rules over a righteous people.

"*Therefore God, thy God, hath anointed thee with the oil of gladness above thy fellows.*" He is an anointed King. Therefore—because He loved righteousness and hated iniquity—*therefore,* God anointed Him. When He ascended to heaven and sat down on the right hand of the throne, He received from the Father anew and in fullest measure, as the Son of Man, the gift of the Holy Spirit to bestow on His people (Acts 2:33). That Spirit was to Him the oil of joy, the joy that had been set before him, the joy of His crowning day when He saw of the travail of His soul. With an anointing above His fellows—for there was none like Him—God gave Him the Spirit without measure. And yet, for His fellows—His redeemed—He made them members of His body with Him as Head. They became partakers of His anointing and His joy. He said, "The Lord has anointed Me to give the oil of joy." Christ, our King and our God, is anointed with the oil of joy. He is anointed, too, to give the oil of joy: His kingdom is one of everlasting gladness, of joy unspeakable and full of glory!

O souls, redeemed by Christ, behold your God and the Son in whom the Father speaks! Let this be the chief thing you live for—to know, to honor, and to serve your God and King. This is the Son in whom God speaks to you in all the divine mystery, but also in all the divine power and blessing, which marks all God's speaking. Let our hearts open wide to receive the King whom God has given us.

And as often as we are tempted, as the Hebrews were, to be slothful, fearful, or disbelieving, let this be our watchword and our strength: My Redeemer is God! In this faith, let me worship Him. My Redeemer is God! Let my whole heart be opened to Him, to receive—as a flower does the light of the sun—His secret, mighty, and divine working in me. My Redeemer is God! Let me trust this omnipotent Lord to work out in me His every promise and to set up His throne of righteousness in my soul in a power that is above all we ask or think. My Redeemer God! Let me wait for Him, and let me count upon Him to reveal Himself in the love that passes knowledge. Blessed be the name of God forever and ever: My Redeemer is God!

Chapter Notes...

1. Who is God? And what is God to us? *"In him we live, and move, and have our being"* (Acts 17:28). He is the Life of the universe. And how wonderfully perfect all that Life is in nature! When we know this God as our Redeemer, in whom *"we live, and move, and have our being,"* what an assurance we have that He will make His new life in us as wonderful and as perfect.

2. *"Thou hast loved righteousness, and hated iniquity; therefore...."* This was Christ's way to the throne, and this is the only way for us—living and doing right while hating everything that is sin.

Eight

The Son—The Everlasting Creator

> *And, Thou, Lord, in the beginning hast laid the foundation of the earth, and the heavens are the works of thy hands: they shall perish; but thou continuest: and they all shall wax old as doth a garment; and as a mantle shalt thou roll them up, as a garment, and they shall be changed: but thou art the same, and thy years shall not fail (see Psalm 102:26–27).*
> —Hebrews 1:10–12

ome and hearken once more to what the divine message has to tell us of the glory of the Son in whom the Father speaks to us. Come and see how truly He is one with God and shares with Him all His glory. The deeper our insight into the true Godhead of our Lord Jesus Christ and His perfect oneness with God, the more confident we will be that He will, in a divine power, make us partakers of His work, His life, and His indwelling.

We find Christ here set before us as the Creator, to whom all creation owes its existence, as the everlasting and unchangeable One, to whom alone, when all waxes old and perishes, can be said,

Andrew Murray

"Thou continuest;...thou art the same, and thy years shall not fail." In Isaiah, God speaks of Himself when He says, *"Hast thou not known? hast thou not heard? the everlasting God, the* LORD, *the Creator of the ends of the earth, fainteth not, neither is weary"* (40:28). In our text, we see the Son as the almighty Creator, the everlastingly unchangeable One, that we may know who it is through whom God speaks to us and to whom He has entrusted the work of our salvation.

The words are taken from Psalm 102. The ordinary reader would not think that the Messiah, or the Son, was spoken of here. Our writer, however, taught by the Holy Spirit, sees how all redemption is wrought only through the Son, and how. Thus he also sees how the building up of Zion and the appearing in His glory (verse 16), as well as the looking down from the sanctuary and the loosing of those who are appointed unto death (verse 20), all points to the Son as Redeemer. And then what follows is true of Him, too. It is: *"Of old hast thou laid the foundation of the earth; and the heavens are the work of thy hands. They shall perish, but thou shalt endure"* (verses 25–26). God is almighty and everlasting. These are the attributes of Him to whom our salvation is entrusted.

Listen, believer! Christ, your Redeemer, is the almighty One. God saw that none but His Son could meet your need. Have you so seen it, too, that this, His almighty power, has been claimed and appropriated for your daily life? Have you learned never to think of Him otherwise than as the One who calls things that are not as though they were and creates what otherwise could not be?

Christ, your Redeemer, is the everlasting and unchangeable One. Have you heard Him speak? "I, Jehovah, change not; therefore you are not consumed" (see Malachi 3:6). Have you learned to trust Him as the One who is each moment to you all that He can be, and who will, without variation or shadow of turning, maintain in unending power His life within you? Oh, learn that God saw it necessary to speak to you through none other than such a One as could reach the heart and fill it with the power of His eternal Word.

The almighty Son—through whom God has created all things
and who upholds and fills all things by the word of His power—
this is He who will, even so, in the power of His Godhead, uphold
and fill your whole life and being. Your Creator is your Redeemer!
One great cause of feebleness and backsliding in the Christian life
is the power of circumstances. We often say that temptations that
come to us from our position in life, from the struggle to live, or
from the conduct of our fellowmen draw us away from God; we say
that these are the causes of our falling into sin. If we but believed
that our Redeemer is our Creator! He knows us. He appoints and
orders our lot. Nothing comes to us but what He has in His hands.
He has the power to make our circumstances, however difficult,
a heavenly discipline, a gain, and a blessing. He has taken them
all up into the life-plan He has for us as Redeemer. If we would
only believe this, how we should gladly meet every event with the
worship of an adoring faith. My Creator, who orders all, is my
Redeemer, who blesses all.

And now, let me once again urge my reader to mark well the
lesson this chapter is teaching us and the object it has in view. Let
no one think, as I myself long thought, that just because we firmly
believe in the divinity of our Savior, this chapter, with its proof-
texts, has no special message for our spiritual life, and that we may
therefore hasten on to what the epistle has to teach further on. No,
let us remember that this is the foundational chapter. The divinity
of Christ is the rock on which we rest. It is in virtue of His divinity that He effected a real cleansing and putting away of sin; that
He can actually communicate and maintain the divine life in us;
and that He can enter into our inmost being and dwell there. If we
open our hearts and give them time to receive the full impression
of the truth, we will see that all that we are to learn of the person
and work of Christ has its value and its power from this—that He
is God. Our Creator, from whom we have our life—it is He who
alone can enter into us to give the new life. It is He, blessed be His
name, who will do it now. As God, He is the hidden ground of all

existence and has the power to enter all and fill it with Himself. Every part of His work has the character and the power of a divine work. If we would but believe that Christ the Son is God—that He is Jehovah, the Eternal, the Creator—how He would make our inner life the proof of His almighty power!

Paul said, *"I count all things but loss for the excellency of the knowledge of Christ Jesus my Lord"* (Philippians 3:8 KJV). Let us do so, too. In the Christian life, the chief thing, the one necessary thing, is the knowledge of Christ. And this knowledge is not the intellectual apprehension of the truth, but the living experiential heart knowledge that comes from faith and fellowship with Him, from love and obedience. May it be ours!

Chapter Notes...

1. God is the incomprehensible One. In all your thoughts of Him, in all your efforts to know Him as revealed in Christ, remember the true knowledge of God is something above sense and reason. As the light reveals itself to the open eye that has been created for it, God reveals Himself to the longing heart. All the teaching of angels and prophets, or of the words and truths of the Bible, can but point the way: Let God, in Christ, speak to your heart. Then you will know Him. Bow in adoring awe and worship Christ. Let all His saints worship Him. It is worship, not study, that will prepare us to know Christ.

2. *"They shall perish;...they all shall wax old."* This is what the creature is, even though created by God, with every experience, even though coming from God. *"Thou continuest:... thou art the same."* This is our security and our joy. Christ, my Redeemer, is the unchangeable—every moment the same, my Keeper and my Life.

Nine

The Son—On the Right Hand of God

But of which of the angels hath he said at any time, Sit thou on my right hand, till I make thine enemies the footstool of thy feet (see Psalm 110)? Are they not all ministering spirits, sent forth to do service for the sake of them that shall inherit salvation?
—Hebrews 1:13–14

"Sit thou at my right hand, until I make thine enemies thy footstool" (Psalm 110:1). These words we have from Psalm 110. Luther called this psalm the chief of all the psalms. The first verse, and the fourth about Melchizedek, contain the hidden mysteries, which we never would have understood without the exegesis of the Holy Spirit. It is from this psalm that the expression, which is become one of the great articles of our faith, "Sitting on the right hand of God," has been taken into the New Testament. Our Lord quoted the words when He taught how David, when he said, *"The Lord said unto my Lord"* (see Matthew 22:44), had acknowledged that the Messiah who was to be His Son would also be his Lord. Before Caiaphas, Christ spoke of Himself as *"the Son of man sitting at the right hand of power"* (Matthew 26:64). Mark, in the narrative of the ascension, used the words, *"The Lord Jesus...was received up into heaven, and sat down at the right hand of God"* (Mark 16:19). At Pentecost, Peter proved from this text that David had prophesied of the Messiah. (See Acts 2:34–36.) Paul applied the words to the final conquest of all the enemies of the Lord Jesus (1 Corinthians 15:25). And to the Ephesians, Paul spoke of the *"working of the strength of his might which he wrought in Christ, when he raised him from the dead, and made him to sit at his right hand in the heavenly places"* (Ephesians 1:19–20). Our epistle, Hebrews, uses the expression five times. Although he could have barely apprehended their full meaning, the words of David, spoken through the Holy Spirit, became, through Jesus and the apostles, the revelation of what is the highest glory of Christ and the greatest strength of our faith and hope.

The word suggests two thoughts. The one is that, as Son of Man, Christ is admitted to perfect fellowship and equality with God. The other thought is that Christ is now possessor of divine, universal authority and power. We are so familiar with the truth that its infinite magnificence hardly strikes us. God is a God who is, and must be, infinitely jealous of His honor. He will not give His glory to another. When Jesus, the crucified Son of Man, takes His place at the right hand of the Majesty on high, it can only be because He is also the Son of God and because He is God. And it assures us that now the power and dominion of God Himself are in Christ's hands—to carry out the work of redemption to its full consummation until all His enemies have been put under His feet and He will deliver up the kingdom to the Father.

When the writer quotes the words, it is with the question, *"But of which of the angels hath he said at any time...?"* And he gives the answer, *"Are they not all ministering spirits, sent forth to do service for the sake of them that shall inherit salvation?"* He would impress deep upon us the thought that angels, though they come from God's throne and are the instruments of His power, are still infinitely distinct from the Son. The redemption from sin, the true fellowship with God, the life and the love of God—angels cannot communicate any of these. It is the Son, sitting at the right hand of God, acting in the power of God, to whom we must look for the everlasting redemption, for the true inward deliverance from sin, and for a complete salvation. The angels, by contrast, all point us to the Son, who is seated as the Man on the throne in proof of, and to impart, that perfect restoration to the fellowship of the Most High in the Most Holy Place.

This is the Son in whom God speaks to us. The words, *"Sit thou on my right hand,"* are spoken in our hearing and on our behalf. In those words, we have all God's speaking concentrated into statement. "See," He says, "how I have exalted Him—your Brother, your Surety, and your Head—to my right hand, in token of My perfect acceptance of His work, which is your perfect admittance into My presence and the enjoyment of all the power of the heavenly life; your full participation, in your inmost being, of what the kingdom of heaven is." *"Sit thou on my right hand."* Let the words enter and master all our hearts and life. I have said that it occurs five times in the epistle. Compare these passages and the others having reference to Christ's place in heaven (see chapter note on the following page), and observe the great truth we are to learn, which is this: The knowledge of Jesus having entered heaven for us and taken us in union with Himself into a heavenly life is what will deliver the Christian from all that is low and feeble; it will lift him to the life of joy and strength. To gaze upon the heavenly Christ in the Father's presence, to whom all things are subject, will transform us into heavenly Christians, dwelling all the day in God's presence and overcoming every enemy. Yes, my Redeemer, seated at God's right hand—if I only know Him aright and trust Him as able to save completely—He will make me more than conqueror.

If we would obtain this blessed knowledge of our Lord and the blessed life in the experience of His power, Scripture has a prayer for us that we will do well to pray often:

Andrew Murray

That the God of our Lord Jesus Christ, the Father of glory, may give unto you a spirit of wisdom and revelation in the knowledge of him...that ye may know...what the exceeding greatness of his power to us-ward who believe, according to that working of the strength of his might which he wrought in Christ, when he raised him from the dead, and made him to sit at his right hand in the heavenly places. (Ephesians 1:17–20)

Let us pray for this spirit of divine illumination; let us study and adore the strength of God's might that lifted Him to the throne; and let us believe joyfully that that power works in us every day to lift us up and enable us to live as those who are set with Him in the heavenlies. And let us sing without ceasing. Praises be to God for such a Savior!

Chapter Notes...

1. *"Now in the things which we are saying the chief point is this: We have such a high priest, who sat down on the right hand of the throne of the Majesty in the heavens"* (Hebrews 8:1). Yes, this is the chief point: Jesus is in heaven, keeping it open for me, drawing me to enter into the Holiest, and keeping me in it, all while He sends down heaven to my heart.

2. *"He that descended is the same also that ascended far above all the heavens, that he might fill all things"* (Ephesians 4:10). On earth, everything is limited by space and matter. In heaven, all is in a divine, all-pervading power. As the light of the sun pervades all the air, the light and spirit of heaven can fill all our hearts. The heavenly Christ fills all things.

3. See how they worship Him who sits on the throne in heaven (see Revelation 5:8–14; 7:9–12) and let every thought of Jesus on the throne lead to worship. It was when the disciples worshiped Him who had just sat down on the right hand of God that they were, within ten days, filled with the Holy Spirit. The Pentecostal gift is ours. Here is the place and the posture in which we will enter into its full experience.

TO TAKE HEED TO WHAT THE SON SPEAKS

Ten

The Danger of Neglecting So Great Salvation

Therefore we ought to give the more earnest* heed to the
things that were heard, lest haply we drift away from them.
For if the word spoken through angels proved stedfast,
and every transgression and disobedience received a just
recompense of reward; how shall we escape, if we neglect
so great salvation? which having at the first been spoken
through the Lord, was confirmed unto us by them that
heard; God also bearing witness with them, both by signs
and wonders, and by manifold powers, and by gifts† of the
Holy Ghost, according to his own will.
—Hebrews 2:1–4

The first chapter has set before us the divine glory of Christ
the Son, in whom God has spoken to us in these days. In the
second chapter, the humanity and the humiliation of Jesus
are to be unfolded. Before the writer proceeded to this, however,
he paused to sound a note of warning. He reminded his readers of

---

* Abundant.

† Marginal note reads, "distributions."

Andrew Murray

the greater responsibility and greater danger in case of neglect—which greater privileges bring—and urged them to take more earnest, more abundant heed to what God is speaking in His Son.

Therefore, this is the link between the teaching of chapter 1, with regard to the Godhead and glory of the Son, and the warning that now comes. The everlasting God speaks to us in His Son; we surely ought to give more abundant heed.

"More abundant heed." The same word is used in Hebrews 6:17: *"Wherein God, being minded to shew more abundantly unto the heirs of the promise the immutability of his counsel."* In what God speaks and does, it is all with the desire to show to us *"more abundantly,"* in full and overflowing measure, what the purpose of His heart is. It is for this that He speaks in none less than His own Son. He has a right to claim that we meet Him with a corresponding wholeheartedness and give "more abundant heed" to what He speaks. Nothing less will satisfy Him. Nothing less, in the very nature of things, will satisfy us, because nothing less than man's "more abundant heed" is capable of receiving God's more abundant grace. It is the lack of this taking more earnest heed—the lack of intense earnestness, the lack of giving God and religion first place and the best powers of our life—which is at the root of the feebleness and sickliness of the Christian life. God is speaking to us in His Son, therefore we ought to take "more abundant heed."

"Lest haply we drift away"—and perish more surely and more terribly than those who sinned under the Old Testament. There in the Old Testament, when the word was spoken, with its threatening, it was steadfast; every transgression was punished. *"How shall we escape, if we neglect so great salvation."* The Gospel does not, as so many think, lessen—in fact, it increases our danger. It does not diminish, but will terribly intensify, the soreness of the punishment in those who neglect it. Oh, let us sound out the warning: It is not only positive enmity or open sin that will be punished. No, simply not taking *"earnest heed"* and instead drifting away unconsciously with the current of worldliness and halfhearted religion while

"neglecting" to give the great salvation that supremacy, that entire devotion, that it claims—it is this that will render escape impossible.

And why? How can we show men that it is right and just that it should be so? And what is the motive that will stir men to take heed? The answer is in these words: *"So great salvation."* The insight into the more abundant glory, the divine, and the all-surpassing greatness of this salvation is what will compel men willingly and joyfully to give up all and buy this pearl of great price.

And where does the greatness of this salvation lie? It is in this: that it comes to us from and through the triune God. The Holy Trinity is revealed as combining to work out this salvation for us. Listen: *"So great salvation...which having at the first been spoken through the Lord, was confirmed unto us by them that heard."* Christ the Son—the brightness of the Father's glory and the express image of His substance—it was He in whom God spoke to us. It was He, the Redeemer, God, and King, who Himself first preached the kingdom that He established when He effected the cleansing of our sins and sat down on the right hand of the throne.

"So great salvation"! First spoken by the Lord, *"God also bearing witness with them, both by signs and wonders, and by manifold powers."* God, the Father Himself, set His seal from heaven on the preaching of the Word. The existence of His church is His standing sign and wonder, the proof of His divine power. Not to take heed, to neglect the great salvation, is nothing less than despising God Himself.

God also bears witness, *"by [distributions] of the Holy Ghost, according to his own will."* Not only did God bear witness to the great salvation by signs and wonders and powers but also, above all, by the Holy Spirit sent down from heaven. The Holy Spirit is God come to dwell on earth, to strive and plead and testify in the hearts of men. There is no fellowship with the Father except through the Son, and no fellowship with the Son and His salvation except through the Holy Spirit in us. Let us enter the study of Christ's person and work in the epistle with this faith. Yes, this is the greatness of the great salvation—in its offer, the three-in-one God comes to us. The Lord preached, the Father bore witness, the Holy Spirit came as the power of God to work. What a salvation! What sin to neglect it! May God reveal to us, as we study this epistle, the glory of the *"so great salvation,"* that we may indeed more abundantly take heed to it.

Chapter Notes...

1. To know the Son who speaks and reveals the Father; to know the Father to whom, and to whose love, the Son brings us in; to know the Holy Spirit with His wonderful gifts of grace and power; to be restored to the image and fellowship of the Holy Trinity: This is salvation.

2. Let every thought of the glory of Christ and of God and of the Spirit and of the great salvation leave this one impression: Take more abundant heed to what you hear! Meet God's abounding grace with abounding desire to listen and believe.

3. God bore witness to the preaching of Christ and the apostles. If this was necessary then, how much more it is needed now, at this long distance from those days of heavenly joy and power. Ask, for the study of God's Word in this epistle, that God bear witness of the Holy Spirit. Claim and expect it. Without this, even the teaching of the apostles by Christ Himself availed little.

4. Once again, this is the greatness of salvation: The everlasting Father in His love speaks to me Himself in the Son. The Son shows and brings and gives me all that the Father speaks. And I have the Holy Spirit in me, fitting me to hear and know and possess and enjoy all that the Father in the Son speaks and gives. Let us, above all, hold this fast: that there is no divine witness, or assurance, or experience of the salvation Christ effected, except as the Holy Spirit, which came from heaven, communicates and maintains within us. Let us, therefore, take more abundant heed to the Holy Spirit in us, in whom the Father and the Son come to us.

JESUS AS MAN MORE THAN THE ANGELS: THE REASONS OF HIS HUMILIATION

Humilitation = to reduce (someone) to a lower position in one's own eyes or other's eyes: to make (someone) ashamed or embrassed
antonyms: elevate, exalt, aggrandize, canonize, deify

Eleven

The World Made Subject to Men, Not to Angels

For not unto angels did He subject the world to come, whereof we speak. But one hath somewhere testified, saying (see Psalm 8:5), What is man, that thou art mindful of him? Or the son of man, that thou visitest him? Thou madest him a little lower than the angels; thou crownedst him with glory and honour, and didst set him over the works of Thy hands: thou didst put all things in subjection under his feet. For in that he subjected all things unto him, He left nothing that is not subject to him. But now we see not yet all things subjected to him. But we behold Him who hath been made a little lower than the angels, even Jesus, because of the suffering of death crowned with glory and honour, that by the grace of God He should taste death for every man.
—Hebrews 2:5–9

82

Andrew Murray

As the Son of God, Christ is more than the angels. As the Son of Man, Jesus is more than the angels, too. He was indeed, as man, made a little lower than the angels. And yet, because the world to come (of which the Spirit of Christ in the prophets had spoken) had been made subject to man, he had a place of honor and dominion greatly excelling the angels. It is not only the divinity, but also the humanity, of Christ that proves how infinitely superior the new dispensation is to what was given by the ministry of angels.

"For not unto angels did he subject the world to come." That world to which the psalm looks forward is the kingdom of the Messiah, the kingdom of heaven upon earth. Psalm 8 does not speak directly of the Messiah but rather of man and his destiny. It is, however, applied most justly to the Messiah, because in Him the psalm and man find the fulfillment of what is promised.

The psalmist first speaks of man's littleness and the wonder that God should notice him. *"What is man, that thou art mindful of him? and the son of man, that thou visitest him?"* (Psalm 8:4). He then points out how high the place is that man occupies. His nature is little less than divine. *"Thou hast made him but little lower than* [the angels], *and crownest him with glory and honour"* (verse 5). And universal dominion is assigned to Him. *"Thou madest him to have dominion over the works of thy hands; thou hast put all things under his feet"* (verse 6). Our epistle points out how this promise, though not yet true of man, has received its fulfillment in Jesus. *"But now we see not yet all things subjected to him. But we behold him...crowned with glory and honour."* What was true of man in promise we see fulfilled in Jesus. And what we see in Jesus will be made true of man. What wonderful thoughts the psalm suggests.

How glorious is the destiny of man! Created in the image of God, he was to bear God's likeness in this, too: that, as king, he was to be ruler of all. The whole world to come was made subject to him. Man has received from God a life, a nature, and a spirit capable of partaking of His own life and spirit. His will and His holiness—we have been made capable of likeness to and fellowship with Himself, even to the sitting on His throne and sharing with Him the dominion over all creation. What a destiny!

How gloriously we see that destiny fulfilled in Jesus! It was because man had been created with a nature capable of such a destiny that the Son of God could become man and not count it unworthy of His divine glory Himself to work out that destiny. He came and proved what the life of man was meant to be—how humility and subjection to God were the sure path to glory and honor. He came and glorified a life of humiliation as the training-school for the exaltation to the right hand of God. Fulfilling man's destiny in Himself as Son of Man, He, as Son of God, fulfilled it for us too.

How gloriously and certainly man's destiny will yet be realized. Jesus, the Son of Man, came as the Second Adam. (See 1 Corinthians 15:45.) He stands in relation to us as close, as real, and as intimate as Adam did. As complete as Adam's communication of a sinful nature was will be Christ's impartation of a new nature—His own. As Son of God, Creator and Upholder of all in whom all things consist, He has a divine power of living within us with all that He was in Himself. His humanity is the revelation of what we can be; His divinity is the pledge that we can be it. *"We see not yet all things subjected to him,"* but—and this is enough—*"but we behold...Jesus...crowned with glory and honour, that by the grace of God he should taste death for every man."*

It was by His union with us in our life in the flesh, by His identifying Himself with our nature, that Jesus was able to claim and to work out and enter into possession of the glory God had promised to man. It is by our receiving His nature and by identifying ourselves with Him in this life on earth, and in heaven, that what He has achieved for us can really become ours. Let us here, at the very outset of our epistle, get a strong hold of the truth that what Christ does for us as our Leader, our Priest, and our

Andrew Murray

Redeemer is not anything external. All that God works in nature in heaven or on earth, in the stars or in the trees, He does from within, by laws that pervade their whole existence. All that Adam wrought in us is from within, by a power that rules our inmost life. And all that Christ does for us, whether as Son of God or Son of Man, is equally and entirely a work done within us. It is when we know that He is one with us and we with Him—even as was the case with Adam—that we will know how truly our destiny will be realized in Him. His oneness with us is the pledge—as our oneness with Him is the power—of our redemption.

Chapter Notes...

1. Your destiny, O man, is to sit with Jesus on His throne. Live as one preparing for it. Cultivate a royal spirit. Abide in Him and He will abide in you.

2. *"All things in subjection under his feet."* How terrible the ruin of sin by which man was made subject to the world. Its king became its slave, and this is so just when he appears most to master it. Christ teaches us to conquer the world by denying it; to hold it in subjection by not being of it. It is in the path of humiliation and self-denial alone that man's destiny can be realized.

3. The epistle has two things to show us in Jesus, as inseparably connected: the place of glory where He is now and the path of humiliation that brought Him there. Make it your care to follow Christ in His humility; He will make it His care to bring you to His glory.

4. Study to see the intimate connection, the real unity, between the two. It is the spirit that is subject to God on earth to which God makes all things subject in heaven. The soul that, in the humiliation of earth, makes God all is fit for the heavens, where God is manifested in glory as the All in All.

Twelve

We See Jesus Crowned with Glory and Honor

But now we see not yet all things subjected to him. But we behold him who hath been made a little lower than the angels, even Jesus, because of the suffering of death crowned with glory and honour, that by the grace of God he should taste death for every man.
—Hebrews 2:8–9

What a glorious contrast! *"We see not yet all things subjected to him,"* that is, to man. But—what is far better—*"we behold...Jesus...crowned with glory and honour."* When we look around upon this world, with all its sin and misery, it indeed does not appear as though man was destined to be higher than the angels and to have dominion over all the works of God's hands. But when we remember that Jesus became man so that He might taste death for all men and that He, the Man upon the throne, now lives as our Surety, our Redeemer, and our Head, it is enough if we see Him crowned with glory and honor. In that, we have the pledge that He will one day bring man to that glory and honor, too. In that, we have the assurance that He is using all that glory and honor even now on our behalf. *"We see not yet all things subjected to him. But we behold...Jesus...crowned with glory and honour."* Blessed contrast!

The right knowledge and use of this antithesis is the secret of the life of faith. *"We see not yet all things subjected to him"*: How exactly this expresses the disappointment and failure that is often the experience of the believer when his first joy and hope begin to pass away. He finds that sin is stronger than he knew, that the power of the world and the flesh and self are not yet made subject to him as he had hoped. At times, he feels as if the promises of God and the expectations they raised in his heart are vain. Or else, if he acknowledges that God is indeed faithful to fulfill them, then the way for one, who is as weak as he is and in his circumstances, to obtain these promises is too hard. The promises of God—to put all things in subjection to us and make us more than conquerors—are indeed most precious. But alas, ever again the bitter experience comes—man sees not yet all things subjected to him.

Blessed the man who knows, then, in living faith to say, *"But we behold...Jesus...crowned with glory and honour."* Blessed is the man who knows to look away from all that he finds in himself of imperfection and failure and to look up and behold all the perfection and glory he finds in Jesus! Yes, blessed is the man who finds his delight and his life in meeting every disappointment and every difficulty with the blessed statement, *"But we behold...Jesus... crowned with glory and honour."* This is all I need! This satisfies the soul and gives it peace and joy and strength.

The epistle is about to expound to us the great mystery of why the Son of God was made a little lower than the angels. It was for the purpose that, by the grace of God, He might taste death for every man and so open up again the entrance into God's presence and favor. The epistle will present to us the necessity and meaning of His sufferings and death in three different aspects. The first aspect is that, in suffering and death, Christ Himself must needs be made perfect so that, as our Leader, He might open up to us the path of perfection and prepare that new nature, that new way of living, in which we are to be led to glory (Hebrews 2:10). The second is that, through death, making propitiation for sin, Christ might destroy the devil, with his power of death, and give us a perfect deliverance from all fear of it (verse 14–15). And the third aspect is that, in what He suffered, He might be made a merciful and faithful High Priest, able to secure our perfect confidence and to give us the comfort we need (verse 16–18). But before the writer thus unfolded the meaning of Christ's humiliation, he first pointed to Christ's glory. It is this that constitutes the excellency of the New Testament, that gives our faith its power of endurance and victory. We see Jesus now at the right hand of the majesty of God. Let us hold this fast as the chief thought of the epistle, as the one great lesson that the Hebrews, and all feeble, backsliding Christians, need: that Jesus, who suffered for us; Jesus, who in His suffering as our Leader opened a way to Father for us; Jesus, who sympathizes with us—this Jesus is crowned with honor and glory. To see Him is to know that we have all we can need.

Would you, my reader, give more abundant heed to the great salvation? Would you experience how completely Jesus is able to save? Do you long for just as much of the love and the presence, the holiness and the joy and the power of God in you as there is in Jesus for you? Here you have the secret of it all! Amid all sin and weakness, all darkness and doubt, all failure and perplexity, hold fast this one truth and engage in this one exercise of faith: *"We see not yet all things subjected to him. But we behold...Jesus...crowned with glory and honour."* This gives peace, victory, and joy unspeakable.

And if you desire to know how to have your heart turned to Jesus, remember this: He came to save His people from their sins. The heart that is weary of itself and its sins, that fully accepts the fact of its utter corruption and utter helplessness of all that is of the old nature and of self, will find itself attracted with strong desire to this mighty Redeemer. In such a heart, Jesus, the crowned One, will not only be a distant object, but, by the Holy Spirit, an indwelling presence. The coming of the Holy Spirit is inseparably connected

Andrew Murray

with and is our only proof of the glorifying of Jesus. (See John 7:38–39; 16:14; 17:10.) It is our only real participation in the blessings that flow from it. Let all our worship of Him, crowned with glory and honor, be in the faith that the Pentecostal Spirit glorifies Him in us so that our whole inner being is filled with His presence.

Chapter Notes...

1. Jesus, *"made a little lower than the angels."* Jesus, *"because of the suffering of death crowned with glory and honour."* Do not look only at the glory but look well at the place of its birth, at the way in which it was gained. It is in the way in which you are walking now. Learn to welcome humiliation and suffering as the seed, the power out of which the glory is brought forth. Accept humiliation as the way in which Jesus, in glory, is preparing you for His glory.

2. We see Jesus crowned with glory and honor. Let every experience of the contrast—*"we see not yet all things subjected to him"*—become a call and a motive and a help to turn to Jesus. Let us take time and gaze and worship until our souls are filled with the faith. This life of humiliation is the bud of the glory everlasting: Jesus, in glory, is proof that it is so, the pledge that it will be so with us. Be this our life. We see Jesus, because of the suffering of death, crowned with glory and honor.

Thirteen

Jesus Tasting Death for Every Man

We behold him who hath been made a little lower than
the angels, even Jesus, because of the suffering of death
crowned with glory and honour, that by the grace of God
he should taste death for every man.
—Hebrews 2:9

Here we have the one great reason why it was fit for Jesus to be made a little lower than the angels. It was that He might taste death for every man. In the counsel of divine grace and in the great plan of redemption, this was one of the first objects of the Incarnation—the birth was for the sake of the death. Without that wonderful birth—the Word, which was God, made flesh (see John 1:1)—the death would not have profited us. Without that wonderful birth, the death would have availed us little. What God has joined together let no man put asunder. Let us beware of exalting the one at the expense of the other. The birth and the death are two inseparable parts of the one process by which He was perfected as the Firstborn from the dead and became our Deliverer and King.

The humanity and humiliation of Jesus were necessary for His death for, or on behalf of, every man.

And what was the meaning of this death? And where does its effectiveness lie? In Scripture there is a twofold aspect in which the death of Christ, as our Head, is set before us. The one is that He died for sin, bearing its curse and suffering death as God's righteous judgment on account of it. His death opened up the way to God for us. It did for us what we cannot and need not do: It wrought out a finished salvation, which we need only to accept and rest upon. According to the other aspect, He died to sin. His death was proof of His resistance to sin and its temptation, of His readiness to give up life rather than yield to sin. His death is proof that there is no way to be entirely free from the flesh and its connection with sin except by yielding the old life to death in order to receive, afresh and direct from God, an entirely new life. In this view, His death was an act of infinite moral and spiritual value—the consummation of the work God wrought when He perfected Him through suffering.

The former aspect—the death for sin on our behalf—has its value from the second, which reveals everything that constitutes its true nature and power. And even so, faith in Christ's death for sin must lead us into our death to sin. The one view is that of substitution, in other words, Christ doing what I cannot do. The other view is that of fellowship, in other words, Christ working in me what I see in Him. The former is a finished work and gives me boldness at once and forever to trust God. The latter is the power of sanctification, as the death and the life of Christ work in me.

Both views are found in the epistle in perfect harmony. See how clearly the former comes out in this chapter. It is because of *"the suffering of death"* that He has been *"crowned with glory and honour."* He was made *"a little lower than the angels"* that He might *"taste death for every man"* and might drink the cup of death, as the fruit of sin, for all. Some men die without tasting the bitterness of death. Jesus tasted its bitterness, as the curse of sin, in full measure. Then we read, in Hebrews 2:14, that He became man, *"that through death he might bring to nought him that had the power of death, that is, the devil."* His death accomplished for us what we never could, what we now need not do. And verse 17 tells us that His being made man was *"that he might be a merciful and faithful high priest in things pertaining to God, to make propitiation for the sins of the people."* All these expressions—suffering death, tasting death for all, bringing to nought the devil, making reconciliation for the sins of the people—refer to the finished work that Christ wrought, the sure and everlasting foundation on which our faith and hope can rest.

In its subsequent teaching, the epistle will show us the building that rests on that foundation—the heavenly power and life, the blessed nearness and service of God to which the High Priest, our Forerunner and Leader, brings us in fellowship with Himself in the way He opened up. But the epistle would have us begin here and strike the roots of our faith deep in the work that Christ, as our Substitute, wrought on Calvary. Let us study the words carefully, remember them well, and believe them fully: Christ has tasted death for all and emptied the cup; Christ has brought the devil to nothing; Christ has made reconciliation for sin. Death, the devil, sin—all these have been put away and brought to nothing. A complete deliverance has been effected. The sufferings and death of Christ have such infinite worth and preciousness in God's sight that no soul who is resolved to have nothing more to do with sin need fear any longer; instead, this soul may, with boldness, meet its God. The death of Christ has worked with mighty power in heaven and earth and hell. It has satisfied and delighted God; it has conquered death and sin and hell; it has redeemed and delivered mankind. Let that death live in your heart; it will work there its mighty wonders, too. And you will find Jesus in your heart, crowned with glory and honor for His suffering of death.

Chapter Notes...

1. The First Adam tasted the forbidden fruit and won death for all. The Second Adam tasted this death and brought life for all. To all who accept Him, the power, the indwelling, and the energy of the life is no less true and real than the power of sin and death has been. *"But we behold...Jesus...because of the suffering of death crowned with glory and honour."*

2. Jesus tasted the bitterness of your sin and death. O my soul, that you might taste the sweetness of His life and love. Oh, taste and see that the Lord is good.

3. *"By the grace of God he should taste death for every man."* *"Where sin abounded, grace did abound more exceedingly: that, as sin reigned in death, even so might grace reign through righteousness unto eternal life through Christ Jesus our Lord"* (Romans 5:20–21).

Fourteen

The Leader of Our Salvation

For it became him, for whom are all things, and through whom are all things, in bringing* many sons unto glory, to make the author† of their salvation perfect through sufferings.
pioneer
—Hebrews 2:10

We have seen that there is more than one reason for the humiliation of the Lord Jesus, even unto the suffering of death. Here we have the first: that as the Leader of our salvation, through whom God leads His sons to glory, He might open up the path, the way of life in which we were to go. For this, He needed to be made perfect through suffering and death. So, only could He become a Leader,‡ in the true and full sense of the word. In suffering, His will was perfected, His character was fashioned, His dependence on God *Father*

---

* Leading.

† Leader.

‡ The Dutch version has, "The Leader-in-Chief." The translation "Leader" makes more clear the connection with what precedes: "God leading (*agagon*) makes the Leader-in-Chief (*Archēgos*) perfect." Of *Captain* in KJV and *Author* in RV, Westcott says, "Neither word gives the fullness of sense. The *Archēgos* Himself first takes part in that which He establishes." In Hebrews 12:1, he adopts the word *"Leader"* in his translation—Jesus the Leader and Finisher of faith.

Andrew Murray

and delight in His will was confirmed and made manifest. In suffering, His obedience unto death opened up the living way in which alone the creature can reach the Creator—the deepest humility and entire surrender. As Leader, He opened up the path of life, a mode of living and acting, in which we are to follow.

It is this that we also spoke of as the second aspect of Christ's death. That death is not only atonement but fellowship. Only in suffering, in being crucified and dead with Christ, do we know Christ and His salvation. Christ was made perfect through suffering, that He might be the Leader—that, in conformity to Him, and in partaking of His Spirit and likeness, we might find the path to God and to glory.

The work of a leader supposes three things. The first is this: He must himself lead the way, passing through all its difficulties and dangers, knowing and showing it to those who follow. The second thing it supposes: Those who follow must yield themselves wholly to his guidance, walking even as he walked. And the third is this: He must take charge of his followers, seeing that all hindrances are removed and providing for all their needs. Let us see how blessedly all this is fulfilled in Jesus and what a comfort it brings us to know that Jesus bears this name, too: the Leader of our salvation.

The leader must walk in the very path his followers have to go. The path we searched for, in vain, was one that could bring us out from under the dominion of sin, both in its guilt as transgression against God and its power as death to all that is holy and good. There was no possible way out of this state of sin, guilt, and death except by submission to the judgment of God and by giving proof, in bearing that judgment, of entire and willing surrender to God's will. There was no way to come out of the fallen nature—with the power of self and self-will ruling it—but by entirely dying to it; suffering anything rather than letting it have its way. This was the way in which Jesus would lead us. And He had to walk in it Himself. *"For it became him,...in* [leading] *many sons unto glory, to make the* [leader] *of their salvation perfect through sufferings."* Christ was perfect from

His birth; every wish and inclination was as it should be. It was only a disposition, a power, that needed to be tested and developed and strengthened by trial. What the suffering and the death effected in Christ personally, in perfecting His character, is the groundwork of what is effected on our behalf. It was necessary that God [*Father*] should make Him perfect through suffering; the perfection that comes through suffering is meekness, gentleness, patience, and complete resignation to God's [*Father's*] will. It was because of the humility, meekness, lowliness of heart that the Lamb of God showed here upon earth that He is now the Lamb on the throne. Through suffering, He was made perfect and found worthy to be our High Priest.

A leader must be followed. His followers must walk in the very path in which He walks. Jesus came and was made like us; we must come and be made like Him. His suffering and death are not only substitution and atonement. They are those things—thank God!—but they are much more, too. His suffering and death call us to fellowship and conformity. The substitution rests on identification; out of that, conformity has its growth and strength. The Lamb of God has no salvation and no perfection to give us but His own meek spirit of entire dependence and absolute submission to God [*Father*]. The meekness and humility that was necessary for God [*Father*] to perfect in Him are as necessary for us. We must suffer and be crucified and die with Him. Death to self and the world, at the cost of any suffering or self-denial, is the only path to glory that the Leader of our salvation has opened up to us.

A leader cares for his followers. He does not say, "Follow me, who can." He watches over everyone, the very feeblest. Remember what care Stanley took in darkest Africa to gather in the stragglers—to leave the feeble ones provided in camp and then to wait for their coming up.* Jesus is a compassionate, sympathetic, and most faithful leader. With all the faithfulness and steadfastness

---

* Henry Stanley was the famous American reporter who led a crew of over one hundred men through modern-day Tanzania in 1871 to find the famous missionary, David Livingstone, who had been missing and persumed dead.

with which He walked that path Himself on earth will He help everyone, who will only, in meekness, trust and obey Him, to walk in that way to the end.

My friends, do you understand what it means that the Father, in leading you to glory, has made Jesus the Leader of our salvation? Jesus is responsible for you. Take Him and trust Him as your Leader. The great need in one who follows a leader is a tender, teachable spirit. Rejoice that you have such a Leader, Himself made perfect in meekness and submission through suffering, that He might lead you in the blessed path that brought Him—and will bring you as surely—to the glory of the Father.

And remember who this Leader is: the Son of God, the divine Maker and Upholder of all things. Not only does the Son of Man guide us as a Leader outside of us, influencing us by example and instruction, by authority and kindness. No, but He also guides us as the Son of God who works in us by His Spirit, yea who Himself dwells within us. Even as it was God who worked in Him and perfected Him, will He, as God, now work in us and perfect us.

Chapter Notes...

1. Christ came to give us an entirely new understanding of what true life is, to show us a new way of thinking and living, to teach us that a heavenly life consists in giving up everything that has the slightest connection with sin—all for the sake of pleasing the Father perfectly. This is the new and living way He opened up through the rent veil of the flesh.

2. *"For it became him,...to make the author of their salvation perfect."* All that Christ wrought, and all that was wrought in Him, was wrought by God. Christ yielded Himself to God; He did nothing of Himself. He allowed God to do all in Him. This is the path of perfection, the path to glory in which Jesus leads. His divinity is inexpressibly precious to

us for what He can be and do in us. But as inexpressibly precious is His humanity—showing us how He was perfected, how God worked in Him, what we must be, and what we can most surely be through Him.

3. Seek to get a very clear grasp of the truth that He is only a Savior as He is a Leader; salvation is being led by Him.

Fifteen

For Whom and Through Whom Are All Things

For it became him, for whom are all things, and through whom are all things, in bringing* many sons unto glory, to make the author† of their salvation perfect through sufferings.
—Hebrews 2:10

"For whom are all things." God is the final cause of all that is. Everything exists with the one purpose of showing forth His Father's glory. Every object in nature has its only reason of existence in this: that the wondrous goodness and power of God may shine out through it. Above all, man was created that the praiseworthy Being, whose very nature is love, might have the opportunity of proving in him how freely and how fully He would make man partaker of the riches of His grace and glory.

"For whom are all things," that in them, His glory and goodness may be made known. "Worthy art thou, our Lord and our God,

---

* Leading.
† Leader.

to receive the glory and the honour and the power: for thou didst create all things, and because of thy will they were created" (Revelation 4:11).

"Through whom are all things." God is the efficient cause of all that is. God is the end and aim of all things because He is their Beginning and Origin. All must return to Him because all came from Him and exist only through Him. There is no life or goodness or beauty that does not rise up to Him again, the only Fountain and Source. *"There is one God, the Father, of whom are all things, and we unto him"* (1 Corinthians 8:6). *"One God and Father of all, who is over all, and through all, and in all"* (Ephesians 4:6).

The apostle might have written, "It became God to make the Leader of our salvation perfect through suffering." Not without good reason did he introduce here the character in which God acted in perfecting the Son as Leader of our salvation. When man sinned and fell from God, he lost together the two blessed truths in which his relation to God had stood. These were his holy allegiance to God, having all things *for* Him, and his blessed dependence on God, having all things *through* Him. Instead of these came the reign of self, with its life for self and through self.

Jesus came to redeem us from this life of self, to bring us back to God, to know and honor Him as the God and Father, for whom are all things and through whom are all things. In doing this, He opened again the only way that could lead to glory. He did it first by showing us in His life as a man how men ought to live for God and through God; and then, by delivering us through His death from the dominion of sin and winning for us the power of the heavenly life.

"For whom are all things, and through whom are all things." It was in this character that God perfected Christ through sufferings. It was in this character that Christ revealed and honored God in His sufferings. It is to win us and to bring us to know, love, and serve God in this character that Jesus is Savior.

"For whom are all things." Throughout His whole life there was nothing that Jesus sought to impress more distinctly on His

disciples than this: that He was the Father's messenger and servant; that He had no thought of doing His own will or seeking His own honor; and that He only sought and did what would be for the Father's pleasure and glory. He gave us the example of a man on earth living absolutely and entirely for God in heaven. His life on earth was the exhibition here in the flesh, the translation into human language of the divine claim, "All things for God." His allegiance to God was absolute. He proved to us that man's destiny and blessedness and everlasting glory are to be found in living wholly for God.

"Through whom are all things." Of this, too, Christ's life was the exposition. He was not ashamed to say continually that He could do nothing of Himself and that only as the Father showed Him or spoke to Him could He work and speak. He counted this His blessedness and strength—not to be able to do anything of Himself but, in continual dependence, to wait on God and His working in Him. He knew and taught us that the man who has said in wholehearted devotion to God, "All things for God," may confidently say, too, "All things by God."

"All for God," and "All by God." Jesus Christ has made it possible for us to make these our watchwords. In all aspirations after a closer walk with God and in all efforts after a purer, truer, and higher life, they are the two poles between which the soul ought to move. They are the sure marks of that true scriptural mysticism that has such attraction for all hungry souls who long to know and please God perfectly.

"All for God!" Absolutely—without a moment, a thought, a word, a person, or a possession excepted—wholly for God: This becomes the soul's one desire. It has been seen that God is worthy of this, that He claims it, and that, in the very nature of things, nothing less can satisfy the heart God made to be filled with Himself.

"All by God!" The clearer the aim becomes to be all for God, and the deeper the soul sinks into its own emptiness and helplessness under the conviction that with man it is impossible, then the sooner faith will rise to see that we will not only be able to say, but that we actually will dare to say, "All for God!" because we may also say, "All by God!" God Himself will work it in us.

This is the God who has revealed Himself to us in His Son. It became Him, for whom all things are and by whom all things are, to make the Leader of our salvation perfect through sufferings. Let us worship Him! Let us adore Him! Let us offer Him the sacrifice of full allegiance and childlike dependence as the words ring through heart and life—"All for God! All by God! God is all!"

Chapter Notes...

1. The practice of the presence of God is a most necessary and most blessed spiritual exercise. As the soul bows in stillness and lowliness, worshiping in silence, it gets into the right spirit for recognizing its own nothingness and realizing that God is all—that all is for Him and that all is by Him.

2. "All for God": That is consecration. "All by God": That is faith. This was the spirit in which Christ yielded Himself to God—consecration and faith.

3. This was the God who perfected Christ. To know and honor God in this character is the secret of perfection, for in such, He can do His work. This is the God who is leading many sons to glory. To know and honor Him is the path to glory. To reveal this God and His claims is to show how to give up everything to Him—this was what Christ came for. This is the life He brought us, the path He opened, and the salvation He gives.

Sixteen

Jesus Calls Us Brethren

For both he that sanctifieth and they that are sanctified are all of* one: for which cause he is not ashamed to call them brethren, saying (see Psalm 22:23), *I will declare thy name unto my brethren, in the midst of the congregation will I sing thy praise. And again, I will put my trust in him* (see Isaiah 8:17). *And again, Behold, I and the children which God hath given me* (see Isaiah 8:18).
—Hebrews 2:11–13

We have here the reason of what precedes. Why was it needful for God, in leading many sons unto glory, to make the Leader of their salvation perfect through suffering? Or how was it that making Him perfect could perfect them and bring salvation to them? The answer is this: He that sanctifies (that is, Jesus) and they who are sanctified (God's sons) are all out of One, that is, of God. In proof of this, three texts are quoted in which Jesus calls us brethren, takes His place with us in trusting God, and speaks of us as the children God has given Him. It is because Jesus (the firstborn Son) and the sons whom He leads to glory are one in their being, begotten of God, that His perfection secures their salvation. It is the oneness of Jesus with us that fits Him to be the Leader of salvation.

* Out of.

This oneness has its root in the truth of the divine life. *"Both he that sanctifieth and they that are sanctified are all* [out] *of one."* Jesus is the Only Begotten, the eternal Son, one with the Father in His divine being and majesty. We are sons of God as we partake of the divine life through and in Him. Notwithstanding the difference between His Sonship and ours—His being original and ours derived—they are at root one. The life of both has its origin in the life of God. This oneness of Christ with us in origin made it possible for Him to become one with us in our humanity and so to be the Leader of our salvation. This oneness makes it possible for Him to communicate to us that perfection, that perfect meekness and delight in God's will, which was wrought out in His human nature through suffering, that holiness of His with which we must be made holy.

"For both he that sanctifieth and they that are sanctified are all of one." Jesus is the Sanctifier; we are the sanctified. The object for which Christ became the Leader of our salvation—the great work He has to do for us, the bond of union between the Son and the sons of God, the proof of their bearing His image and likeness, and the mark of their real oneness—is holiness.

The word *holy* is one of the deepest in Scripture. It means a great deal more than separated or consecrated to God. The triune God is the Thrice-Holy One: Holiness is the deepest mystery of His being, the wondrous union of His righteousness and His love. To be holy is to be in fellowship with God, possessed by Him. Therefore, the Spirit specially bears the name *Holy* because He is the bearer to us of the love of God, and the maintenance of the divine fellowship is His special work. Jesus is the Holy One of God, who makes us holy in filling us with His Holy Spirit.* The difference

---

* Here, and throughout the epistle, the words *holy* and *sanctify* include much more than is ordinarily meant by the doctrine of sanctification. *"Sanctify,* here, includes all that God does for our restoration, as He calls, justifies, and glorifies." —Rieger in Lange on Hebrews 10:10 (compare 9:13, 14; 10:10, 14, 29; 13:12)

between Jesus and us is great—the oneness is greater. He and we are of one, together partakers of God's life and God's holiness. Let us give abundant heed to so great a salvation.

This oneness finds its manifestation in the brother-name that Jesus gives us. *"For which cause he is not ashamed to call them brethren, saying, I will declare thy name unto my brethren."* The writer had spoken of our inner oneness with Jesus. But, oh, what a difference in actual life—such a terrible difference that He might well be ashamed of us! Yes! Before angels, as well as before the world, how often His saints have put Him to shame and have given Him reason to be ashamed of His relationship! But—blessed be His name— His becoming man was an act of condescension, which had its root in the sense of His oneness with us as being one with Him out of God, which had its strength in the love as of an elder Brother.

Three texts are now quoted. The one is from Psalm 22:23, in which the suffering Messiah promises to make known the Father's name to His brethren. The second and third are from Isaiah 8:17– 18, in which His fellowship with all His people in the life of faith and trust, and His place at the head of those whom God has given Him as children, find expression in prophetic types.

What wonderful thoughts! We, as truly as Jesus, are of God! It is in the light of this truth that Jesus looks on us, loves us, and deals with us! It is in the light of this truth that we must look on Jesus, love Him, and deal with Him. And let us look on ourselves in the light of this truth, too. This is the life of faith—to see Jesus and ourselves as He sees us, to think as He thinks, and to live in His heart. Then will the promise be fulfilled to us, *"I will declare thy name unto my brethren"* *"that the love wherewith thou hast loved me may be in them, and I in them"* (John 17:26 KJV). As we bow in lowly, waiting silence before Him, the soul will hear Him say, "My brother! Let me reveal to you the Father." And the name and the love and the nearness of the Father will have new meaning when I can say, "Jesus calls me His kin! God has spoken to me in His

Son!" And I will understand that, to faith, the incomprehensible reality of oneness with Jesus becomes the blessed, conscious experience of the soul in its daily life.

Chapter Notes

1. Union with Jesus in being born of God, in being holy, in being acknowledged by Him as a brother or sister! What a blessed life! What a full salvation!

2. *"Whosoever shall do the will of God, the same is my brother"* (Mark 3:35). Would you know the holy joy of Jesus saying to you, "Brother"? Let your life be what His was—the doing of the will of God! It was in this that He was perfected in suffering. It was in this that His Spirit and life in you will manifest itself and the brother-name will be the index, not only of His compassion but also of the oneness in Spirit and the likeness in conduct that prove you to be a son of God.

3. Sanctification, or holiness, is nothing more than a life in union with Jesus. Nothing more and nothing less. *"He that sanctifieth and they that are sanctified are all of one."* To live in that oneness, to have Jesus living in us, is the way to be holy.

4. *"And again, I will put my trust in him."* Jesus lived by faith in God. He is the Leader and Perfecter of faith. He opened up to us the path of faith and leads us in it.

Seventeen

That He Might Bring to Nought the Devil

Since then the children are sharers in flesh and blood,
he also himself in like manner partook of the same; that
through death he might bring to nought him that had the
power of death, that is, the devil; and might deliver all
them who through fear of death were all their
lifetime subject to bondage.
—Hebrews 2:14–15

The previous verses spoke of the oneness of Jesus and His brethren from the divine side: They are all of One. Here we have it put before us from its human side: *"Since then the children are sharers in flesh and blood, he also himself in like manner partook of the same."* We have already said that for this, Christ becoming man, there was more than one reason. The first was that, as our Leader, He might Himself be perfected and so prepare a way—or state of living, a nature, a life—in which we might draw nigh to God. The second reason was so that He might deliver us from the power of death and the devil. The third reason was that in all His work for us and in us, He might be a merciful High Priest in things pertaining to God, able to understand and sympathize with us, and ready to bear and to succor. Here, in this verse, it is the second of these three aspects of Christ's incarnation that is brought out: He became man that He might meet and conquer and destroy the power of death and the devil.

"Since then the children are sharers in flesh and blood, he also himself in like manner partook of the same." However familiar the thought of the Incarnation is, let us again seek to realize fully all that it means. As Adam never could have brought us under the power of sin and death if he had not been our father, communicating to us his own nature, so too Christ never could save us except by taking our nature upon Him, doing in that nature all that we would need to do—had it been possible for us to deliver ourselves—and then communicating the fruit of what He effected as a nature within us to be the power of a new and eternal life. As a divine necessity, without which there could be no salvation, and as an act of infinite love and condescension, the Son of God became a partaker of flesh and blood. So, He alone could be the Second Adam, the Father of a new race.

"That through death he might bring to nought him that had the power of death, that is, the devil." Death is a power that has its sanction from God Himself. In the very nature of things it could not be otherwise than that man, when he turned from God, the fountain of life, to Satan and to self, fell under the power of death. He had yielded himself to Satan, and Satan had power over him. As the jailer keeps the prisoner under the authority of the king, Satan holds the sinner in the power of death as long as no true legal release is given. The only way for us to come from under the power of Satan and death was to lay off that fallen nature over which they had power, to come out of that sinful life by dying to it, and, in dying, to be entirely freed from it. We had no power to do this. Jesus entered into all the conditions of our fallen humanity. He entered into our death and endured it as the penalty of sin; and, in enduring it, He satisfied the law of God. And so, because the law had been

the strength of sin, He took from sin and the devil the power of death over us. He endured death as the end of the life of the flesh, in full acknowledgment of God's righteous judgment, yielding up His spirit to the Father. Death, as the penalty of the law; death, as the end of the life of nature; death, as the power of Satan over man—death as all of these was destroyed, and he that had the power of death was brought to nothing. And now, as little claim or power as death has on Him, the same it has on those who are in Him, on those in whom the power of His life now works. *"He also himself in like manner partook of the same; that through death he might bring to nought him that had the power of death, that is, the devil."*

"And might deliver all them who through fear of death were all their lifetime subject to bondage." The power of death and the devil has been so completely broken that there is now perfect deliverance from that fear of death that keeps so many in bondage. Under the Old Testament, life and immortality had not yet been fully brought to light. No wonder the older saints often lived and spoke as those subject to bondage. But how sad that the redeemed of Jesus Christ, His brethren, so often prove that they know but little of the reality and power of His deliverance, or of the song of joy: *"Death is swallowed up in victory....Thanks be to God, which giveth us the victory through our Lord Jesus Christ"* (1 Corinthians 15:54, 57).

My friend, are you living in the full experience of this blessed truth? Because you share in flesh and blood, Christ came and likewise partook of the same, that there might be perfect oneness between Him and you. Do you live in this oneness? By His death He destroyed the devil, that you might be entirely freed from his power. Is your life in this liberty? He delivers from the fear of death and the bondage that it brings, changing it into the joy of the hope of glory. Is this joy yours? Let us believe that He who is now crowned with glory and honor is indeed able to make all a reality to us so that, as those who are one with Him by the double bond of the birth from God and the birth in flesh and blood, we may be His ransomed, His sanctified ones, and His beloved brethren.

He gave Himself to be wholly like us and for us—will we not give ourselves to be wholly like Him and for Him?

Chapter Notes...

1. *"Through death he might bring to nought him that had the power of death."* Death had its power from the law. There was no way of conquering it but by fulfilling its claim. Through death, He destroyed death. This is the way for us, too. As I give myself up to death, as I give up the sinful life and die to self in the power of Christ's death, the power of His deliverance will work in me.

2. Through death to life. This is the law of nature, as seen in every corn of wheat. This is the law of the life of Christ, as seen in His resurrection. This is the law of the life of faith, to be felt and experienced every day, as the power of the new death that He died and the new life that He lives works in us.

3. The first chapter revealed to us the divinity of Christ as the foundation of the Gospel, that we might know that all that He accomplished in His humanity has been effected in divine reality and works in us in divine creative power.

Eighteen

A High Priest Able to Succor

For verily not of angels doth he take hold, but he taketh hold of the seed of Abraham. Wherefore it behoved him in all things to be made like unto his brethren, that he might be* a merciful and faithful high priest in things pertaining to God, to make propitiation for the sins of the people. For in that he himself hath suffered being tempted, he is able to succour them that are tempted.
—Hebrews 2:16–18

In the first chapter, we saw the writer quoting text after text from the Old Testament in order that he might bring us to full apprehension of the truth and meaning of our Lord's divinity. In this chapter, we see him in the same way, time after time, reiterate the fact of our Lord's humanity lest we would not fully realize all that it means. So it is here. He had just said, *"Since then the children are sharers in flesh and blood, he also himself in like manner partook of the same"* (2:14). It is almost as if he felt the insufficiency of words and

---
* Become.

therefore, once again, repeated and confirmed his statement: *"For verily not of angels doth he take hold, but he taketh hold of the seed of Abraham."* Man may have been made lower than the angels, but this honor the angels do not have: that He took hold of them. *"He taketh hold of the seed of Abraham."* And how does He take hold? There is no way in which God can take hold of a creature other than by entering into him with His life and Spirit, so imparting His own goodness and power and bringing him into union with Himself. So did Jesus take hold of man. He entered into humanity and became one with it. And so He takes hold of individual souls by entering with each into personal union and fellowship.

"Wherefore"—being thus minded to take hold of man—*"it behoved Him"*—in other words, it was divinely right and proper and, in the nature of things, an absolute necessity as a consequence of His purpose—*"it behoved him in all things to be made like unto his brethren."* The laying hold implied His identifying Himself with them, and this, again, was impossible without being made like them in all things. Only in this way could He save them. It was indeed necessary, so that He might become a merciful and faithful High Priest in things pertaining to God, to make propitiation for the sins of the people.

Here we have, for the first time, the phrase *"high priest"*—a phrase that is used in no other book of the New Testament in reference to our Lord Jesus; in this epistle, however, this is its central thought. We will see later, in chapter 5, how inseparably His divine sonship and His priesthood are linked. Here we are taught that His real humanity is just as much essential to it. It is one of the remarkable things in the epistle that it unfolds so wonderfully the value of the personal development in our Lord's life. It ever connects the person and the work as inseparable.

See it here. The work He had to do was to make propitiation for the sins of the people. Sin had incurred the wrath of God, and His love could not flow forth toward men until the sin had been covered up, atoned for, and taken away. In fulfillment of all that had

(This was done before the foundation of the world.)

been taught to us in the Old Testament sacrifices, Christ came to do this. He put away sin by the sacrifice of Himself and obtained everlasting redemption. Of this, the epistle will speak later on. What it here seeks to impress is that Christ became man, not merely to die and atone but also that, in doing this, He might be a faithful and merciful High Priest. His relation to us was to be a personal one. He must Himself minister to us the salvation He worked out. Everything would depend upon His winning our confidence; getting possession of our hearts and love; and, as a living Leader, guiding us into the path to God. It is this that makes His human life on earth so precious to us. It proved Him faithful; we can dare to fully trust Him. It showed Him to be merciful; we need not fear coming to Him. *"Wherefore it behoved him in all things to be made like unto his brethren, that he might be a merciful and faithful high priest."*

For in that He Himself has suffered being tempted, He is able to succor those who are tempted. The work of our High Priest does not only consist in His atonement, nor even in the advocacy and intercession that is the fruit of that atonement. Above all, as the result of all these, His work consists in that personal charge of our spiritual life that He takes and in that never-ceasing succor that He is able to give in every temptation. This is the greatest and most blessed part of His work in bringing us to God; that, as the Leader in the path of suffering and perfection, He inspires us with His own dispositions and, by the mighty operation of His Spirit within us, gives us His help in every time of need. The one thing we need is to know and trust Him fully. To know Him as our High Priest who not only has opened a way to God for us to walk in and not only prays for us in heaven, but who also undertakes to keep us so in fellowship with Himself, under the covering of His power, and in the experience of His full redemption that temptation can never conquer us. His divinity secures to us His unfailing and never-ceasing presence. His humanity assures us of His sympathy and compassion. More ever-present and more mighty than the temptation, His unfailing love is always near to give the victory. He can and will do it. Our High Priest is a living, faithful helper: Let us trust Him. Salvation is not a thing He gives us apart from Himself. Full salvation is nothing but Jesus Himself, most compassionately and most faithfully watching over us in daily life, and most really and fully giving and living His life in us. The abiding, indwelling presence of Jesus, able to succor, is the true secret of the Christian life. Faith will lead us into the experience that Jesus is and does all that is said of Him.

Chapter Notes...

1. What a chapter! Jesus crowned with glory and honor. Our Leader, our Sanctifier, our Brother, made like to us; our merciful and faithful High Priest, tempted as we are, our Helper in temptation. What a Savior!

2. No member of my body can be hurt without my feeling it and seeking to guard it. No temptation can touch me without Jesus feeling it at once and giving succor. Isn't this what we need: to know Him better, in faith to realize His ever-present nearness, and to count on His help?

3. The knowledge of Jesus that sufficed for conversion will not suffice for sanctification. For the growth of the spiritual life it is essential that we enter more deeply into the knowledge of all that Jesus is. Jesus is the bread of heaven, the food of our spiritual life. Knowing Him better is the only way to feed upon Him.

4. Learn to regard every temptation as the blessed opportunity for trusting and realizing the succor of your ever-present High Priest.

Third Section—Hebrews 3:1–6
CHRIST JESUS MORE THAN MOSES

Nineteen

Consider Jesus

Wherefore, holy brethren, partakers of a heavenly calling,
consider the Apostle and High Priest
of our confession, even Jesus.
—Hebrews 3:1

Consider Jesus!" This is the central thought of the verse and of the passage of which it is a part, as it is indeed of the whole epistle. It is the one aim of the writer to persuade the Hebrews that, if they only knew aright the Lord Jesus as the faithful, compassionate, and almighty High Priest in heaven, they would find in Him all they needed for a life such as God would have them lead. Their lives would be in harmony with their faith, in harmony with the life of Him whom their faith would apprehend. The words might have been taken as the title of my book: "Consider Jesus!" is indeed the keynote of the epistle.

The word *consider*, from the root of the Latin word for *star*, originally meant to contemplate the stars. It suggests the idea of the astronomer and the quiet, patient, persevering, concentrated gaze with which he seeks to discover all that possibly can be known of the stars that he studies. And Jesus—who is God, who became man and perfected our human nature in His wonderful life of suffering and obedience, and who now dwells in heaven to communicate to us its life and blessedness—oh, what reason there is for saying, "Consider Jesus!" Gaze upon Him. Contemplate Him. For increased knowledge of the stars, what devotion, enthusiasm, and sacrifices are oftentimes witnessed. Oh, let the study and possession of the Son of God waken our devotion and our enthusiasm that we may be able to tell men what beauty and what glory there is in Jesus.

"Holy brethren." Thus the Hebrews were addressed. In the previous chapter, the word *"brethren"* had been used twice. Christ is not ashamed to call them brethren. *"It behoved him in all things to be made like unto his brethren"* (2:17). The sacred name is now applied personally: Christ's brethren are brethren in Christ. And the heart of the writer warmed to them personally, as he sought to urge them to what, with him, was indeed the one aim of the epistle—*"Consider...Jesus."*

"Holy brethren"! The word *"holy"* had also just been used. *"For both he that sanctifieth* [maketh holy] *and they that are sanctified* [made holy] *are all of one: for which cause he is not ashamed to call them brethren"* (2:11). We saw how holiness is the common mark of Christ and His people; it is their bond of union and the great object they both aim at. One of the great mysteries the epistle will reveal to us is that our great High Priest has opened the way for us into the Most Holy Place, or the Holiest of All. In Hebrew, it is the Holiness of Holinesses. There, we have boldness of access; there, we are to have our dwelling encircled by the holiness of God. We must know that we are holy in Christ; this will give us courage to enter into the Holiness of Holinesses, to have God's holiness take complete possession of and fill our whole being. It is Jesus who makes holy; it is we who are to be made holy. What is more natural than that the thoughts should be coupled together—*"Holy brethren,...consider...Jesus"*?

"Holy brethren, partakers of a heavenly calling, consider...Jesus." What is elsewhere spoken of as "a holy calling" is here named *"a heavenly calling."* That does not only mean a calling from heaven, or a calling to the heaven from where the call proceeds. No, there

is much more in it. Heaven is not only a place but also a state, a mode of existence, the life in which the presence of God is revealed and experienced in its unhindered power. And the heavenly calling is that in which the power of the heavenly life works to make our lives heavenly. When Jesus was upon earth, the kingdom of heaven was close at hand. After He had ascended into heaven and received the kingdom from the Father, the kingdom of heaven came to this earth in power, through the descent of the Holy Spirit. Christians, at Pentecost, were people who, by the new birth, entered into the heavenly kingdom or state of life. And the kingdom entered into them. And they were *"partakers of a heavenly calling,"* because the spirit and the life and the power of heaven was within them.

It is to such men that the invitation comes. "Holy brethren, partakers of the heavenly calling, consider Jesus!" If you would know what it is to be holy and to live holy, consider Jesus, who makes us holy! If you would know the privileges and powers that belong to you as partakers of a heavenly calling, consider Jesus! He is God, the King of heaven! He is the Man who has ascended to heaven as your Priest and Savior, has opened it for you and can communicate its life and blessedness. Oh, consider Jesus! Set your hearts on Him; He will make you holy and heavenly.

There is more than one of my readers, I suppose, who mourns that he knows so little of what it is to live a holy and a heavenly life. Listen, God's word speaks to you. "Holy brethren, partakers of a heavenly calling, consider Jesus!" This is your weakness: You have looked at yourselves and your own strength; you have not studied Jesus! This will be your cure: Each day, each hour, consider Jesus; and in Him you will find all the holiness and the heavenliness you need.

Chapter Notes...

1. In the latter part of the epistle, all the glory of Jesus as He entered heaven and opened it for us; as He became a minister of the heavenly sanctuary; and as He led us to dwell in the

Father's presence—all of these will be opened to us. But let us even now, from the commencement, hold fast to this truth: that the knowledge of Jesus seated in heaven is the power of the heavenly calling and the heavenly life.

2. Do not think that you know all that can be told about Jesus. Believe that there are wonders of heavenly joy to be revealed to you if you know Him better: His divine nearness and oneness with man; His ever-present indwelling to succor and lead you; and His power to bring you into the Holiest of All, into the Father's presence and love, and to keep you there, will be revealed.

Twenty

Christ and Moses

Wherefore, holy brethren, partakers of a heavenly calling,
consider the Apostle and High Priest of our confession, even
Jesus; who was faithful to him that appointed him, as also
was Moses in all his house. For he hath been counted worthy
of more glory than Moses, by so much as he that built the
house hath more honour than the house. For every house is
builded by some one; but he that built all things is God.
And Moses indeed was faithful in all his house as a servant,
for a testimony of those things which were afterward to be
spoken; but Christ as a son, over his house; whose house are
we, if we hold fast our boldness and the glorying of
our hope firm unto the end.
—Hebrews 3:1–6

The writer had just spoken of Christ as *"a merciful and faith-*
ful high priest" (2:17). Later (4:14–5:7), he will speak again
of Him as merciful. Here he wished first to set before us His
faithfulness. To this end he compared Christ to Moses, of whom
God Himself had spoken: *"My servant Moses is not so; he is faithful*
in all mine house" (Numbers 12:7). But, at the same time, he went
on to prove that Christ the Son is more than Moses the servant.
We have seen that Christ is more than the angel through whom

the Law was given; we will yet see that He is more than Aaron, through whom the Law was ministered; He is more than Moses too, the mediator of the Law, the servant in the house of God. In every aspect, the New Testament has more glory than the Old.

Moses and Aaron together represented God in Israel; the one as apostle or messenger, the other as high priest. In the person of Jesus, the two offices are united. As High Priest, He is merciful as Aaron; as Apostle of our profession, He is faithful as Moses. Moses was the great apostle or messenger of God, the Old Testament type of Christ as prophet. He had access to God and brought the word of God to the people. Christ is the great Apostle or Prophet of the new covenant. He ever spoke of Himself as the One whom the Father had sent. In Him, the Son, God speaks to us. As Apostle, He is God's representative with us, making God known to us. As High Priest, He is our representative with God, bringing us into His presence. As High Priest, He stands linked to us by His mercy and compassion, as He now, having died for us, helps us in our temptation and weakness. As Apostle, He pleads for God with us and proves Himself entirely faithful to Him. We need to consider Christ Jesus not only as a High Priest in His mercy but also as the Apostle of our profession who was faithful to Him who appointed Him, just as Moses was in all his house. Faithfulness is trustworthiness. As we see Jesus faithful to Him who appointed Him, our faith and trust will rise into perfect and joyful assurance that He will indeed most faithfully fulfill all God's promises in us; that in us, too, He will be faithful as a Son over His own house. Nothing gives such strength to faith as resting on the faithfulness of Jesus. The glory of Jesus is the glory of Christianity, the strength and glory of the Christian life.

Moses was in every respect a type of Christ. In what he suffered from his brethren; in his rejection by his brethren; in his zeal and his sacrifice of all for God; in his willingness to die for his people; in his fellowship with God—in all these, we see the marks of an apostle, as they were to be perfectly revealed in Christ Jesus. And yet, it was all only a shadow and a prophecy, a testimony of things to come.

> *For he hath been counted worthy of more glory than Moses, by so much as he that built the house hath more honour than the house. For every house is builded by some one; but he that built all things is God. And Moses indeed was faithful in all his house as a servant, for a testimony of those things which were afterward to be spoken; but Christ as a son, over his house.*

Moses was himself but a part of the house; Jesus Christ is the Builder. Moses was a servant in the house; Jesus was a Son over His own house.

"Whose house are we." The true house, the true dwelling of God, is His people. In Christ, we are built together for a habitation of God in the Spirit. Of the church, as His body, and of the individual soul, Christ says, *"Will come unto him, and make our abode with him"* (John 14:23). It is the characteristic of spiritual things that each part is also a living whole. Collectively and individually, we are Christ's house. He that would know the faithfulness of Christ in His house must yield himself to be His house. He must allow Christ as Son to be Master over His house, to have the keys alone, and to hold undisturbed possession and rule.

"Whose house are we." Later on, we will see how the great work of Christ, as the great High Priest over the house of God, is to open the way into the Holiest of God's dwelling, His living and loving presence. The Word we have here today tells us beforehand that the Holiest is not only with God and that we must enter into it; the Word tells us that the Holiest is also with us and that God will come in to us, too. God's heart is our habitation; our heart is God's habitation. When Jesus spoke, *"Abide in me, and I in you"* (John 15:4), He taught us that mutual relationship. The more my heart goes out to Jesus and lives in Him, the more He comes to live in me.

"Whose house are we." Would you have the full experience of all that means and brings? Holy brethren, partakers of the heavenly calling, consider Jesus, who is faithful to Him who appointed Him, as a Son over His house. Yield yourselves to Him as His house, and trust His faithfulness to do His work. And, remember, as the epistle teaches us the spiritual meaning of the external symbols of the Old Testament that we must not seek their fulfillment again in other external things, however much we conceive of them as infinitely higher and greater, but in that inward spiritual experience that comes when Jesus dwells in us as His house. He does His work as the indwelling Savior, whether it be Prophet, Priest, or King. *"Whose house are we."*

Chapter Notes...

1. *"Faithful to him that appointed him."* This is the spirit of God's house, the mark of being of His household. It was so with Moses the servant. It was so with Christ the Son. It must be so through the whole household. Be it so with us; may we be faithful to God.

2. *"Whose house are we."* Not like a house of stone and wood, in which the dweller has no living connection with it. No, Christ dwells in us as a life within a life, inspiring us with His own temper and disposition. Our moral and spiritual being, our power of willing and living and acting—within these He comes and dwells in us a divine, hidden, but mighty power and operation.

3. *"Faithful,...as a son, over his house."* But He must be Master in His own house, not just an honored guest while you have the keys and the care. So it is with many Christians, and so it should not be. No, give Him the keys; give Him entire control over the whole being, as Son over His house. He will blessedly prove how faithful He is to God and to you.

4. Consider well the faithfulness of Christ; this will work in you the fullness of faith.

Twenty-One

If We Hold Fast Our Boldness Firm to the End

Whose house are we, if we hold fast our boldness and the glorying of our hope firm unto the end.
—Hebrews 3:6

A mong the Hebrews there were not a few who had gone back and were in danger of falling away. They had given way to sloth and had lost the joy and confidence of their first faith. The writer was about to sound a note of solemn warning (3:7–4:13), to call them to beware of that evil heart of unbelief that departs from the living God. For the transition, he wrote—making the words, as it were, the text for what follows—"*Whose house are we, if we hold fast our boldness and the glorying of our hope firm unto the end.*"

Holding fast and firm to the end. Steadfastness and perseverance; this is indeed the great need of the Christian life. There is no question that exercises the earnest minister of the Gospel in our days, as in early times, more deeply than what may be the reason why so many converts grow cold and fall away, and what can be done so that we may have Christians who can stand and conquer. How often does it happen—both after times of revival and special effort, and also in the ordinary work of the church—that those who ran well for a time get so entangled in the business or the pleasure of life, or the literature, politics, or friendships of the world, that all the life and the power of their profession is lost? They lack steadfastness; they miss the crowning grace of perseverance.

The words of our text teach us what the cause of backsliding is, and from where the lack of power to stand comes, even in those who strive after it. They show us, at the same time, what the secret is of restoration, as well as of strength to endure unto the end. *"Whose house are we,"* he said, *"if we hold fast our boldness and the glorying of our hope firm unto the end."* Or, as it is expressed a few verses further on, *"if we hold fast the beginning of our confidence firm unto the end"* (verse 14). A boldness and confidence that make us abound in hope, that make us glory in hope of the glory of God, and glory in tribulation, too—this makes us strong to resist and overcome. Nothing can make us conquerors but the bold and joyful spirit that, day by day, glories in the hope of what God will do.

It is in this that so many fail. When first they found peace, they learned that they were saved by faith. They understood that pardon, acceptance, peace, and life all come by faith alone. But they did not understand that we can stand only by faith; that we must always walk by faith; that ever and increasingly we must live by faith; and that every day and every hour nothing can help us but a clear, definite, habitual faith in God's power and working, as the only possibility of growth and progress. They sought to hold fast to the light and the blessing and the joy they had found; they knew not that it was their boldness of faith, the glorying of their hope, the beginning of their confidence—they knew not that it was this that they needed to hold fast firm to the end. And even when they learned something of the need of faith and hope, they did not know how indispensable the boldness of faith and the glorying of hope were. No one can conquer without the spirit of a conqueror. The powers of sin and Satan, of the world and the flesh, are so great that only he who is bold and glories in his hope upon what God will do will have strength to resist them. And only he who has learned to be bold with God, and to glory in Him, can be bold to face the enemy. It is when faith becomes a joy, and hope is a glorying in God, that we can be more than conquerors.

The lesson is one of the most important the Christian has to learn. We will see later how our whole epistle has been written to teach us that boldness is the only root of steadfastness and perseverance and, therefore, the true strength of the Christian life. We will also see that its one object is to show what abundant ground for the boldness we have in the work, person, and glory of our Lord Jesus.

"Whose house are we, if we hold fast our boldness and the glorying of our hope firm unto the end." If you would know the blessedness of all this means, then see here the open gate. In spite of all the enemies that surround you, yield yourself boldly to Jesus Christ as His—your heart a home for Him to dwell in. Glory in the hope of all that He has promised to perfect in you. *"Hold fast the beginning of* [your] *confidence firm unto the end"* (verse 14). Was not that beginning this—that you confessed yourself to be nothing and Christ to be all? Did you not just cast yourself on His mighty saving power? Hold fast this beginning with the greatest confidence. He will each moment guard and keep His house and maintain His work within it. Claim boldly and expect confidently that Christ the Son will be faithful over His house as Moses the servant was over his. And when the difficulty arises, the way to maintain this boldness and glorying of hope is always the same. Just remember the answer the epistle gives: Consider Jesus, who was faithful. Yes, just consider Jesus! How faithful, even unto death, He was to God in all that He had given Him

to do for us. Let that be to us the assurance that He, who is still the same Lord, will be no less faithful in all the blessed work He can now do in us, if we hold fast our boldness and the glorying of our hope firm to the end.

Chapter Notes...

1. Faith is the mother of hope. How often a daughter can be a help and a strength to her mother. So, as our hope reaches out to the future and glories in it, our faith will grow into the boldness that can conquer all.

2. Hold fast together what this passage has joined: the faithfulness of Jesus and the boldness, or confidence, of our faith. His faithfulness is our security.

3. *"The glorying of our hope."* Joy is not a luxury or a mere accessory in the Christian life. It is the sign that we are really living in God's wonderful love and that that love satisfies us. *"Now the God of hope fill you with all joy and peace in believing, that ye may abound in hope, in the power of the Holy Ghost"* (Romans 15:13).

4. Christ is faithful as a Son over His house: How confidently I may trust Him to keep charge and rule in it.

NOT TO COME SHORT OF THE PROMISED REST

Twenty-Two

On Hearing the Voice of God

*Wherefore, even as the Holy Ghost saith, To-day if ye shall
hear his voice, harden not your hearts, as in the provocation,
like as in the day of the temptation in the wilderness,
wherewith your fathers tempted me by proving me, and saw
my works forty years. Wherefore I was displeased with this
generation, and said, They do alway err in their heart: but
they did not know my ways; as I sware in my wrath,
They shall not enter into my rest.*
—Hebrews 3:7–11

The writer had such a deep impression of the low and dangerous state into which the Hebrews had sunk, that, having
mentioned the name of Moses, he made a long digression
to warn them against being like their fathers and hardening themselves against Him who is so much more than Moses. From Psalm
95, he quoted what God said of Israel in the wilderness, hardening
its hearts against Him so that He swore that they should not enter
into His rest. The words of the quotation first point us to what is
the great privilege of God's people: they hear His voice. Then it

points us to their great danger: hardening the heart against that voice. These words of warning are not directed to the unbelieving Jews but rather to the Christian Hebrews. Christians in our day have no less need of them. Let us take more abundant heed to the Word: *"Wherefore, even as the Holy Ghost saith, To-day if ye shall hear his voice, harden not your hearts."*

When God spoke to Israel, the first thing He asked of them was a heart that did not harden itself but that, in meekness and gentleness, in tenderness and docility, turned itself to listen to His voice. How much more may He claim this, now that He speaks to us in His Son. As the soil must be broken up by the plow and softened by the rain, so a broken, tender spirit is the first requisite for receiving blessing from God's Word or being, in truth, made partakers of God's grace. As we read in Isaiah, *"To this man will I look, even to him that is poor and of a contrite spirit, and that trembleth at my word"* (Isaiah 66:2). When this disposition exists, and the thirsty heart truly waits for divine teaching, and the circumcised ear opens to receive it, God's voice will bring real life and blessing and be the power of living fellowship with Himself. Where it is lacking, the Word remains unfruitful, and we go backward, however much our heads and mouths are filled with Bible truth. *"Wherefore, even as the Holy Ghost saith, To-day if ye shall hear his voice, harden not your hearts."*

It is not difficult to say what it is that hardens the hearts. The seed sown by the wayside could not enter the soil because it had been trodden down by the passersby. When the world, with its business and its interests, has at all times a free passage, the heart loses its tenderness. When we trust too much to the intellect in religion, and very great care is not taken to take each word as from God into the heart, into its life and love, then the heart gets closed to the living voice of God. The mind is satisfied with beautiful thoughts and pleasant feelings, but the heart does not hear God. When we are secretly content with our religion, our sound doctrine, and Christian life, the heart gets hardened, unconsciously but surely.

Andrew Murray

When our life does not seek to keep pace with our knowledge, and we have more pleasure in hearing and knowing than in obeying and doing, then we utterly lose the meekness to which the promise is given, and, amidst all the pleasing forms of godliness, the heart is too hard to discern the voice of the Spirit. Furthermore, when unbelief—which walks by sight and looks at itself and all around in the light of this world—is allowed to have its way, and the soul does not seek in childlike faith to live in the invisible, as revealed in the Word, then the heart gets so hardened that God's Word never enters. Yes, it is an unspeakably solemn thought that—with a mind occupied with religious truth, with feelings stirred at times by the voice and words of men, and with a life apparently given to religious works—the heart may be closed to the humble, direct communion with God, and it may be a stranger to all the blessing the living Word can bring. *"Wherefore, even as the Holy Ghost saith, To-day if ye shall hear his voice, harden not your hearts."*

Let all who would seek the blessing to be found in this epistle beware of studying it simply as an inspired treatise on divine things. Let it be to us a personal message, the voice of God speaking to us in His Son. Let us—under a sense of the spiritual mystery there is in all divine truth and of the helplessness of the human mind rightly to apprehend spiritual things—open our hearts in great meekness and docility to wait on God. The whole of religion, and the whole of salvation, consists in the state of the heart. God can do nothing for us, in the way of imparting the blessings of redemption, but as He does it in the heart. Our knowledge of the words of God will profit nothing until the heart is opened to receive Himself to fulfill His words in us. Let our first care be a meek and lowly heart that waits on Him. God speaks, in His Son, to the heart, and in the heart. It is in the heart that the voice and the Son of God must be received. The voice and the word have weight according to how much we esteem the speaker. As we realize the glory and the majesty of God, His holiness and perfection, His love and tenderness, we will be ready to sacrifice everything to hear what He speaks and receive what He gives. We will bid all the world around us, all the world within us, to be silent that we may hear aright the voice of the Divine Being speaking to us in the Son of His love.

Chapter Notes...

1. Salvation will be found in these two things—God speaking to me in His Son, and my heart opening to hear His voice. It is not only in order to salvation, as a means to an end that is something different and higher, that He speaks. No, His speaking gives and is salvation, the revelation of Himself to my soul. Let the work of my life be to hearken with a meek and tender spirit.

2. The Lord opened the heart of Lydia to give heed to the things that were spoken. This is what we need. God Himself will draw our hearts away from all else and open them to take heed. Let us ask this very earnestly.

3. Nothing so effectually hinders hearing God's voice as opening the heart too much to other voices. A heart too deeply interested in the news, the literature, and the society of this world cannot hear the divine voice. It needs silliness, retirement, and concentration to give God the heed He claims.

Twenty-Three

Even as the Holy Ghost Saith

Wherefore, even as the Holy Ghost saith,
To-day if ye shall hear his voice.
—Hebrews 3:7

In quoting the words of Psalm 95, the writer used the expression, *"as the Holy Ghost saith."* He regarded that psalm as simply the language of the Holy Spirit. He looked upon the Scriptures as truly inspired by God, God-breathed, because men spoke from God, being moved by the Holy Spirit. (See 2 Timothy 3:16; 2 Peter 1:21.) He regarded them as the very voice of God, and he attached to the words all the weight of divine authority and all the fullness of meaning they have in the divine mind. On this ground he saw in them a deeper meaning than we would have looked for and taught us to find in the words, *"enter into my rest"* (Hebrews 3:11), the revelation of a deep spiritual mystery and a prophecy of what Christ would bring. As it was the Holy Spirit who of old first gave the Word, so it was the same Spirit who taught the apostle to set forth to us its spiritual meaning and lessons, as we have them in the fourth chapter. And even now it is that same Spirit alone who can reveal the truth spiritually within us and make it life and power in our experience. Let us wait on Him as we meditate on these words, *"as the Holy Ghost saith."* The words of the Holy Spirit need the Holy Spirit as their interpreter. And the Holy Spirit interprets only to those in whom He dwells and rules.

In the opening words of the epistle, we were told that it was the same God who had spoken to the fathers in the prophets who has now spoken to us in His Son. The inferiority of the Old Testament did not consist in that the words were less the words of God than in the New. They are equally the words of the Holy Spirit. But the superior excellence of the new dispensation lies in this: that, in virtue of the mighty redemption attained by Christ, taking away the veil between God and us and the veil from our eyes and hearts (see Hebrews 10:20; Isaiah 25:7; 2 Corinthians 3:16), the Word can enter more fully into us with its life-giving power. The Son of God, as the living Word dwelling in us through the Holy Spirit, brings the truth and the power of the Word as a divine reality into our living experience. The Old Testament was like the bud; in the New, the bud has opened and the flower is seen. *"As the Holy Ghost saith."* These words assure us that the Holy Spirit will Himself unfold in the New what He had hidden in the words of the Old.

This brings us to a lesson of great importance in our spiritual life: that what the Holy Spirit has spoken, He alone can make plain. He uses human words and thoughts, and, as regarded from the human side, human reason can understand and expound them. But even in one who may be a true Christian, this does not bring him further than the Old Testament, the preliminary stage: *"The prophets sought and searched diligently, who prophesied of the grace that should come unto you: searching what time or what manner of time the Spirit of Christ which was in them did point unto"* (1 Peter 1:10–11). Beyond this, they did not come to the real possession and experience of the redemption they proclaimed. It was only when Christ was glorified and the Spirit was given as an indwelling fountain of light and life that the divine meaning and power could be known. And so it is with us. To understand the words of the Holy Spirit I must have yielded myself to be led by the Spirit, and I must be living in the Spirit. Only one who knows Hebrew can expound a Hebrew writing; only the Spirit of God knows the mind of God and can reveal it to us. Take, for instance, what is said of entering into the rest of God. Anyone who will take the trouble to study it carefully will be able to form some concept of what it means. But truly to know the rest of God, to enter into it, and to enjoy it in living power—none but the Holy Spirit can teach us this.

"Wherefore, even as the Holy Ghost saith, To-day if ye shall hear his voice." Here is the first lesson the Holy Spirit teaches. He calls us not to harden or close the heart but to hearken to the voice of God there. The Holy Spirit cannot possibly lead us into the power and the blessing of God's Word unless we hearken to the voice with our whole hearts. The Holy Spirit can teach in nothing but a heart that is given up to hearken and obey. When the Son came into the world he said, *"Lo, I am come...to do thy will, O God"* (Hebrews 10:7). The proof of the Spirit's presence in Him, the sacrifice in the power of the Eternal Spirit, and the way to the outpouring of the Spirit was that of hearkening and obedience. The first message of the Holy Spirit and the condition of all further teaching is always, *"If ye will hear his voice, harden not your heart"* (Psalm 95:7–8 KJV). God has sent the Spirit of His Son into our hearts. God asks each of us to yield our whole hearts to His leading. It is as the indwelling Spirit that He will call us and fit us to listen to God's voice.

We are commencing the study of an epistle of which the key-note is, "God speaks to us now in His Son." The wonderful truths of the heavenly priesthood of our Lord Jesus and of our access into the Holiest of All, by the blood, to dwell and worship there. And there, in God's presence, to be made partaker of the full union with Christ—these wonderful truths are to be unfolded. Let us seek a deeper sense of the need, and also the certainty, of the teaching of the Spirit within us: Let us pray *"that the God of our Lord Jesus*

Christ, the Father of glory, may give unto [us] *a spirit of wisdom and revelation in the knowledge of him"* (Ephesians 1:17). Let us hear God's voice in meekness and tenderness of heart. Let us in deep humility yield ourselves to the Spirit's guidance. We can count upon it that the same Spirit who first of old inspired the words of the psalm, who then in this epistle revealed their fullness of meaning, will reveal to us in power all the light and truth they are meant to bring into the believing heart.

Chapter Notes...

1. God speaking to us in His Word, and in His Son, is all by the Holy Spirit. Everything depends upon our right relation to the Spirit. Let the Word be as a seed in which the life of God dwells. Let us receive the Word, in the faith that the Holy Spirit will open it and make it work mightily in us who believe.

2. And as we wait on the Spirit to open the Word, we will, through the Word, be led to receive the Spirit of heaven, as the divine seal of our faith in the Word.

3. So will we learn to speak the Word in the power of the Spirit. The disciples, however much they knew of Jesus through His communion and teaching and as the witnesses of His death and resurrection, were not allowed to go and preach Him until they received the Spirit from on high. The Spirit-breathed Word, the Spirit-opened Word, must also be a Spirit-spoken Word. We, too, must speak out of a living communication of the Spirit from the throne of the glorified Christ. From beginning to end, everything connected with God's Word must be in the power of the Holy Spirit.

Twenty-Four
Today

*Wherefore, even as the Holy Ghost saith, To-day if ye shall
hear his voice, harden not your hearts.*
—Hebrews 3:7–8

These words are generally applied to the unconverted; the psalm in which they occur and the context in which they stand in this epistle both prove that they are meant for God's people. In all the dealings of the Holy Spirit with believers, be they weak and erring or strong and glad, His great word to them is, *"To-day."*

"The Holy Ghost saith, To-day." What does this mean? God is the Eternal One. With Him there is no yesterday or tomorrow. What we call past and future are with Him an ever-present now. His life is an ever-blessed, neverending "today." One of the great words of this epistle in regard to Christ and His salvation is the word *eternal,* or *forever.* He has become the Author of eternal salvation—that is, a salvation that bears the character of eternity. Its chief mark is that it is an ever-present now, that there is not a moment in which Christ, who ever lives to pray for us, is not able to maintain us in it, in the power of an endless life.

Man is the creature of a moment. The past has gone from him and he has no control over the future; it is only the present moment that is his. Therefore, it is such that when he is made partaker of Christ, the High Priest forever, and of the eternal salvation He imparts, God's great word to him is *"To-day."* In Christ, all the blessedness of the great eternity is gathered up in an ever-present now. The one need of the believer is to know it, to respond to it, and to meet the "Today, the now, My child!" of God's grace with the "Today, the even now, my Father!" of his faith.

If you would understand the meaning of this divine *"to-day,"* look at it in its wondrous setting. *"Wherefore, even as the Holy Ghost saith, To-day."* Satan's word is ever *tomorrow*. Man's favorite word, too, is *tomorrow*. Even with the child of God, the word of unbelief is too often *tomorrow*. God's demand is too great for today; God's promise too high; we hope it will come easier later on. *"The Holy Ghost saith, To-day."* That means that He who is the mighty Power of God is Himself ready to work in us all that God wills and asks; it is He who is each moment pleading for immediate surrender, for a present trust, because He bears with Him the power of a present salvation.

Today! It is a word of wonderful promise. It tells that today, this very moment, the wondrous love of God is for you—it is even now waiting to be poured out into your heart. It says that *today*, all that Christ has done and is now doing in heaven and is able to do within you—this very day it is within your reach. Today the Holy Spirit—in whom there is the power to know and claim and enjoy all that the Father and the Son are waiting to bestow—today the Holy Spirit is within you, sufficient for every need, equal to every emergency. With every call we find in our Bible to full and entire surrender; with every promise we read of grace for the supply of temporal and spiritual need; with every prayer we breathe; and with every longing that rules in our hearts, there is the Spirit of promise whispering, *"To-day."* *"As the Holy Ghost saith, To-day."*

Today! It is a word of solemn command. It is not here a question of some higher privilege that you are free to accept or reject. It is not left to your choice, O believer, whether you will receive the fullness of blessing the Holy Spirit offers. The *"To-day"* of the Holy Spirit brings you under the most solemn obligation to respond to God's call and to say, "Yes, today, Lord—complete and immediate submission to all Thy will. Today, the surrender of a present and perfect trust in all Thy grace. *'As the Holy Ghost saith, To-day.'*"

Today! It is a word, too, of earnest warning. *"Wherefore, even as the Holy Ghost saith, To-day if ye shall hear his voice, harden not your hearts,...They shall not enter into my rest."*

There is nothing so hardening as delay. When God speaks to us, He asks for a tender heart, open to the whispers of His voice of love. The believer who answers the *"To-day"* of the Holy Spirit with the "tomorrow" of some more convenient season does not know how he is hardening his heart. The delay, instead of making the surrender and obedience and faith easy, makes it more difficult. It closes the heart for today against the Comforter and cuts off all hope and power of growth. O believer, *"As the Holy Ghost saith, To-day."* When you hear His voice, open your heart in great tenderness to listen and obey. Obedience to the Spirit's today is your only certainty of power and of blessing.

To all Christians whose life has been one of feebleness and of failure, who have not yet entered into the rest of faith, into God's own rest, this word, *today,* is the key to all their disappointments and to all their failures. You waited for strength to make obedience easier and for feeling to make the sacrifice less painful. But you did not listen to the voice of God breathing through every word. He speaks that wondrous note—even through the living Word, Jesus Christ—that wondrous note of hope, *"To-day."* You thought it meant for the sinner a call to immediate repentance; you did not know that it means immediate wholehearted submission to all God says each time the believer hears His voice, as well as immediate trustful acceptance of all He gives. And yet, this is exactly what it does mean.

The Holiest of All

In the epistle to the Hebrews, we have a very wonderful exhibition of what Christ, as a High Priest at the right hand of God, can do for us in the power of an endless life. The entering into the rest of God; the perfect cleansing of the conscience in the blood through which He entered into the presence of God; our access within the veil into the presence of God; the being brought close to the very heart of God; the being taken up and kept in Christ in the love of God—these blessings are all ours. And over each of them is written the words, *"Now is the accepted time"* (2 Corinthians 6:2 KJV). *"As the Holy Ghost saith, To-day."*

Chapter Notes...

1. Brother, let you and me bow in great stillness before God to hear this wonderful message, the Holy Spirit whispering, "Today, today." Let our whole hearts open up to take it in. Let all fear and unbelief pass away as we remember that it is the Holy Spirit Himself—the Giver of strength, the Dispenser of grace, and the Revealer of Jesus—who says *"To-day."*

2. Let our faith simply listen to God's voice, until it rings through our souls day by day and all day long. We will take God's word *"To-day,"* and make it our own. We will meet this wonderful *"To-day"* of God's love with the confident *"To-day"* of our faith. And it will become to us a foretaste of that eternal *"To-day"* in which He dwells.

3. The Holy Spirit's *"To-day,"* accepted and lived in, will be within us the power of an endless life, the experience of an eternal salvation, as an ever-present, never-ceasing reality. *"As the Holy Ghost saith, To-day."*

4. Just yesterday I heard a servant of God testify that at his conversion he was led to say, "I am going to do the will of God today, without thinking of tomorrow," and he had found the unspeakable blessing of it. Let anyone begin to live a wholehearted life, by the grace of God, for one day. For tomorrow will be as today, and still better.

Twenty-Five

An Evil Heart of Unbelief

*Take heed, brethren, lest haply there shall be in any one of you
an evil heart of unbelief, in falling away from the living God.*
—Hebrews 3:12

The great practical aim of the epistle is to call us to faith. It is
with this view that it will show us what a sure ground we have
for it in the Word and oath of God, in the person and power
of our heavenly High Priest. It will remind us how unbelief has been
the cause of all falling away from God and of all failing to enter into
the enjoyment of His promise and rest—as faith has, in all ages,
been the one power in which God's saints have lived and worked. It
has already spoken of *"hold*[ing] *fast our boldness and the glorying of
our hope firm unto the end"* (3:6); it here uses the word *believe,* for
the first time, in the call to beware of *"an evil heart of unbelief."*

"An evil heart of unbelief." Think a moment of what the expression means. And note first the place the heart takes in religion. We
have heard the warning, *"Harden not your hearts"* (verse 8). It is in
the heart that God speaks and that He longs to give His blessing.
On that there followed God's complaint, *"They do alway err in their
heart: but they did not know my ways"* (verse 10). A heart that goes
wrong cannot know God's ways. And so, here again, it is the evil

heart that cannot believe, that falls away from the living God. Do let us, in our study of the epistle, and in our whole religious life, beware of rejoicing in beautiful thoughts and happy feelings, while the heart, with its desire and will and love, is not wholly given up to God. In our communion with God, everything depends on the heart. It is with the heart that man believes and receives the salvation of God.

"An evil heart of unbelief." Many think and speak of unbelief as a frailty. They wish to believe but do not feel capable of doing so; their faith, they say, is too weak. And, of course, they have no sense of guilt or shame connected with it; in their minds, not being able to do a thing is counted as a sufficient excuse for not doing it.

God, however, thinks differently. The Holy Spirit speaks of the *"evil heart of unbelief."* The heart is the organ God created in man for holding fellowship with Himself. Faith is its first natural function; by faith and love, the heart lives in God. Faith is the ear that hears the voice of God, the eye that can ever see Him and the unseen world, and the capacity for knowing and receiving all that God can communicate. Faith begins as trust in the spoken Word; it grows into fellowship with the Person who speaks; and its fruit is the reception of all God has to bestow. Sin turned the heart from the unseen to the seen, from God to self; faith in God lost the place it was meant to have and instead became a faith in the visible world and its good. And now, unbelief, whether avowed and definite or more secret and unconscious, is the great mark of the evil heart, the great proof of sin, the great cause of everlasting darkness and damnation. There is no warning the professing Christian church needs to have sounded more loudly than this one to the Hebrews: *"Take heed, brethren, lest haply there shall be in any one of you an evil heart of unbelief, in falling away from the living God."*

"In falling away from the living God." This is the terrible evil of unbelief; it incapacitates a man for holding fellowship with God as the living One. The expression, *"the living God,"* occurs four

times in this epistle. In the Old Testament, the expression contrasted God with the dead idols that could not hear or speak or help. Alas, how often it is that professing Christians, instead of a graven image, have the more dangerous idol of a thought-image—a concept of the Mind to which they bring their worship. *"The living God,"* speaking in His Son, hearing them when they speak, working out in them His mighty salvation—the living God who loves and is loved—Him, they do not know. With all their Christian profession and religious exercises there is *"an evil heart of unbelief"* in falling away from the living God.

Let us take the warning. Before we come to the deeper truth the epistle has to teach us, let us learn our first lesson well: The one thing God looks to, the one thing we need to receive, and the fullness of blessing that our great High Priest has for us and waits to bestow is a heart of faith—a true heart drawing near to God in fullness of faith (see Hebrews 10:23).

"Take heed." We ought to give more abundant heed, lest there be in any of us, even for a moment, *"an evil heart of unbelief."* Let us cast out everything that can cause or can strengthen it—whether it be worldliness or formality; too little knowledge or too much head-knowledge of God's Word; too little looking to the state of our hearts or too much occupation with self; let us take heed lest there be at any time in us *"an evil heart of unbelief."* Let a tender heart—hearkening to His voice, listening to and trusting His Word—ever be the sacrifice we bring Him.

"With the heart man believeth" (Romans 10:10), whether in God or in the world. As our heart is, so is our faith and our life. Our enjoyment of Christ, our spiritual strength and fruitfulness, our nearness to God, and our experience of His working in us, all depend, not upon single, isolated acts of faith but rather upon the state of the heart. Therefore, God breathes into us the Spirit of faith, to keep our hearts ever tender and open toward Him. Oh, let us above everything beware of *"an evil heart of unbelief."*

And if we would know how true living faith is to be obtained and increased, we must note the connection. As unbelief falls away from the living God, so does faith draw near to Him and is fed and nourished in His presence. Practice the presence of God in deep humility and stillness of heart. Thirst for God, the living God. *"My soul, wait thou only upon God; for my expectation is from him"* (Psalm 62:5). He is the living God. He sees and hears and feels and loves. He speaks and gives and works. He reveals Himself. His presence wakens and strengthens and satisfies faith. Bow in lowly meditation and worship before the living God, and faith will waken up and grow into boldness and the glorying of hope. He is the living God, who makes alive and out of whom life comes into them who draw near to Him. Tarry in His presence: That, and nothing else—but that, most surely—will free your from the *"evil heart of unbelief."*

Chapter Notes...

1. *"Unbelief, in falling away from the living God."* Remember with holy fear the close connection between unbelief and departing from God. They act and react with each other.

2. The faithfulness of Jesus fills the heart with the fullness of faith. You remember the lesson? Here it is the same again: Drawing near to the living God will fill the heart with living faith. And the epistle is going to teach us how God draws near to us in Jesus and how, in Jesus, we draw nigh to God.

3. Never speak or think of unbelief as a weakness but always as the sin of sins, the fruitful mother of all sin.

4. The living God in heaven, and the believing heart on earth: Those are the two powers that meet and satisfy each other. Let your faith know of no other measure or limit than the living God. Let it be living faith in a living God.

Twenty-Six

Exhort One Another Day by Day

But exhort one another day by day, so long as it is called To-day;
lest any one of you be hardened by the deceitfulness of sin.
—Hebrews 3:13

In the previous verse we read, *"Take heed, brethren, lest haply there shall be in any one of you an evil heart of unbelief, in falling away from the living God."* That is, let each one not only look to himself but let all look to it that there isn't in any one of you the evil unbelieving heart. The church is one body; the sickness of one member is a danger to the whole body. Each one must live to care for those around him. Each member is entrusted by Christ to the love and care of his brethren and is dependent on their help. Believers who are joined together in one house—in a neighborhood, in a church—are responsible for one another. They must take heed that there isn't in anyone the unbelief that falls away from God. They are called to help and encourage each other so that all may at all times continue steadfast in the faith.

In our meditation on verse 6, we spoke of the painful fact that, in so many cases, the first boldness and joy of hope is not held fast firm to the end. Here is one cause: There is not the care and help for each other that the Lord intended. In caring solely for ourselves, not only does our brother suffer but we lose much ourselves, as well. The healthy life of the individual member is dependent on the life around him and on the part he takes in maintaining that life. The warning has a deeper significance than we think: *"Take heed, brethren, lest haply there shall be in any one of you an evil heart of unbelief."*

It is this thought that our text seeks to enforce: *"But exhort one another day by day, so long as it is called To-day; lest any one of you be hardened by the deceitfulness of sin."* Christians are bound to exhort one another; it is their duty and their right. It is implied in the whole constitution of the body of Christ that the members care for one another. Its life is entirely dependent on the Spirit of Christ, who pleased not Himself; and that Spirit is a love that seeks not its own but has its very being in loving and blessing others. As each member humbly yields himself to be helped and to help, the safety and the vigor of all will be secured. The communion of saints in all our church circles must be proved in the cultivation of a practical ministering love and care for each other.

"Exhort one another day by day, so long as it is called To-day." We saw what solemn meaning there was in the Holy Spirit's call, *"To-day,"* if we hear His voice. We sought to apply that personally. Here we are taught that all the urgency that call implies must be applied by each one of us to our neighbor as well as to ourselves. We must think of the danger of delay, of the time when it will be no longer *"To-day"* for those around us who are forgetting it, and exhort them *"day by day."* Today! The work is urgent and must be done immediately. It may be difficult, but He who commands will enable. Our conscious unfitness must drive us to Him who can fill us with the love, the boldness, and the wisdom we need. *"Day by day."* The work is slow and must be done unceasingly, *"so long as it is called To-day."* The Spirit of Jesus can give us grace and patience and faith to persevere. *"In due season we shall reap, if we faint not"* (Galatians 6:9).

"Day by day." This word of the Holy Spirit is the complement of that other *"To-day."* The *"To-day"* of the Holy Spirit must *"day by day"* be accepted and obeyed afresh. It is only as we are ready, every day without one exception, to live fully in obedience to the voice of God and the faith of Jesus that our life can grow. What has once—or for a time—been done will not avail. *"Day by day"* our fellowship with Jesus, our consecration to Him, and our service for Him must be renewed. So will we, in our care for others as much as in our personal walk, hold fast our boldness firm to the end. (See Hebrews 3:6.)

"But exhort one another...lest any one of you be hardened by the deceitfulness of sin." We heard the warning, *"Harden not your hearts"* (verse 8). Here is its exposition, *"Hardened by the deceitfulness of sin"* (verse 13). All sin is deceit; its promised pleasures are all a lie. But there are some sins that are open and unmistakable. There are others that are specially deceptive. Where the sanction of the Christian world, or the force of habit and custom, or the apparent insignificance of what we do makes us think little of the sin, it has a terrible power to deceive the professing Christian. And through this deceitfulness of sin—be it worldliness, or unlovingness, or pride, or want of integrity—hearts are hardened and become incapable of hearing the voice of God. What a call to all who are awake to their own danger to listen, *"But exhort one another day by day, so long as it is called To-day; lest any one of you be hardened by the deceitfulness of sin."*

Let me impress upon everyone who would study this epistle the solemn obligation resting upon him to care for those around him—not only the outcast but those with whom he is associated in church fellowship, especially any who are in danger of being *"hardened by the deceitfulness of sin."* The Christ unto whom we are to grow up in all things is the Christ *"from whom all the body fitly framed and knit together through that which every joint supplieth, according to the working in due measure of each several part, maketh the increase of the body unto the building up of itself in love"*

(Ephesians 4:16). Our connection with the Head, the power of our growth unto Him in all things, must be maintained in our love to the members of His body around, however feeble or backward.

And if we would know where the grace for this work is to be found, the answer is not far to seek: It is in Jesus Christ, our Head, and in His love shed abroad in our hearts. As we study in this epistle the compassion of Jesus, as our High Priest and Leader, let us believe that He makes us partakers of His Spirit. He forms us in His own likeness, He leads us in His footsteps, He makes each of us what He was—a Priest with a priestly heart ready to live and die for those around us. Therefore, brethren, *"exhort one another day by day."*

Chapter Notes...

1. This work is most difficult. But strength for it will come as for any other work. First of all, accept the command; get the heart filled with the sense of obligation. Yield yourself to your Master in willing obedience, even though you do not see the slightest prospect of doing it. Then wait on Him for His light and strength—for wisdom to know how to begin, for boldness to speak the truth in love. Present yourself unto God as one alive from the dead, and your members as instruments of righteousness in His hands. Let the fire within your heart be kept burning: The grace of obedience will not be withheld.

2. This epistle is an exposition of the inner life, the life of faith. But with this, work is considered as a matter of course that needs no vindication. Let every Christian give himself to his Lord to watch over others: Let all the fresh grace and the deeper knowledge of Jesus that we seek be for the service of those around us. *"Exhort one another day by day."*

Twenty-Seven
Partakers of Christ

*For we are become partakers of Christ, if we hold fast the
beginning of our confidence firm unto the end: while it is
said, To-day if ye shall hear his voice, harden not
your hearts, as in the provocation.*
—Hebrews 3:14–15

In the second chapter, the twofold oneness of our Lord Jesus and
His believing people was set before us. On the divine side, they
are one, *"For both he that sanctifieth and they that are sanctified
are all of one"* (Hebrews 2:11). On the other, the human side, they
are one, because He became man, and took our nature upon Him.
*"Since then the children are sharers in flesh and blood, he also himself
in like manner partook of the same"* (2:14). There we have the same
word as here. Just as truly, as Christ became a partaker *"in flesh and
blood,"* we become *"partakers of Christ"* (3:14). In partaking with
us of flesh and blood, Christ entered into perfect fellowship with
us in all we were; our life and our death became His. When we
become partakers of Christ, we enter into perfect fellowship with
Him in all He was and is; His death and His life become ours.

We are become *"partakers of Christ"*! What a mystery! What a
treasure! What a blessedness! The whole object of the epistle is to

show what there is in the Christ of whom we are become partakers and what He can do for us. But here, at the outset, amid needful words of remonstrance against giving way to sloth or unbelief, believers are reminded of what their portion and possession is: They are become partakers of Christ. There is often danger, as we listen to the teaching of Scripture about Christ as our High Priest, of regarding Him as an outward person and His work as something that is done outwardly for us in heaven. This precious word reminds us that our salvation consists in the possession of Himself, in the being one life with Him, in having Himself as our own. Christ can do nothing for us but as an inward Savior, Himself being our life as He personally dwells and works in us. As truly and fully as Christ, when He became partaker *"of flesh and blood,"* was entirely and eternally identified with man and His nature so that He and it were inseparably united in one life, so surely, when we become *"partakers of Christ,"* do we become indissolubly identified with Him. Since Christ became partaker *"of flesh and blood,"* He is known and will be to all eternity, even upon the throne, as the Son of Man. No less will we, when we truly become *"partakers of Christ,"* be known, even now and to all eternity, as one with Christ on the throne of glory. Oh, let us know ourselves as God knows us—as *"partakers of Christ."*

It is the one thing God desires. When God set forth His only begotten Son as the only possible way of access to Himself, it meant that He can delight in, or have fellowship with, nothing in which the likeness of His Son is not to be seen. We can have no further entrance into God's favor or good pleasure than to the extent that He can see Christ in us. If God has called us to the fellowship of His Son and made us participators of all there is in Christ—the sonship, the love, and the Spirit of the Father—let us live worthy of our privilege. Let us live as men who are—oh, the riches of grace!—become *"partakers of Christ"*!

And how can we know in full assurance that it is so and ever rejoice in the blessed consciousness of all it implies? Just as it was said before, where our blessed relation to Christ was set forth in another aspect—we are *"his house...if we hold fast our boldness and the glorying of our hope firm unto the end"* (3:6)—so we have the answer here again: *"For we are become partakers of Christ, if we hold fast the beginning of our confidence firm unto the end."* The beginning of our confidence must be held fast. We must not, as many think, begin with faith and then continue with works. No, the confidence with which we began must be held fast firm to the end. We must see that when we are made *"partakers of Christ"*—that includes all, and that, as at first, so all the way unto the end—we can receive out of Christ only by faith and according to our faith. Apart from faith receiving Christ's strength, our works avail not. God works nothing but through Christ, and it is as by faith that we live in our riches in Christ that God can work into us all there is in Him for us. It is this faith through which God can work all our works for us and in us.

For *"we are become"*—note, not "we will become"—*"we are become partakers of Christ, if we hold fast the beginning of our confidence firm unto the end."* Our perseverance will be the seal of our being *"partakers of Christ."* The faith by which, at conversion, we knew at once that we had Christ, grows clearer, and brighter, and more mightily effectual in opening up the treasures of Christ as we hold it fast firm unto the end. Persevering faith is the witness that we have Christ because, through it, Christ exercises His keeping and perfecting power.

Believer, would you enjoy the full assurance and the full experience that you are a partaker of Christ? It is alone to be found each day in the living fellowship with Christ. Christ is a living person; He can be known and enjoyed only in a living personal communion. Christ is my Leader; I must cling to Him—I must follow Him—in His leading. Christ is my High Priest; I must let Him lift me into God's presence. Christ is the living Son of God, our life; I must live Him. I am His house; I can only know Him as Son in His house as I yield myself to His indwelling.

But, all and only through faith, we are become *"partakers of Christ, if we hold fast the beginning of our confidence firm unto the end."* Begin each day, meet each difficulty, with the renewal of the confidence you placed in Jesus when first you came to Him; with a brightness that shines unto the perfect day, you will know what boundless blessing it is to be a partaker of Christ.

Chapter Notes...

1. When Christ became partaker of human nature, how entirely He identified Himself with it, that all could see and know it. I am become a partaker of Christ: Let me be so identified with Him that my whole life may be marked by it. So may all see and know that I am a partaker of Jesus Christ.

2. How did Christ become partaker of our nature? He left His own state of life, forsook all, and entered into our state of life. How do I become a partaker of Christ? By coming out from my state of life, forsaking all, giving myself wholly to be possessed of Him and to live His life.

3. *"If we hold the beginning of our confidence firm."* Christ maintained His surrender to be man, firm to the end, even unto death. Let me maintain my surrender to Christ, live one life with Christ, at any cost.

4. Partaker of Christ—of His life, His dispositions as man, His meekness and lowliness of heart. Partaker of a living Christ—who will live His life out in me.

Twenty-Eight

The Rest in Canaan

For who, when they heard, did provoke? nay, did not all
they that came out of Egypt by Moses? And with whom was
he displeased forty years? was it not with them that sinned,
whose carcases fell in the wilderness? And to whom sware
he that they should not enter into his rest, but to them that
were disobedient? And we see that they were not able
to enter in because of unbelief.
—Hebrews 3:16–19

In the opening verses of the epistle we saw that God has two dispensations, or ways of dealing with man, and that these find their counterpart in the Christian life. There are believers who always walk in the twilight and bondage of the Old Testament; there are others who truly know the joy and the power of the New Testament and have fellowship with God, not as through the prophets but truly and directly in the Son Himself.

In the words we are now to meditate on, we have the same truth in another aspect. The writer had spoken of Christ as more than Moses. This gave him the occasion to speak, in the tone of solemn warning, of the people of Israel who came out of Egypt. They did not all enter Canaan. A separation developed between those whom God had redeemed out of Egypt. Some perished in the wilderness; others did indeed enter and possess the Promised Land. The cause of this failure to enter Canaan was, we are told, disobedience arising out of unbelief. When God commanded them to go up and possess the land, they gave way to fear. They did not believe God's promise, and they were disobedient. Unbelief is ever the cause of disobedience; they could not enter in because of unbelief and disobedience.

The story has deep spiritual significance and teaches a lesson of great solemnity. In our chapter, we have heard twice already that it is not enough to begin well; we must hold fast *"unto the end"* (verses 6, 14). Of Moses and the people of Israel, we read, *"By faith he kept the passover, and the sprinkling of the blood, that the destroyer of the firstborn should not touch them. By faith they passed through the Red sea as by dry land: which the Egyptians assaying to do were swallowed up"* (11:28–29). There was the initial faith to go up out of Egypt. But when they were tested to see if they would *"hold fast the beginning of our confidence firm unto the end"* (3:14), the great majority failed. Their faith was but for a time: They had faith to leave Egypt, but they had not faith to enter Canaan.

Among the Hebrews, there were Christians who were in the same state. They had begun well but had been hindered. Some were standing still; some had already turned back. And even so, there are many Christians in our churches who never come further than the initial faith of conversion. They say they know God has saved them from Egypt. They rest content with the thought of having been converted. There is no hearty desire, no earnest purpose to press on to a life of holiness, no readiness at any sacrifice to go up into the Promised Land of rest and of victory.

When Israel was about to enter the land of Canaan, Moses used the words, *"And he brought us out from thence, that he might bring us in, to give us the land which he sware unto our fathers"* (Deuteronomy 6:23). It is to be feared that there are many Christians who put asunder what God has joined together. They would gladly be brought out from the land of bondage; they are not ready to go all the length with God, to enter the land and conquer every enemy. They would gladly be made happy in being delivered from bondage; they long not to be made holy in a life of separation and service. They do not listen to the voice that calls to enter into God's rest but harden their hearts instead.

It was not in Egypt—let us note this well—it was on the very borders of Canaan that the men God had begun to harden their hearts. It is among Christians who profess conversion—who have not only begun the Christian life but have even made some progress in it—that the hardening of the heart is now still found. The call to holiness; the call to cease from the life of wandering and murmuring and enter into the rest of God; the call to the life of victory over every enemy and to the service of God in the land of promise—these are not obeyed. They say it is too high and too hard. They do not believe with Caleb that "we are well able to possess the land" (Numbers 13:30); they fear the sacrifice and cling to the carnal life. In not hearkening to God's voice their hearts are hardened. God has sworn that they will not enter into His rest.

I cannot with too much earnestness urge every Christian reader to learn well the two stages of the Christian. There are the carnal, and there are the spiritual. There are those who remain babes and those who are full-grown men. There are those who come up out of Egypt but then remain in the wilderness of a worldly life, and there are those who follow the Lord fully, entering the life of rest and victory. Let each of us find out where we stand and, taking earnest heed to God's warnings, with our whole hearts press on to go all the length in following Jesus and in seeking to stand perfect and complete in all the will of God.

What do all these warnings in our epistle—specially dedicated to the unfolding of the heavenly life and power, the complete salvation of our great High Priest—mean? It means this: that no teaching of what Christ is can profit, unless our hearts are longing and ready to follow Him fully. The epistle will sum up all its teachings in its call to enter into the Holiest of All, into the rest of God. But it wants us to feel deeply that there can be no entering in, except in the path of faith and full obedience with a heart that is ready to forsake all its own will and to follow Him who bore the cross—a heart that will be content with nothing less than all that God is willing to give.

Chapter Notes...

1. *"They were not able to enter in because of unbelief." "Take heed, brethren, lest haply there shall be in any one of you an evil heart of unbelief"* (verse 12). Everything depends upon faith. At each step in the teaching of our epistle, let faith be exercised. Faith in the God who speaks to us; faith in the blessed Son, in the divine power and all-pervading nearness in which He works, in His true humanity and the heavenly life He perfected for us and imparts from heaven; faith in the Holy Spirit who dwells within us and is God's power working in us. Let faith be the habit of our soul, the every breath of our life.

2. *"Because of unbelief."* Just what Jesus says, "Because of your unbelief," in answer to our, "Why?" Let us cultivate the deep conviction that the root of all disobedience and failure, of all weakness and trouble in the spiritual life, is unbelief. Let us not think that there is some inexplicable mystery about our prayers not being heard; it is simply unbelief that will not trust God, will not yield itself wholly to God, will not allow God to do what He promises. God save us from unbelief!

Twenty-Nine
The Rest of Faith

Let us fear therefore, lest haply, a promise being left of
entering into his rest, any one of you should seem to have come
short of it. For indeed we have had good tidings preached
unto us, even as also they: but the word of hearing did not
profit them, because they were* not united by faith with them
that heard. For we which have believed do enter into that rest;
even as he hath said, As I sware in my wrath, They shall not
enter into my rest: although the works were finished
from the foundation of the world.
—Hebrews 4:1–3

We have seen that, with Israel after its deliverance from Egypt, there were two stages. The one was the life in the wilderness, with its wanderings and its wants, its unbelief and its murmurings, its provocation of God and its exclusion from the promised rest. The other was the Land of Promise, with rest instead of the desert wanderings, with abundance instead of want, and the victory over every enemy instead of defeat. These are both symbols of the two stages in the Christian life: the one in which we only know the Lord as the Savior from Egypt, in His work on the

---
* It was.

provocation = provoking

155

cross for atonement and pardon; the other where He is known and welcomed as the glorified Priest-King in heaven, who, in the power of the endless life, sanctifies and saves completely, writes God's laws in the heart, and leads us to find our home in the holiest of God's presence. The aim of the writer in this whole section is to warn us not to rest content with the former, the preparatory stage, but to show all diligence to reach the second and enter the promised rest of complete deliverance. *"Let us fear therefore, lest haply, a promise being left of entering into his rest, any one of you should seem to have come short of it."*

Some think that the rest of Canaan is the type of heaven. This cannot be, because the great mark of the Canaan life was that the land had to be conquered and that God gave such glorious victory over enemies. The rest of Canaan was for victory and through victory. And so it is in the life of faith, when a soul learns to trust God for victory over sin and yields itself entirely—as to its circumstances and duties—to live just where and how He wills, that it enters the rest. It lives in the promise, in the will, in the power of God. This is the rest into which it enters, not through death, but through faith; or rather, not through the death of the body, but through the death to self in the death of Christ through faith. *"For indeed we have had good tidings preached unto us, even as also they: but the word of hearing did not profit them, because they were not united by faith with them that heard."*

The one reason why they did not enter Canaan was their unbelief. The land was waiting: The rest was provided and God Himself would bring them in and give them rest. One thing was lacking: They did not believe and so did not yield themselves to God to do for them what He had promised. Unbelief closes the heart against God, withdraws the life from God's power; in the very nature of things, unbelief renders the word of promise to no effect. A Gospel of rest is preached to us as it was to them. We have in Scripture the most precious assurances of a rest for the soul to be found under the yoke of Jesus, of a peace of God that passes all understanding, of a peace and a joy in the soul that nothing can take away. But when they are not believed, they cannot be enjoyed. Faith is, in its very nature, a resting in the promise and the Promiser until He fulfills it in us. Only faith can enter into rest. The fullness of faith enters into the full rest.

"For we which have believed do enter into that rest." It is not, "will enter." No. Today. *"As the Holy Ghost saith, To-day"* (Hebrews 3:7), now and here, we who have believed do enter into rest. It is with the rest of faith— here as it was with what we heard of being *"partakers of Christ"* (verse 14)—that the blessing is enjoyed *"if we hold fast the beginning of our confidence firm unto the end"* (verse 14). The initial faith, that passes out of Egypt through the Red Sea, must be held fast firm, then it comes to the fullness of faith that passes through Jordan into the land.

Let every student of this epistle realize how intensely personal its tone is, and with what urgency it appeals to us for faith, as the one thing needful in our dealings with the Word of God. Without this, the Word cannot profit us. We may seek by thought and study to enter into the meaning of the promise, but God has sworn that we never will enter into its possession, or into His rest, but by faith. The one thing God asks in our communion with Him and His Word is the habit of faith that ever keeps the heart open toward God and longs to enter in and abide in His rest. The soul that thirsts for God, for the living God, will have the spiritual capacity for receiving the revelation of how Jesus, the High Priest, brings us into God's presence. What is to be taught us later on of our entering into the Holiest of All is nothing but the clearer unfolding of what is here called "entering into rest." Let us, in studying the epistle, above everything have faith.

Would you enter into the rest? Remember what has been taught us of the two stages. They are represented by Moses and Joshua. Moses the leader, Joshua the perfecter, or finisher, of the faith of Israel. Moses brought the people out; Joshua brought them in. Accept Jesus as your Joshua. Do not let past failure and wandering and sin cause either despair or contentment with what you are. Trust Jesus who, through the sprinkling of the blood, brought you out of Egypt to bring you as definitely into the rest. Faith is always rest in what another will do for me. Faith ceases to seek help in itself or its efforts, to be troubled with its need or its weakness; it rests in the sufficiency of the all-sufficient One who has undertaken all. Trust Jesus. Give up and forsake the wilderness. Follow Him fully: He is the Rest!

Chapter Notes...

1. Let no one imagine that this life in the rest of faith is something that is meant only for a favored few. I cannot too earnestly press it upon every reader: God calls you—yes, you—to enter the rest. He calls you to a life of entire consecration. If you rest content with the thought of having been converted, it may be at the peril of your soul; with Israel, you may perish in the wilderness. *"As I sware in my wrath, They shall not enter into my rest."*

2. If God be indeed the Fountain of all goodness and blessedness, it follows that the nearer we are to Him and the more we have of Him, the deeper and the fuller our joy will be. Has not the soul that is not willing at all costs to yield to Christ when He offers to bring us into the rest of God, reason to fear that all its religion is simply the selfishness that seeks escape from punishment and that it is content with as little of God here as may suffice to secure heaven hereafter?

Thirty

The Rest of God

For he hath said somewhere of the seventh day on this wise,
And God rested on the seventh day from all his works; and
in this place again, They shall not enter into my rest. Seeing
therefore it remaineth that some should enter thereinto, and
they to whom the good tidings were before preached failed
to enter in because of disobedience, he again defineth a
certain day, saying in David, after so long a time, To-day,
as it hath been before said, To-day if ye shall hear his voice,
harden not your hearts. For if Joshua had given them rest,
he would not have spoken afterward of another day.
—Hebrews 4:4–8

We speak, with Scripture, of the rest of faith. Faith, however, only gives rest because it rests in God; it rests because it allows God to do all. The rest is in God Himself. It is His own divine rest into which we enter by faith. When the Holy Spirit says, *"my rest"* or *"God rested,"* it teaches us that it is God's own rest into which we enter and of which we partake. It is, as faith sees, that the creature was destined to find its rest nowhere but in the Creator and that, in the entire surrender to Him—to His will and His working—the creature may have perfect rest, that it may dare to cast itself upon God and have no care. It sees that God, the cause of all movement and change, is Himself the immovable and unchangeable One, and that His blessed rest can never be disturbed by what is done either by Himself or by others. Hearkening to the loving offer, it forsakes all to find its dwelling place in God and His love. Faith sees what the rest of God is; faith believes that it may come and share in it; faith enters in and rests, yielding itself to Jesus to lead it in and make it partaker. Because it honors God and counts Him all, God honors it; He opens the door, and the soul is brought in to rest in Him.

This faith is faith in Jesus. It is the insight into His finished work, the complete salvation He bestows, the perfection that was wrought in Him personally, and in which we share as *"partakers of Christ"* (3:14). The connection between the finishing of a work and the rest that follows is clearly seen in what is said of Creation. God rested on the seventh day from all His works. (See Genesis 2:3.) *"For he that is entered into his rest hath himself also ceased from his own works, as God did from his"* (Hebrews 4:10). The rest of God was His glad complacency in what He had finished in Creation and the beginning of His blessed work of providence to care for and bring on to perfection what He had wrought. And so it is the finished work of Jesus that is ever set before us in the epistle as the ground of our faith, the call for us in fullness of faith to draw near and enter in and rest. Because Christ put away sin, rent the veil, and is set down on the right hand of the throne—because all is finished and perfected—and we have received the Holy Spirit from heaven in our hearts to make us the partakers of that glorified Christ, we may, with confidence and boldness, rest in Him to maintain and perfect His work in us. And, resting in Him, He becomes our Joshua, perfecting our faith, bringing us in, and giving us a home in the rest of God with Himself, now to go no more out forever.

And if you would know why so few Christians enjoy this rest, it is because they do not know Jesus as their Joshua. We will see later how Aaron was only a type of Christ in His work on earth. Melchizedek is needed as a type of His work in heaven, in the power and joy of the heavenly life. Moses and Aaron both shadow forth the beginning of Christ's work—His work on earth. Melchizedek and Joshua foreshadow His work in heaven. They show us clearly how, just as in the type that God ordained, so in reality there are two stages in Christian knowledge and experience. All the feebleness of our Christian life is owing to one thing: We do not know Jesus in heaven. We do not know that Jesus has *"entered in"* (9:12) and that this secures to us boldness and the power of entrance into a heavenly state of life that He sits there upon the throne as our High Priest in power, maintaining in us His own heavenly life and keeping us in personal fellowship with the living Father so that, in Him, we too enter the rest of God. It is because we do not know Jesus in His heavenly life and power that our lives are feeble. If we learn to know Him as He is revealed in this epistle, as our heavenly Joshua, actually bringing us and our inmost nature into the rest of God, then we cannot but enter into that rest. When Joshua went before, the people followed at once in fellowship with him. Entering the rest of God is a personal, practical experience of the soul that receives the Word in living faith because, in it, it receives Jesus on the throne.

Let us do what Israel did in crossing Jordan: They allowed Joshua to bring them in; they followed him. Let us follow Jesus in the path He trod. In heaven, God's will is all. On earth, Jesus made that will all. He lived in the will of God, in suffering and doing, in meeting trial, in waiting for the Father's guidance. In giving up everything to it, He proved that God's will was His path. Follow Him. Yield yourself, in the death to self, to the will of God; have faith in Jesus on the throne, as your Head and life, that He has brought you in and will make it true in your experience; trust Jesus, as being partaker of His nature and life, to work all in you that the Father seeks. Do these things and you will know how blessed it is to enter the rest of God.

Chapter Notes...

1. Deep restfulness, even amid outward activity, is one of the most beautiful marks and aids of the life of faith. Cultivate that holy stillness that seeks to abide in God's presence and does not yield too much to things around.

2. This rest is God's rest: It is found in His fellowship. Think of all He sees, of all He feels, and has to bear; think of the divine peace and patience with which He guides all; and learn to be patient and trustful, to rest in Him. Believe in Him, as the one God who works all in all and works in you what is well-pleasing in His sight. And you will have perfect rest in letting Him do all for you and in you.

3. God is a supernatural, incomprehensible Being. We must learn to know Him in a way that is about reason and sense. That way is the adoration of faith and the deep humility of obedience. Through these, the Holy Spirit will work the work of God in us.

4. All entering in means a coming out from the place we were in before. Forsake all, and follow Jesus into God's presence.

5. O my soul, listen to this word of the great God, and let His unspeakable love draw you—"Today, enter into My rest."

Thirty-One

Rest from Works

There remaineth therefore a sabbath rest for the people of
God. For he that is entered into his rest hath himself also
rested from his works, as God did from his.
—Hebrews 4:9–10

There remaineth therefore a sabbath rest for the people of God."
Taken in connection with what precedes about the seventh
day, or Sabbath, the rest is here called a "sabbatism" or *"sab-*
bath rest." It is spoken of as "remaining," with reference to the
rest in Canaan. That was but a shadow and symbol: The real Sabbath rest remained, waiting its time, until Christ, the true Joshua,
should come and open it to us by Himself entering it.

In verse 10, we have here another proof that the rest does
not refer to heaven. How needless it would be in that case to say
of those who have died, *"There remaineth therefore a sabbath rest*
for the people of God. For he that is entered into his rest hath himself
also rested from his works, as God did from his." The remark would
have no point. But what force it has in connection with the rest of
faith in this life, pointing us to the great secret of this entrance into
rest—the ceasing from works, as God did from His.

In God we see, as it were, two distinct stages in His relation to His work. The first was that of Creation—until He had finished all His work that He created and made. The second, His rest when Creation was finished; and He rejoiced in what He had made, now to begin the higher work of watching the development of the life He had entrusted the creature with and securing its sanctification and perfection. It is a rest from work that is now finished so that higher work can be carried on. Even so, there are the two stages in the Christian life. There is the one in which, after conversion, a believer seeks to work what God would have him do. And there is the second, in which, after many a painful failure, he ceases from his work and enters the rest of God, there to find the power for work in allowing God to work in him.

It is this resting from their own work that many Christians cannot understand. They think of it as a state of passive and selfish enjoyment, of still contemplation that leads to the neglect of the duties of life and unfits for that watchfulness and warfare to which Scripture calls. What an entire misunderstanding of God's call to rest! As the Almighty, God is the only Source of power. In nature, He works all. In grace, He waits to work all, too, if man will but consent and allow. Truly to rest in God is to yield oneself up to the highest activity. We work because He works in us to will and to do. As Paul said of himself, *"I labour…, striving according to his working, which worketh in me mightily"** (Colossians 1:29). Entering the rest of God is the ceasing from self-effort and the yielding up of oneself in full surrender of faith to God's working.

How many Christians there are who need nothing so much as rightly to apprehend this word. Their life is one of earnest effort and ceaseless struggling. They long to do God's will and to live to His glory. Continued failure and bitter disappointment is their too frequent experience. Very often, as the result, they give themselves

---

* Literally, "agonizing according to His energy who energizes in me with might."

up to a feeling of hopelessness: "It never will be otherwise." Theirs is truly the wilderness life—they have not entered into God's rest. Would that God might open their eyes and show them Jesus as our Joshua, who has entered into God's presence, who sits upon the throne as High Priest, bringing us in living union with Himself into that place of rest and of love and, by His Spirit within us, making that life of heaven a reality and an experience.

"He that is entered into his rest hath himself also rested from his works, as God did from his." And how does one rest and cease from his works? It is by ceasing from self. It is the old self-life that always insists upon proving its goodness and its strength and that presses forward to do the works of God. It is only in death that we rest from our works. Jesus entered His rest through death; each one whom He leads into it must pass through death. *"Reckon ye also yourselves to be dead unto sin, but alive unto God in Christ Jesus"* (Romans 6:11). Believe that the death of Christ, as an accomplished fact, with all that it means and has effected, is working in you in all its power. You are dead with Him and in Him. Consent to this, and cease from dead works. *"Blessed are the dead which die in the Lord from henceforth: yea, saith the Spirit, that they may rest from their labours"* (Revelation 14:13). That is as true of spiritual dying with Christ as of the death in the body. To the sinful nature, there is no rest from work but through death.

"He that is entered into his rest hath himself also rested from his works." Ceasing from our works and entering the rest of God go together. Read the first chapter of Joshua, and hear God's words of strength and encouragement to everyone who would enter. Exchange the wilderness life with your own works for the rest life in which God works. Fear not to believe that Jesus came to give it, and that it is for you.

Chapter Notes...

1. *"Not I, but Christ"* (Galatians 2:20 KJV). This is the rest of faith in which a man rests from his works. With the unconverted

man it is, "Not Christ, but I." With the feeble and slothful Christian, "I and Christ: I first, and Christ to fill up what is wanting." With increasing earnestness it becomes, "Christ and I: Christ first, but still I second." With the man who dies with Christ it is, *"'Not I, but Christ:'* Christ alone and Christ all." He has ceased from his work: Christ lives in him. This is the rest of faith.

2. God says of His dwelling among His people, *"This is my rest for ever: here will I dwell"* (Psalm 132:14 KJV). Do not be afraid to say this too. It is the rest of God in His delight and pleasure in the work of His Son, in His love to Jesus and all who belong to Him. It is the rest of Jesus in His finished work, sitting on the throne, resting in the Father's love. It is the rest of our faith and love in Jesus, in God, in His love.

Thirty-Two

Give Diligence to Enter into the Rest

Let us therefore give diligence to enter into that rest, that
no man fall after the same example of disobedience.
—Hebrews 4:11

O ur epistle is intensely practical. How it detains and holds us fast in hope of persuading us not to be content with the knowledge or the admiration of its teaching, but personally to listen to the message it brings from God by the Holy Spirit and indeed to do the thing God would have us do—enter into His rest. *"Let us...give diligence to enter into that rest."*

"Let us...give diligence." The word *diligence* means, "make haste, be in earnest, put your whole heart into it, see that you do it." *"Enter into that rest, that no man fall after the same example of disobedience."* The danger is imminent—the loss will be terrible. God has sworn in His wrath that unless we hearken and obey, we will not enter His rest. Let us give diligence to enter in. All the wonderful teaching the epistle contains further on—as to the Holiest that is opened for us as the place where God wants to receive

us into His rest and live, and as to the great High Priest who has opened the way and entered in and lives as our Joshua to bring us in—will profit us nothing unless there be the earnest desire, the willing readiness, and the firm resolve to enter in. It is this disposition alone that can fit a man spiritually to apprehend the heavenly mysteries the epistle opens up.

And surely it shouldn't be necessary to press the motives that should urge us to obedience. Ought not the one motive suffice— the unspeakable privilege God offers me in opening to me the entrance into His own rest? No words can express the inconceivable greatness of the gift. God speaks to me in His Son as one who was created in His image, capable of fellowship with Himself; as one whom He has redeemed out of the awful captivity of sin and death because He longs to have me living with Him in His love. As one for whom He has made it possible to live the outer life in the flesh with the inner life in Christ lifted up, kept safe in the Holiest of All, in God's own rest. Oh, can it be that anyone believes this and does not respond? No, let each heart say, "Blessed be God. Into this rest would I enter; here would I dwell."

We are so accustomed to the wilderness life of stumbling and sinning that we have learned to take the words God speaks of that life—*"They do alway err in their heart"* (3:10)—as descriptive of what must be daily Christian experience so that we hardly count it a practical possibility to enter into the rest. And even when the desire has been awakened, the path appears so dark and unknown. Let me, for the sake of such, once again gather up what has been said as to the way to enter in. God, in His great mercy, may even help some to take the step. The instructions are very simple.

First, settle it in your mind. Believe with your whole heart that there is such a rest, and do so today. It is God's rest, in which He lives; into which Jesus, as your Joshua, has entered. It is your rest, prepared for you; your Land of Promise; the spiritual state of life that is as surely yours as Jesus is, into which Jesus will bring you and

Andrew Murray

where He will keep you. It is the rest in which you can live every hour, free from care and anxiety, free from weariness and wanderings, always resting in the rest that trusts God for all. Believe this.

Then, cease from your own works. Not as if you had to attain this perfectly before entering into God's rest, but consent, yield, and be willing that all self-working should come to an end. Cease from self. Where there is life, there is action; the self-life will seek to work unless you give up self into the death of Christ. With Him you are buried, in Him you live. As Christ said, "Hate your own life; lose it" (Luke 14:26). Cease from your own works, and bow in deep humility and helplessness of all good, as nothing, before God.

Trust Jesus as your Joshua, who brings you in, even now. Israel had simply to trust and obey and follow Joshua. Set your heart on Him who has entered the heavens to appear before God for us. Claim Jesus as yours, not only in His cross and death and resurrection, but above all in His heavenliness and in His possession of the rest of heaven. Claim Him, and leave Him to do His blessed work. You need not understand all. Your feelings may not be what you would wish. Trust Him, who has done all for you in earth and heaven, to do all in your heart, too.

And then be a follower of them who, through faith and patience, have inherited the promises. Israel passed through Jordan and into Canaan in one day, but they did not come to perfect rest in one day. At the end of Joshua's life, we read, *"The LORD gave them rest round about"* (Joshua 21:44). Enter today into the rest. Though all may not be bright at once, look to Jesus, your Joshua, and leave all in His hands. Come away, out of self, and live in Him. Rest in God, whatever happens. Think of His rest, and of Jesus who has entered it in your name and who, out of it, fills you with its Spirit. Think of Jesus, and fear not. Today, if you hear His voice, enter in.

Chapter Notes...

1. Jesus said, *"Take my yoke upon you, and learn of me; for I am meek and lowly in heart: and ye shall find rest unto your souls"* (Matthew 11:29). It was through meekness and lowliness of

heart that Jesus found His rest in God. He allowed God to be all, trusted God for all—the rest of God was His abode. He invites us to share His rest and tells us the secret. In the meekness and lowliness of Jesus is the way to rest.

2. Israel did not enter Canaan. And why? It is twice said because of disobedience and thrice because of unbelief. The two things always go together. Yield yourself in everything to obey. This will strengthen you to trust for everything He has promised to do.

3. The rest includes victory: *"The LORD...giveth you rest from all your enemies round about, so that ye dwell in safety"* (Deuteronomy 12:10). *"And the LORD gave them rest round about... the LORD delivered all their enemies into their hand"* (Joshua 21:44).

Thirty-Three

The Heart-Searching Word of God

*For the word of God is living, and active, and sharper
than any two-edged sword, and piercing even to the
dividing of soul and spirit, of both joints and marrow, and
quick to discern the thoughts and intents of the heart. And
there is no creature that is not manifest in his sight: but
all things are naked and laid open before the eyes of him
with whom we have to do.*
—Hebrews 4:12–13

They have been earnest words with which the writer warned the Hebrews against unbelief and disobedience, hardening the heart and departing from God, and coming short of the promised rest. The solemn words of God's oath in Psalm 95:11, *"I sware in my wrath, that they should not enter into my rest,"* have been repeated more than once to urge all to give diligence lest any man fall after the same example of unbelief. He was about to close his warning. He did so by reminding them of the power of the Word of God as the Word of the omniscient One—of Him with whom we have to do and before whose eyes all things, our hearts and lives too, are naked and open. Let each student of the epistle make a very personal application of the words. Let us take the oath of God concerning His rest, and the command to labor that we may enter in, home to our heart, and say whether we have indeed entered in. And if not, let us all the more yield ourselves to the Word to search and try us: It will, without fail, do its blessed work in us and prepare us for following with profit the further teaching concerning our Lord Jesus.

"For the word of God is living, and active." At times it may appear as if the Word effects so little. The Word is like seed: Everything depends on the treatment it receives. Some receive the Word with the understanding; there it cannot be quickened. The Word is meant for the heart, the will, the affections. The Word must be submitted to, must be lived, must be acted out. When this is done, it will manifest its living, quickening power. It is not we who have to make the Word alive. When the heart, in faith in the life and power of the Word, yields itself in humble submission and honest desire to its action, it will prove itself to be life and power.

"And sharper than any two-edged sword, and piercing even to the dividing of soul and spirit, of both joints and marrow." The first action of God's Word is to wound, to cut, to divide. In the soul, the natural life has its seat; in the spirit, the spiritual and divine life has its place. Sin has brought confusion and disorder; the spirit is under the mastery of the soul, the natural life. God's Word divides and separates; wakens the spirit to a sense of its destiny as the faculty for the unseen and eternal; brings the soul to a knowledge of itself as a captive to the power of sin. It cuts deep and sure, discovering the deep corruption of sin. As the knife of the surgeon, who seeks to heal, pierces even to the dividing of the joints and marrow where it is needed, so the Word penetrates all; there is no part of the inner being to which it does not pass.

"And quick to discern the thoughts and intents of the heart." It is especially with the heart that God's Word deals. In chapter 3,

we read of the hardened heart, the evil heart of unbelief, the erring heart. When the word *"heart"* occurs later in the epistle, we will find everything changed; we will read of a heart in which God's law is written, of a true heart, a heart sprinkled with the blood, a heart established by grace. (See 8:9–10; 10:22.) We have here the transition from the one to the other. God's appeal was, *"To-day if ye shall hear his voice, harden not your hearts"* (3:7–8). The heart that will but yield itself to be searched by God's Word, to have its secret thoughts and intents discerned and judged by it, will be freed from its erring and unbelief. It will be quickened, cleansed, and made a living table on which the Word is written by God Himself. Oh, to know how needful it is, but also how blessed, to yield our hearts to the judgment of the Word.

"And there is no creature that is not manifest in his sight." God's Word bears the character of God Himself. He is the all-knowing and all-pervading: Nothing can hide itself from the judgment of His Word. If we will not have it judge us now, it will condemn us hereafter. *"But all things are naked and laid open before the eyes of him with whom we have to do."* Yes, the God with whom we have to do is He of whom we later read, *"It is a fearful thing to fall into the hands of the living God"* (10:31). And again, *"For our God is a consuming fire"* (12:29). It is this God who now pleads with us to enter into His rest.

Let each of us gladly yield ourselves to have to do with Him. If perhaps there be a secret consciousness that all is not right, that we are not giving diligence to enter into the rest, oh, let us beware of setting such thoughts aside. It is the first swelling of the living seed of the Word within us. Do not regard that thought as coming from yourself, or from the man who brings you God's Word; it is God Himself, waking you out of sleep. Have to do with Him. Be willing for the Word to show you what is wrong. Do not be afraid of its revealing to you your sin and wretchedness. The knife of the physician wounds to heal. The light that shows you your sin and wrong will surely lead you out. The Word is living and will give you life.

Chapter Notes...

1. God has spoken to us in His Son. This is the keynote of the epistle. *"To-day if ye shall hear his voice, harden not your hearts"* (3:7–8): This is the keynote of this long and solemn warning. Let us hearken and let us yield to the Word. As we deal with the Word, so we deal with God; and so will God deal with us.

2. Judge your life not by what your heart says, or the church, or the so-called Christian world—but by what the Word says. Let it have its way with you: It will greatly bless you.

3. *"All things are naked and laid open before the eyes of him with whom we have to do."* Why, then, through indifference or discouragement, do you shut your eyes to them? Oh, lay everything open before God, the God with whom we have to do, whether we will or not.

4. *"The word of God is living, and active."* Have great faith in its power. Be sure that the Holy Spirit, that the living Word, that God Himself works in it. The Word ever points to the living God, who is present in it and makes it a living Word in the heart that is seeking for life and for God.

Jesus Our High Priest More than Aaron

Thirty-Four

A Great High Priest

Having then a great high priest, who hath passed through
the heavens, Jesus the Son of God, let us hold
fast our confession.*
—Hebrews 4:14

After his digression, in the warning to the Hebrews not to harden their hearts through unbelief like their fathers with Moses, our writer returned to his argument. He had already twice used the words *"high priest"* (see Hebrews 2:17; 3:1) and was preparing the way for what is the great object of the epistle—the exposition of the heavenly priesthood of the Lord Jesus and the work He has accomplished by it for us (7:1–10:18). In this section (4:14–5:10), he first gave the general characteristics of that priesthood, as typified by Aaron and exhibited in our Lord's life here on earth. In chapters 1 and 2, he had laid the foundation of his structure in the divinity and the humanity of our Savior; here he first spoke of Him in His greatness as a High Priest passed through the heavens, then in His sympathy and compassion, as having been tempted as we are.

* Therefore.

Phil

"*Having* [therefore] *a great high priest.*" The "therefore" refers to the previous argument, in which Christ's greatness had been set forth, and in view of the dangers against which the writer had been warning, the readers had been urged to steadfastness in holding fast their confession. The force of the appeal lies in the word "*Having.*" We know the meaning of that word so well in earthly things. There is nothing that touches men so nearly as the sense of ownership of property. I *have* a father, I *have* money, I *have* a home—what a world of interest is awakened in connection with such thoughts. And God's Word comes here and says: You *have*— oh, best and most wonderful of all possessions—you *have* a "*great high priest.*" You own Him; He is yours, your very own, wholly yours. You may use Him with all He is and has. You can trust Him for all you need, know and claim Him as indeed your great High Priest, to bring you to God. Let your whole walk be the proof that you live as one "*having...a great High Priest.*"

"*A great high priest, who hath passed through the heavens.*" We have said more than once, and will not weary of repeating it again, that one of the great lessons of our epistle has been to teach us this: The knowledge of the greatness and glory of Jesus is the secret of a strong and holy life. Its opening chapter was nothing but a revelation of His divine nature and glory. At the root of all it has to teach us of Christ's priesthood and work, it wants us to see the praiseworthy omnipotent divinity of Christ—in that our faith is to find its strength and the measure of its expectation, and by that our conduct is to be guided. That is to be the mark of our life—that we have a Savior who is God. "*A great high priest, who hath passed through the heavens.*" Later on we read, "*Such a high priest became us,...and made higher than the heavens*" (7:26). It is difficult for us to form any idea of what heaven is, so high, and bright, and full of glory. But all the heavens we can think of were only the vestibule through which He passed into what is behind and above and beyond them all—the light that is inaccessible, the very life and presence of God Himself. And the Word calls us to follow our great

High Priest in thought—and when thought fails, in faith and worship and love—into this glory beyond and above all heavens and, *"having"* Him as ours, to be sure that our life can be the counterpart of His, the proof of what a complete redemption He has wrought, the living experience of what he has effected there.

"A great high priest,...Jesus the Son of God." The name *"Jesus"* speaks of His humanity and of His work as a Savior from sin. This is the first work of the priest—the cleansing, the putting away of sin. The name *"Son of God"* speaks of His divinity and His power as High Priest to bring us to God, into the very life and fellowship of the Holy One. It is in His Son that God speaks to us; it is to the perfect fellowship and blessedness of the ever-blessed One that our great High Priest, who is passed through the heavens can, and does indeed, bring us.

"Having [therefore] *a great high priest,...let us hold fast our confession."* He is *"the Apostle and High Priest of our confession"* (3:1). The knowledge of what He is is our strength to hold fast to our confession. Twice, the Hebrews had been told how much would depend on this: *"Whose house are we, if we hold fast"* (3:6) and *"We are become partakers of Christ, if we hold fast"* (3:14). Our faith in Christ must be confessed. If we have Him as our great High Priest, He is worthy of it; our souls will delight in rendering Him this homage. Without it, failure will speedily come; without it, the grace of steadfastness, perseverance, cannot be maintained.

O brethren, having a great High Priest, who is passed through the heavens, let us hold fast our confession. Let every thought of Jesus, in heaven for us, urge us to live wholly for Him and, in everything, to confess Him as our Lord.

Chapter Notes...

1. Ought it not to fill our hearts with worship, and trust, and the incarnation love without end, this wondrous mystery: the Son of God, become man—the Son of Man, now God on the throne—that we might be helped.

2. *"Who hath passed through the heavens"* beyond all thought of space and place, into the mystery of the divine glory and power. And why? That He might, in divine power, breathe that heavenly life into our hearts. His whole priesthood has, as its one great characteristic, heavenliness. He communicates the purity, the power, the life of heaven to us. We live in heaven with Him; He lives with heaven in us. With Him in our hearts, we have the kingdom of heaven within us, in which God's will is done, as in heaven, so on earth. Let us believe it can most surely be.

3. After all the solemn warning about falling in the wilderness and coming short of the rest, see here your safety and strength—*"Wherefore, holy brethren, partakers of a heavenly calling, consider the Apostle and High Priest of our confession, even Jesus"* (3:1). Having Jesus, let us hold fast.

Thirty-Five

A High Priest, Able to Sympathize

For we have not a high priest that cannot be touched with*
the feeling of our infirmities;† but one that hath been in
all points tempted like as we are, yet without sin.
—Hebrews 4:15

May God in His mercy give us a true insight into the glory of what is offered to us in these words—even this, that our High Priest, whom we have in heaven, is one who is able to sympathize with us because He knows, from personal experience, exactly what we feel. Yes, so that God might give us courage to draw nigh to Him, He has placed upon the throne of heaven one out of our own midst, of whom we can be certain that, because He Himself lived on earth as man, He understands us perfectly and is prepared to have patience with our weakness and to give us just the help we need. It was to effect this that God sent His Son to become man and, as man, perfected Him through suffering. That not one

---

* Who is not able to sympathize with.
† Weaknesses.

single feeble soul should be afraid to draw nigh to the great God or, in drawing nigh, should doubt as to whether God is not too great and holy fully to understand or to bear with his weakness. Jesus, the tried and tempted One, has been placed upon the throne as our High Priest. God gives us a glimpse into the heart of our compassionate, sympathizing High Priest!

"For we have not a high priest [who is not able to sympathize] *with* [our weaknesses]." The writer used the two negatives to indicate how common the thought is that he wished to combat. Can a rich king, who lives every day in luxury—even though he hear of it—can he fully realize what it means for the poor sick man, from year to year, never to know where his daily bread is to come from? Hardly. And God, the glorious and ever-blessed, can He truly feel what a poor sinner experiences in his daily struggle with the weaknesses and temptations of the flesh? God be praised! Jesus knows and is able to sympathize. He is *"one that hath been in all points tempted like as we are, yet without sin."*

In all things! The thought of Jesus as a sympathizing High Priest is ordinarily applied to those who are in circumstances of trial and suffering. But the truth has a far deeper meaning and application: It has special reference to the temptation that meets the soul in the desire to live wholly for God. Jesus suffered, being tempted; it was the temptation to refuse the Father's will that caused His deepest suffering. As the believer, who seeks in all things to do the will of God, understands this, the truth of the sympathizing High Priest becomes doubly precious.

What is the ordinary experience of those who set themselves with their whole hearts to live for God? It happens very often that it is only then that they begin to find out how sinful they are. They are continually disappointed in their purpose to obey God's will. They feel deeply ashamed at the thought of how often, even in things that appear little and easy, they fail entirely in keeping a good conscience and in pleasing God. At times it is as if the more they hear of the rest of God and the life of faith, the fainter the hope of attaining it becomes. At times they are ready to give up all in despair: A life in the rest of God is not for them.

What comfort and strength comes at such a time to a soul when it sees that Jesus is able to sympathize and to succor because He Himself has been thus tempted. Or did it not become so dark in His soul that He had to wrestle and to cry, *"If it be possible"* (Matthew 26:39) and *"Why hast thou forsaken me?"* (Matthew 27:46)? He, too, had to trust God in the dark. He, too, in the hour of death had to let go His spirit and commit it, in the darkness of death, into God's keeping. He knew what it was to walk in darkness and see no light. And when a man feels utterly helpless and in despair, Jesus can sympathize with him. He is *"one that hath been in all points tempted like as we are, yet without sin."* If we would but rest in the assurance that He understands it all, that He feels for us with a sympathy in which the infinite love of God and the tenderness of a fellow-sufferer are combined, and is able to succor him, we would soon reach the rest of God. Trusting Jesus would bring us into it.

Holy brethren, partakers of a heavenly calling, would you be strong to hold fast your confession and know, in full, the power of your Redeemer God to save? Listen today to the voice of the Holy Spirit. Jesus was in all things tempted just as you are. And why? That He might be able to help you. His being able to sympathize has no other purpose than that He should be able to succor. Let the one word, *sympathize*, be the food of your faith; the other, *succor*, will be its fruit, your blessed experience. Just think of God giving His Son to come and pass through all the temptations that come to you, so that He might be able to sympathize, and then lifting Him up to the throne of omnipotence that He might be able to succor, and say if you have not reason to trust Him fully. And let the faith of the blessed High Priest in His infinite and tender sympathy be the foundation of a friendship and a fellowship in which we are sure to experience that He is able to save completely.

Chapter Notes...

1. Some time ago I asked a young lady who had come from Keswick and had spoken of her having been a happy Christian for years before and of having found such a wonderful change in her experience, how she would describe the difference between what she had known before and what she now enjoyed. Her answer was ready at once: "Oh, it is the personal friendship of Jesus!" And here is one of the gates that lead into this blessed friendship: He became a man just that I might learn to trust His gentle, sympathizing kindness.

2. Study well the three "ables" of this epistle. Jesus able to sympathize, able to succor, able to save completely. And claim them all. *to go to the aid of, help*

3. Tempted as we are—He was made like to us in temptation so that we might become like Him in victory. This He will accomplish in us. Oh, let us consider Jesus, who suffered being tempted, who experienced what temptation is, who resisted and overcame it and brought to nought the tempter, who now lives as High Priest to succor the tempted and glue the victory—let us consider Jesus, the ever-present Deliverer. He will lead us in triumph over every foe.

Thirty-Six

Let Us Draw Near with Boldness

*Let us therefore draw near with boldness unto the throne of
grace, that we may receive mercy, and may find grace
to help us in time of need.**
—Hebrews 4:16

In the first two chapters, the true divinity and the real humanity of our Savior were set before us as the very foundation of our faith and life. In the two verses that we have just been considering, these two truths are applied to the priesthood of Christ. *"Having then a great high priest, who hath passed through the heavens"* (Hebrews 4:14) and having a High Priest who is able to sympathize, let us draw near. The one work of the High Priest is to bring us near to God. The one object of revealing to us His person and work is to give us perfect confidence in drawing near. The measure of our nearness of access to God is the index of our knowledge of Jesus.

"Let us therefore," with such a High Priest, *"draw near with boldness unto the throne of grace."* The words, *"draw near,"* are the

* For timely help.

same used of the priests in the Old Testament. It is this one truth the epistle seeks to enforce: that we can actually, in spiritual reality, draw near to God, and live in that nearness, in living fellowship with Him, all the day. The work of Christ, as our High Priest, is so perfect, and His power in heaven so divine, that He not only gives us the right and liberty to draw near, but by His priestly action, He does in very deed and truth so take possession of our inmost being and inward life to draw and bring us nigh so that our life can be lived in God's presence.

"Let us draw near." The expression occurs twice—here and in 10:22. The repetition is significant. In the second passage, after the deeper truths of the true sanctuary, the rent veil, and the opening of the Holiest have been expounded, it refers to the believer's entrance into the full blessing of a life spent in the power of Christ's heavenly priesthood, in the presence of God. Here, where all this teaching has not yet been given, it is applied more simply to prayer, to the drawing near to the throne of grace, in a sense that the feeblest believer can understand it. As we are faithful in the lesser—the tarrying before the throne of grace in prayer—we will find access to the greater, which is the life within the veil, in the full power of the Forerunner who has entered there for us.

"Let us therefore draw near...that we may receive mercy." This refers to the compassion that we need when the sense of sin and guilt and unworthiness depress us. In drawing near to the throne of grace, to the mercy seat, in prayer, we first receive mercy; we experience that God pardons and accepts and loves. And we *"find grace* [for timely help]." This refers to that strengthening of the inner life by which He, who was tempted in all things just as we were, meets us and enables us to conquer temptation. Grace is the divine strength working in us. *"My grace is sufficient for thee: for my power is made perfect in weakness"* (2 Corinthians 12:9). The Holy Spirit is *"the Spirit of grace"* (10:29). The believing supplicant at the throne of grace not only receives mercy—the consciousness of acceptance

and favor—but also finds grace in that Spirit whose operation the Father always delights to bestow. And that grace is for "timely help," literally, "well-timed help"—just the special help we need at each moment. The infinite mercy of God's love resting on us and the almighty grace of His Spirit working in us will ever be found at a throne of grace if we but come boldly, trusting in Jesus alone.

And now comes the chief word, *"Let us therefore draw near with boldness."* We have already been taught to *"hold fast our boldness"* (3:6). We will later on be warned, *"cast not away therefore your boldness"* (10:35). And the summing up of the epistle will tell us that the great fruit of Christ's redemption is that we have *"boldness to enter* [in]*"* (verse 19). It is the expression of the highest form of confidence, in the unhesitating assurance that there is nothing that can hinder, and in a conduct that corresponds to this conviction. It suggests the thought of our drawing near to God's throne without fear, without doubt, with no other feeling but that of the childlike liberty that a child feels in speaking to its father.

This boldness is what the blood of Christ, in its infinite worth, has secured for us, and what His heavenly priesthood works and maintains in us. This boldness is the natural and necessary result of the adoring and believing gaze fixed on our great High Priest upon the throne. This boldness is what the Holy Spirit works in us as the inward participation in Christ's entrance into the Father's presence. This boldness is of the essence of a healthy Christian life. If there is one thing the Christian should care for and aim at, it is to maintain, unbroken and unclouded, the living conviction and practice of this *"draw*[ing] *near with boldness."*

"Let us therefore draw near with boldness." Jesus, the Son of God, is our High Priest. Our boldness of access is not a state we produce in ourselves by meditation or effort. No, the living, loving High Priest, who is able to sympathize and give grace for timely help, He breathes and works this boldness in the soul that is willing to lose itself in Him. Jesus, found and felt within our heart by

faith, is our Boldness. As the Son, whose house we are, He will dwell within us. And by His Spirit's working, He Himself will be our Boldness and our Entrance to the Father. *"Let us therefore draw near with boldness"*!

Chapter Notes...

1. Do take hold of the thought that the whole teaching of the epistle centers in this: that we should so be partakers of Christ and all He is, that we should so have Him as our High Priest that we may, with perfect boldness and with most undoubting confidence, enter into, dwell in, and enjoy the Father's presence. It is in the heart that we partake of and have Christ. It is Christ, known as dwelling in the heart, who will make our boldness perfect.

2. Each time you pray, exercise this boldness. Let the measure of Jesus' merit—yea more!—let the measure of Jesus' power to work in you and lead you on to God be the measure of your boldness.

3. What tenderness of conscience, what care, what jealousy, what humility this boldness will work, lest we allow anything for which our hearts can condemn us and thus lose our liberty before God. Then it will truly be our experience—

> *So near, so very near to God,*
> *More near I cannot be.*

TPT 5:1 A KING-PRIEST LIKE MEL

① For [every High Priest] was chosen from among the people & appointed to represent ~~them~~ before God by presenting their gifts to God & offering sacrifices on their behalf ② since [the High Priest] is also [one] who is clothed in weakness, [he humbles himself] by showing compassion to those who are ignorant of God's ways & stray from them.

Thirty-Seven

The High Priest Bearing Gently with the Ignorant

For every high priest, being taken from among men, is appointed for men in things pertaining to God, that he may offer both gifts and sacrifices for sins: who can bear gently with the ignorant and erring, for that he himself also is compassed with infirmity;* and by reason thereof is bound, as for the people, so also for himself, to offer for sins.
—Hebrews 5:1–3

We know how much the epistle has already said of the true humanity and sympathy of the Lord Jesus. In chapter 2 we read,

It became him,...to make the author of their salvation perfect through sufferings. (verse 10)

Since then the children are sharers in flesh and blood, he also himself in like manner partook of the same. (verse 14)

Wherefore it behoved him in all things to be made like unto his brethren. (verse 17)

---

* Weakness.

In that he himself hath suffered being tempted, he is able to succour them that are tempted. (verse 18)

And in chapter 4 we have just heard, *"For we have not a high priest that cannot be touched with the feeling of our infirmities; but one that hath been in all points tempted like as we are"* (verse 15). And yet, the truth is counted of such importance that once again our attention is directed to it. It is not enough that we have a general conviction of its truth; we need to have it taken up into our hearts and life until every thought of Jesus is permeated by such a feeling of His sympathy that all sense of weakness will at once be met by the joyful consciousness that all is well because Jesus is so very kind and cares so lovingly for all our feebleness and all our ignorance.

Let us listen once again to what the Word teaches. *"Every high priest, being taken from among men, is appointed for men in things pertaining to God, that he may offer both gifts and sacrifices for sins."* Here we have the work of a high priest and the first essential requisite for that work. His work is *"in things pertaining to God"*: He has charge of all that concerns the access to God—His worship and service—and has, for this, to offer gifts and sacrifices. And the requisite is that he must be a man because he is to act for men. For this great reason, he must also be one *"who can bear gently with the ignorant and erring, for that he himself also is compassed with infirmity; and by reason thereof is bound, as for the people, so also for himself, to offer for sins."* At the root of the priestly office, there is to be the sense of perfect oneness in weakness and need of help. In priestly action, this is to manifest itself in sacrificing, *"as for the people, so also for himself."* And all this is so that the priestly spirit may ever be kept alive for the comfort and confidence of all the needy and weary—*"who can bear gently with the ignorant and erring."*

Glory be to God for the wondrous picture of what our Lord Jesus is. A priest must be God's representative with men. But he cannot be this without being himself, a man encompassed with weaknesses and so identified with and representing men with God.

This was why Jesus was made a little lower than the angels. The high priest is to offer *"as for the people, so also for himself."* Offering for himself was to be the bond of union with the people. Even so, our blessed Lord Jesus offered *"prayers and supplications with strong crying and tears"* (verse 7)—yea, in all that, He offered Himself unto God. And all this so that He might win our hearts and confidence as one *"who can bear gently with the ignorant and erring."* God has indeed done everything to assure us that, with such a High Priest, no ignorance or error need make us afraid of not finding the way to Him and His love. Jesus will care for us. He bears gently with the ignorant and erring.

Have we not, in our faith in the priesthood of Christ, been too much in the habit of looking more at His work than at His heart? Have we not too exclusively put the thought of our sins in the foreground and not sufficiently realized that our weaknesses, our ignorance and errors—that for these, too, a special provision has been made in Him who was made like us and Himself encompassed with weaknesses that He might be a merciful and faithful High Priest, *"who can bear gently with the ignorant and erring."*

Oh, let us take in and avail ourselves to the full of the wondrous message: Jesus could not ascend the throne as Priest until He had first, in the school of personal experience, learned to sympathize and to bear gently with the feeblest. And let our weakness and ignorance henceforth, instead of discouraging and keeping us back, be the motive and the plea that lead us to come boldly to Him for help, *"who can bear gently with the ignorant and erring."* In the pursuit of holiness, our ignorance is often our greatest source of failure. We cannot fully understand what is taught of the rest of God, and the power of faith, of dwelling within the veil, or of Christ dwelling in our hearts. Things appear too high for us, utterly beyond our reach. If we but knew to trust Jesus, not only as He who made propitiation for our sins, but also as One who was specially chosen and trained and prepared and then elevated to the throne of God to be the Leader of the ignorant and erring, bearing gently with their every weakness! Let us this day accept afresh this Savior, as God has here revealed Him to us, and rejoice that all our ignorance need not be a barrier in the way to God, because Jesus takes it into His care.

Chapter Notes...

1. Oh, the trouble God has taken to win our poor hearts to trust and confidence. Let us accept the revelation and have our hearts so filled with the sympathy and gentleness of Jesus that, in every perplexity, our first thought will always be the certainty and the blessedness of His compassion and help.

2. How many souls there are who mourn over their sins, and do not think that they are making their sins more and stronger by not going with all their ignorance and weakness boldly to Jesus.

3. Do learn the lesson: The whole priesthood of Jesus has but this one object—to lead you boldly and joyfully to draw near to God and live in fellowship with Him. With this view, trust Jesus as definitely with your ignorance and weakness as with your sins.

③ And for this reason, he has to not only present the sin offering for others, but also to bring a sin offering for himself.

Thirty-Eight

The High Priest Called by God

And no man taketh the honour unto himself, but when he is called of God, even as was Aaron. So Christ also glorified not himself to be made a high priest, but he that spake unto him, Thou art my Son, this day have I begotten thee: as he saith also in another place, Thou art a priest for ever after the order of Melchizedek.
—Hebrews 5:4–6

A priest sustains a twofold relationship—to God and to man. Every high priest is appointed for men in things pertaining to God. We have just seen what the great characteristic is of his relation to men: He must himself be a man, like them and one with them, with a heart full of gentleness and sympathy for the very weakest. In his relation to God, our epistle now proceeds to say, the chief requirement is that he should have his appointment from God. He must not take the honor to himself: He must be called by God. All this is proved to be true of Jesus.

The truth that Jesus had His appointment from God was not only of importance to the Hebrews to convince them of the divine and supreme right of Christianity; it is of equal interest to us, to give us an insight into what constitutes the real glory and power of our religion. Our faith needs to be fed and strengthened, and this can only be as we enter more deeply into the divine origin and nature of redemption.

"And no man taketh the honour unto himself, but when he is called of God." It is God against whom we have sinned, in separation from whom we are fallen into the power of death. It is God we need; it is to Him and His love that the way must be opened. It is God alone who can say what that way is, who is able to have it opened up. And this now is what gives the Gospel and our faith in Christ its security and sufficiency—that it is all of God. Christ has been called by God to be High Priest. The very God who created us, against whom we sinned, gives His Son as our Redeemer.

"So Christ also glorified not himself to be made a high priest, but he that spake unto him, Thou art my Son, this day have I begotten thee: as he saith also in another place, Thou art a priest for ever after the order of Melchizedek." Here it is not merely the fact that Christ was called by God to be High Priest, but also the ground upon which He was chosen, that we must especially notice. The passages quoted teach us that it was as Son of God that He was appointed High Priest. This opens up to us the true nature and character of the priesthood. It shows us that the priesthood is rooted in the sonship: The work of the priesthood is to reveal and communicate the blessed life of sonship.

As Son, Christ alone was heir of all that God had. All the life of the Father was in Him. God could have no union or fellowship with any creature but through His beloved Son, or as far as the life and spirit and image of the Son was seen in it. Therefore, no one could be our High Priest but the Son of God. If our salvation was not to be a merely legal one—external and, I may say, artificial—but an entrance anew into the very life of God with the restoration of the divine nature we had lost in Paradise, it was the Son of God alone who could impart this to us. He had the life of God to give; He was able to give it; He could only give it by taking us into living fellowship with Himself. The priesthood of Christ is the God-devised channel through which the ever-blessed Son could make us partakers of Himself, and with Himself, of all the life and glory He has from and in the Father.

And this now is our confidence and safety—that it was the Father who appointed the Son High Priest. It is the love of the God against whom we had sinned that gave the Son. It is the will and the power of this God that ordained and worked out the great salvation. It is in God Himself that our salvation has its origin, its life, its power. It is God drawing near to communicate Himself to us in His Son.

"Christ also glorified not himself to be made a high priest." It was God who gave Him this glory. Just think what this means. God counts it an honor for His Son to be the Priest of poor sinners. Jesus gave up His everlasting glory for the sake of this new glory, which He now counts His highest—the honor of leading guilty men to God. Every cry of a penitent for mercy, every prayer of a ransomed soul for more grace and nearer access to God— He counts these His highest honor, the proofs of a glory He has received from His Father above the glory of sonship, or rather the opening up of the fullness of glory that His sonship contained.

O doubting troubled soul, will you now believe this: that Jesus counts it His highest honor to do His work in any needy one that turns to Him? The Son of God, in His glory, counts His priesthood as His highest glory, as the power of making us partake as brethren with Him in the life and love of the Father. Let Jesus now become your confidence. Be assured that nothing delights Jesus more than to do His work.

Do what God has done: Glorify Him as your High Priest. And, as you learn to turn from yourself and all human help to trust the Son of God, He will prove to you what a great High Priest He is; He will, as Son, lead you into the life and love of the Father.

Chapter Notes...

1. Could God have bestowed a more wondrous grace upon us than this, to give His own Son as our High Priest? Could He have given us a surer ground of faith and hope than this, that the Son is Priest? And will we not trust Him? And give Him the honor God has given Him?

2. What is needed is that we occupy and exercise our faith in appropriating this blessed truth: Jesus is the eternal Son, appointed by the Father as our Priest to introduce us into His presence and to keep us there. He was Himself so compassed with weaknesses and tried with temptations that no ignorance or weakness on our part can weary Him or prevent Him from doing His blessed work—if we will only trust Him. Oh, let us worship and honor Him. Let us trust Him. Let our faith claim all He is able and willing to do—our God-appointed High Priest.

3. Faith opens the heart—through faith, this divine Being fills and pervades the whole heart and dwells in it. He cannot bring you near to God except as He brings your heart near. He cannot bring your heart near except as He dwells in it. He cannot dwell in it except as you believe. Oh, consider Jesus until your whole heart is faith in Him and what He is in you.

Thirty-Nine

The High Priest Learning Obedience

Who in the days of his flesh, having offered up prayers and
supplications with strong crying and tears unto him that
was able to save him from death, and having been heard for
his godly fear, though he was a Son, yet learned obedience
by the things which he suffered.
—Hebrews 5:7–8

We have already noticed with what persistence the writer sought to impress upon us the intense reality of Christ's humanity—His being made like unto His brethren, His partaking of flesh and blood in like manner as ourselves, His being tempted in all things as we are. In the opening verses of our chapter, he has again set before us the true High Priest—Himself compassed with weaknesses. He now once more returns to the subject. In verse 6, he already quoted the promise in regard to the order of Melchizedek, as the text of his further teaching, but felt himself urged to interpose before repeating the quotation in verse 11. He did this in order to unfold, still more fully, what the full meaning is of the blessed humiliation of the Son of God. He led us in spirit down into Gethsemane and spoke of the wondrous mystery of the agony there, as the last stage in the preparation and the perfecting of our High Priest for the work He came to do. Let us enter this holy place with hearts bowed under a consciousness of our ignorance but thirsting to know something more of the great mystery of godliness, the Son of God become flesh for us.

"Who in the days of his flesh." The word *"flesh"* points to human nature in the weakness that is the mark of its fallen state. When Jesus said to His disciples that dark night, *"Watch and pray...the spirit indeed is willing, but the flesh is weak"* (Matthew 26:41), He spoke from personal experience. He had felt that it was not enough to have a right purpose but that, unless the weakness of the flesh were upheld, or rather overcome, by power received in prayer from above, that weakness would so easily enter into temptation and become sin. The days of His flesh, encompassed with its weaknesses, were to Him a terrible reality. It was so that He would not to yield to this that He watched and prayed.

"Who in the days of his flesh, having offered up prayers and supplications with strong crying and tears unto him that was able to save him from death, and having been heard for his godly fear," having gained the strength to surrender His will and fully accept the Father's will and the renewed assurance that He would be saved and raised out of it, *"though he was a Son"*—the form of the expression implies that no one would have expected from the Son of God what is now to be said—*"yet learned obedience by the things which he suffered."* Gethsemane was the training-school where our High Priest, made like to us in all things, learned His last and most difficult lesson of obedience through what He suffered.

"Though he was a Son." As the Son of God, come from heaven, one would say that there could be no thought of His learning obedience. But so real was His emptying Himself of His life in glory, and so complete was His entrance into all the conditions and likeness of our nature, that He did indeed need to learn obedience. This is of the very essence of the life of a reasonable creature, of

man—that the life and the will he has received from God cannot be developed without the exercise of a self-determining power and without the voluntary giving up to God in all that He asks, even where it appears to be a sacrifice. The creature can only attain his perfection under a law of growth, of trial, and of development, in the overcoming of what is contrary to God's will and the assimilating of what that will reveals.

Of Jesus it is written, *"The child grew, and waxed strong, filled with wisdom"* (Luke 2:40). What is true of His childhood is true of His maturer years. At each stage of life, He had to meet temptation and overcome it; He came out of each victory with His will strengthened; His power over the weakness of the flesh, and the danger of yielding to its desire for earthly good, or its fear of temporal evil, increased. In Gethsemane, His trial and His obedience reached their consummation.

"[He] *learned obedience by the things which he suffered."* Suffering is something unnatural, the fruit of sin. God has made us for joy. He created us with not only the capacity but also the power of happiness, so that every breath and every healthy movement should be enjoyment. It is natural to us, and it was so to the Son of God, to fear and flee suffering. In this desire, there is nothing sinful. It only becomes sinful where God would have us submit and suffer and we instead refuse. This was the temptation of the power of darkness in Gethsemane—for Jesus to refuse the cup. In His prayers and supplications, with strong crying and tears, Jesus maintained His allegiance to God's will: In wrestlings and bloody sweat, He became obedient unto death, even the death of the cross. The deepest suffering taught Him the highest lesson of obedience: When He had yielded His will and His life, His obedience was complete and He Himself was perfected forevermore.

This is our High Priest. He knows what the weakness of the flesh is. He knows what it costs to conquer it and how little we are able to do it. He lives in heaven, able to succor us—sympathizing with our weaknesses, bearing gently with the ignorant and erring—

a High Priest on the throne who we may boldly draw near to find grace for timely help. He lives in heaven and in our hearts, to impart to us His own spirit of obedience so that His priesthood might bring us into the full enjoyment of all He Himself has and is.

Chapter Notes...

1. *"Heard for his godly fear."* How it becomes me then to pray in humble, holy reverence, that I may pray in His spirit and be heard, too, for His godly fear. This was the very spirit of His prayer and obedience.

2. "[He] *learned obedience by the things which he suffered."* Learn to look upon and to welcome all suffering as God's message to teach obedience.

3. "[He] *learned obedience."* This was the path in which Christ was trained for His priesthood. This is the spirit and the power that filled Him for the throne of glory; the spirit and the power that alone can lift us there; the spirit and the power that our great High Priest can impart to us. Obedience is of the very essence of salvation. Whether we look at Christ being perfected personally, or at the merit that gave His death its value and saving power, or at the work wrought in us—obedience, the entrance into the will of God, is the very essence of salvation.

4. "[He] *learned obedience."* Jesus was obedience embodied, obedience incarnate. I have only as much of Jesus in me as I have of the spirit of obedience.

Obedience - Phil 2:8 (NASB) Being found in appearance as a man, He humbled Himself by becoming obedient to the point of death, even death on a cross.

perfect - Heb 2:10 (NASB) For it was fitting for Him for whom are all things, through Whom are all things, in bringing many sons to glory, to perfect the author of their salvation through suffering

Forty

The High Priest Perfected Through Obedience

Though he was a Son, yet learned obedience by the things which he suffered; and having been made perfect, he became unto all them that obey him the author of eternal salvation.
—Hebrews 5:8–9

Our Lord Jesus *"learned obedience by the things which he suffered."* Through this obedience, He was *"made perfect"* and *"became unto all them that obey him the author of eternal salvation."* So he entered heaven as our High Priest, a Son, perfected forevermore.

The word *"perfect"* is one of the keywords of the epistle. It occurs thirteen times, four times in regard to the Old Testament, which could make nothing perfect.

For the law made nothing perfect. (7:19)

Sacrifices that cannot, as touching the conscience, make the worshipper perfect. (9:9)

The law...can never...make perfect them that draw nigh. (10:1)

That apart from us they should not be made perfect. (11:40)

199

As great as the difference between a promise and its fulfillment, or hope and the thing hoped for—between the shadow and sub-stance—is the difference between the Old and New Testament. The law made nothing perfect: It was only meant to point to something better, to the perfection Jesus Christ was to bring. With the New Tes-tament, perfection would come. Three times the word is used of our Lord Jesus, who in Himself prepared and wrought out the perfection He came to impart.

> *For it became him,...to make the author of their salvation perfect through sufferings.* (2:10)

> *And having been made perfect, he became unto all them that obey him the author of eternal salvation.* (5:9)

> *For the law appointeth men high priests, having infirmity; but the word of the oath, which was after the law, appointeth a Son, perfected for evermore.* (7:28)

The perfection brought by Christ was what was revealed in His own personal life. He came to restore to us the life of God we had lost—a life in the will and love of God. This alone is salvation. God per-fected Him through suffering—wrought out in Him a perfect human character, in which the divine life was fully united with the human will. He learned obedience through suffering and manifested perfectly the humility and submission and surrender to God that is man's duty and blessedness. So, when He had been perfected, He became the Author of eternal salvation to all who obey Him because He now had that per-fected human nature that He could communicate to them. And so He was appointed High Priest—a Son, perfected forevermore.

As Son of God, He was to take us up into the very life of God; as High Priest, He was to lift us, in actual spiritual reality, into God's fellowship and will and presence. The way in which He was perfected through obedience was the living way in which He is to lead us—as the Son, perfected through obedience, who had found and opened and walked the path of obedience as the path to God. He animates us with His own Spirit to do it, too. He, the perfected One, can alone be our Salvation.

Then twice we have the word used for what Christ has done for us.

For by one offering he hath perfected for ever them that are sanctified. (10:14)

Jesus the author and perfecter of our faith. (12:2)

Christ's perfecting us forever is nothing but His redeeming us by His one sacrifice so that we may have perfect possession of Himself, the perfected One, as our life. His death is our death to sin, His resurrection as the perfected One is our life, His righteousness is ours, His life is ours; we are put in possession of all the perfection that the Father wrought out in Him through suffering and obedience.

And once, the word is used to describe the spiritual sanctuary opened by Christ:

The greater and more perfect tabernacle, not made with hands. (9:11)

And three times it is used in regard to Christian character:

Solid food is for full-grown [perfected] *men.* (5:14)

Let us...press on unto perfection. (6:1)

Now the God of peace...make you perfect* in every good thing. (13:20–21)

Those who receive solid food are those who are not content with the mere beginnings of the Christian life but have given themselves wholly to accept and follow the perfected Master. These are they who press on to perfection—nothing else than the perfection that Christ revealed as God's claim on men, and as what He has won and made possible for them.

He learned obedience and, being perfected, became the cause of eternal salvation. Perfection in God is His will. There is no perfection for man but in union with that will. And there

---

* In the Greek here the word used is not the same as in the other passages.

is no way for attaining and proving the union with that will but by obedience. Obedience to the good and perfect will of God transforms the whole nature and makes it capable of union with Him in glory. Obedience to God's will on earth is the way to the glory of God's will in heaven. The everlasting perfection of heaven is nothing but the obedience of earth transfigured and glorified. Obedience is the seed, the power, the life of Christ's perfection and ours.

We are approaching the threshold of the Holiest of All, as this epistle is to open it up to us as the sphere of the heavenly priesthood of Him who was made after the order of Melchizedek. Before we proceed there, let us learn this lesson well: The distinguishing mark of the earthly life of our High Priest; the source of His heavenly glory and His eternal salvation; the power of His atonement of our disobedience; the opening of the living way in which we are to follow Him, our Leader; the inner disposition and spirit of the life He bestows—of all this, the secret is obedience. Through obedience, He was perfected, His sacrifice was perfect, He perfected us forever, and He carries us on to perfection.

Chapter Notes...

1. When the perfect heavenly life of the Lord Jesus comes down from heaven into our hearts, it can assume no form but what it had in Him—obedience.

2. God must be obeyed: In that one word, you have the key to the life and death of Jesus, His sitting at God's right hand, His priesthood, His dwelling in our hearts, as well as to the whole of the Gospel—God must be obeyed.

3. Christ, the obedient One who inaugurated for us the new way of obedience unto death as the way to God—is this the Christ you love and trust? Is this your delight in Him, that He now has delivered you from your disobedience and makes you strong to live only to obey God and Him? Is Christ precious to you because the salvation He gives is a restoration to obedience?

Forty-One

The High Priest Saving the Obedient

Though he was a Son, yet learned obedience by the things which he suffered; and having been made perfect, he became unto all them that obey him the author of eternal salvation.
—Hebrews 5:8–9

The death of Jesus has its value and efficacy in obedience—ours as well as His. With Him, obedience was God's great object in His suffering; the root and power of His perfection and His glory; the real efficient cause of our eternal salvation. And with us, the necessity of obedience is no less absolute. With God and with Christ, our restoration to obedience was the great aim of redemption. It is the only way to that union with God in which our happiness consists. Through it alone God can reveal His life and power within us. Again, I say: The death of Jesus has its value and efficacy in nothing but obedience—ours as well as His. He *"learned obedience by the things which he suffered; and having been made perfect, he became unto all them that obey him the author of eternal salvation."* Our obedience is as indispensable as His. As little as He could work out salvation without obedience, can we enjoy it. In us as much as in Him, obedience is the very essence of salvation.

Let us try and grasp this. God is the blessedness of the creature. When God is all to the creature, when He is allowed in humility and dependence to work all, and when all returns to Him in thanksgiving and service, nothing can prevent the fullness of God's love and joy entering and filling the creature. The creature has but one thing to do—to turn its desire or will toward God and give Him free scope; then nothing in heaven or earth can prevent the light and the joy of God filling that soul. The living center around which all the perfections of God cluster, the living energy through which they all do their work, is the will of God. The will of God is the life of the universe. The universe is what it is because God wills it; His will is the living energy that maintains the universe in existence. The creature can have no more of God than he has of God's will working in him. He that would meet and find God must seek Him in His will, for union with God's will is union with Himself.

Therefore, it was that the Lord Jesus, when He came to this world, always spoke of His having come to do one thing—the will of His Father. This alone could work our salvation. Sin had broken us away from the will of God. In doing the will of God, He was to break the power of sin. He was to prove where the service of God and true blessedness consisted; He was to work out in Himself a new nature to be communicated, a new way of living to be followed; He was to show that the doing of God's will at any cost is blessedness and glory everlasting. It was because He did this, because He was obedient unto death, that God highly exalted Him. It was this disposition, His obedience, that made Him worthy and fit to sit with God on the throne of heaven. Union with the will of God is union with God Himself and must—it cannot be otherwise—bring glory to God.

And this is as true of us as of Him. It is to be feared that there are many Christians who seek salvation and have no understanding of what salvation consists—a being saved from his own will and being restored to do the will of God alone. They seek after Christ and trust in Him; but it is not the true Christ but rather a Christ of whom they have framed their own image. The true Christ is the incarnate will of God, the incarnate obedience, who works in us what God wrought in Him. Christ came as the Son, to impart to us the very same life and disposition that animated Him on earth. Christ came to be a High Priest, to bring us to God in that very same way of obedience and self-sacrifice in which He drew near to God. As Son and Priest, Christ is our Leader and Forerunner; it is only as we follow Him in His path on earth that we can hope to share His glory in heaven. *"He became unto all **them that obey him** the author of eternal salvation"* (emphasis added).

Let us beware that no wrong or one-sided views of what salvation by faith means lead us astray. There are some who think that salvation by faith is all and obedience not so essential. This is a terrible mistake. In our justification, there is indeed no thought of obedience in the past. God justifies the ungodly. But repentance is a return to obedience. And without repentance, there can be no true faith. Justification, and the faith by which it comes, are only for the sake of obedience, as means to an end. They point us to Christ and the salvation that is to be found in union with Him. And He has no salvation but for those who obey Him. Obedience, as the acceptance of His will and life, is our only capacity for salvation. This is the reason there is so much complaining that we cannot find and do not enjoy a full salvation. We seek it in the wrong way. Jesus Himself said that the Father would give the Holy Spirit, that is, salvation as it is perfected in Christ in heaven, to *"them that obey Him."* To such, He would manifest Himself; with such, the Father and He would dwell. The salvation of Christ was wrought out entirely by obedience; this is its very essence and nature; it cannot be possessed or enjoyed but by obedience. Christ, who was perfected by obedience, is the cause of salvation to none but *"them that obey Him."*

God grant that the obedience of Jesus—with the humility in which it roots—may be seen of us to be the crowning beauty of His character, the true power of His redemption, the bond of union and likeness between Him and His followers, and the true and real salvation in the salvation He gives to those who obey Him.

Chapter Notes...

1. Salvation to obedience. Let us draw our eyes and desires from the too exclusive thought of salvation as happiness and fix them more upon what is its reality—obedience. Christ will see to it that a full salvation comes to the obedient.

2. Let no wrong thoughts of our sinfulness and inability secretly keep us back from the surrender to entire obedience. *"We are become partakers of Christ"* (3:14), of Himself, with the very life and spirit of obedience that constitutes Him, the Savior. The Son of God came not only to teach and to claim but also to give and to work obedience. Faith in this Lord Jesus may claim, and will receive, the grace of obedience—indeed, will receive Himself.

3. Jesus personally learned and exercised obedience; personally He communicates it in fellowship with Himself. It becomes a personal link with Himself to those who obey Him.

AGAINST SLOTH, STANDING STILL, AND APOSTASY

Forty-Two

Of the Sin of Not Making Progress in the Christian Life

*Named of God a high priest after the order of
Melchizedek. Of whom we have many things to say,
and hard of interpretation, seeing ye are become dull of
hearing. For when by reason of the time ye ought to be
teachers, ye have need again that some one teach you the
rudiments of the first principles* of the oracles of God; and
are become such as have need of milk, and not of solid food.
For every one that partaketh of milk is without experience
of the word of righteousness; for he is a babe.*
—Hebrews 5:10–13

W e have here the commencement of the third of the five
warnings to be found in the epistle. The first was against
indifference and neglect; the second against unbelief and
disobedience; the third deals specifically with the sloth that prevents

---

* Beginning.

all progress in the Christian life, renders the soul incapable of entering into the full meaning of gospel truth and blessing, and often leads to an entire falling away. In the previous part of the epistle, the author has been dealing with what he considers more elementary truths—the divinity and humanity of the Savior and His fitness as a merciful and faithful High Priest for the work He has to do for us. The author is about to enter on the higher teaching he has to give us on the heavenly priesthood of Christ (7:1–10:18) but feels that many of his readers are incapable of following or appreciating such spiritual truth. He feels it necessary first to rouse them by words of earnest reproof and exhortation, because no teaching can profit where the heart is not wakened up to hunger for it as its necessary food.

In the Christian church, there are, alas, too many whom we hope are believers and who are living in this state. They are content with the thought of pardon and the hope of heaven; they rest in their orthodoxy, their attachment to the church and its services, their correct deportment. But as to any strong desire for the deeper truths of God's Word—they have no understanding of what is meant, or why these deeper truths should be needed. When our author speaks of the power of Jesus' blood in heaven, of the opening of the Holiest of All, of our entering in to dwell there and then of our going out to Him without the camp, the words find no response because they meet no need of the soul. Let every reader listen earnestly to what God says of this state.

"We have many things to say, and hard of interpretation, seeing ye are become dull of hearing." The writer's complaint is not that they do not have sufficient education or mental power to understand what he says. By no means. But spiritual things must be spiritually discerned. Spiritual truth can only be received by the spiritual mind, by a heart that thirsts for God and sacrifices this world for the knowledge and enjoyment of the unseen One. They were content with their knowledge of the crucified Christ; the heavenly

Andrew Murray

Christ and His power to draw them up out of the world and to give heaven into their hearts had but little attraction.

He further says, *"By reason of the time ye ought to be teachers."* In the Christian life, every one who makes real progress feels himself constrained to teach others. Christ's love in the heart must overflow to those around. The Hebrews had been Christians so long that they ought to have been teachers. The very opposite of this, however, was the case. *"Ye have need again that some one teach you the rudiments of the first principles of the oracles of God."* So there are numbers of Christians whose Christian life consists very much in always learning. Sermons and books are a delight, but they never get beyond the stage of being fed; they know not what it is to feed others. There is no effort to appropriate God's Word like this, compared to the strength required to impart it to others. There is no real longing for deliverance from the power of sin, and the great incentive to the fuller knowledge of Jesus and His heavenly power is wanting.

"And [ye] *are become such as have need of milk, and not of solid food."* Where there is no hunger for solid food (the higher truth of Christ's heavenly priesthood) or where there is unwillingness to use what is received in helping others, the spiritual faculties are dwarfed and enfeebled; such a Christian never gets beyond the use of the milk meant for babes. In the Christian life, as in nature, there are two stages—the one of infancy or childhood, the other of manhood. In nature, the growth out of the one into the other comes spontaneously. In grace, this is not so. It is possible for a Christian to remain in a sickly infancy all his life, always needing help instead of being a help. The cause of this is sloth, reluctance to make the sacrifice needed for progress, unwillingness to forsake all and follow Jesus. And this again is very much owing to the fatal mistake that, in religion, our only thought is often of safety, that we may be content when some assurance of that is attained. Such a soul cares not for the heavenly blessedness of conformity to Jesus, of living fellowship with God, and of the godlike privilege of bringing life and blessing to men.

It is one of the great needs of the teachers in the church in our day that they should have a clear insight into the feeble and sickly state in which most Christians live, as well as into what constitutes a healthy life that goes on to perfection. As they themselves enter into the full experience of the power of Christ's priesthood, as the Holy Spirit imparts it in their hearts, they will be able to reprove with authority and effectually to help all upright souls into the full salvation Christ has provided. God give His church such teachers.

Chapter Notes...

1. Have we not here the reason there is so little earnest pursuit after holiness? So little true consecration to living to bless others? So little of the power of the Holy Spirit in the life of the church? Let us plead with God to discover the evil and to visit His church. Let us exhort one another daily to rest content with nothing less than a wholehearted enthusiastic devotion to Jesus.

2. In preparing to go on to the study of the inner sanctuary in what is to follow (7–10), do let us consider it a settled thing that unless we are really hungering after righteousness and longing for a very close fellowship with Jesus, our further study of the epistle will do us very little good. Let us pray God to convince us of our sloth, our contentment with the beginnings of grace, and to stir in us a burning thirst after Himself.

Forty-Three

Solid Food for the Perfect

*For every one that partaketh of milk is without experience
of the word of righteousness; for he is a babe. But solid food
is for full-grown* men, even those who by reason of use
have their senses exercised to discern good and evil.*
—Hebrews 5:13–14

perfect

We have here the contrast between the two stages in the
Christian life. Of the first, we have already spoken.
The second stage is that of manhood—the full-grown,
mature, perfect man. This does not, as in nature, come with years,
but consists in the wholeheartedness with which the believer yields
himself to be all for God. It is the perfect heart that makes the
perfect man. The twenty years needed for a child to become a full-
grown adult are no rule in the kingdom of heaven. There is indeed
a riper maturity and a mellowness that comes with the experience
of years. But even a young Christian can be of "the perfect" of
whom our epistle speaks, with a heart all athirst for the deeper and

* Perfect.

more spiritual truth it is to teach and a will that has indeed finally broken with sin and counted all things loss for the perfect knowledge of Christ Jesus.

The contrast is expressed in these words: The babe *"is without experience of the word of righteousness."* He has not yielded himself to the discipline that *"the word"* demands and brings; he has not, in the struggle of practical obedience, had experience of what *"the word"* can do to search and cleanse, to strengthen and bless. His religious life has been, as with a babe, the enjoyment of being fed. He is without real experience of *"the word of righteousness."*

With the perfect, the full-grown man, it is the very opposite: *"by reason of use* [they] *have their senses exercised to discern good and evil."* Just as in nature, the use of the limbs, with plenty of exercise for every sense and organ, is one of the surest conditions of a healthy growth, so with the Christian, too. It is when the faculties God gives us in the spiritual life are put to the use He meant them for, and our spiritual senses are kept in full exercise, that we pass from feeble infancy to maturity. This exercise of the senses has special reference to what we have been saved to—a life of obedience and holiness; it is to *"discern good and evil."* The eye is exercised to see and know God's way and Him who leads in it; the ear to hear His voice; the conscience to reject everything that is not well pleasing to God or even doubtful; the will to choose and do only what is His will.

It is of the utmost consequence that we note this well. The capacity for entering into the deeper truths to be unfolded does not depend on talent or study, on sagacity or genius, but on the tenderness with which the soul has exercised itself in daily life in discerning good and evil. The redemption in Christ is to save us from sin and bring us back to the perfect obedience and unhindered fellowship with God. It is as the desire not to sin becomes more intense; and the acceptance of Jesus as an indwelling Deliverer from sin more entire; and the surrender to the operation of God in working His will in us more complete that the spiritual teaching of our epistle will be appreciated. It is a holy sensitivity to the least sin, arising from the faithful use and exercise of the senses as far as there was light, that is the spiritual sense or organ for spiritual truth, the mark of the perfect man. In the things of God, a tender conscience and a surrendered will are more than the highest intellect.

Such are the perfect. The word *"perfect"* means here just what it meant when used of Jesus a few verses previously. His perfection came through obedience. Ours comes in no other way—the exercise of the senses to discern good and evil. In temptations, Jesus Himself was exercised to discern between good and evil; in the wilderness and the garden, He had to fast and watch and pray, lest the lawful desire of His human nature lead to sin. Thus, He was perfected. And this is Christian perfection—the fellowship with Christ, through the indwelling Spirit, in His obedience.

"Solid food is for full-grown men." And what is this solid food? The context leaves no doubt as to the answer. It is the knowledge of Christ as Melchizedek, as it is now to be expounded. To know Christ as Aaron—to believe in His atonement on earth and in pardon through His blood—this is often found with Christians who are content to remain mere babes, entirely slothful and stationary. But to know Christ as Melchizedek in His heavenly priesthood, working in us in the power of an endless life; as a Savior able to save completely; as Minister of the sanctuary who has opened the Holiest of All and brings us in to dwell there; as Mediator of the new covenant, who does actually fulfill its promise and write God's law in living power in our hearts—this is the solid food for the perfect. The teaching in the Word is open and free to all, but only those who have given themselves to be perfect feel the need and hunger for it; only they are capable of receiving and assimilating it, because it is only they who have, in very deed, determined to rest content with nothing less than all Christ can do for them and to count all things loss for the possession of this pearl of great price. All the outward teaching and knowledge of the words of

the prophets and of Christ must give way to the inward speaking of Christ in the soul by the Holy Spirit. It is to souls who break through the husk and hunger to feed on the kernel, on the very life of God in Christ, who will become perfect in Christ Jesus.

Chapter Notes...

1. These Hebrew Christians are reproved for not being perfect. It is not left to their choice whether they are to be eminent Christians. God expects each child of His to be as eminent in grace and piety as it is possible for Christ to make him.

2. *"Till we all attain...unto a fullgrown man, unto the measure of the stature of the fulness of Christ"* (Ephesians 4:13). This ought to be our aim. We have the motive and the power to seek this in our Lord Jesus.

3. Let nothing satisfy us but living wholly for Christ; He is worthy.

Forty-Four
Let Us Press On to Perfection

Wherefore let us cease to speak of the first principles* of Christ, and press on unto perfection; not laying again a foundation of repentance from dead works, and of faith toward God, of the teaching of baptisms, and of laying on of hands, and of resurrection of the dead, and of eternal judgement. And this will we do, if God permit.
—Hebrews 6:1–3

a list

W e have seen how among the Hebrews there were two classes of Christians. They are to be found in every Christian church—some who, instead of growing up to be teachers and helpers of others, always remain babes and have need that someone again teach them the rudiments of the beginning of the oracles of God; and others who are perfect, or fully grown, men, who have had their spiritual senses exercised in discerning good and evil and are able to receive the solid food of the knowledge of the perfection of Christ and His work. Let us listen

---

* Leave the word of the beginning.

215

as the Word calls us to come out of all sloth and feebleness and to press on to the perfection Christ has come to reveal.

First, we hear what it is we are to give up. *"Let us* [leave the word of the beginning] *of Christ."* In Hebrews 3:14, we were urged to *"hold fast the beginning of our confidence firm unto the end."* These two expressions are not at variance. The beginning is the seed, or first principle, out of which the further life must grow and expand into perfection. This beginning, as the root of all that is to come, must be held fast to the very end. But the beginning, as being only a commencement of something better, must be left. It is a terrible misunderstanding of the words, "Hold fast what you have," to imagine that we simply need to preserve what we already have. By no means. We must realize that the knowledge of Christ and the measure of grace we receive at conversion cannot suffice for our further life. We need each day to learn more of Christ, to make new advances in obedience, to gain larger experience of the power of the heavenly life. There can be no healthy life without growth and progress. We must "leave the word of the beginning of Christ."

"Not laying again a foundation." A builder, when he has laid his foundation, leaves working at it any more and builds upon it. There are Christians who never get beyond the foundation, who never know what the house is —for the sake of which alone the foundation is!—what it is to be a habitation of God through the Spirit and to dwell in the love and the power of God. The writer mentioned, in three pairs, six points that belong to the foundation truths in which the young beginner has to be instructed. *"Repentance from dead works, and of faith toward God."* These are, in very deed, only the rudiments of the Word of Christ. Then follow two points that have reference to the public confession of faith and the connection with the church: *"of the teaching of baptisms, and of laying on of hands."* And then there are two more, which relate to the future life: *"and of resurrection of the dead, and of eternal judgement."* Without these elementary truths, one could hardly be a Christian; but the man who rests content with them and cares not

to know more cannot be a Christian as God would have him; he has reason to doubt whether he is a Christian at all.

"Wherefore let us [leave the word of the beginning] *of Christ, and press on unto perfection."* It is not difficult to know what *"perfection"* here means. Perfect is what corresponds to its ideal, what is as it should be, and what answers to what its Maker intended. No parent is content that his child should remain a babe; he educates the child to be a full-grown man or woman. God has set before us, in His Word, the life He actually means us to live; and He calls every true child of His to leave the beginnings and press on to perfection, to press on to be all that He has promised to make us. God would not have us seek more; and with less, we dare not be content, lest we deceive ourselves.

In Christ Jesus and His life on earth we have the embodiment of that perfection, as it consists in a life given up to obedience to God's will; the proof that it is possible for a true man to live a life that is well-pleasing to the Father; the promise that from His throne in heaven He will now impart and work in us. In suffering, He yielded Himself to God to perfect Him. In suffering, He learned obedience and was made perfect, thereby to be the cause of eternal salvation to us. He is now, as *"a Son, perfected for evermore"* (7:28), our High Priest, in heaven working in us in the power of the heavenly life, that perfection, through which, as our Leader, He opened the path to glory. Our perfection can be none other than Christ's: His perfection our model, His perfection our life and strength. God desires and can be satisfied with nothing in us but what He sees of His beloved Son, and His perfection through suffering and obedience.

"Wherefore let us [leave the word of the beginning] *of Christ, and press on unto perfection....And this will we do, if God permit."* It is as if he said, "The following chapters are to be the teaching of Christian perfection. We will, with you, press on and help you on by giving the solid food that is the nourishment and strength of

the perfect: the heavenly priesthood of Christ in the power of an endless life." His glory and power as Mediator of the new covenant, writing God's law into our very hearts, the infinite efficacy of the blood as opening the Holiest of All to us, and cleansing us to enter in and serve the living God—these and such like truths, revealing the perfection that Christ attained in His human life and into which He lifts us in His divine power, these constitute the solid food for the perfect. The perfection of Christ, as truth revealed, becomes the perfection of the believer, as a life experienced, in those who count all things loss for the excellency of the knowledge of Him our Lord.

Chapter Notes...

1. Let us hold fast the distinction between foundation doctrine and perfection doctrine. There are truths of the beginning of Christ, which we have had in the first half of the epistle—His divinity and humanity, His substitution, tasting death for all, and His entering into heaven, as far as that was typified by Aaron. In the second half, we have what is needed for the completion of the Christian life—the power of the heavenly life as it is secured in the heavenly priesthood and the heavenly sanctuary. *"Wherefore let us...press on unto perfection."*

2. *"Let us...press on unto perfection."* Do take this as a distinct injunction of the God who speaks to us in His Son. Hear His voice, do not rest content with the beginnings—press on to perfection, to the perfect man, to the measure of the stature of the fullness of Christ.

3. Compare Paul: *"I press on, if so be that I may apprehend that for which I also was apprehended by Christ Jesus...forgetting the things which are behind,...I press on toward the goal....Let us therefore, as many as be perfect, be thus minded."* (Philippians 3:12–15). *"Let us...press on unto perfection."*

Forty-Five

The Danger of Falling Away

For as touching those who were once enlightened and tasted
of the heavenly gift, and were made partakers of the Holy
Ghost, and tasted the good word of God, and the powers of
the age to come, and then fell away, it is impossible to renew
them again unto repentance; seeing they crucify to themselves
the Son of God afresh, and put him to an open shame. For
the land which hath drunk the rain that cometh oft upon
it, and bringeth forth herbs meet for them for whose sake it
is also tilled, receiveth blessing from God: but if it beareth
thorns and thistles, it is rejected and nigh unto a curse;
whose end is to be burned.
—Hebrews 6:4–8

"L *et us...press on unto perfection....For as touching those who were*
once enlightened...and then fell away, it is impossible to renew
them again" (Hebrews 6:1, 4–6). The argument is one of
unspeakable solemnity. It is in the Christian life as with all progress
amid difficulties. In commerce, in study, in war, it is so often said,
"There is no safety but in advance." To stand still is to go back. To

cease effort is to lose ground. To slacken the pace before the goal is reached is to lose the race. The only sure mark of our being true Christians, of our really loving Christ, is the deep longing and the steady effort to know more of Him. Tens of thousands have proven that to be content with beginning well is but the first step on a backward course that ends in losing all. The whole point of the argument from the case of those who fall away is, *"Let us...press on unto perfection."*

To realize its force, we must specifically note two things with regard to those who fall away: the height that they may have attained and the irrecoverable depth into which they sink. As to the former, five expressions are used. They

- *"were once enlightened"*
- *"tasted of the heavenly gift"*
- *"were made partakers of the Holy Ghost"*
- *"tasted the good word of God"*
- *"[tasted] the powers of the age to come"*

As to the latter, we are told,

It is impossible to renew them again unto repentance; seeing they crucify to themselves the Son of God afresh, and put him to an open shame.

The question that always suggests itself at once here has reference to the Scripture truth of the perseverance of the saints, in which so many saints of God have found their strength and their joy. Our Lord Jesus spoke of His sheep: *"I give unto them eternal life; and they shall never perish, and no one shall snatch them out of my hand. My Father, which hath given them unto me, is greater than all; and no one is able to snatch them out of the Father's hand"* (John 10:28–29). Where He gives the eternal life to a soul, that life cannot be lost.

This is the divine side of the truth. Every truth has two sides. The only way to apprehend the truth fully is to look at each side as if it were the whole and yield ourselves to its full force. There is a human side, too. Scripture speaks most solemn words of warning in regard to the possibility of receiving the grace of God in vain, of beginning well and then falling away from grace. (See 2 Corinthians 6:1, Galatians 5:4.) Our Lord spoke more than once of the man who receives the Word with joy but has no roots in himself; he only believes for a while. In a time of revival, of mighty spiritual influences, as in Corinth and Galatia, many were mightily affected and even manifestly changed who, in after times, proved that they never had been truly born again; they had not received eternal life. It is of such that our text speaks. It is possible to have the emotions touched and the will affected without the heart being truly renewed. The gifts of the Spirit may be received without His graces. The joy of light in the mind may be mistaken for life in the soul. And so some, who were counted true believers by man, may fall away beyond hope of renewal.

And how, then, are we to know who truly has received eternal life? And what is the mark of its being no mere superficial or temporary change? There is no mark by which man can decide. The only sure sign that the perseverance of the saints will be ours is perseverance in sainthood, in sanctification and obedience. We are His house (Hebrews 3:6), and *"we are become partakers of Christ, if we hold fast the beginning of our confidence firm unto the end"* (verse 14). My assurance of salvation is not something I can carry with me as a railway ticket or a bank note, to be used as occasion calls. No, God's seal to my soul is the Holy Spirit; it is in a life in the Spirit that my safety lies; it is when I am led by the Spirit that the Spirit bears witness with my spirit and that I can cry, *"Abba, Father"* (Romans 8:15; see verses 14–16). Jesus not only gives His life but is, Himself, our life. My assurance of salvation is alone to be found in the living fellowship with the living Jesus in love and obedience.

This is what we see in verses 7 and 8. *"The land which hath drunk the rain that cometh oft upon it, and bringeth forth herbs meet for them for whose sake it is also tilled, receiveth blessing from God: but if it beareth thorns and thistles, it is rejected."* The soul that is content with drinking in the rain and only seeks its own happiness, without bearing fruit, has every reason to fear. It is in growth and fruitfulness—in exercising the senses to discern good and evil, in pressing on to perfection, in following our Forerunner in the path in which He was perfected, by obedience to God's will—that we know that we have eternal life.

"The word of God is...sharper than any two-edged sword" (4:12). Let each one of us yield to its searching power. Anything like sloth, and resting content in our beginnings, is unspeakably dangerous. Nothing will do but *"to give the more earnest heed"* (2:1), to *"give diligence to enter into that rest"* (4:11), and with our whole hearts to *"press on unto perfection"* (6:1).

Chapter Notes...

1. Self-deception is a solemn possibility. Our only safeguard is God, the surrender to His searching light, the trust in His faithfulness, the giving up to His will. At the footstool of the throne, no soul can perish.

2. To *"press on unto perfection"* is a command not meant for a select few, but for all, and especially the backward and feeble ones. Beware of any suggestion that would make you evade the force of this command and immediate obedience to it. Let your only answer be, "Yes, Lord." Open your eyes and heart to the state of all around you, who are slothful and at ease, lagging behind, and help them. *"By reason of the time ye ought to be teachers"* (5:12).

Forty-Six

Of Diligence and Perseverance

*But, beloved, we are persuaded better things of you, and
things that accompany salvation, though we thus speak:
for God is not unrighteous to forget your work and the love
which ye shewed toward his name, in that ye ministered unto
the saints, and still do minister. And we desire that each one
of you may shew the same diligence unto the fulness of hope
even to the end: that ye be not sluggish, but imitators of them
who through faith and patience* inherit the promises.*
—Hebrews 6:9–12

In every Christian community, you have two classes. There are
some who give themselves up with their whole hearts to seek
and serve God. There are others—too often the majority—
who, like Israel, are content with deliverance from Egypt and settle
down in sloth without striving for the full possession of the promise, the rest in the Promised Land. In speaking to such a church,
one might address the two classes separately. Or one might address
the whole body from each of the two standpoints. This is what the

------

* Longsuffering.

epistle does. In its warning, it speaks to all as if all were in danger. In its exhortation and encouragement, it speaks as if all shared the sentiments of the better half.

"But, beloved, we are persuaded better things of you, and things that accompany salvation, though we thus speak" of falling away and the impossibility of renewal. We have the hope that our word of warning will bear fruit and that, by the grace of God that has already been wrought in you, you will be stirred to rise up out of all sloth and unbelief and press forward. We look to God Himself to perfect His work in you.

"For God is not unrighteous to forget your work and the love which ye shewed toward his name, in that ye ministered unto the saints, and still do minister." If there was much in the present state to make him anxious, the writer encouraged himself and them by pointing to the past. When the Gospel was preached among them, they had received Christ's messengers with joy and stood by them in sharing reproach and spoiling for His name. Even now there was still among them a love toward God's people. And God is not unrighteous to forget what has been done for His name and people; the reward of the cup of cold water may be remembered by God even when the giver has grown cold, and it may come in the form of a blessing that restores him again. God does not only remember sin; He much rather remembers the work of love.

"And we desire that each one of you may shew the same diligence unto the fulness of hope even to the end." In all worldly business, diligence is the secret of success. Without attention and trouble and hearty effort, we cannot expect our work to prosper. And yet, there are many Christians who imagine that in the Christian life things will come right of themselves. When they are told that Jesus undertakes to do all, they count this as a pass into a life of ease. Truly, no. Jesus will indeed do all; but He undertakes it just to inspire us with His own spirit of self-sacrifice and devotion to the Father's will, His own readiness to forsake all ease and comfort to please God and

man, His own unwearying diligence in working while it was day. And so, our writer urges his readers to show the same diligence they had formerly manifested, *"unto the fulness of hope even to the end."*

We have here the same three words we had in the second warning. There we read, *"Let us therefore give diligence to enter into that rest"* (4:11); *"if we hold fast our boldness and the glorying of our hope firm unto the end"* (3:6); and *"if we hold fast the beginning of our confidence firm unto the end"* (3:14). The great marks of Christian perseverance are here once again joined together. Hope looks again forward and lives in the promises; it glories beforehand in the certainty of their fulfillment. Bright hopefulness is one of the elements of a healthy Christian life—one of the surest preservatives against backsliding. This hopefulness must be cultivated; diligence must be given unto the fullness of hope—a hope that embraces all the fullness of God's promises and that fills all the heart. And all this to the end, with a patience and perseverance that knows no weariness, that waits on God's time and seeks in patience until the fulfillment has come.

"That ye be not sluggish." This is what had done so much harm—they had been slothful in hearing. (See 5:11.) This is the danger that still threatens. *"But* [be] *imitators of them who through faith and patience inherit the promises."* The writer had spoken in warning of the example of the fathers in the wilderness; he here encouraged them by reminding them of those who, *"through faith and* [longsuffering] *inherit*[ed] *the promises."* Longsuffering is the perseverance of faith. Faith grasps at once all that God promises but is in danger of relaxing its hold. Longsuffering comes to tell how faith needs daily to be renewed; it strengthens the soul, even when the promise tarries, still to hold fast firm unto the end. This is one of the great practical lessons of our epistle and one that the young believer especially needs. Conversion is but a beginning, a step, an entrance on a path. Day by day, its surrender must be renewed; every day, faith must afresh accept Christ and find its strength in Him. Through faith and longsuffering, we inherit—enter into the possession of—the promises. Salvation consists in what Christ Jesus

is to us and does in us. There must, each day, be personal communion with Him, distinct personal surrender to His teaching and working, if He is indeed to be our life. Let us beware, above everything, of unconsciously resting or trusting in what we have or enjoy of grace. It is alone by faith and longsuffering, by the never-ceasing daily renewal of our consecration and our faith in our quiet time with our beloved Lord, that the heavenly life can be maintained in its freshness and power.

Chapter Notes...

1. *"For God is not unrighteous to forget your work."* How often God spoke to Israel of its first love. What an encouragement to any who have grown cold to return and trust Him to restore them. God cannot forget what has passed between you and Him.

2. *"That ye be not sluggish,"* not for a single day. We may lose in an hour by unwatchfulness what we have gained in a year. Christ and His service ask for your undivided, unceasing attention.

3. Let not God's way appear too slow or too difficult. Let patience have its perfect work. As the husbandman has long patience with the seed, God is patient with you. Be patient with Him. Just remember this simple lesson. Day by day, renew your surrender to Jesus and your faith in Him—your hope in God. Faith and patience must inherit the promises.

Forty-Seven

Inheriting the Promise

For when God made promise to Abraham, since he could
swear by none greater, he sware by himself, saying, Surely
blessing I will bless thee, and multiplying I will multiply
thee. And thus, having patiently endured,*
he obtained the promise.
—Hebrews 6:13–15

The epistle deals with one of the greatest dangers in the spiritual life. All experience amply confirms what was seen in the first Christian churches, that many who began well stood still and then turned back. The Christian life is a race: To begin profits nothing unless we run to the end and reach the goal. Faith may accept, but only longsuffering inherits the promise. Day by day, without intermission, rather with ever-growing zeal and diligence, our allegiance to Jesus our Leader must be maintained or else backsliding must inevitably ensue. And the church of Christ is a very hospital of backsliding Christians, who meant honestly, in the joy of their first love, to live wholly for God, and who yet gradually sank down into a life of formality and feebleness. There is nothing the church needs more than the preaching of daily diligence and

---
* Suffered long.

perseverance as the indispensable condition of growth and strength. Let us learn from the epistle how these virtues can be fostered in ourselves and others. It had spoken of those who, through faith and longsuffering, inherit the promises. It will now show us, from the example of Abraham, what this means. It first points us, as ever, to what God promises; it then shows us the disposition that it will work in man.

"For when God made promise to Abraham, since he could swear by none greater, he sware by himself, saying, Surely blessing I will bless thee, and multiplying I will multiply thee." The deeper our insight into the certainty and the fullness of the blessing of God, the more will our hearts be roused to believe and to persevere. The word fom God is our assurance of what we are to expect. How much greater must our confidence be when that word is an oath? It is of this that the following verses are to speak. Here the fullness of God's blessing is set before us in the promise given to Abraham; as his seed, we are his heirs, and what God promised him is for us, too. We need be content with nothing less; nothing less will stimulate us to a life like his in faith and patience.

"Surely blessing I will bless thee, and multiplying I will multiply thee." In Hebrew, the repetition of a verb is meant to give force to what is said, to express the certainty and the greatness of what is asserted. In the mouth of God, the repetition, *"Blessing I will bless thee, multiplying I will multiply thee,"* was meant to waken in Abraham's heart the confidence that the blessing was indeed to be something very wonderful and worthy of God, blessing in divine power and fullness. What that blessing was to be is shown by the second half of the sentence: *"Multiplying I will multiply thee."* Scripture teaches us that the highest blessing God can bestow, what makes us truly godlike, is the power of multiplying ourselves—of becoming, as God is, the source and the blessing of other lives. So the two words are connected in passages like the following:

And God blessed them, saying, Be fruitful and multiply.
(Genesis 1:22)

And God blessed them: and God said unto them, Be fruitful and multiply.
(Genesis 1:28)

So of Noah, too:

And God blessed Noah and his sons, and said unto them, Be fruitful, and multiply, and replenish the earth.(Genesis 9:1)

It is the glory of God that He is the Dispenser of life—that in His creatures He multiplies His own life and blessedness. And it is one of His highest blessings when He communicates this power of increase to those whom He chooses for His service. The power of His blessing to Adam is seen in the race that sprang from him, as of His blessing to Abraham in his seed, even in Jesus Christ Himself. And to each child of Abraham, to each true believer, the promise still comes in divine power: *"Surely blessing I will bless thee, and multiplying I will multiply thee."* Every believer who will but claim and give himself up to the blessing of God will find that the blessing is a power of the divine life that will make him fruitful in blessing to others; and it will make it true of him, too—*"multiplying I will multiply thee."* Even we, like Christ, can become priests, bringing the blessing of God to those who know Him not.

It is when this fullness of blessing in its divine energy—when this *"blessing I will bless thee"* begins to be understood and the soul sees that there is something beyond the mere being saved from wrath—that the soul becomes the recipient, the channel, and the dispenser of life and blessing to others. It becomes willing to sacrifice everything and, in longsuffering, to endure until it obtains the promise.

Christian, would you be an imitator of Abraham and let the God who spoke to him speak to you? Remember it is not so easy to receive and claim this promise. Abraham received it in the way of faith and obedience and self-sacrifice, in the entire surrender to God's will and leading. It was when he had sacrificed Isaac—yea, more, when in doing so, he had sacrificed himself—that this promise was given him with an oath. God will speak to you as truly as to Abraham. Learn with him to go out of your country and your home; give yourself to God's leading; be prepared to sacrifice all. God will meet you, too, with His double blessing. And your heart will become strong to hear His voice, *"Blessing I will bless thee, multiplying I will multiply thee."* And it will be true of you as of Abraham: *"And thus, having patiently endured, he obtained the promise."* We will not only be the heirs, but the actual inheritors of the promise.

Chapter Notes...

1. This promise comes after the most terrible warning. Until the slothful Christian is roused, the most precious promise finds no entrance. When he is roused, it is the preaching of the promise in its fullness that will give him courage and strength.

2. Does your heart condemn you? Do you fear that there is but little hope of your becoming a bright, growing, holy child of God, blessed and made a blessing? Come and learn from Abraham the secret that God spoke to him! Listen to God. Let God speak to you. Follow where He leads, and obey what He commands. He will bring you to the place of blessing, the place of the revelation of Himself.

3. And put at once into practice the lesson of today. Do not be discouraged if you feel feeble and cold and if there appears to be no progress. Listen to God's, *"Blessing I will bless thee."* Feed on what God says, and trust Him to work in you all you need.

4. Are you a worker in God's service? Wait upon God to speak this word to you, too: *"Multiplying I will multiply thee."* He can make even you a blessing to many. But such a promise needs an oath to find entrance to the heart. Accept and live on the oath of God.

Forty-Eight

The Oath of God

*For men swear by the greater: and in every dispute of theirs
the oath is final for confirmation. Wherein God, being
minded to shew more abundantly unto the heirs of the
promise the immutability of his counsel, interposed* with an
oath: that by two immuatable things, in which it is impossible
for God to lie, we may have a strong encouragement, who
have fled for refuge to lay hold of the hope set before us.*
—Hebrews 6:16–18

For any serious man, it is always a solemn thing to take an oath and appeal to the omniscient God for the truth of what He says. But there is something more solemn even than taking an oath before God, and that is God's taking an oath before man. And this is what our writer proceeded to speak of. He had already spoken of God's oath in His wrath, *"They shall not enter into my rest"* (3:11). He would, in the next chapter, point out the deep significance of Christ's appointment as High Priest being confirmed by an oath. Here he wished to show believers what strong encouragement they have in God's oath to expect most confidently the fulfillment of the promise. It is this confidence alone that will enable the Christian to endure and conquer.

---

* Mediated.

Let us once more consider this. The oath of God plainly proves that the thing He seeks above everything is faith; He wishes to be trusted. Faith is nothing but depending on God to do for us what we cannot do—what He has undertaken to do. God's purpose concerning us is something of infinite and inconceivable blessedness. He is ready—He longs!—as God Himself to work in us all that He has promised. He cannot do this except as we open our hearts to Him and yield ourselves in stillness and surrender to Him so He can do His work. Until this faith takes possession of us, we are always seeking to do His work and we hinder Him. Faith teaches us, in deep humility and dependence, in meekness and patience, to place ourselves in God's hands, to make way for Him, and to wait for His time. Faith opens the whole heart and life in expectation and hope. Then God is free to work; faith gives Him His place as God, and it honors Him; and He fulfills the promise, *"Them that honour me I will honour"* (1 Samuel 2:30). Oh, do learn the lesson that the first and the last—the one thing—God asks is that we trust Him to do His work.

It is for this that He mediates, or comes in between, with an oath. Just notice the expressions that are used: *"God, being minded to shew."* They had shown their love toward His name; they had been urged to show diligence unto the fullness of hope; and here they are told what God will show them—*"being minded to shew more abundantly unto the heirs of the promise the immutability of his counsel."* God wills to show us how unchangeable His purpose to bless us is if we will but let Him, if we will but trust Him and, by trusting, let Him work. And He wills to show us this *"more abundantly."* He wants us to have such more abundant proof of it that we may, as we had it in Hebrews 2:1, *"give the more earnest heed"* and see that there can be no possibility of a doubt: God will do it. It was for this that He confirmed the promise with an oath.

"That by two immutable things"—His promise and His oath —*"in which it is impossible for God to lie, we may have a strong encouragement."* Just notice the expression—*"impossible for God to*

lie"! It is as if God asks if we do not think His Word is enough; if we think it is possible that He, the faithful and the unchangeable One, would lie. He knows how little our darkened hearts trust Him; His promises are so large, so divine, so heavenly that we cannot take them in. And so, to waken and to shame us out of our unbelief, He comes and, as if it were possible for God to lie, calls us to listen as He takes an oath in our presence that He will do what He has said: *"Blessing I will bless thee, and multiplying I will multiply thee"* (6:14). And all this so that we, the heirs of salvation, might have a strong encouragement. Surely every vestige of fear and doubt ought to pass away and our whole souls fall down to worship and to cry out: "O God! We do trust Thee. Never, never, will we doubt Thy word again."

"For when God made promise to Abraham, since he could swear by none greater, he sware by himself" (verse 13). Yes, by Himself! In that lies the power of the oath and the power of our faith in our oath. God points to Himself—His divine Being, His glory, His power—and pledges Himself, gives Himself as security and hostage that, as sure as He lives, He will fulfill His promise. Oh, if we would but take time to tarry in the presence of this God and to listen to Him swearing to us that He will be faithful, surely we would fall down in confusion that we ever harbored for a moment the doubt that thinks it possible He may be untrue and not keep His word. Will we not kneel and vow that, by His grace, we would rather die than again make such a God a liar?

And now let us pause and realize what all this argument about the blessing and the oath of God means. In the Christian life, there is lack of steadfastness, of diligence, of perseverance. Of all, the cause is simply this—lack of faith. And of this again, the cause is simply this—lack of the knowledge of what God wills and is: of His purpose and His power to bless most wonderfully: and of His faithfulness to carry out His purpose. It is to cure these evils, and to tell His people that He will do anything to win their trust and anything for them if they will trust Him, that God has taken

His oath of faithfulness. Oh, will we not this day believe God and believe in the fullness of His blessing? And will we not count it our most sacred duty, our most blessed privilege, to honor God every day by a life of full and perfect trust?

Chapter Notes...

1. *"The oath is final for confirmation."* The same word is in Hebrews 3:6, 14; 6:19—*"firm"* or *"stedfast."* As we see how firm and how steadfast God's promise and the hope He gives us is, our confidence will grow more firm, too. The fullness of my faith depends upon my being occupied with the faithfulness of God.

2. "By faith and longsuffering" (6:12). "Having suffered long" (verse 15). God is often very slow. "He bears long with His elect" (Luke 18:7). This is the patience of the saints: to let God take His time and, through all, ever to trust Him.

3. *"That ye be not sluggish"* (Hebrews 6:12). It is the faith that God will work all that rouses to diligence both in waiting on Him and in doing His will.

6:18-20

[Handwritten annotations:] TPT God did this so that, by 2 unchangeable things in which it is impossible for God to lie, we who have fled to take hold of the hope set before us may be greatly encouraged. 19. we have this [anchor for the soul], FIRM + SECURE. It enters the inner sanctuary behind the curtain 20 where OUR FORE RUNNER, → Jesus, YYYYYY! has entered on our (my) behalf. He has become a high priest forever in the order of melchizedek.

Forty-Nine

The Forerunner Within the Veil

That by two immutable things, in which it is impossible for God to lie, we may have a strong encouragement, who have fled for refuge to lay hold of the hope set before us; which we have as an anchor of the soul, a hope both sure and stedfast* and entering into that which is within the veil; whither as a forerunner Jesus entered for us, having become a high priest for ever after the order of Melchizedek.
—Hebrews 6:18–20

In chapter 5, speaking of the priesthood of Jesus, the writer had twice cited the words of Psalm 110, with its prophecy of a Priest after the order of Melchizedek (Hebrews 5:6, 10). But he feared that the Hebrews were, by reason of sloth, too far back in the Christian life to be able to receive this higher teaching. On this account he interposed his words of reproof and warning. From these he passed to exhortation and encouragement and was then ready to address himself to what is the central teaching of

---

* Firm.

the epistle. There are specifically two great heavenly mysteries that he was commissioned to unfold. The one is that of the heavenly priesthood of Christ; the other is that of the heavenly sanctuary in which He ministers and into which He gives us access. In the two last verses of our sixth chapter, we have the transition to the new section and, in it, these mysteries are both mentioned as the hope set before us. Hope enters within the veil; it finds there *"forerunner Jesus* [who has] *entered for us, having become a high priest for ever after the order of Melchizedek."*

We *"who have fled for refuge to lay hold of the hope set before us."* The hope sometimes means the object of hope, or what God sets before us, and sometimes the subjective grace or disposition of hope in our hearts. Here it specifically refers to the former, the object of hope. And what that hope is is clear from the next chapter (7:19), where we read of the *"bringing in...of a better hope, through which we draw nigh unto God."* This *"better hope"* is the access our High Priest in heaven gives us into God's very presence, into the enjoyment of His fellowship and blessedness, even while we are here on earth.

"Which we have as an anchor of the soul, a hope both sure and stedfast and entering into that which is within the veil." The hope is an anchor. A ship is held by the anchor cast into the unseen depth beneath. So, too, the hope in the unseen within the veil, which God has given us, holds us fast. And as our hearts are fixed upon it, hope as a subjective grace is stirred and drawn and enters within the veil, too. Where our hope lives, there the heart lives. There we, our real selves, are living, too.

"Whither as a forerunner Jesus entered for us." The Forerunner. Here we have another of the key words of the epistle, without the right understanding of which our view of the work of Jesus as High Priest must be defective. It points us to the work He did in opening up the way, by Himself walking in it; to our following Him in that way to the place into which He has entered and into which we now have access. We have had His name as Leader. We will yet have the new and living way He has opened up. (See

10:21.) We will hear of the race we have to run, looking to Jesus
who went on before, enduring the cross, and is now set down at the
right hand of God. (See 12:1.) There is nothing that will so much
help us to understand the work Jesus does as Son and High Priest
as the acceptance of Him as Leader and Forerunner, bringing us
into the very presence of the Father.

"Entered for us." We are so familiar with all the blessed meaning there is in these words for us in reference to Christ on the cross.
What He did there was all for us; by it and in it we live. No less is it
true of Christ within the veil. It is all for us, and all that He is and
has there is for us; it is our present possession, and by it and in it we
live with Him and in Him. The veil was rent that the way through
it might be opened for us; that we might have access to what is
within the veil; that we might enter into a new world, an entirely
new way of living in close and intimate fellowship with God. A
high priest must have a sanctuary in which he ministers. The mystery of the opened sanctuary is that we can enter, too. The inner
sanctuary, the Holiest of All, the presence of God, is the sphere of
Christ's ministry and our life and service.

The Forerunner, even Jesus! It is as if the writer delighted to
repeat this name that our Savior bears as Son of Man. Even in the
glory of heaven, He is still Jesus, our Brother.

*"Having become a high priest for ever after the order of Melchize-
dek."* We have yet to learn all that is contained in this Melchizedek
priesthood. But this will be its chief glory—that He is a Priest forever, a Priest in the power of an endless life, a Priest who opens
to us the state of life into which He Himself has entered in, and
a Priest who brings us there to live here on earth with the life of
eternity in our bosom.

Christian reader, do you know the power of this hope, entering into what is within the veil, where the Forerunner has already
entered for us? Jesus is in heaven for you, to secure you a life on
earth in the power and joy of heaven, to maintain the kingdom of

heaven within you by that Spirit through whom God's will is done on earth as it is in heaven. All that Jesus is and has is heavenly. All that He gives and does is heavenly. As High Priest at God's right hand, He blesses with all heavenly blessings. Oh, prepare yourself, as the glory of His person and ministry in the heavenly places are now to be opened up to you, to look upon it and appropriate it all as your personal possession. And believe that His high priesthood not only consists in His having secured certain heavenly blessings for you but also in his fitting and enabling you to enter into the full personal experience and enjoyment of them.

Chapter Notes...

shining place TPT

1. There is a sanctuary in which God dwells. There was a veil that separated man from God. Jesus came from within to live without the veil—and to rend it and open a way for us. He is now there for us as Forerunner. We may now enter in and dwell there, in the power of the Holy Spirit. This is the Gospel according to the epistle to the Hebrews.

2. Hope enters within the veil, rejoices in all that there is to be found there, and counts upon the revelation in the heart of all that is there prepared for us.

3. Jesus is the Forerunner; follow Him. Even though you cannot understand all, follow Him in His path of humility and meekness and obedience. He will bring you in. This is the promise that, even in this life, you will inherit through patience and longsuffering.

TPT 7:1 [The Melchizedek Priesthood]
Melchizedek's name means "King of righteousness." He was the King of Peace, because the name of the city he ruled as king was Salem, which means "peace." And he was also a priest of the Most High God. Now when Abraham was returning from defeating many kings in battle, Melchizedek went out to meet him & blessed him. Then Abraham took 1/10 of every

THE NEW PRIESTHOOD AFTER THE ORDER OF MELCHIZEDEK

[handwritten: he had won in battle & gave it to Mel. This Mel. has no father or mother, + no record of any of his ancestors. He was never born & he never died, but his life is like a picture (resembles) made to]

Fifty

Melchizedek Made like unto the Son of God

[handwritten: of the Son of God, a King-Priest forever!]

> For this Melchizedek, king of Salem, priest of God Most
> High, who met Abraham returning from the slaughter of
> the kings, and blessed him, to whom also Abraham divided
> a tenth part of all (being first, by interpretation, King of
> righteousness, and then also King of Salem, which is, King
> of peace; without father, without mother, without genealogy,
> having neither beginning of days nor end of life, but made
> like unto the Son of God), abideth a priest continually.
> —Hebrews 7:1–3 *[handwritten: Gen 14:17–20]*

I n chapter 5, we read that Jesus was called by God, even as Aaron
was. In many points, Aaron was a type of Christ. But there were
other respects in which the priesthood of Aaron utterly failed
even to prefigure that of Christ. By a special divine provision, the
name of another is found, in whom all that was wanting in Aaron
as type was foreshadowed. The difference between the priesthood
of Aaron and Melchizedek is a radical one. In the right understanding of what that difference is, and in the knowledge of that in
which Melchizedek has been made like unto the Son of God, lies

the secret of this epistle and the secret of the Christian life in its power and perfection. The secret may be expressed in one phrase— *"Priest for ever"* (Hebrews 5:6; 7:17, 21).

The whole place Melchizedek occupies in sacred history is one of the most remarkable proofs of the inspiration and the unity of Scripture, as written under the direct supernatural guidance of the Holy Spirit. In the book of Genesis, all we know of him is told in three short, very simple verses. A thousand years later, we find a psalm with just one single verse, in which God Himself is introduced, swearing to His Son that He is to be a High Priest after the order of Melchizedek. Another thousand years pass, and that single verse becomes the seed of the wondrous exposition, in this epistle, of the whole work of redemption as revealed in Christ Jesus. All its most remarkable characteristics are found enveloped in the wondrous type. The more we study it, the more we exclaim, "This is the Lord's doing! It is marvelous in our eyes!" We see in it nothing less than a miracle of divine wisdom, guiding Melchize-dek and Abraham with a view to what was to take place with the Son of God two thousand years later; revealing to the psalmist the secret purpose of the divine mind in the promise made to the Son in heaven; and then, by the same Holy Spirit, guiding the writer of our epistle to his divinely inspired exposition. To the believing mind, no stronger proof of inspiration could possibly be given. It is indeed the Eternal Spirit, the Spirit of Christ Himself, through whom all was wrought and in due time recorded.

In the first three verses of our chapter, we are reminded of the story of Melchizedek, and the exposition is given of his name and history. His name signifies, *"King of righteousness."* He is also called, from the city where he reigned, Salem, meaning "peace"— the *"King of peace."* The two titles thus combined proved how he was destined by God to be the figure of His Son. Righteousness and peace are mentioned together both in the Old Testament and in the New as characteristic blessings of the kingdom of Christ. Righteousness is the only foundation of peace; peace is its sure and blessed result. The kingdom of God is righteousness and peace, and, as the sure fruit of these, joy in the Holy Spirit

Rom. 14:17

Melchizedek was priest and king—a thing unknown in the entire history of Israel. What was always kept asunder in God's people had, by the divine forethought, been united in Him who had been made like unto the Son of God. It is the glory of Christ as the Priest-King that our epistle is specifically to unfold.

The silence of Scripture as to his genealogy and birth and death is then interpreted as proof of how different his priesthood was from that of Aaron and the priests in Israel, where descent was everything. So had God prepared in him a wondrous prophecy of His Son, whose right to the priesthood lay in no earthly birth but in His being the Son of God from eternity to eternity. *"Made like unto the Son of God..., abideth a priest continually."*

"A priest for ever after the order of Melchizedek" (Psalm 110:4). This word of God is in the psalm that forms the connecting link between Genesis and our epistle. The Holy Spirit who first inspired it, and then expounded it, is waiting to lead us into the mystery of its glory as a living experience. That phrase *"for ever"*—which we meet in the expressions *"priest for ever," "eternal salvation"* (5:9), *"eternal redemption"* (9:12), and *"perfected for ever"* (10:14) —not only signifies "without end" but infinitely more. God is the Eternal One; His life is eternal life. Eternal is what is divine, in which there is no change or decay but only everlasting youth and strength, because God is in it. The everlasting priesthood of Christ means that He will do His work in us in the power of the eternal life, as that life is lived in God and heaven. He lives forever; therefore, He can save completely.

May God teach us to know what it means that Christ is our Melchizedek, a priest forever. The spiritual apprehension of this everlasting priesthood—as communicating even here and maintaining an everlasting, unchangeable life in us—lifts our inner experience out of the region of effort, change, failure, and into the rest of God so that the immutability of His counsel is the measure of that of our faith and hope.

Chapter Notes...

1. In this chapter, we have now the beginning of the things that are hard to be understood except by the perfect. It is only those who *"press on unto perfection"* (6:1), who long to possess the very utmost of what God is able to work in them through Christ; it is these who can inwardly appropriate the revelation of the eternal priesthood. Neither talent nor genius can suffice—it is the heart that thirsts for the living God that will understand this teaching about our being brought near to God.

2. The Holy Spirit—through whom the history was recorded, and the oath to the Son revealed, and the exposition inspired—can alone lead us into the spiritual power and blessing here revealed. And the Holy Spirit only leads when He is known as the Indwelling One; is waited on in deep humility; and is yielded to in meek resignation. What a solemn, holy, blessed thing to believe that the Spirit of God is leading us into this perfection-truth as a possession and experience.

3. He *"abideth...continually"*: an unchanging, neverending life. This is the characteristic of Melchizedek—who was made like to Christ—of Christ in His heavenly priesthood and of the life of the believer who learns rightly to know and trust Him.

Fifty-One

Melchizedek More than Abraham

*Now consider how great this man was, unto whom Abraham,
the patriarch, gave a tenth out of the chief spoils. And they
indeed of the sons of Levi that receive the priest's office have
commandment to take tithes of the people according to the
law, that is, of their brethren, though these have come out of
the loins of Abraham: but he whose genealogy is not counted
from them hath taken tithes of Abraham, and hath blessed
him that hath the promises. But without any dispute the less is
blessed of the better. And here men that die receive tithes; but
there one, of whom it is witnessed that he liveth. And, so to say,
through Abraham even Levi, who received tithes, hath paid
tithes; for he was yet in the loins of his
father, when Melchizedek met him.*
—Hebrews 7:4–10

Now consider how great this man was. If we rightly apprehend the greatness of Melchizedek, it will help us to understand the greatness of Christ, our great High Priest. The
Hebrews gloried in Abraham, as the father of the chosen people;

in Aaron, who, as high priest, was the representative of God and His worship; and in the law, as given from heaven in token of God's covenant with His people. In all these respects, the superiority of Melchizedek is proven. He was more than Abraham (see Hebrews 7:4–10), more than Aaron (see verses 11–14), and more than the law (see verses 11–19).

Melchizedek was more than Abraham; of this, a double proof is given. Abraham gave tithes to Melchizedek, and Melchizedek blessed Abraham. According to the law, the priests received tithes from their brethren, but here a stranger receives them from the father of the whole people. There is more; in Israel, men who die receive tithes, but here, one of whom it was witnessed that *"he liveth"* receives the tithes. And in Abraham, even Levi, who received tithes, paid tithes. All was so ordered of God as a hidden prophecy, to be unfolded in due time, of the greatness of Christ our High Priest. Consider how great this man was.

There is a second proof of his greatness; Melchizedek blessed Abraham. *"But without any dispute the less is blessed of the better."* Abraham had already been blessed by God Himself. (See Genesis 12:2.) He here accepted a blessing from Melchizedek, acknowledging his own inferiority, subordinating himself and the whole priesthood that was to come from him to this priest of the Most High God.

The unfolding of this divinely ordained type not only reveals the superiority of Christ to the Levitical priesthood but sets before us most suggestively two of the characteristics of our relation to Christ as Priest. We receive blessing from Him; He receives tithes from us.

Christ comes to bring us God's blessing. We have seen in Hebrews 6:14 what God's blessing is. In Christ the blessing is confirmed and imparted. And if we would know fully what the blessing is that Christ brings us, we have only to think of the priestly blessing in Israel.

> *On this wise ye shall bless the children of Israel; ye shall say unto them,*
> *The LORD bless thee, and keep thee: the LORD make his face to shine*

Andrew Murray

upon thee, and be gracious unto thee: the LORD *lift up his counte-*
nance upon thee, and give thee peace. (Numbers 6:23–26)

These are indeed the spiritual blessings in the heavenlies with
which God has blessed us in Christ and that, as High Priest, Christ
dispenses. He brings us to the Father, and we learn to know that
He blesses and keeps us. In Him, the Son, God's face shines upon
us, and the grace of our Lord Jesus Christ is our portion. In Him,
God lifts up His countenance upon us and, by the Holy Spirit,
gives His peace to our hearts. Christ, the High Priest, makes every
part of this blessing a divine reality, a living experience in the power
of a life that abides continually.

Christ gives us the blessing; we give Him the tithes. The tithes
to God are the acknowledgment of His right to all. Our High
Priest has a right to the surrender of all we have, as belonging to
Him, to the willing sacrifice of all He asks or needs for His service.
The connection between the tithes and the blessing is closer than
we know. The more unreservedly we place all that we have at His
disposal, the more we in very deed forsake all for His sake and the
richer will our experience be of the fullness and the power with
which our High Priest can bless.

"Without any dispute the less is blessed of the better." This is the
true relation. The more we know of that better name that Jesus has
received, and the more we have our hearts filled with His glory,
the lower we will bow and the less we will become in our own
eyes—and, thereby, the fitter and the more willing to be blessed we
will become. And the more ready, too, to render Him not only the
tithes but also the whole of all we are and possess. As in our spiritual
lives, this twofold relation to our great High Priest is maintained,
and a deep faith and dependence on His divine fullness of blessing is cultivated, along with an absolute surrender to His disposal
and service. The mighty power of His priesthood will be revealed
in our hearts. And we will see with ever-increasing clearness that
the two dispositions, faith in Him who blesses and consecration to
His service, have their root in the one cardinal virtue of humility,

Levi was yet unborn, the seed from which Levi came was present in Abraham when he paid his tithe to Mel.

making us ever less and less in our own eyes until we sink into that nothingness that is the death to self and makes room for Him to be all. Then this word will be fulfilled in us in a new meaning: *"Without any dispute the less is blessed of the better."*

Chapter Notes...

1. Melchizedek blessed Abraham. The work of your High Priest, O my soul, is simply blessing. Learn to think this of Jesus, and seek to have a great confidence that He delights to bless. He is nothing but a Fountain of blessing; rejoice greatly in this and trust Him for it.

2. Remember that the all-comprehensive blessing of your Melchizedek in heaven is the Holy Spirit from heaven in your heart. As it is written : *"Christ redeemed us...that upon the Gentiles might come the blessing of Abraham in Christ Jesus; that we might reeive the promise of the Spirit through faith"* (Galatians 3:13–14). The Holy Spirit abiding continually in the heart is the blessing of the High Priest.

3. This day He comes to meet you, as you return from the battle weary and faint. Bow before Him, and let Him bless you! *"Even as the Holy Ghost saith, To-day"* (Hebrews 3:7). Believe that Jesus is all to you.

6 But Mel was not Abraham's Jewish relative, + yet abe still paid tithes
— Mel imputed a blessing on mighty Abe who had received the promises of God.
7 and no one could deny the fact that the one who has the power doing a blessing is superior to the one who recieves it.
8 although the Jewish priests recieved tithes they all died — they were mortal. But Mel lives on
9 It could even be said that Levi, the ancestor of every Jewish priest who recieves tithes, actually paid tithes to Mel through abe 10 For although

Fifty-Two

Melchizedek More than Aaron and the Law

*Now if there was perfection through the Levitical priesthood
(for under it hath the people received the law), what further
need was there that another priest should arise after the
order of Melchizedek, and not be reckoned after the order of
Aaron? For the priesthood being changed, there is made of
necessity a change also of the law. For he of whom these things
are said belongeth to another tribe, from which no man hath
given attendance at the altar. For it is evident that our Lord
hath sprung out of Judah; as to which tribe Moses spake
nothing concerning priests.*
—Hebrews 7:11–14

When God, in Psalm 110, spoke with an oath of a priest
after the order of Melchizedek, it was a prophecy of deep
spiritual meaning. Why should the order of Aaron, whom
God Himself had called, whose work took such a large place in
the purpose of God and of Scripture, be passed over for the order
of another of whom we knew nothing save one single act? *"What
further need was there that another priest should arise after the order*

of Melchizedek, and not be reckoned after the order of Aaron?" The
answer is this: Because the order of Aaron was only the figure of
the work of Jesus upon earth; for His eternal and almighty priesthood in heaven something more was needed.

Let us see and grasp this. Aaron's work was the shadow of
Christ's work upon earth, of sacrifice and blood-shedding, of atonement and reconciliation with God. Aaron entered indeed within
the veil with the blood, in token of God's acceptance of the atonement and the people. But he might not tarry there; he had to come
out again at once. His entering only once a year—and that only
for a few moments—served mostly, as we see in Hebrews 9:7–8, to
teach the people that the way into the Holiest was not yet opened;
that, for this, they would have to wait until another dispensation
came. Of a life in the Holiest of All, of a dwelling in God's presence and fellowship with Him there, of a communication to the
people of the power of a life within the veil—of all this there was
no thought. The glory of Christ's priesthood consists in His rending the veil and entering in for us; of His sitting at the right hand
of God to receive and impart the Spirit of God and the powers of
the heavenly life; of His being able to bring us in, that we, too, may
draw nigh to God; of His maintenance in us of the life of heaven
by His unceasing intercession and ministry in the power of an endless life. Of all this, the ministry of Aaron could afford no promise.

It was in all this that Melchizedek was made like unto the Son
of God. As priest of the Most High God, he was also king, clothed
with honor and power. As such, his blessing was in power. And
as one of whose death and the end of whose priesthood Scripture
mentions nothing—one who *"abideth...continually"* (7:3)—he is
the image of the eternal priesthood, which is ministered in heaven,
in eternity, in the power of an endless life.

The revelation of the mystery and the glory of the Melchizedek
priesthood of our Lord Jesus is the great object of the epistle. And
I cannot urge my reader too earnestly to see that he entered fully
into the infinite difference between the two orders, or ministries,

of Aaron and Melchizedek. The apparently simple question, *"What further need was there that another priest should arise after the order of Melchizedek?"* has more to do with our spiritual lives than we think.

In the opening of our epistle, in 1:3, we found the work of Christ divided into two parts: *"When he had made purification of sins"* (that was, after the order of Aaron), He *"sat down on the right hand of the Majesty on high"* (that was, after the order of Melchizedek). There are too many Christians who see in Christ only the fulfillment of what Aaron typified. Christ's death and blood are very precious to them; these Christians do seek to rest their faith upon His death and blood. And yet they wonder that they have so little of the peace and joy, of the purity and power, that the Savior gives and that faith in Him ought to bring. The reason is simple: because Christ is only their Aaron, not their Melchizedek. They do indeed believe that He is ascended to heaven and sits upon the throne of God; but they have not seen the direct connection of this with their daily spiritual lives. They do not count upon Jesus working in them in the power of the heavenly life and imparting it to them. They do not know their heavenly calling with the all-sufficient provision for its fulfillment in them secured in the heavenly life of their Priest-King. And as a consequence of this, they do not see the need for giving up the world to have their lives and walk in heaven.

The work of redemption was accomplished on earth in weakness (see 2 Corinthians 13:4); it is communicated from heaven in resurrection and ascension power. The Cross proclaims the pardon of sin; the throne gives the power over sin. The Cross, with its blood-sprinkling, is the deliverance from Egypt; the throne, with its living Priest-King, brings us into the rest of God and its victory. With Aaron there is nothing beyond atonement and acceptance, nothing of kingly rule and power; it is with Melchizedek that the fullness of power and blessing comes, the blessing that abides continually. It is as the soul no longer ever again seeks the foundation, but resting on it and it alone is built up into Christ Jesus, the perfected and

[handwritten note:] For though He was crucified through weakness, yet He lives by the power of God. For we also are weak in Him, but we shall live with Him by the power of God towards you. (KJV)

exalted One, that it will be delivered from its feebleness and know the power of the heavenly life. The more we consider and adore our blessed King-Priest, our Melchizedek, the stronger will our confidence become that from His throne in heaven He Himself will, in divine power, apply to us all the blessed fruits of His atonement and make a life in God's presence and nearness our daily experience.

Chapter Notes...

1. *"When he had made purification of sins"* (Hebrews 1:3). God be praised for our Aaron! Glory be to the Lamb that was slain! He *"sat down on the right hand of the Majesty on high"* (verse 3). God be praised for our Melchizedek! Glory to the Lamb in the midst of the throne! The Holiest is now opened, with our great High Priest to bring us in and keep us there.

2. The effecting of the cleansing of sins by Jesus preceded His sitting on the throne. But the application in us in power follows. This is the reason why we are here first taught about the High Priest in heaven; then, in chapter 8, about the heavenly sanctuary; and after that is chapter 9 about the power of the blood in heaven and from heaven in us. It is only in the knowledge of Jesus in heaven that we will know the full power of the cleansing blood.

3. *"Wherefore, holy brethren, partakers of a heavenly calling, consider the Apostle and High Priest of our confession, even Jesus"* (3:1) on the throne in heaven! The worship and the fellowship of a heavenly Christ makes heavenly Christians.

(15) And all of this is made even clearer if there was another King-Priest raised up in the rank of Mel. (16) This priest did not arise because of a geneological right under the law to be a priest, but by the power of an indestructible resurrection life. For it says in Ps YOU ARE like Mel, a King Priest FOREVER!

Fifty-Three

A Priest Forever—In the Power of an Endless Life

And what we say is yet more abundantly evident, if after the likeness of Melchizedek there ariseth another priest, who hath been made, not after the law of a carnal commandment, but after the power of an endless life: for it is witnessed of him, Thou art a priest for ever after the order of Melchizedek.
—Hebrews 7:15–17

In the words of Psalm 110, each expression is full of meaning. We saw (see Hebrews 5:4–6) that the word, *"Thou art a priest"* is the proof that Christ did not glorify Himself to become Priest but was appointed by God. We have seen the deep significance of the words, *"after the order of Melchizedek."* We now come to what is implied in its being said, *"Thou art a priest for ever."*

The word *"ever,"* or *eternal,* is one of the most important in the epistle. It is used repeatedly. It contains all that distinguishes the New Testament from the Old; the healthy Christian life of the perfect from the stunted sickly growth of the babes. To understand what it means, we must connect it with God, the Eternal One.

Eternity is an attribute of the Deity and of the divine life and has its true existence only in the fellowship of that life. In God, there is no change, aging, or fading; He is all that He is in an ever-fresh, never-changing youth. As someone has said, "He is the Ancient of Days, and yet the youngest of all, for He lives ever in the freshness of the eternal strength that knows no past." The eternal life is what always remains the same because it is always in God. And when God speaks to His Son, *"Thou art a priest for ever,"* it not only means that the priesthood will never cease but also points to what is the root and cause of this—it roots in the life and strength of God. Christ is become a Priest *"after the power of an endless life."* Unceasingly, without one moment's cessation, in unbroken continuity, He lives and works in the power of the divine life.

The contrast will make the meaning clear. He is made Priest— *"not after the law of a carnal commandment,"* as Aaron—*"but after the power of an endless life,"* even as Melchizedek, who *"abideth a priest continually"* (7:3). Law and life are the contrasts. Every creature naturally acts according to the life that is in it, without any law or compulsion from without. The bird needs no law to bid it fly, or the fish to make it swim: Its life makes it a delight. A law is a proof that the life is wanting. The law that forbids stealing is a proof that the life of those for whom it is made is wrong. And a law is not only a proof that the right life is wanting, but it is also helpless to produce it. It may check and restrain, but it cannot inspire. It can demand but cannot give; it has power to command but not to create what it seeks. Aaron became priest *"after the law of a carnal commandment,"* a law that made nothing perfect, and was disannulled for the weakness and unprofitableness thereof; Christ, *"after the power of an endless life."* Every act of His holy and blessed priesthood, every application of the fruits of His eternal redemption, is wrought in *"the power of an endless life."*

These two principles mark two systems of religion, two ways of worshiping God, two experiences of the inner life. The one is that of the law, with atonement and acceptance with God as typified in

Aaron. The Christian who lives under this system trusts in Christ as his Redeemer and seeks, by the great motive of gratitude, to compel himself to love and obedience. His life is one of unceasing effort, but he is painfully conscious of failure; obedience is not his life and delight. The New Testament offers a better life. Through unbelief and sloth, the majority of Christians know little of it. But here it is, opened up by the Holy Spirit, as the mystery of Melchizedek. Jesus Christ is become a Priest *"after the power of an endless life."* These precious words are the key to the higher life. Jesus lives in heaven as High Priest in *"the power of an endless life."* And as He lives so He works in that power. This is the meaning of His being *"a priest for ever."* His work does not consist, like that of Aaron, in a series of successive acts that ever cease and ever need to be renewed. No, each work He does for us He is able to do in *"the power of an endless life."* He works it within us as a life, as our own life, so that it is our very nature to delight in God and in His will. His priesthood acts as an inner life within us, lifting us up, not in thought but in spirit and in truth, into a vital fellowship with God. He breathes His own life in us, and He works it in as the power of life, a life that is strong and healthy because it is His own life from heaven. And He works it in *"the power of an endless"*—an indissoluble—*"life,"* a life that never for a moment needs know a break or an interruption because it is the life of eternity, the life maintained in us by Him who is *"a priest for ever,"* a priest who *"abideth...continually."*

And why is it so many Christians experience and prove so little of this *"power of* [the] *endless,"* the unchanging life that *"abide... continually"*? Some know nothing of it; they only know of Christ as Aaron. And some hear of it but are not willing to give up all to purchase this pearl of great price; to give up the world for this heavenly life. And some, who would fain give up all, cannot, dare not, and will not believe that Christ is indeed Melchizedek, *"a priest for ever,"* a Priest who does everything in eternal life power.

He *"abideth a priest continually."* The continuity of His priesthood is never interrupted or broken, nor is the continuity of the action of His priesthood or the experience of that action. Everything Christ as my High Priest in heaven does for me He does in *"the power of an endless life,"* as a Priest who abides continually; what He works can abide continually, too. Oh, for faith to consider and know and trust Christ Jesus, *"priest for ever,"* Priest after *"the power of an endless life"*!

Chapter Notes...

1. *"The power of an endless life."* There is not a more significant or important expression in the whole epistle. It is life we need, a strong life and a life that never gives way. Here we have it—the life more abundant.

2. We will often have occasion to refer to these words. We are so accustomed to think of a priest as a man who does certain things on behalf of other men, separate from himself, that we apply this mode of thinking to the Lord Jesus. Christ is no outward Savior, nor can He give us any salvation as an outward thing. All He does for us and to us, He puts into our hearts and makes it our life. We need to know that all He does as High Priest for us in heaven, He also does within us as He gives life. He is Priest and can save in no other way than *"after the power of an endless life."* It is only as a life within us that His priesthood can attain its object.

3. Jesus was crucified in weakness but raised in the power of God. He won the power through the weakness, the sacrifice of all unto the death. Let all who would know Him in the power of the endless life enter into the fellowship of His death and walk in deep humility and meekness and dependence upon God, in the path in which He trod to reach the throne.

(18) The old ORDER OF PRIESTHOOD has been SET ASIDE!!! as weak + powerless (useless!) (19) For the law (Torah) has never made anyone perfect, but in its place is a far better hope which gives us confidence to experience intimacy with God!

Fifty-Four

A Better Hope, Through Which We Draw Nigh to God

For there is a disannulling of a foregoing commandment because of its weakness and unprofitableness (for the law made nothing perfect), and a bringing in thereupon of a better hope, through which we draw nigh unto God.
—Hebrews 7:18–19

In Hebrews 7:12 we read, *"For the priesthood being changed, there is made of necessity a change also of the law."* When the order of Aaron had to give way to that of Melchizedek, the law, under which Aaron had ministered, had to give way to the new order—to the law not of commandment but to the law of *"the power of an endless life"* (verse 16). The reason of this is now given. *"There is a disannulling of the foregoing commandment because of its weakness and unprofitableness (for the law made nothing perfect)."* Perfection was what God and man sought as deliverance from sin and its effects: perfect restoration and perfect fellowship. The law could make nothing perfect, neither the conscience nor the worshiper. Jesus came to work out, to reveal, and to impart that perfection that the law could only foreshadow.

And what this perfection is, we are now told: *"There is a disannulling of a foregoing commandment...and a bringing in thereupon of a better hope, through which we draw nigh unto God."* To bring man near to God, into full favor and actual fellowship, is the object of every priest. Aaron could not do it; Jesus has done it. This is the glory of the New Testament; it brings in a better hope, a real drawing near to the living God, a communion of the Holy Spirit with Him. This is the perfection that, not the law, but Jesus gives. In chapter 6, hope was already mentioned as that through which we enter within the veil, where our Forerunner has gone for us. (See verses 19–20.) In *"the power of the endless life"* (7:16), He has opened the veil and opened the way; He has brought in the *"better hope, through which we draw nigh unto God."*

Draw nigh to God! This expression is one of the fingerposts on the way to the higher teaching that is to come. It gives us the main object of Christ's work: to enable us to live our lives in the nearness of God. There are Christians who, in seeking salvation, only think of themselves and their own happiness: Christ is simply a means to an end. There are others who go further: They feel a personal relation to Christ and desire greatly to know and serve Him better, but even with these, there is something lacking that is indispensable to a whole and vigorous Christian character. They do not know that Christ is only the Way, the Door to the Father, and that His great desire is to lead us through and past Himself to the Father, really to bring us to God! He wants us to live the same life He lived upon earth—always looking up to, depending upon, and honoring a God in heaven above Him.

Draw nigh to God! Nothing but this can satisfy God and His love. He longs to have His children come to dwell in that love and to delight in His presence. He sent His Son to bring us to Him. This is what constitutes full salvation. God, as the Author of our being, longs to have us yield ourselves and wait upon Himself to work His work in us. As the righteous and Holy One, He seeks to have us wholly given up to His will and wisdom. As the unseen and hidden One, He asks that we withdraw ourselves from the visible and hold fellowship with Him. Man was created for the presence of God. The nearness of God was to be his native atmosphere. It is this that God is willing to vouchsafe to each of us; it is this that the heavenly priesthood makes possible; and it is this that God would have us seek.

As God is no outward Being, so is nearness to Him nothing external but an inner spiritual harmony of disposition, a fellowship and unity of will. As His Spirit gives us more of the divine nature and God works His will more freely and fully in us, we come nearer to Him, we become truly united to Him.

Draw nigh to God! Nothing less than this is what the redemption of Christ has won and set open for us. This was the weakness of the law, that it made no provision for God's people entering into His sanctuary, His immediate presence. The way into the Holiest has been opened by Jesus. We may boldly enter in and appear before God. Seated on the throne, our High Priest has the power by His Holy Spirit to make the drawing nigh to God our continual abiding experience. He does this in *"the power of an endless life"* (7:16). Life never works from without, always from within. Our High Priest by His life-power enters our lives and renews them, lifts them up; His heavenly life becomes our actual life, and the presence of God surrounds and shines on us as the sunlight shines on our bodies. He is able so to shed abroad the love of God in our hearts that His presence is our joy all the day.

Draw nigh to God! Nothing less than this must be what our faith claims. The redemption in Christ is so perfect and all-prevailing, His salvation so complete, the power of His life in us so heavenly and indissoluble, the action of His priesthood so unceasing and unbroken, and the working of His Spirit so sure and so divine that it is indeed possible for us to dwell all the day in the enjoyment of God's love and fellowship. It is a life-state He has entered into, has opened to us, and lives to keep us in. Let us believe it. Yes, let faith be the one habit of our soul—a faith that honors our King-Priest on the throne in expecting from Him what is impossible to man, what is possible only to God: to keep our hearts all the day within the veil before the face of God.

Christ is the Door. The door of what? The Door to the heart of God. Through Him, I can enter in and abide in God's love; can dwell in God and God in me. He is the living Door who takes me up and brings me in to God. He does it most surely because He is High Priest in *"the power of an endless life"* (7:16).

Chapter Notes...

1. A life *"nigh unto God."* This is the better hope, which enters into that *"which is within the veil"* (6:19). Hold fast the glorying of this hope. Give diligence unto the fullness of the hope; hope does not shame.

2. God near, the world far; the world near, God far. Jesus entered the presence of God in the path that He opened up for us. That path was humility and meekness, obedience and death. It cost Jesus entire and intense self-surrender to open the path and enter in. He has won for us the power to follow Him and communicates it to all upright souls in *"the power of an endless life"* (7:16).

3. *"Nigh unto God"*! Is this your life? Is this your desire? Is this your expectation? It is the salvation Christ has prepared for you and waits to give you.

(20) and he confirmed it to us with his solemn vow. For the former priests took their office WITHOUT an oath, but with Jesus; (21) God ordained his royal priesthood with His promise, saying the LORD has made a solemn oath & will never change His mind, "You are a king-priest forever. (22) So all this magnifies the truth that we have a superior covenant with God than what they experienced, for Jesus Himself is its guarantor.

Fifty-Five

Jesus, the Surety of a Better Covenant

And inasmuch as it is not without the taking of an oath (for they indeed have been made priests without an oath; but he with an oath by him that saith of him, The Lord sware and will not repent himself, Thou art a priest for ever); by so much also hath Jesus become the surety of a better covenant.
—Hebrews 7:20–22

In chapter six, the deep meaning of God's oath was set before us. On His side, it is a proof of His unchangeable purpose concerning something that He binds Himself faithfully to perform. On our side, it points to something in which there is special need of faith, and it calls us to the exercise of full and unhesitating confidence as to the certainty of God's fulfillment of the promise. In the words of the appointment of Christ as High Priest, we have already found three significant expressions—there is a fourth one we are now to notice: *"The Lord sware and will not repent himself."* This oath of God is a new proof of the glory of Christ's priesthood and its superiority to the old. God confirmed His blessing to Abraham with an oath; that blessing is eternal and unchangeable. Aaron was

259

made a priest without an oath; his priesthood was only temporary, a shadow of what was to come. At the first announcement of
a priest after the new order, God again interposed with an oath:
*"Inasmuch as it is not without the taking of an oath...by so much also
hath Jesus become the surety of a better covenant."* The oath points
us to the covenant, to its being a better covenant, to Jesus being its
surety, and to the priesthood as that in which the covenant and the
suretyship have their power.

"A better covenant." The object of a covenant is to define and
settle the relation between the two parties who enter into it and
to give security for the faithful fulfillment of their engagements to
each other. The old covenant that God made with Israel had proved
a failure. At its establishment, they were most ready to promise,
"All that the LORD *hath spoken will we do, and be obedient"* (Exodus
24:7). But how soon was the covenant forgotten and the promise broken! They had undertaken what they could not perform;
the vow and the purpose availed nothing without the strength. In
course of time, God promised to establish a new covenant, and in
it to provide for what had been wanting—for the power to obey
and so to keep the covenant. It would be a covenant of life—giving
that new life into the heart out of which obedience would naturally
spring. Of this *"better covenant,"* established on better promises, we
will hear in the next chapter.

"The surety of a better covenant." It is this that Jesus has come
to do—to give the covenant its security and to undertake that its
engagements will indeed be fulfilled. He is surety of the covenant
on both sides. Surety to us that God will keep His promise and give
us His life and law and Spirit in our hearts; and surety to God for
us that He will ensure our obedience and our keeping the covenant.

"But he with an oath." It is in the priesthood of Jesus that the
covenant and the suretyship have their power. It is the *"priest for
ever"* who deals with sin and takes it away in *"the power of an endless life"* (Hebrews 7:16). It is the *"priest for ever,"* the Son of God,
perfected forevermore, who has opened a new and living way, a

new state of life, and works all in the power of an endless life—it is in Him that we have a divine surety that every promise and every obligation of the better covenant will be fulfilled by God and by us.

It is to give us a living and most complete assurance that all this will be so that the installation of Jesus in the Priest's office was announced by an oath from heaven. God does so long that we should, in very deed, become the full partakers of the eternal redemption His Son has obtained for us; because He sees it is impossible for Him to work out His will in us except as our hearts open to Him in faith and expectation, He is ready to do anything He can to awake our confidence and compel us to trust Him perfectly. And so, His Spirit reminds us that the priesthood of Jesus, and all the blessings that come from it in the power of our eternal life, are absolutely sure and certain.

As if it is not enough that we know that, as the Son of God He is the almighty One; as Son of Man, the merciful and faithful High Priest; as the exalted One, a King upon God's throne—God calls us to consider the oath He took. He swears by Himself. He points to Himself and His honor as God, to Himself as the eternal and almighty God, and charges us to believe that this *"priest for ever"* He has given us does indeed save with an everlasting salvation, with a salvation in which the power of eternity works.

When God confirmed by oath to Abraham His promise of blessing, Abraham, though he knew but little of what that blessing would yet be, believed God; he was strong in faith giving glory to God. And we, who know the Son in whom God has now revealed Himself, and in regard to the efficacy and eternal life-power of whose work for us God has now sworn His oath to us, will we doubt or hesitate? God forbid! Oh, that our hearts were opened to understand! The one thing God asks us is that faith that sees what He has promised to do and that sinks down before Him to let Him work what He has undertaken. The one thing we have to strive after, as we move on in the path the epistle opens up to the inner sanctuary, is that our faith stands not in the wisdom of men, in our own thoughts of the way, or in the measure in which God will fulfill His promise—but only and entirely in the power of God. What needed an oath of God to assure us of it needs and has the power of God to work it.

Chapter Notes...

1. Do hold fast these two things. Faith must see what God promises and then allow God to fulfill the promise in us. Pray for the enlightening of the Holy Spirit, to get delivered from all partial and defective views of what our High Priest can work in us, and then regard as your highest work to wait upon God and yield to His operation in adoring trust.

2. The content and substance of the oath of God is the living, personal Christ, as Son and Priest—that is, as Priest in the power of the divine and eternal life that He imparts. He that clings to Christ will be led on to know all that God has promised in Him.

PP The former priests, on one hand, existed in greater numbers because they were prevented by death from continuing, (24) but Jesus, on the other hand, because He continues forever, holds His priesthood permanently. (25) Therefore He is able also to save forever those who draw near to God through Him, since He always lives to make intercession for them.

Fifty-Six

A High Priest Able to Save Completely

And they indeed have been made priests many in number, because that by death they are hindered from continuing: but he, because he abideth for ever, hath his priesthood unchangeable. Wherefore also he is able to save to the uttermost* them that draw near unto God through him, seeing he ever liveth to make intercession for them.
—Hebrews 7:23–25

In the order of Aaron, there was a continual succession of priests, one dying and another taking his place. That characterized the whole system; it bore the mark of change, weakness, and death. It could not effect anything that was really abiding and permanent, much less anything that was eternal. The whole inner life of the worshiper was what the system was—subject to change and decay. *"But he, because he abideth for ever, hath his priesthood unchangeable."* He Himself is the Eternal One, who abides as Priest forever. His priesthood is unchangeable; the life—in the

---

* Completely.

power of which He ministers—and the life that He ministers is a life that abides unchangeable, too. His priesthood is an everlasting one, ever living, ever active.

"*Wherefore also he is able to save* [completely] *them that draw near unto God through him.*" "*Wherefore*"—that is, "*because he abideth for ever,*" because there is never a single moment in which His priestly action, His watchful care of us, His loving sympathy and succor, His working in us in the power of our endless life, is not in full operation. Therefore, He can save completely; that is, there need never be a moment in which the experience of His saving power is disrupted, in which the salvation He has wrought does not save. To confirm this, it is added, "*seeing he ever liveth to make intercession for them.*" Without ceasing, there streams forth from Him to the Father the prayer of His love for everyone, and every need of those that belong to Him; His very person and presence is that prayer, so closely and so inseparably is He identified with those He calls His brethren. And without ceasing, there streams forth to Him from the Father the answer of His good pleasure, and the power of the Holy Spirit, bearing that answer. And even so, without ceasing, there streams forth from Him to each member of His body the grace for timely help. "*Because...he ever liveth to make intercession,*" without one moment's intermission, therefore, "*he is able to save* [completely]."

"*He is able to save* [completely]." The connection of the promise with the character and work of Christ shows us what it means. The great complaint of Christians is that their experience is so changeful—that the blessed sense of God's love and grace passes away and that what they know of the keeping, cleansing power of Christ does not last; the sense of nearness to God does not abide continually. It is somehow as if there is a necessity of its being lost. With change of circumstances, alas, comes too often change in the nearness of God and His saving power. Could what Christ does for them at times but be maintained continuously, could it but abide, then their joy would be full and their salvation complete. We have here the very promise that such Christians need. *"Because he abideth for ever,"* because *"he ever liveth to make intercession,"* because He is *"a priest for ever"* (7:21) who exercises every function of His office in an endless life-power that never for a moment disrupts its action, *"he is able to save* [completely]*."* In Himself, He has been *"perfected for evermore"* (7:28); with Himself, *"he hath perfected for ever them that are sanctified"* (10:14). The salvation He has wrought out is a life in the opened sanctuary of God's presence in the power of God's Spirit; all that is needed is that the believer be kept abiding forever, always living in this salvation life that Jesus has opened up. And this he can do when once he learns to trust Jesus for it because he understands that *"he ever liveth to make intercession."* He prayed for Peter that his faith might not fail. Because His work of intercession never pauses or ceases, our faith and our experience of the power of that intercession need never fail. *"He is able to save* [completely]*"*!

"Them that draw near unto God through him." In verse 19, we saw that, to enable us to *"draw nigh unto God"* is *"the better hope"* the Gospel brings—the one aim of Christ's priesthood. Here we have it again. One reason why so many have no understanding of Christ as *"able to save* [completely]*"* is simply that they have never understood fully what salvation is. The following chapters will open it up to us—and may God's Spirit truly open it!—that to come to God through Christ, to *"draw nigh unto God"* means nothing less than an entering into the Holiest of All and dwelling there all the day, spending our lives there, abiding there continually. It is only those who believe it is possible that will give themselves up to it. It is only those who forsake all to give themselves up to it to whom it will be possible. But for all who come to God through Him, the promise is sure: *"He abideth for ever"* and *"He is able to save* [completely]*."*

Oh, let us fix our eyes and hearts on Jesus in heaven, our Melchizedek, our Priest-King on the throne of power, and on His unceasing intercession. And let our one desire be to believe that the God who has sworn by Himself, by His own life as God, means to do for us something above all we can ask or think.

Chapter Notes...

1. *"Able to save* [completely]." This is that *"solid food"* for the perfect (5:14) that only the truly consecrated soul can apprehend. It is of the things *"hard of interpretation, seeing ye are become dull of hearing"* (5:11).

2. Like priest, like people. The character of a priest determines the character of the people whose worship he leads. The character of Christ's priesthood determines the character of those who belong to Him. And our view of what that priesthood can affect will determine our religious character. Of what infinite importance to worship and to trust Him, as *"able to save* [completely]." That will determine our Christian characters and lives.

3. What a view of the place and power of intercession! Christ's whole life is given up to it. His power as Priest-King on the throne has no other channel for its exercise. You long to save others; give yourself to prayer and intercession. Present yourself before God as a sacrifice for your fellowmen, offering to be filled with His Spirit and consumed by His fire. Count intercession the secret of bringing down the blessing of heaven. Connect the two things inseparably together—unceasing intercession and power to save completely in Christ. Complete salvation and unceasing intercession in us.

Fifty-Seven
Such a High Priest, the Son Perfected Forevermore

For such a high priest became us, holy, guileless, undefiled,
separated from sinners, and made higher than the heavens;
who needeth not daily, like those high priests, to offer up
sacrifices, first for his own sins, and then for the sins of
the people: for this he did once for all, when he offered up
himself. For the law appointeth men high priests, having
infirmity; but the word of the oath, which was after the law,
appointeth a Son, perfected for evermore.
—Hebrews 7:26–28

"For such a high priest became us"—was suited to us, as being what we needed. The words refer to the whole chapter, but especially to the verse that just precedes—"such a high priest," one who "abideth for ever" (Hebrews 7:24), one who is "able to save [completely]" (verse 25). It also refers to what now follows, in which His personal characteristics are summed up. "Holy," in fellowship and harmony with God; *"guileless,"* in the purity of His disposition; *"undefiled,"* in His having conquered all temptation from sin and the world; *"separated from sinners,"* a true man among men and yet One who had kept Himself free from their sin; *"made higher than the heavens,"* now exalted in the glory of God to communicate to us the life and the blessings of the heavenly world.

"Who needeth not daily, like those high priests, to offer up sacrifices, first for his own sins, and then for the sins of the people: for this he did once for all, when he offered up himself." We saw that the glory of Christ's priesthood—in contrast with that of the many who had, by reason of death, to succeed each other—was that He alone is Priest because He abides forever. Here we have the same truth from another side: In contrast with the daily ever-repeated sacrifices, He accomplished all *"once for all, when he offered up himself."* Whatever has to be repeated is imperfect; whatever needs to be done only once is perfect and lasts forever. Further on we will find the word *"once"* again as having the same meaning with regard to His sacrifice that *"for evermore"* has with regard to His priesthood.

"He offered up himself." We have here the first mention of the sacrifice of Christ. In chapter 2, we had mention of His death; here we see that it was death upon the altar. He is both Priest and sacrifice. His divine priesthood, as it is exercised in heaven, is the application of the blood and the virtue of that sacrifice that He brought upon earth. The *"once for all"* of the sacrifice is the counterpart of the *"henceforth"* (10:13) and *"for ever"* (10:12) of the throne of the heavens.

"For the law"—this is the conclusion of the whole—*"appointeth men high priests, having infirmity; but the word of the oath, which was after the law, appointeth a Son, perfected for evermore."* The law was a preparation, to waken the need and the hope of that true, supernatural, heavenly communion with God, which should be not in words or wishes but in the power of the eternal life. What the law could not do, God has done, appointing as High Priest the *"Son, perfected for evermore."*

In these last words, we have the summing up of the whole preceding teaching of the epistle. In chapter 1, it had spoken of the Son of God and His glory: He came from God, He is God, and He has the life of God in Him; He is able to bring us near, into the true possession and enjoyment of the very life of God. In chapters 2–5, we had His humanity, His being made perfect through suffering and obedience. He so perfected a new human nature, which He imparts to us from heaven in the power of the Holy Spirit. In chapter 7, we have now been taught what it means that He is the *"priest for ever after the order of Melchizedek"* (verse 17), whose person and priesthood and work are all in *"the power of an endless life"* (verse 16), and who, because He ever abides and ever intercedes, *"is able to save* [completely]" (verse 25), and to make our drawing nigh to God a life that abides continually. *"Such a high priest became us,...a Son, perfected for evermore."*

And if such a High Priest became us, what becomes us now toward Him? Surely one thing—that we fully seek to know and to trust and to experience His saving power. If your heart does indeed long for deliverance from sin, for true near fellowship with God, for complete salvation, for a life in the power and the likeness of the Son of God, our Leader and Forerunner within the veil—you must learn to know Jesus both as Son of God and as your High Priest. You must pray for the Spirit of wisdom and revelation so that you may know the exceeding greatness of God's power toward us who believe, according to the working of His mighty power in Christ Jesus when He raised Him from the dead and set Him at His own right hand. You must believe that the mighty power by which He was thus *"perfected for evermore,"* and is seated at God's right hand, is working in you. Yield yourself up in faith to this mighty working of God in Christ, to the power of the eternal life with which He will work, from heaven, in you to draw you near to God and keep you there. As you believe this and trust Jesus for it, He Himself will make it your experience. Oh, beware of thinking that these are beautiful words and images that Scripture gives; they are meant by

God as the most downright, actual realities for daily life and walk. God has given you such a High Priest that you might live an impossible life, a life above sense and reason, a supernatural life in the power of His Son. When Jesus ascended the throne His disciples were to wait for a communication direct from Himself of the Spirit and power of the heavenly life into which He had entered for them. It is the same Holy Spirit, dwelling in us in Pentecostal power, who alone can make all the blessed objective truth of the epistle a living reality within us.

Chapter Notes...

1. Before we part from this chapter, note well the three words in which its practical teaching gathers up what our Melchizedek, who abides as a Priest continually, is to us. The law of His working is: He does all *"after the power of an endless life"* (verse 16). The object of His work: the *"better hope, through which we draw nigh unto God"* (verse 19). The measure of His work: *"He is able to save* [completely]" (verse 25). The power of eternal life, the nearness of God, and complete salvation are what He has to bestow.

2. The eternal priesthood of Christ: This is the first of the perfection truths that lead us to the perfection life. A Son, *"perfected for evermore,"* is our High Priest, who out of Himself and in Himself gives us the life we are to live.

3. The one thought of God in His Word here is to make us feel what a complete salvation there is for us with such a Savior. God speaks to us in His Son, giving us in Him His own life.

Sixth Section—Hebrews 8:1–13

THE NEW SANCTUARY AND THE NEW COVENANT

Fifty-Eight

The Priest-King on the Throne in the Heavens

Now in the things which we are saying the chief point is this: We have such a high priest, who sat down on the right hand of the throne of the Majesty in the heavens.
—Hebrews 8:1

In every pursuit, it is always most important to keep the eye fixed on whatever is the main thing and to make everything else subservient to it. A Christian often feels perplexed by the variety of truths and duties set before him in Scripture; to see clearly what the central thought is is like finding the key to some building around which one had vainly wandered seeking an entrance. Our author here is careful in summing up what we have had thus far, to fix our view on what is *"the chief point"*: *"We have such a high priest"* as has been set before us, the very Son of God, a true man in His obedience to God and sympathy with us, become *"a priest for ever after the order of Melchizedek"* (Hebrews 7:17), *"after the power of an endless life"* (verse 16). And we have Him as One *"who sat down on the right hand of the throne of the Majesty in the heavens."* It is as our faith apprehends and holds this truth that we have the key that opens the door into the heavenly life upon earth.

Jesus, our Priest-King, on *"the throne of the Majesty in the heavens."* What does this mean, and teach, and give? It reminds, first of all, that Jesus is not only Priest but also King. This was part of what was included in His appointment after the order of Melchizedek, whose name meant *"King of righteousness, and then also King of Salem, which is, King of peace"* (verse 2). The psalm in which the word of the oath is spoken began thus: *"The Lord saith unto my lord, Sit thou at my right hand"* (Psalm 110:1). In Israel, the office of king and priest had been kept separate; it was only one of the latest prophets who foretold, *"He shall be a priest upon his throne"* (Zechariah 6:13). It was part of the defect in the character of the preparatory dispensation that the function of priest, the representative of the religious life, should be so distinct from that of the king, the guide of the civil life of the people. The priest represents purity; the king, power. It is the glory of the new dispensation that the Priest is King—the cleansing from sin, and the access to God that it gives, is all in a power that goes through the whole life. Religion is no longer to be a thing of times and seasons, of special acts or emotions: In kingly power, our High Priest rules over all. Blessed is the man to whom it is given to see that this is *"the chief point,"* that this is all.

And that, because He is a King, He *"sat down on the right hand of the throne of the Majesty in the heavens."* The Son of God became man that He might win for Himself and us—for humanity, His own and ours—the power He had with the Father before the world began, and so as our High Priest, to serve and rule us *"after the power of an endless life"* (Hebrews 7:16), in the power of the heavenly life. He *"sat down on the right hand of the throne."* His position is now one of perfect fellowship with God, in a nearness in which nothing can intervene, in an equality that gives Him complete possession and disposal of all power in heaven and on earth. This is *"the chief point"* to know in faith—that we have such a High Priest!

Andrew Murray

"Of the throne of the Majesty in the heavens." We have said before that the great characteristic of our Priest-King, of His salvation and His life, is its heavenliness. It will reward the reader each time the thought occurs to go over the passages we have marked and seek to come fully under the power of the thought. Jesus is *"passed through the heavens"* (4:14), *"made higher than the heavens"* (7:26), and now seated on *"the throne of the Majesty in the heavens,"* in order that He might open the kingdom of heaven to us. Heaven, we have said before, is not only a place but also a state of life; the kingdom of heaven can come to us here on earth in power and be set up within our hearts. The will of God can be done on earth as in heaven. All Jesus is, is heavenly; all the gifts He bestows, all the work He does, all the life He breathes, and all the power He exercises is exclusively heavenly. This is the *"solid food"* (5:14) for the perfect; as our faith receives and feeds upon this, it becomes partaker of the very spirit of heaven, in *"the power of an endless life"* (7:16). As the heavenliness of the redemption and the life in Jesus is revealed by the Holy Spirit in the heart, then heavenliness—its purity, its power, its love, its worship, and its blessedness—will be the characteristic of our religion.

He *"sat down on the right hand of the throne of the Majesty in the heavens."* We know how this blessed truth was revealed and sealed to the first disciples—it was by the Holy Spirit sent down from heaven. The Spirit of heaven is the Spirit in the power of which the angels do God's will there. The Spirit of heaven is the Spirit that came down from the opened heaven on the Son of Man. The Spirit of heaven was sent down to His disciples by the Son of Man when He had *"sat down on the right hand of the throne of the Majesty in the heavens,"* as their share in His exaltation; not as the Spirit of conversion but as the Spirit to seal their faith; as their experience of fellowship with Him in His glory; as their participation in the joy and holiness of the heavenly life; as their power to conquer sin and the world. To those who are willing to come and be separate and utterly forsake this world, this Spirit of heaven still comes as the gift of our heavenly Priest-King. Let us believe the Word, let us cling to Him and worship Him as seated on the throne in the heavens. It will become our blessed heart experience, not only that this is *"the chief point"*—that *"such a high priest became us"* (verse 26)—but also that we have—yes, not only in thought and in gift, but in living enjoyment—*"We have such a high priest, who sat down on the right hand of the throne of the Majesty in the heavens."*

Chapter Notes...

1. The spirit of a king imparts itself to his subjects. As he devotes himself to war or peace, to noble pursuits or to luxury and pleasure, his example leads his people. Perfect heavenliness, heavenly perfection, is the mark of our King; it is meant to be the mark of His people. The true knowledge of a heavenly Christ makes a heavenly Christian.

2. "Our Forerunner has carried away our hearts with Him. We have no heart left for anyone but Him, or for anything without or within the veil that He is not, or is not in."*

3. Ever connect Christ's entering the heavenly life and His ascending the throne with the descent of the Spirit to be the life of the disciples. And remember that all our knowledge and faith in the Priest-King is only preparatory to the true blessing—the Holy Spirit revealing Him and making Him present in the heart. Ascension and Pentecost are inseparable.

---

* Author unknown.

Fifty-Nine

The Priest-King, the Minister of the True Sanctuary

Now in the things which we are saying the chief point is this:
We have such a high priest, who sat down on the right hand
of the throne of the Majesty in the heavens, a minister of
the sanctuary, and of the true tabernacle, which the Lord
pitched, not man. For every high priest is appointed to offer
both gifts and sacrifices: wherefore it is necessary that this
high priest also have somewhat to offer. Now if he were on
earth, he would not be a priest at all, seeing there are those
who offer the gifts according to the law; who serve that which
is a copy and shadow of the heavenly things; even as Moses
is warned of God when he is about to make the tabernacle:
for, See, saith he, that thou make all things according to the
pattern that was shewed thee in the mount.
—Hebrews 8:1–5

The chief point is this: We have such a high priest, who sat down
on the right hand of the throne of the Majesty in the heavens."
Thus the writer had summed up his teaching. He has now
one more thought to add, revealing still more distinctly and fully

the work our Lord does for us in heaven. He is *"a minister of the sanctuary, and of the true tabernacle, which the Lord pitched, not man."* The heavens, with the heavenly life of Christ there, are here shown to be the true counterpart of the tabernacle Moses built; and He, the Priest-King on the throne, is seen to be the Minister of the sanctuary, of the true tabernacle that God pitched and not man.

He then proceeds to remind us that, as every high priest is appointed to offer gifts and sacrifices, so Christ must have something to offer, too. *"Now if he were on earth, he would not be a priest at all, seeing there are those who offer the gifts according to the law."* Christ belongs to an entirely different sphere. With the body that He offered on earth and the blood He shed, He has passed away out of the visible into the invisible realm of spiritual worship and life. Heaven is the sphere of His ministry. When God said to Moses to make all according to the pattern showed him in the mount to serve as a *"shadow of the heavenly things,"* in the very appointment of the tabernacle there was the indication that it was but a copy and promise of the true tabernacle, with its heavenly sanctuary. The heavens where Jesus sits on the throne, they are the *"true tabernacle"*; and the High Priest on the throne is, at the same time, the *"minister of the sanctuary."*

"A minister of the sanctuary." The King is still a servant. All the ministry or service of the priests in the tabernacle had its fulfillment in Him. The priests served in the tabernacle day by day and ordered everything for the service of God according to His will. As representatives of the people, they received the assurance of God's favor and brought them God's blessing. Jesus is the Minister of the heavenly sanctuary. He represents us there. He has opened up the way, and brought us in, and sends down into our hearts the life and spirit of the true sanctuary; without ceasing, He maintains the cleansing of His precious blood in our conscience, and *"in the power of an endless life"* (Hebrews 7:16), enables us to worship in spirit and in truth and to live our earthly lives in the presence and the favor of God. As the exalted Priest-King, He does it all in an infinite, a divine, power. As

Andrew Murray

the *"minister of the sanctuary,"* He does it with all the sympathy and the gentle forbearance that we have seen to mark Him as *"made like unto his brethren"* in all things (2:17).

A priest must have a sanctuary in which he dwells, to receive all who come to seek his God. Our great High Priest has His sanctuary in the heavens; there He dwells, there we find Him; there He receives us, there He introduces us to meet God; there He proves that He is a Priest who abides continually and who gives those who come to God through Him the power to do it, too—to abide continually in His presence. The nearness to God and fellowship with Him I cannot partake of except through my heart. My heart is my life, is myself; my only blessedness is in the state of the heart. And, therefore, Jesus as High Priest cannot do His priestly work of bringing me near to God except as He dwells in my heart by the power of the Holy Spirit. All our thought, faith, and adoration of Him in heaven bring us back to the riches of the glory of the mystery—Christ in you. He is Priest after *"the power of an endless life"* (7:16), a Priest whose presence and power are known and enjoyed in the life of the heart.

These are indeed spiritual mysteries of which we speak—things hard to be understood by those who, through sloth or worldliness, are dull of hearing. Oh, let us not imagine that these are things that reason can grasp or hold; they are a supernatural wisdom, a divine revelation that none can receive but those who receive it from the Spirit of God. Let us remember that it is God who has pitched this tabernacle; that it cost the Son of God a life of humility and suffering, cost Him His death and blood, to open it for us; that it needed the almighty power of God in the Resurrection and Ascension to bring Him there; that it needed ten days of unceasing prayer, and the coming down of the blessed Spirit at Pentecost, before the High Priest could impart even to His elect circle the power of the life within the veil. And let us then pause to think that it is no wonder if most Christians rest content with the easier and more external worship, as typified by Aaron, and never press on unto perfection, in the full knowledge of our Melchizedek and the mystery of the heavenly life into which He leads them. Let us, above all, remember that it was through death, through the offering up of Himself, that Jesus entered in and opened a way for us to follow. To enter in demands a very entire renunciation of the world and of self, a very real and true participation in Christ's humbling of Himself and *"becoming obedient even unto death, yea, the death of the cross"* (Philippians 2:8)—in His death to sin. And it demands no less than a very real experience of the mighty operation of God that raised Him from the dead and set Him at His right hand. But let us praise God, too, that for every soul who truly wills it, our almighty King-Priest, able to save completely, will surely give it.

Chapter Notes...

1. How many Christians think of heaven as the place where Jesus is, as the place to which they have a title, the place they hope to go when they die? But they think not of heaven as a life, and of God's nearness as an experience for every hour of our daily walk. And how many are there who think of Jesus as the blessed One in whom they are there, by imputation, but know not of Him as lifting them and their whole lives into heaven and, by the Holy Spirit, bringing heaven into them?

2. Every priest has his temple where he receives the worshipers and leads them to find the God they seek. Jesus must have a temple, too. The heavens are the true sanctuary. Do not attempt to separate between the priest and the place of his dwelling. As His life in heaven is the life of our heart, we know the power of His priesthood.

Sixty

The Priest-King, the Mediator of the New Covenant

But now hath He obtained a ministry the more excellent, by as much also He is the mediator of a better covenant, which hath been enacted upon better promises. For if that first covenant had been faultless, then would no place have been sought for a second. For finding fault with them, He saith, Behold, the days come, saith the Lord, That I will make a new covenant with the house of Israel and with the house of Judah; not according to the covenant that I made with their fathers in the day that I took them by the hand to lead them forth out of the land of Egypt; for they continued not in my covenant, and I regarded them not, saith the Lord.
—Hebrews 8:6–9

I n our chapter, there are two titles given to our Priest-King, describing two functions that He discharges. The one is "a minister of the sanctuary" (Hebrews 8:2), the other, "the mediator of a better covenant." The epistle, having mentioned the sanctuary

279

in which Christ ministers, is about to proceed in the next chapter with the work that Christ did in opening and entering the sanctuary with His own blood. He does not, without good reason, first interpose here the member of the new covenant and Christ's work as its Mediator. The two designations, *"minister of the sanctuary"* (verse 2) and *"mediator of a better covenant,"* represent two aspects of Christ's work that are the complements of each other and that are each necessary to the right understanding of the other. The sanctuary is God's dwelling; a *"minister of the sanctuary"* has specifically to do with bringing us near to God and the blessedness we find there. The covenant deals with our relation and duty toward God; *"the mediator of a better covenant"* has specifically to do with our preparation for entering the sanctuary and being made fit to meet God.

In chapter 7, we heard that Jesus is *"the surety of a better covenant"* (verse 22). We said there that a covenant is meant to define the mutual relation of the two contracting parties and to secure the fulfillment of their engagements to each other. In the passage from Jeremiah quoted in our chapter, we are told that the covenant God made with Israel, when He brought them up out of Egypt, was not faultless and that, therefore, a second was needed. The fault or insufficiency of the first—*"its weakness and unprofitableness"* (verse 18)—would be avoided in the new. A different provision would be made. The fault of the old covenant is stated to be: *"They continued not in my covenant, and I regarded them not, saith the Lord."* Israel began well, and accepted the covenant, and promised obedience. But *"they continued not."* There was no power to continue; no power to conquer temptation or the evil heart; no power to remain faithful. Against this, the new covenant would provide something better, because it was better, enacted in better promises. It would, by the blood of Christ, provide such an actual putting away and cleansing of sin that God would actually remember them no more forever. With this, He would, by His Holy Spirit, so put His laws into their hearts (see 8:10) so that they would delight in doing them. God would Himself work both to will and to do. And then, in this power of Christ's blood and the renewal of the Holy Spirit, they would no longer be dependent on men for their knowledge of God but have direct access and direct intercourse with Him. They would, in spiritual reality, draw near to God in the Holiest of All.

This is the new, the better covenant, of which Jesus was to be the Mediator. It is easy now to see of what importance it is that the epistle should here introduce this name and function of our blessed Lord, *"the mediator of a better covenant."* When the message comes to us of drawing near to God, of entering into the Holiest and abiding there, the thought always comes that our sinful, faithless hearts render it impossible. It would be very easy, we say, and very blessed to dwell all the day consciously in God's presence if we could just all the day remain occupied with spiritual things. But we cannot—our earthly duties render unbroken communion an impossibility. And if it be said that, "If we trust this to Jesus, He will care for us, even when we have to be occupied with earthly things," the answer comes again: "But oh, the sinfulness of our hearts! Before we know, tempers and dispositions come and bring a cloud; to abide always in the light of God, not only to enter God's presence but to continue there—it is not possible!"

Come and listen. But *"they continued not in my covenant."* This is the experience of the old covenant, to which there now can be an end. The whole provision of the new covenant is to fit us for continuing in it, for abiding continually. It is indeed true that the sanctuary is the dwelling-place of the Holy One, the Holiest of All, and that sinning clouds God's presence. There must be correspondence, harmony, between the sanctuary with the God that dwells there and the worshiper. But it is for this very purpose that Jesus, the Minister of the true sanctuary, is also the Mediator of the new covenant. He engages so as to reveal the power of His blood and the boldness of access that it gives you; so to put God's law into your heart in that *"power of an endless life"* (7:16) in which He does all His priestly work; so to fit you to know the Lord that you will indeed know that, as *"minister of the sanctuary"* (8:2), He does in very truth secure your entrance and your abiding there. The work done by Jesus in the heavenly sanctuary must have its counterpart in the heart that is to enter that sanctuary. And because it is one Jesus who is both Minister of the new sanctuary and Mediator of the new covenant, we may be confident that He will do His work in our hearts as effectually as He does it in heaven. And, therefore, the deeper our insight into the perfection of His work in heaven above, the more confident our expectation may be of the perfection in our lives within.

Chapter Notes...

1. Let us pray to God very earnestly that, as we now proceed to study the better promises of the better covenant, our hearts may be opened to receive them in all their fullness.

2. "No omnipotence can make you partaker of the life of the outward world without having the life of this outward world born in your own creaturely being. And, therefore, no omnipotence can make you a partaker of the beatific life in presence of the Holy Trinity unless that life stands in the same triune state within you that it does without you."

3. A heavenly sanctuary and a heavenly High Priest ask for a heavenly Christian and a heavenly heart. And this is what the new covenant promises and what the Mediator of the new covenant gives indeed.

Sixty-One

The Central Blessing of the New Covenant—The Law Written in the Heart

For this is the covenant that I will make with the house of Israel after those days, saith the Lord; I will put my laws into their minds and on their heart also will I write them: and I will be to them a God, and they shall be to me a people.
—Hebrews 8:10

Jer 31:33
Rom 11:27
Heb 10:16
2 Cor 3:3

We have seen what the fault of the old covenant was: *"They continued not in my covenant"* (Hebrews 8:9). We have seen that the one objective of the new covenant is to repair the fault of the old. There is, henceforth, no more need of the word, *"They continued not."* The one distinguishing characteristic of the new covenant is to be, "There is grace for those who enter it to continue." The great mark of the priest after the order of Melchizedek is this—He *"abideth...continually"* (7:3). The great mark of each of His people is meant to be, too, that they abide continually.

But are we not, someone will say, all living under the new covenant; and yet, is not the ordinary experience of Christians still the same as of old in that *"They continued not"* (8:9)? Alas, it is so. And how, then, with the provision of the covenant? Is it really to be taken so literally? And if so, has not the new covenant failed, just as the old did, of securing the continual obedience God desired? The answer will be found in what we have more than once pointed out. The Hebrews were Christians under the new covenant but with their lives in the old. The new covenant does not do violence to man's will. It is only present where the heart sees and believes what God has promised and is ready, at any cost, to claim and possess it that any blessing can be realized. With most Christians, there is not even the intellectual belief that God means His promise literally. They are so sure that their views of man's sinfulness and the necessity of always sinning are correct that the teaching of God's Word in regard to His purpose to make an end of the *"they continued not"* can never enter the mind. There are others who accept the truth but, through unbelief, enter not into the full possession. And the whole state of the church of Christ is such that very few live in the full experience of what the covenant means.

Let us meditate on its promises and especially on its chief promise, its central blessing—*"I will put my laws into their mind, and on their heart also will I write them"*—in the adoring faith of our great High Priest upon the throne who, as Mediator of the new covenant, is its Surety that every word will be made true. It is in Him, whom He has by oath appointed Priest in *"the power of an endless life"* (7:16), that God says, *"This is the covenant that I will make with the house of Israel after those days, saith the Lord; I will put my laws into their mind, and on their heart also will I write them."* In 7:16, we saw what the difference is between an external law and an inner life. The one is helpless, the other mighty. And we saw how even God's law failed to secure obedience because the heart was not right. The promise of the new covenant is to convert the external law into an inner life, to put it so in the heart that it will be its inmost life; so that, as naturally as the heart wills and lives and acts on earth, it shall will and live and do what God demands. Why does an acorn so spontaneously grow up into an oak? Because the law of the oak is written in the heart of the acorn. The life of every creature acts with delight in accordance to the law of its Creator—that is, its inner nature. God and His holiness, Christ and His Holy Spirit, if they belong to us, must be as near to us and as essentially within us and as truly inherent in our own lives as our own thinking, willing, and feeling. And so God promises that He will put His law in our minds and write it in our hearts in such a way that it will be our inner nature, our very life, and we will act according to it as naturally as we think or live. Yes, He will do it. So that we can say, even as His Son did, *"I delight to do thy will, O my God; yea, thy law is within my heart"* (Psalm 40:8).

"This is the covenant that I will make…, saith the Lord." And God has given His own Son with an oath to be the Surety of that covenant! And of that covenant He, the High Priest upon the throne, is the Mediator! Oh, what do you think? Will God fail in the very thing the covenant was devised to provide? Will He disappoint us in the one thing in which, as it deals with our experience, the new covenant is to be better than the old? In the one thing His heart and our hearts long for—to serve Him in righteousness and holiness all the days of our lives—is this one thing the very thing we are not to realize? God forbid. He has said, *"This is the covenant that I will make,"* and He will do it.

Let us look up to the Mediator of the covenant, our High Priest upon the throne in the heavens. When He was with His disciples on earth, the law was not yet put into their hearts. How often they failed in humility and love and boldness. But when He sat down upon the throne, He sent down the Holy Spirit from heaven in their hearts and all was new. They were full of humility and love and great boldness. The law of God was in their hearts as the power of a life that knew, and loved, and they did His will. Christ dwelt in their hearts by faith. The power of the endless life from the throne of God had taken possession of them. Oh, let us not doubt. Let us plead God's promise, *"I will make a new covenant"* (Hebrews 8:8). Let us trust God's Son, the Surety of the covenant, and receive God's Spirit. We will be brought into the covenant, and into the sanctuary together, and have grace to continue, to abide continually.

Chapter Notes...

1. Just as truly as there is a sanctuary above, there is a sanctuary within. In the old sanctuary, the chief object in the Holiest of All was the law, in the ark covered by the mercy-seat sprinkled with blood. It is the law written in the heart sprinkled with the blood that makes it a sanctuary. It is the heart that is thus made a sanctuary that enters the true sanctuary.

2. Is not the reason that some, who seek earnestly, fail to receive the blessing because they seek to grasp it in their own power and do not yield to the Holy Spirit to work it in them? It is God who says, *"I will make a new covenant"* (verse 8). He must, by His mighty operation, do it in each heart. Our place is deep dependence, patient waiting, and implicit reliance on His mighty power.

3. Remember that all He has to do as Mediator of the new covenant, He does because He is Minister of the true sanctuary. He sends out of the sanctuary the Spirit of heaven into our hearts. It is this that puts God's law within us.

4. The whole law is fulfilled in one phrase: *"Thou shalt love"* (Mark 12:30–31, for example). Where the love of God is shed abroad in the heart by the Holy Spirit, the law of love is written in the heart.

5. The soul of man has no one else, near or far from God, but as its will unites with God's will and works with it.

Sixty-Two

The Crowning Blessing of the New Covenant— Fellowship with God

*And I will be to them their God, and they shall be my
people: and they shall not teach every man his fellow-
citizen, and every one his brother, saying, Know the Lord:
for all shall know me, from the least to the greatest of them.*
—Hebrews 8:10–11

God created man to find his blessedness in Himself. This is
the nobility and the greatness of man, that he has a heart
capable of fellowship with God, a heart so great that nothing less than God can really satisfy it. This is held out to him as his
highest blessedness through eternity.

There is but one thing that can hinder the fellowship, and that
is sin. Where there is no sin, the creature lives in the Creator as
naturally as a bird in the air or a fish in the water. For this reason,
the two promises of the new covenant go together as cause and
effect: "I will write my law in their hearts," and, *"I will be to them*

287

a God, and they shall...know me." The deliverance from the evil, wandering heart will be followed by close personal access to God. *"They shall not teach every man his fellow-citizen, and every man his brother, saying, Know the Lord: for all shall know me, from the least to the greatest of them."*

Personal, direct fellowship with God: This is the crowning blessing of the new covenant to which the epistle to the Hebrews very specifically points the way. In Israel, only the priests could enter the Holy Place, and then they went out again to teach the people. Into the Most Holy, only the High Priest could come. In Christ, every believer has access to the Holiest of All. Christ has redeemed us, not to bring us to Himself but to bring us to God. He is the Door in which we are not to remain standing but through which we are to enter to God Himself, to His heart and His love. *"God, having of old time spoken unto the fathers in the prophets...hath at the end of these days spoken unto us in his Son"* (1:1–2); in Him, there is an immediate living fellowship with the living God. All that the epistle has to teach of the rending of the veil, and our boldness in the blood, and the entrance into the Holiest of All—it has all to do with this one thing: direct, personal, living fellowship with the living God. As the Minister of the true sanctuary, Jesus sends the Spirit to do the work He has in our hearts as Mediator of the covenant and to prepare us to enter the sanctuary. As Mediator of the covenant, He then reveals Himself more fully as the Minister of the sanctuary, who does indeed bring us near to God.

And how does He do this? In the way in which He Himself entered there: the way of obedience. *"I will put my laws into their mind, and on their heart also will I write them:...and they shall... know me"* (8:10–11). The law written on the heart is the condition of fellowship with God. Without holiness no man will see the Lord. (See Hebrews 12:14.) *"Blessed are the pure in heart: for they shall see God"* (Matthew 5:8). *"Thy will be done, as in heaven, so on earth"* (Matthew 6:10). To be brought by the heavenly High Priest within the veil and to dwell before God's face, we must learn to do

Andrew Murray

His will on earth as it is done in heaven. This is the true heavenly mindedness that renders us capable of fellowship with the God of heaven. Union with God's will was the way by which Jesus entered. Union with God's will is the way by which Jesus brings us in to the love and the joy of the Father.

And how, again, do we obtain this double blessedness—of the law written in the heart, and the entrance into God's presence in Jesus? It is God who must do it. It is He who swore to Abraham, *"Blessing I will bless thee"* (Hebrews 6:14). It is He who swore to our High Priest, *"Thou art a priest for ever"* (7:17). It is God Himself who will fulfill His oath. Jesus is not now on the throne to take the place of God, or to be to us *instead* of God. Truly, no; He brings us *to* God. Through Him we draw near to God that God may perfect His work in us. Our first access to God in the pardon of sin, before we even know what the access of abiding fellowship is, has this one sole object: that God may reveal His Son in us so that we look up to and love and serve the Father even as the Son did. And so the one thing required of us is that we bow ourselves and abide and live in deep dependence and humility before God. However clearly we see the blessed truth of the promises of the new covenant, however earnestly we desire them, however firmly we think we grasp them as faith, all will not avail—God Himself must do it. God Himself must admit us to His presence and make His face to shine upon us. And as for the path to this, God Himself must write His law in our hearts and give us the new nature in such power of the Holy Spirit that He works both to will and to do. God Himself must, by the Holy Spirit, so shed abroad His love in our hearts so that to love becomes as natural to us as it is for the dove to be gentle. God has promised, on His oath, to do this for us in Jesus, *"the surety of a better covenant"* (7:22). It is God who strengthens us mightily by His Spirit, then gives Christ to dwell in our hearts by faith; it is in God that we are rooted in love and then—this is the full entrance into His presence in the Holiest of All—filled with all the fullness of God.

Once again, how do we obtain this double blessedness of the law of God written in the heart and the presence of God filling our lives? There is no way but utterly ceasing from ourselves, dying to self, and waiting in absolute dependence and deep humility upon God. Christ's priesthood is not of earth but of heaven. All means and ordinances, all thoughts and purposes in man, are but shadows of the heavenly things. It is from God in heaven that the heavenly life must come, through Christ who brings us near to Him. And Christ cannot bring us near to God, cannot make our drawing near acceptable, in any other way than by working in our hearts a faith and love and obedience that are pleasing to Him—that is, by His fulfilling, as Mediator of the new covenant, its promises within us. This brings us to the true knowledge of God.

Chapter Notes...

1. If you would realize the need of absolute dependence upon God and His direct operation, I know not of anything that will be more helpful than to read what William Law says on humility, meekness, patience, and resignation to God's will, as the one only and infallible way to God.*

2. *"When he had made purification of sins, sat down on the right hand of the Majesty on high"* (1:3). The removal of sin is the path to God's presence with Christ and with us.

---

* See William Law, "The Spirit of Love," Part II, Dialogue 3. <http://www.ccel.org/l/law/love/Spirit_of_Love.txt>.

Sixty-Three

The Initial Blessing of the New Covenant— The Pardon of Sin

For I will be merciful to their iniquities. And their sins will I remember no more. In that he saith, "A new covenant," he hath made the first old. But that which is becoming old and waxeth aged is nigh unto vanishing away. —Hebrews 8:12–13

O f the blessings of the new covenant, the one that is here mentioned last, is in reality the first. *"For I will be merciful"*—this is what precedes and is the ground of the renewal of the heart and the fellowship with God. Pardon is the door; holiness of heart and life, the pathway; the presence of God, the blessedness of the Christian life. The first leads to the second, the first and second to the third. To live in God's presence and fellowship, two things must be clear: The thought of sin must be put away out of God's heart, and the love of sin must be put away out of our hearts. These two blessings are together secured in the new covenant. First, the

forgiveness of sins is so complete that He remembers them no more
forever; they never more enter into God's heart. And second, the
renewal of our hearts and wills is so complete that the law of God is
written there by the Holy Spirit so that the will of God is our will.

The three blessings—the pardon of sin, the purity of heart, and
the presence of God—are so joined that, as our views and our acceptance of one is feeble, our hold on the others will suffer. In Jesus,
the Mediator of the new covenant, they are offered and secured to
us in their fullness, in *"the power of an endless life"* (Hebrews 7:16).
But our experience of this depends upon our knowledge, our faith,
and our surrender. And it is because our understanding and acceptance and experience of the first two blessings is so defective that
our fellowship with God—our entrance into the holy presence and
our abiding there—is still so much in Old Testament failure. *"They
continued not"* (8:9). Let us try and realize this.

Take the first of the three covenant blessings: *"I will be merciful
to their iniquities. And their sins will I remember no more."* In more
than one respect, the Christian's thought of what this pardon is
may be defective. With some, it is nothing more than the remission
of punishment. They think only of acquittal; they know not that it
implies acceptance, complete restoration to the favor—to the heart
and the home—of the Father. They are content with pardon as the
escape from great danger; of the surrender to, and of the life abiding
in the love that pardoned—of these they know little. With others,
the thought of pardon is mostly connected with individual or daily
sin. They have no concept of the entire and eternal putting away of
sin out of God's sight and thought, which is assured to us in the
words: *"Their sins will I remember no more."* And with still others,
whose views may be more accurate, the pardon of God exercises
so little power because it has been accepted more with the mind
than the heart. They consent to and claim what God's Word says
of it, but they have never—mostly owing to the want of any deep
sense of sin or any powerful workings of the Holy Spirit—realized
the overwhelming glory of God's mercy as they came to Him to

receive from His own mouth the pardon from their sins. In all these cases, the further blessings are scarcely understood or sought; or, if claimed, their full meaning and power are never known.

It is even so with the second covenant blessing. There are not a few who know indeed what the greatness of God's pardoning love is who yet never reach out to claim, as equally sure, the greatness of His sanctifying grace. The necessity of daily sinning, the impossibility of living for one day without actual transgression, is such a deeply rooted conviction, and there is such confidence that God's Word teaches it, that the mind cannot for a moment enter into what the Word has said of the radical difference between the old covenant and the new in this respect. The confounding of the freedom from any sinful tendency, and freedom in the power of Christ's indwelling from actual sinning, even with the sinful tendency still remaining, is so universal that every attempt to press home the promise of the law written in the heart, in its contrast to the Old Testament life, is regarded as dangerous. The wonderful promise is leveled down to the ordinary experience of the ordinary Christian life. No wonder, then, that the crowning promise, *"They shall not teach every man his fellow-citizen, and every man his brother, saying, Know the Lord"* (8:11), with its direct teaching of the Holy Spirit and its direct fellowship with God through the Spirit, is neither valued nor claimed; instead, the entrance through the rent veil into the Holiest of All and the presence of God is postponed to another world.

Let us pray the Father to give us enlightened eyes of the heart, to know what is the hope of His calling, to a life in His love and will; and what are the riches of the glory of His inheritance in the saints—the direct and full access to His presence and fellowship; and what is the exceeding greatness of His power in us who believe, according to the working of His mighty power that He wrought in Christ when He raised Him from the dead and set Him on His own right hand. Let us believe that that exaltation of Christ out of the dead to His throne—and the assurance that that same mighty power works in us—means, even for this earth, a life of heavenly power and joy, and of holiness and happiness that has not yet entered into the heart for it to conceive. Jesus, the Priest-King on the throne, is the surety of the covenant. Let us, like Him, yield ourselves to that death to sin and to self, out of which God raised Him. Let us sink into the death of emptiness and nothingness and helplessness; let us, as dead, wait for the mighty operation of God. He who gave Jesus as Mediator of the new covenant, and Surety for its promises, will reveal Him, and fulfill them in us; will bring us in Him within the veil and give us our life there in the secret of His blessed presence.

Chapter Notes...

1. Pardon of sin is the door, the entrance to the Father's home. The law in the heart is the life and walk there, the fitness to draw near to God. Direct fellowship with God; this is the blessedness to be found in God's presence.

2. All the three blessings are in Him, the Surety of the covenant. In Him, our justification and the assurance that our sins no more come up before Him. In Him, our sanctification with the Holy Spirit breathing His will into our very hearts. In Him, our complete redemption, the fitness to dwell in God's presence forevermore.

THE POWER OF CHRIST'S BLOOD IN THE OPENING OF THE NEW SANCTUARY AND THE NEW COVENANT

Sixty-Four

The Holy Place and the Most Holy

[handwritten: =where I dwell! 3/6/18]

[handwritten right margin: rest unspeak-able joy oceans of love PEACE PAPA's face speak in detail and loving arms + smile + warmth]

Now even the first covenant had ordinances [handwritten: regulations] *of divine service* [handwritten: worship]*, and its sanctuary, a sanctuary of this world* [handwritten: earth]*. For there was a tabernacle prepared, the first* [handwritten: outer one]*, wherein were the candlestick, and the table, and the shewbread* [handwritten: sacred bread]*; which is called the Holy place. And after the* [handwritten: behind] *second veil, the tabernacle which is called the Holy of the holies; having a golden censer* [handwritten: altar of]*, and the ark of the covenant overlaid round about* [handwritten: all over] *with gold, wherein* [handwritten: in which] *was a golden pot holding the manna, and Aaron's rod that budded, and the tables of the covenant; and above it cherubim of glory overshadowing the mercy-seat; of which* [handwritten: but of these] *things we cannot now* ~~speak severally~~*. Now* [handwritten: when] *these things having been thus prepared* [handwritten: so]*, the priests go in continually into the first* [handwritten: outer] *tabernacle,* [handwritten: performing] ~~accomplishing~~ [handwritten: divine worship] *the services, but into the second the high priest* ~~alone~~*, once* [handwritten: only] *in the year, not without* [handwritten: taking] *blood, which he offer*~~eth~~ *for himself, and for the* ~~errors of the~~ [handwritten: ignorance] *people.*

—Hebrews 9:1–7 *[handwritten: sins of people committed in ignorance.]*

In chapter 7, the eternal priesthood of Jesus has been revealed
to us. In chapter 8, we have seen Him, as Priest seated on the
throne of heaven in His twofold work: He is the Minister of the
sanctuary in the heavens, and He is the Mediator of the covenant in
the heart of man on earth; we thus know the Priest and the sanctuary in which He ministers. We are now invited in this chapter to
look at the blood that He presents and what it effects. Up to this
point, the word *"blood"* had not been used; in this chapter, we have
it twelve times. In the first half (1–14), we have its efficacy in opening the Most Holy Place and in sprinkling our consciences to enter
there; then (15–22), in dedicating the covenant and cleansing all
connected with it; and after that again (23–28) in opening heaven
and putting away all sin.

The first portion begins with a description of the worldly
sanctuary, the tabernacle and its furniture, *"of which things,"* the
writer says, *"we cannot now speak severally,"* Just as he said in 8:1,
"The chief point is this: We have such a high priest," so here, too, in
speaking of the sanctuary, he has one great thought that he wishes
to press home. The tabernacle was so constructed by Moses, after
the heavenly pattern, to shadow forth one great truth; in that truth
lies the mystery and the glory of the New Testament, the power
and joy of the Christian life. That truth is the opening of the way
into the Holiest, the access into the presence of God.

We read: *"There was a tabernacle prepared, the first,...which is
called the Holy place. And after the second veil, the tabernacle which
is called the Holy of the holies....The priests go in continually into the
first tabernacle, accomplishing the services; but into the second the
high priest alone, once in the year, not without blood."* The one thing
the writer wished to direct our attention to is the difference and the
relation between the two compartments into which the tabernacle
was divided and the meaning of the veil that separated them.

The inner sanctuary was called the Holiest of All or, as it is
in Hebrew, the Holiness of Holinesses. It was the highest embodiment there could be of holiness; it was the place where God Most

Holy dwelt. His holy presence filled it. No man might enter there on pain of death but the high priest, and even he only once a year. In the Holy Place, separated from the Most Holy by a heavy veil, the priests entered and served. The truths embodied in the house thus made after a heavenly pattern were very simple. In the Most Holy, God dwelt, but man might not enter. In the Holy Place, man might enter to serve God, but God did not dwell there. The veil was the symbol of separation between a holy God and sinful man: They cannot dwell together. The tabernacle thus expressed the union of two apparently conflicting truths. God called man to come and worship and serve Him, and yet he might not come too near; the veil kept him at a distance. His worship in the tabernacle testified to his longing for the restoration to the fellowship with God he had lost in Paradise but also to his unfitness for it and his inability to attain it. The two truths find their reason and their harmony in the holiness of God, that highest attribute of the divine Being. In it, righteousness and love are combined. Love calls the sinner near; righteousness keeps him back. The Holy One bids Israel build Him a house in which He will dwell but forbids them entering His presence there. The entrance of the high priest once a year for a few moments was a faint foreshadowing that the time would come when access to the Holiest would be given. In the fullness of time, righteousness and love would be revealed in their perfect harmony in Him, in whom those types and shadows would find their fulfillment.

The first and second tabernacles are symbols of two degrees of the divine nearness, two stages of access to God's presence, two modes of fellowship with God, two ways of serving Him. The one, to which the high priest had access only once a year, is the promise of what would one day be in Christ, who was the nearer, the more direct and immediate approach into the presence and fellowship of God. The other is the symbol of the service of God as at a distance, with a veil between, without the full light of His countenance. The one thing the writer wanted us to learn is the difference between the two stages, and the way by which God leads us from the lower to the higher.

Chapter Notes...

1. *"Of which things we cannot now speak ~~severally~~,"* in detail, one by one. There is a time for doing this, too. But when souls are to be led on into the perfection of Christ and His work, we must turn then from the multiplicity of truths to the simplicity and unity of one truth: that Christ has opened heaven. Let this be our one question: What has the heavenly High Priest effected for me? Love from the Father + peace + rest + joy = LIFE. Dwell with Jesus in our Father's bosom.

2. I know what Christ has done. I need to know what He had to do. There was a Holy Place into which man might enter. There was a Most Holy into which he might not enter. The veil shut him out. And Christ's one work was to tear down that veil and give us the right and the fitness to enter, even to dwell, in that heretofore inaccessible place. The mystery of the rent veil, of the opened entrance into the Holiest, is the one thing we need to learn.

Sixty-Five

The Holy Spirit and the Way into the Holiest

The Holy Ghost this signifying, that the way into the holy place hath not yet been made manifest, while as the first tabernacle is yet standing; which is a parable for the time now present; according to which are offered both gifts and sacrifices that cannot, as touching the conscience, make the worshipper perfect, being only (with meats and drinks and divers washings) carnal ordinances, imposed until a time of reformation.
—Hebrews 9:8–10

We said that the Holiest of All, or as it is literally, the Holiness of Holinesses, was the very embodiment of the holiness of God, the place of His presence. The Holy Spirit specially bears the epithet *Holy* because He is the Bearer of the divine holiness to impart it to man—He is the Spirit of holiness. It will appear no more than natural that there should be a close connection between the sanctuary as the revelation of God's holiness and the Holy Spirit as the Revealer. This is what we are taught here: The whole construction of the tabernacle and the appointment of the high priest's entrance once a year was so ordered by the Holy Spirit as to be a great object lesson in which the truth was taught that, so long as the veil hung there, the way into the Holiest was not yet open.

"The Holy Ghost this signifying, that the way into the holy place hath not yet been made manifest." The words teach us that the truth about the way into the Holiest was entirely in the charge of the Holy Spirit. It was He who devised and revealed to Moses the heavenly pattern. It was He who ordered the veil as the token that the way was not open. It was He who, by the yearly entrance of the high priest, gave the prophecy that it would one day be opened. It was He who prepared a body for Him and later on filled Him who was to be the Opener of the way. It was He, the Eternal Spirit, through whom Christ offered Himself as the Sacrifice with whose blood He might enter in. It was He, the *"spirit of holiness"* (Romans 1:4), through whom Christ was raised from the dead and exalted to the throne of God. It was the Holy Spirit who, when the way had been opened, came out from the Holiest of All on the day of Pentecost to impart to men the life and the power of the glorified Christ. It is He who today still presides over the way into the Holiest, leading in all who are willing to dwell there.

The lesson for our spiritual lives is one of deep suggestiveness. The Holy Spirit has charge of the way into the Holiest—both while that way is not yet manifest and when it is opened up. He alone has the knowledge and the power to reveal this mystery. For it is still a spiritual mystery. Though everything that Scripture reveals of it can be studied and understood by any man of intelligence—and a clear understanding can be formed or an exposition given of what it means—the living power of the truth, the actual experience of entering in through the opened veil into the presence of God, can only be communicated and wrought in the life within by the Holy Spirit. The Holy Spirit alone can reveal in the heart what the way means, both where it is not yet made manifest and where it is. He can work in a man the deep conviction that he does, or does not know, the true nearness of God in his own experience.

Andrew Murray

We have seen that the two compartments of the tabernacle represent two degrees of nearness to God, two dispensations of God's grace, or two stages in the Christian life: a lower and a higher. Into the Holy Place, every priest might come daily to do there the service God had appointed. Into the Most Holy, he might not enter until Christ had opened it for all believers. Many believers never in experience enter into this life of the inner sanctuary, the more complete and abiding nearness to God. They have, in the outer court, seen the altar and received the pardon of sin; they have entered upon the service of God; they seek to do His will, but the joy of His presence as their abiding portion they know not. And very often, they do not know that there is a better life, that there is an entering within the veil, a real dwelling in the secret of God's presence; they need the Holy Spirit to signify to them, to work in them, the conviction *"that the way into the holy place hath not yet been made manifest"* to them. They need—oh, let us, if we have not yet entered in, let us give ourselves to pray for—the discovery that there is an inner chamber; that there is still the veil of the flesh, the life of the carnal Christian, that prevents access; that only the possession of the Pentecostal blessing, the Spirit who came from the throne when Jesus had rent the veil and who reveals Him and links man to Him, is what will bring us in.

When He has signified this to us, and we yield ourselves to the full conviction that we are still outside the veil, and strong desire has been awakened at any cost to enter in, then the same Spirit—who, at Pentecost, when our High Priest had just entered with His blood, came forth from the Holiest of All—will come to us in power and bring us in, too. As He reveals Jesus Himself as having gone in for us, and as He makes us willing for that perfect surrender in which nothing less than the direct and continual fellowship with God can satisfy us, our hearts will open to the wondrous mystery that what is impossible to men is possible with God; and that God, of His free grace and in His mighty power, does indeed grant it to His child, even now in Christ, to dwell with Him in unbroken communion.

O God, let the Holy Spirit witness to every reader who needs it that the way into the Holiest *"hath not yet been made manifest"* to him; and to everyone who is ready for it, that in Christ the way into the Holiest is indeed open. With Pentecost, and the participation it brought of the Spirit of the glorified Jesus, began true Christianity, as a ministration of the Spirit. The enjoyment of the Pentecostal gift—as the communication of the heavenly life and the abiding presence of Jesus, the glorified One—in all its Pentecostal freshness and fullness is the only power that can enable us to live within the veil, in the living experience that the way into the Holiest has now been opened. It is the Spirit dwelling in us who will fit us for dwelling in God's presence.

Chapter Notes...

1. Should we any longer fear and doubt? The Father in heaven beckoning us into His presence; the Son—our Brother, Prophet, Priest, and King—pointing to the way He opened for us; and the Holy Spirit within us to be our light and strength, to enable us to walk in that way: Should we fear? No, let us hear the voice that gives the power: "Rise up and walk. Enter in."

2. Do get it very clear that the two compartments are two stages in religious life and worship and service. The one is when the power of the rent veil is not yet understood, and the other is where the Holy Spirit has brought us in.

Sixty-Six

The Opening Up of the Holiest

*But Christ having come a high priest of the good things
to come, through the greater and more perfect tabernacle,
not made with hands, that is to say, not of this creation,
nor yet through the blood of goats and calves, but through
His own blood, entered in once for all, into the holy place,
having obtained eternal redemption!*
—Hebrews 9:11–12

I n studying the meaning of the Mosaic ritual, there are specifically four things through which the Holy Spirit shadows
forth to us the mysteries of redemption, the good things
to come of the new dispensation that Israel was to look for.
These are the priest, the sanctuary, the blood, and the way into
the Holiest. We have these four things here together. There is
Christ, *"a high priest of the good things to come"*; there is *"the
greater and more perfect tabernacle"*; there is *"his own blood"*;
and there is His entering *"into the holy place."* As we apprehend
the power of these things, we will know the meaning of His
"having obtained eternal redemption." Let us hear what the Holy

303

Spirit speaks of the opening up of the Holiest and of the wonderful path in which this was effected.

The writer used a very remarkable expression: *"Christ...through the greater and more perfect tabernacle,...entered in once for all into the holy place."* The two compartments of the sanctuary are the symbols of two states of life, the two degrees of fellowship with God. The epistle teaches us that Christ knew this difference in His own life experience; in entering into and opening up the higher one for us, He passed through the lower. He entered into the Holiest *"through the greater and more perfect tabernacle,"* through the experience of that spiritual reality of which the tabernacle was the shadow. The Holiest is God's immediate presence; the Holy Place, a drawing near to God with a veil between. The flesh—man's fallen nature in its weakness and its exposure to all the consequences of sin—is the veil. Christ has dedicated for us a new and living way through the veil, that is to say, His flesh. When He came in the likeness of sinful flesh, that life in flesh—with its liability to temptation and its weakness, with its possibility of suffering and death, with its life of faith and prayer and tears, with its need of learning obedience and being made perfect, with its subjection to the law and its curse—was the Holy Place, the first tabernacle through which He had to pass to have the veil rent in His death, so to enter in and appear before God. Christ lived with His people in the Old Testament; He passed through the first tabernacle as a spiritual experience in perfect reality; it was only with that Resurrection and Ascension that the New Testament began.

Yes, Christ passed from the Holy Place into the Holiest of All. When He died, the veil was rent in two; the two compartments were made one. The priest who was in the Holy Place could see, could enter into, the Holiest. All that was in the Holiest, the light of God's presence between the cherubim, could shine unhindered into the Holy Place. In Christ, the veil of the flesh was rent asunder and taken away. The free access to God was opened up, not only as a thing of right and title in virtue of our pardon but also as a thing of power and living reality. *"Ye are not in the flesh, but in the spirit, if so be that the Spirit of God dwelleth in you"* (Romans 8:9). When the veil was rent and Christ entered in, the two abodes— what had been the dwelling of God and what had been the dwelling of the priests—were thrown into one. The eyes and the hearts of men might freely and boldly look up and rise up and greet their God and Father; in Christ, they had their place before Him. All the light and love and holiness of the Most Holy shone into the Holy Place. The Spirit of God, as He was received by Christ from God the Father on His ascension, passed down into the worshipers. The Pentecostal gift brought down from above, the higher life into which the blessed Son had entered; the Holy Spirit made the light and love and holiness of the inner sanctuary not only a vision and a revelation but a possession and an experience.

The veil of the flesh has been rent; Christ has entered once for all, having obtained everlasting redemption; the dwelling of God and man has been thrown into one; the Spirit of heaven has been given to signify to us, and to give us the living experience, that the way into the Holiest has been made manifest. Our entering in, our dwelling in God's presence in the light and nearness and holiness of the Most Holy, is a spiritual, a heavenly reality. It can only be apprehended by the tender, by the perfect, conscience that the Holy Spirit gives to him who is willing to give up all to be saved completely, by the perfect whose senses are exercised to discern good and evil. But to all who are willing to pass through the rent veil of Christ's flesh, to die with Him as He died and live with Him as He lived, the Holy Spirit will show it; the way into the Holiest is opened up.

"Christ having come...entered in once for all." Four thousand years after man's loss of fellowship with God in Paradise had to pass. For fifteen hundred years, the veil had to hang with its solemn injunction not to draw near. For thirty-three years, the Son of God Himself had to live on this side of the veil. But at length, once for all and forever, the way was opened. Fear not, O Christian to whom these things appear too high, fear not. Be faithful; through faith

and longsuffering, we inherit the promises. Persevere in the faith of what Christ has accomplished once for all. He entered in—the Second Adam, in whom our life is and whose members we are. Persevere in the faith of the infinite meaning of that great transaction. And to you, too, there will come a day when, in your experience, you will enter in and go out no more forever.

Chapter Notes...

1. This entering in and opening up of the Holiest was solely and entirely on our behalf, that we might live and serve there. Therefore, the practical part of the epistle commences at once; *"Having therefore, brethren, boldness to enter into the holy place... let us draw near"* (10:19, 22). That is the summing up of the whole epistle. God is not content that we serve Him with a veil between. Let us know clearly which of the two positions we occupy as Christians—within or still outside the veil.

2. "After I had lived for thirteen years in the Holy Place, seeking to serve God there, it pleased Him who dwells between the cherubim, to call me to pass through the veil and to enter the Holiest of All, through the blood of Jesus."*

---
* Author unknown.

Sixty-Seven

The Power of Christ's Blood to Open the Holiest

And not

Nor yet through the blood of goats and calves, but through his own blood, He entered in once for all into the holy place, having obtained eternal redemption.
—Hebrews 9:12

T*hrough his own blood."* We have seen our great High Priest on the throne of God, a Priest after the order of Melchizedek, in the power of an endless life. When He rose from the dead and ascended into heaven, it was according to that working of the strength of His might whereby God had raised Him from the dead and set Him at His own right hand. He entered God's presence as the living One who was dead; and behold, He lives forevermore. And yet, strange to say, it was not enough that He should present Himself at the gate of heaven as the Conqueror of death and hell and ask admission. He had to take with Him His own blood, as it had been shed upon earth, as the power by which alone, as the Surety of sinners, He could claim access to the presence of God. *"Through his own blood, [Christ] entered in once for all into the holy place."*

And what does this phrase, *"His own blood,"* mean? To Moses God had said that He gave the blood upon the altar to be an atonement, *"for the life of the flesh is in the blood"* (Leviticus 17:11). That is, the living blood in the body is the life. And the shed blood? That means death. More than that, it means an unnatural, a violent, death. There are only two ways in which this unnatural bloodshed comes: by malice or by justice. We have the two together in the words: *"Whoso sheddeth man's blood, by man shall his blood be shed"* (Genesis 9:6). In the death of Christ, the malice of men and the righteousness of God met. He was slain, a sacrifice to the evil passions of men, because He resisted unto blood, striving against sin. He was slain, a sacrifice unto God, because He was the Lamb of God who takes away the sin of the world. (See John 1:29.) Death is inseparably connected with sin and the curse that God pronounced upon it. When Jesus, as the Second Adam, tasted death for all; when, in Gethsemane, He pled to His Father with strong crying and tears that the cup might pass from Him; when, on the cross, He cried, *"My God, my God, why hast thou forsaken me?"* (Matthew 27:46), He tasted death in all its bitterness—both as the terrible fruit of sin, the revelation of what sin is in its very nature, and as the penalty God had attached to it. He died, as Scripture says, *"the just for the unjust"* (1 Peter 3:18 KJV); He bore our sins; His blood was shed for us; He gave His life as a ransom for many. (See Matthew 20:28.) And the word *"blood"* in this epistle includes all that is meant by the death of Christ: The blood is the expression and embodiment of His obedience unto death, of His death for our sins, of the atonement that He made for us as the victim on the altar, as our Substitute.

It is this blood now of whose power our epistle says such wondrous things. It was in *"the blood of the eternal covenant"* (Hebrews 13:20) that God brought again our Lord Jesus from the dead; the blood was the power of the Resurrection. It was through His blood that He cleansed the heavenly things themselves and entered the Holiest on our behalf. In those heavenly places, our sins were in God's book; our sins had, as a thick cloud, darkened God's presence.

For the sake of the blood, the sin was blotted out, and access was given to Him—and in Him to us—to appear before the very face of God. And now, in the vision of the heavenly glory to which he has given us access, as we have it later in the epistle, we find in heaven not only God as the Judge of all, and Christ as the Mediator of the new covenant, but also *"the blood of sprinkling that speaketh better than that of Abel"* (12:24). Everywhere we see beside and along with Jesus Christ, the living One Himself—in His resurrection, in His entering heaven, in His sitting on the throne—as a separate existence and power, the blood, the symbol of the death in which we have our ransom and redemption.

"Through his own blood." Let us especially note how the blood is connected with the heavenly priesthood of Christ. We are too apt to think only of the fulfillment of the type of Aaron, the bloodshed on earth. The epistle does not speak of it. Where it mentions the blood, it is in connection with the Resurrection and the entrance into heaven, as it works in *"the power of an endless life"* (7:16). It is as the Holy Spirit reveals this to the soul—the heavenly power of the blood as ministered by our Melchizedek, the Minister of the heavenly sanctuary—that we see what a power that blood must have, as so sprinkled on us from heaven, in the power of the Holy Spirit, at once to give us a real, actual, living access into the presence of God.

"His own blood." I know of no word in the Bible or in human speech that contains such mysteries! In it are concentrated the mysteries of the Incarnation, in which our God took flesh and blood; of the obedience unto death, in which the blood was shed; of the love that passes knowledge, which purchased us with His own blood; of the victory over every enemy and the everlasting redemption; of the Resurrection and the entrance into heaven; of the atonement and the reconciliation and the justification that came through it; of the cleansing and perfecting of the conscience; of the sprinkling of the heart and sanctifying the people. Through that blood, Christ entered *"once for all"* into heaven; through that blood, we enter,

too, and have our home in the Holiest of All. As the Holy Spirit from heaven, dwelling in us, imparts to us the boldness that the blood gives and the love into which it opens the way, our whole inner being will be brought under its power, and the cleansing of the blood in its full extent will be our experience.

Chapter Notes...

1. *"As in heaven, so on earth"* (Matthew 6:10). You have more interest than you think in knowing what the blood has wrought in heaven. As you enter by the Spirit into its power there, will your faith to receive its power within you.

2. The inner sanctuary—deeper, nearer in to God. He who seeks after this will have the inner sanctuary opened within himself. To such a one, a deepening sense of the life of God in the soul and of the law within the heart will be given to the inner life, in the inward parts.

3. There are two aspects of Christ's death in Scripture—that of atonement and that of fellowship. He died for us, for our sin, that we might not die. What our Substitute did in bearing the curse of sin we cannot do and we need not do. He died to sin, and we died with Him and in Him. The blood is the divine expression for the former aspect: His own blood is the power and the worth of His death taken up and presented and forever preserved in its energy and action before God. The sprinkling with the blood includes the transition to the second aspect. As the blood, as a heavenly reality, through the Holy Spirit works in us, the very disposition that animated Jesus in the shedding of it will be imparted to us.

4. Christ can bring us into the Holiest in no other way than He went in Himself: *"through his own blood."* Oh, seek to know the power of Christ's blood.

Sixty-Eight

The Power of Christ's Blood to Cleanse the Conscience

For if the blood of goats and bulls, and the ashes of a heifer sprinkling them that have been defiled, sanctify unto the cleanness of the flesh: how much more shall the blood of Christ, who through the eternal Spirit offered himself without blemish unto God, cleanse your conscience from dead works to serve the living God?
—Hebrews 9:13–14

The high priest went into the Holiest once a year, not without blood. Christ, the High Priest of good things to come, entered the greater and more perfect Holiest of All *"through his own blood"* (Hebrews 9:12), opening up to us in very deed the way into God's presence. The entrance of the high priest on earth effected a certain external and temporary cleansing and liberty of access. The blood of Christ, which had power to open heaven, is able to effect, in its heavenly, eternal power, a heavenly and a divine cleansing in the heart.

To illustrate this, we are referred to Numbers 19 and the cleansing with the ashes of the heifer. Anyone who had touched a dead body was unclean and had to be excluded from the camp. To meet the need, the ashes of a heifer that had been sacrificed, and of which the blood had been sprinkled toward the tabernacle, were mingled with water and sprinkled on the one who had been defiled. The sprinkling restored him to his place and privileges; with a clear conscience he could now take part in the life and worship of God's people. And the question is asked, If the blood of a sacrifice had such power, *"how much more shall the blood of Christ...cleanse your conscience from dead works to serve the living God?"* The infinite efficacy of Christ's blood, and the infinite blessedness of the cleansing it effects, can only be measured by what that blood really is.

The power of Christ's blood consists in two things: The one element that gives the blood its value is the holy obedience of which its outpouring was the proof—the blood of Christ *"who through the eternal Spirit offered himself without blemish unto God."* He came to live the life of man, such as God had meant Him to be in creating Him. He gave up His will to God; He pleased not Himself but sought only God's pleasure; He yielded His whole life that God might reveal Himself in it as He pleased; He offered Himself unto God. He took and filled the place the creature was meant to fill. And that, without spot or blemish. His self-sacrifice was complete and perfect. And His blood, even as the blood of a man, was inexpressibly precious in God's sight. It was the embodiment of a perfect obedience. The other element is that the Eternal Spirit was in the life of that blood. It was *"through the eternal Spirit* [he] *offered himself."* It was the Word that became flesh, the eternal Son of God who was made man. It was the life of God that dwelt in Him. That Life gave His blood, each drop of it, an infinite value. The blood of a man is of more worth than that of a sheep. The blood of a king or a great general is counted of more value than hundreds of common soldiers. The blood of the Son of God! It is in vain that the mind seeks for some expression of its value; all we can say is that it is His own blood, the precious blood of the Son of God!

It was this twofold infinite worth of the blood that gave it such mighty power—first, in opening the grave and then, in opening heaven. It was this that gave it the victory over all the powers of death and hell beneath and gave Him the victor's place on high on the throne of God. And now, when that blood from out of the heavenly sanctuary is sprinkled on the conscience by the heavenly High Priest, how much more—with what an infinitely effectual cleansing!—must our consciences be cleansed.

We know what conscience is. It tells us what we are. Conscience deals not only with past merit or guilt but also with present integrity or falsehood. A conscience fully cleansed with the blood of Christ, fully conscious of its cleansing power, has the sense of guilt and demerit removed to an infinite distance. And no less is it delivered from that haunting sense of insincerity and double-heartedness, which renders boldness of access to God an impossibility. It can look up to God without the shadow of a cloud. The light of God's face, to which the blood gave our Surety access, shines clear on the conscience and, through it, on the heart. The conscience is not a separate part of our hearts or inner natures that can be in a different state from what the whole is. By no means. Just as a sensibility to bodily evil pervades the whole body, so the conscience is the sense that pervades our whole spiritual nature and at once notices and reports what is wrong or right in our state. Hence it is that when the conscience is cleansed or perfected, the heart is cleansed and perfected, too. And so it is in the heart that the power the blood had in heaven is communicated here on earth. The blood that brought Christ into God's presence brings us and our whole inner beings there, too.

Oh, let us realize it. The power of the blood in which Christ entered heaven is the power in which He enters our hearts. The infinite sufficiency it has with God to meet His holy requirements is its sufficiency to meet the requirements of our hearts and lives. It is the blood of the covenant. Its three great promises—pardon and peace in God's forgetting sin; purity and power in having the law of life in our hearts; and the presence of God set open to us—are not only secured to us by the blood, but the blood has its part, too, in communicating them. In the power of the Holy Spirit, the blood effects a mighty, divine cleansing, full of heavenly life and energy. The Spirit that was in Christ when He shed the blood makes us partakers of its power. His victory over sin, His perfect obedience, His access to the Father—the soul that fully knows the cleansing of the blood in its power will know these blessings, too.

Chapter Notes...

1. The blood that cleanses my conscience is the blood that gave Christ access into the Holiest. If I truly desire, if I know and honor and trust the blood, it will give me access, too.

2. How completely every vestige of an evil conscience can be taken away and kept away by the redeeming power of this precious blood! Let us believe that our High Priest, Whose entrance into the sanctuary and Whose ministry there is all in the power of the blood, will make it true to us.

3. This cleansing is what is elsewhere spoken of as Christ's washing us in His blood. A piece of linen that is to be washed is steeped and saturated until every stain is taken out. As we in faith and patience allow the blood to possess our whole inner beings, we will know what it means that it washes whiter than snow.

Sixty-Nine

Through the Eternal Spirit

How much more shall the blood of Christ, who through the
eternal Spirit offered himself without blemish unto God,
cleanse your conscience from dead works
to serve the living God?
—Hebrews 9:14

O ne might well ask for the reason why the blood of Christ, which has had such infinite power in conquering sin and death and in opening heaven to Christ and to us, does not exercise a mightier influence even in earnest Christians, in cleansing our hearts and lifting us into a life in the joy of God's presence. The first answer must be that we seek too little for a real insight into its divine and infinite worth. The blood of the heavenly Son, shed in the power of the Eternal Spirit, could not but again return heavenward; as God's Spirit leads us by faith to gaze on its power in heaven, and to see how through all heaven its power is manifest, we will learn to expect and to receive its working to keep us in God's presence, in a power above all that thought can conceive. The same Eternal Spirit, through whom the blood-shedding took place, will effect in us the blood-sprinkling, too, and make us indeed partakers of what it has accomplished in God's presence above.

This is a lesson of the utmost consequence. If the blood is His who offered Himself to God through the Eternal Spirit; if it is in the power and life of that Spirit that the blood was brought into heaven; and if it now has its place there, we may be sure that that Spirit will ever work with and in that blood. *"There are three who bear witness, the Spirit, and the water, and the blood"* (1 John 5:8). The Spirit and the blood must and will ever go together. We must not limit our faith in the power of the blood in our hearts to what we can understand. Our faith must ever be enlarging, to expect that the Holy Spirit, according to His hidden but almighty and uninterrupted working, can maintain the heavenly efficacy of the blood in a way that is, to us, inconceivable. Just as Christ is the visible revelation on earth and in heaven of the invisible God, so the Holy Spirit again is the communication of the life and redemption of the unseen Christ. The Holy Spirit is the power of the inner life. Within us, down in the depths of our being inaccessible to ourselves, He is able, as the Eternal Spirit, to maintain in those who yield to Him the divine power of the blood to cleanse from sin and to give abiding access to the presence of God. Let him who would know to the full, the mighty, the divine, and the inexpressible power and blessing that the blood each moment can bring in Him remember that it was through the Eternal Spirit it was shed.

In connection with this, there is still another lesson. The Spirit not only applies the power of the blood but, in doing so, He reveals its spiritual meaning. The blood has its value not from the mere act of physical suffering and death but from the inner life and disposition that animated Christ in shedding it. It is the blood of the Lamb who *"offered himself without blemish unto God"* with which our hearts are brought into a divine and living contact. Self-offering and self-sacrifice were the dispositions of which the blood was the expression and from which alone it had its worth. Where the Eternal Spirit communicates the power of the blood, He communicates this disposition.

Christ humbled Himself and became obedient to death. Therefore, as the Lamb of God who gave His blood, He was the embodiment of meekness and humility and submissive surrender to God's

Andrew Murray

will. It was our pride and self-will that was the very root and life of sin in us; as we are washed in the blood of the Lamb, His spirit of meekness and submissiveness and obedience will work in us because the same Eternal Spirit, through which the blood was shed, applies it in our hearts. We know what it means to wash our clothes in water, how they are plunged into it and saturated with it until the water carries off all defilement. The blood of Jesus Christ cleanses from all sin because the Eternal Spirit imparts the very life and power of which that precious blood-shedding was the outcome and the fruit. This is the power that cleanses the conscience from dead works to serve the living God. It is not the blood only, as shed upon earth and as the first object of our faith for pardon, but also the blood as shed through the Eternal Spirit and glorified in the spirit life of heaven—it is this that brings us truly into the inner sanctuary, and empowers us to serve Him as the living God. "As nothing but the Eternal Spirit could have overcome or redeemed fallen nature, as Christ took it upon Him, so nothing can possibly overcome or redeem the fallen soul or body of any child of Adam, but that same overcoming and redeeming Spirit, really living and acting in it, in the same manner as it did in the humanity of Christ."*

We live in the dispensation of the Spirit—the Spirit of God's Son, who has been sent for this into our hearts. It is the dispensation of the inner life, in which we are brought into the inner sanctuary, the secret of His presence, and the inner sanctuary is found within us—in that secret inner place that none but God's Spirit can search out. In that hidden depth is the house God has prepared for Himself; there, in the inner man, the Holy Spirit will reveal, in a way that sense and reason cannot apprehend, the power of Christ's blood to cleanse and bring God near. Oh, let us believe the infinite mysteries with which we are surrounded. And above all, this mystery, too—that within us, the blood of Christ, the Lamb of God, that mystery of mysteries, is being applied and kept in full action by the Eternal Spirit, cleansing us and revealing God's presence in us.

---

* Author unknown.

Chapter Notes...

1. What a mystery! What blessedness! A heart sprinkled with the blood of the Son of God! To walk before God day by day with the blood of His Son upon us! To know that the Lamb of God sees us washed in His own blood! Oh, we need—let us ask—the Eternal Spirit to make all this clear to us.

2. If our faith is only to believe what our reason can make clear to us, then no wonder the power of the blood effects so little. Let us have faith, not in what we understand, but let us have faith in God, and the heavenly, the inexpressibly glorious realities, of the blood and Spirit of the Son.

3. What a tender, careful, holy fear comes upon a soul that lives in the full and living consciousness of this blessed reality—a heart sprinkled with the blood of the Lamb.

4. Beware of trying to comprehend all the blood means or of being discouraged when you fail to do so. The blood in heaven is a divine and inscrutable mystery. Be content to believe in its efficacy. When the Holy Spirit comes into the heart in power, He applies the blood in a power far beyond what we can think or understand.

Seventy

The Power of the Blood to Fit for the Service of the Living God

How much more shall the blood of Christ, who through the
eternal Spirit offered himself without blemish unto God,
cleanse your conscience from dead
works to serve the living God?
—Hebrews 9:14

We must not regard the cleansing in the blood of Christ as the end, the final aim, of redemption. It is only the beginning, the means to a higher end—the fitness for the service of the living God. It is the restoration to the fellowship of Him who has life and gives life. The blood gives cleansing *"from dead works,"* the works of the law and of self with its own efforts; it brings us into a living relation to the living God. God and His fellowship, a life in His love and service, the living God and the enjoyment of His presence—this is the aim of redemption.

"The living God"! This name was used in the Old Testament as a contrast to the dead idols of the heathen. In the New Testament, it points us to the danger of our forming an image of God, not in wood or stone, but in our minds and imaginations—a thought-image—in which there is neither life nor truth. What we need first of all in religion is that we believe that God is and that our faith realizes Him as the living One, who is all that He is in the power of an infinite life and energy. He is *"the living God"*! He speaks and hears. He feels and acts. He has the power to make us know that He is near to us and that He receives us when we come near to Him. The knowledge of the living God is the ground of a living faith, a living fellowship, a living service. As the living God, He is all, and does all and fills all—the ever-present, ever-working God.

"To serve the living God"! The glory of the creature is to serve God, to be a vessel in which He can pour His fullness, a channel through which He can show forth His glory, an instrument for working out His purposes. This was what man was created for in the image of God. The whole object of redemption is to bring us back to a life in the living service of God. It is for this that the Holiest of All was opened to us by the blood as the place of service. It is for this that our consciences are cleansed in the blood, as the fitness for service. A life in the Holiest of All is a life in which everything is done under the sense of God's glory and presence, and to His glory; it is a life that has no object but the service of God.

It was thus with the priests in Israel. They were set apart by the sprinkling of blood. (See Exodus 29:19–20.) The object of this was to fit them *"to stand before the LORD to minister unto him, and to bless in his name"* (Deuteronomy 10:8). One great reason why many Christians never enter into the full joy and power of redemption, into the life within the veil, is that they seek it for themselves. Let us beware lest we seek the access into the Holiest, the joy of unclouded fellowship with God, the power of the blood to cleanse, only for the sake of our advance in holiness or in happiness. The whole appointment of the sanctuary and the priests was that there might be men who could come before God to minister to Him and then go out and bless their fellowmen. Christ entered through His blood within the veil, to go and serve; to be a minister of the sanctuary in the power of the blood, by which He could cleanse others and admit them, too, within the veil. To know the power of the blood to cleanse and admit within the veil, and to give us part in the priests' ministry of blessing men— this will come as we seek it as fitness to serve the living God.

"How much more shall the blood of Christ...cleanse your conscience from dead works to serve the living God?" The cleansing is for service. There was a great difference between the people in the outer court and the priests within the tabernacle. The former saw the blood sprinkled on the altar and trusted for forgiveness; the blood was not applied to their persons. The priests were sprinkled with the blood; that gave them access to the sanctuary to serve God there. We still have outer-court Christians, who look at Calvary and trust for forgiveness but know nothing of the access to God that the more direct and powerful application of the blood from heaven by the Holy Spirit gives. Oh, let us give ourselves to be priests, wholly separated to the service of God, wholly given up to God, for Him to work in us and through us what perishing men need; our consecration to this service will urge us mightily to claim an ever mightier experience of the blood because we will feel that nothing less than a full entrance into, and a true abiding in God's presence, can fit us for doing God's work. The more we see and approve that the object of the cleansing must only be for service, the more will we see and experience that the power for service is only in the cleansing.*

---

* "The blood contains that which makes white (Revelation 7:14). Not only the man, but his garments, are made white. This is more than cleansing. It is the Word used regarding Christ's transfiguration garments (Matthew 17:2); the angel robes (Matthew 28:3); the heavenly clothing (Revelation 4:4); the judgment throne (Revelation 20:11), whiter than snow, white as the garments of Christ. What potency, what excellency, what virtue does this blood contain! How it beautifies! How it glorifies!" —H. Bonar

"How much more shall the blood...cleanse...from dead works to serve the living God?" If we experience in ourselves, or in those around us, that there is little of the power and presence of the living God in our religious service, we have here the reason. If we find that in that service dead works still prevail and that in prayer and preaching, in home life and work around us, the duties of the religious life are performed without the power of the life and Spirit of God, let us learn the lesson—it is only the effectual cleansing, through the Eternal Spirit, of the blood that has been taken into the Holiest, that can fit us to serve the living God. That blood, witnessed to by the Holy Spirit, brings us into the Holiest and makes God to us a living God! That blood brings the life of the Holiest into our hearts, cleanses our consciences from every dead work— from every attempt and every hope to do anything in our own strength—gives the consciousness that we are now ransomed and set free and empowered from heaven to serve the God of heaven in the power of a life that comes from heaven. The blood of Christ does indeed cleanse us to serve the living God!

Chapter Notes...

1. How vain it would have been for anyone to seek the priestly consecration with blood and the entrance into the sanctuary if he were not to do the priest's service. Let us give up the vain attempt. Let us seek the power of the blood to serve the living God as His ministers to our fellowmen. The whole inward life of our High Priest, which He imports to us, consisted of these two things: It was a life in the will of God and in self-sacrificing love to men.

2. The priests honored the blood sprinkled on them by boldly entering the tabernacle. Oh, let us honor the blood of the Lamb by believing that it gives the power for a life in the Holiest, in the service of the living God!

3. Conscience tells me what I must think of myself. The blood tells me what God thinks of me. A conscience cleansed with

the blood is a conscience that glories in this—that in holiness and in sincerity of God, we behave ourselves in the world.

4. Oh, to realize it! Christ went into the Holiest, not for Himself, but for us. And we go in, too, by His blood and in His Spirit, not only for ourselves but for others.

Seventy-One

The Power of Christ's Death Ratifying the Covenant and the Testament

15 reason
And for this cause he is the mediator of a new covenant,
so that a *death having taken place for the redemption of*
since has committed
the transgressions that were under the first covenant,
those
they that have been called *may receive the promise of the*
covenant
eternal inheritance. 16 *For where a testament is, there must of*
one who
necessity be the death of him that *made it.* 17 *For a* testament
valid covenant
is of force *where there hath been death: for doth it ever avail*
when men are dead, *while he that made it liveth?*
for it is never in force
while the one who made it —**Hebrews 9:15–17**
lives.

Y
ou remember how, in chapter 8, we found two names given
to our Lord Jesus, indicating the twofold work He does, with
God in heaven and in our hearts on earth. As *"a minister of
the sanctuary"* (8:2), He is in God's presence, ministering the grace
of the sanctuary to us and giving us the enjoyment of that presence. As Mediator of the new covenant (see verse 6), He works in

our hearts on earth, giving God's law within us, as the law of the Spirit of His own life, and fitting us for the worship and fellowship of the sanctuary. In the first half of chapter 9, we have had the exposition of how Christ, as *"minister of the sanctuary"* (8:2), opened and entered into it through His own blood and there ministers the everlasting redemption. He does it by cleansing our consciences, in the power of that blood that has prevailed to open heaven, to enter in boldly and freely to serve the living God. In the second half of the chapter, the author now proceeds to speak of Christ as the Mediator of the new covenant. With the same blood with which He dedicated the sanctuary, He has dedicated the covenant, too.

"And for this cause he is the mediator of a new covenant, that a death having taken place for the redemption of the transgressions that were under the first covenant, they that have been called may receive the promise of the eternal inheritance." The word *"promise"* reminds of what was said of the *"better covenant, which hath been enacted upon better promises"* (8:6). The word *"inheritance"* is of the oath of God and the inheriting of the promise through faith. The word *"eternal"* is of all we have heard of our Melchizedek, as a Priest forever, who does all His work in the power of an endless life. Christ has become a Mediator of this new covenant, that the promise of the eternal inheritance, that blessed heritage of eternal life even now made manifest in the promises of the law written in the heart and full personal fellowship with God, might be our portion; it is the work of the Mediator to ensure our inheriting the promises. But this could not be until a death had taken place for the redemption of the transgressions that were under the old covenant. The first covenant had its sanction in God's appointment; the new covenant could not take its place until the first had met with full satisfaction for its claims. There was no way for this, for the redemption of the transgressions it had seen and condemned, but by a death. All the writer had meant in speaking of the blood he then included in the expression, *"the death."* The change of the expression reminds us how the two are one. The blood is through the death; the death

is for the blood. The bloodshed and the death are the redemption and the ransom that, by sin-bearing and atonement, deliver us from transgressions and their power. All the transgressions of the old covenant had been treasured up; the death of Christ gave satisfaction to all that that covenant could claim and brought release. So the Mediator of the new covenant begins an entirely new economy, with sin put away by the sacrifice of Himself and an open path to the beginning of a new life in the favor and power of God.

Now follow two verses that have caused no little difficulty. In English, we have for one word in Greek two words of entirely different meaning. The word "covenant," a treaty between two parties, and "testament," the last will by which one party leaves his property to another, are the same in Greek. Through the whole of Scripture, the word may always best be translated "covenant," with the exception of the two following verses; here, the argument renders the meaning "testament" or "will" necessary. *"For where a testament is, there must of necessity be the death of him that made it. For a testament is of force where there hath been death: for doth it ever avail while he that made it liveth?"* It is as if the author turned aside for a moment, led to it by what he had just said of them who receive the eternal inheritance, to use the other meaning of the Greek word in order to prove how, in every connection, a death is indispensable. He had spoken of Christ's death as the sacrifice by which the covenant was ratified. To confirm the thought, it's as if he added, "When one who has made a testament dies, he passes away, and the heir takes his place. Even so, Jesus, the Heir of all things, gave up all in His death that we might stand in His place and inherit all."

Oh, that our hearts might take it in! A death having taken place! Now the covenant is sure. The redemption of past transgressions is sure; we may now claim and take the promise of the eternal inheritance. A death having taken place! Now the testament avails. The maker of the testament has died, to put us in complete possession of all He had and all He won for us. And, praise God! He lives again, as no other maker of a testament ever lives, to put us in full possession of the inheritance and to be Himself its chiefest measure and joy; as Minister of the true sanctuary, to keep us in God's presence; as Mediator of the new covenant, to keep our hearts in the full enjoyment of all its blessings.

Chapter Notes...

1. Everyone can understand how absolutely a last will or testament needs a death. This must help me to believe that a covenant needs it as much for the redemption of transgressions. As sure as the death of a maker of a testament puts the heir in complete possession of the promise, so surely has the death of the Mediator made a perfect redemption from all transgression.

2. Let us get firmly ahold of this: In virtue of His death, the first covenant could be set aside and the second dedicated with His blood. The second covenant has entirely to do with keeping our hearts and lives in a right state for entering the sanctuary and abiding there. Let me believe it can and will be fulfilled.

Seventy-Two

Even the First Covenant— Not Without Blood

*Wherefore even the first covenant hath not been dedicated
without blood. For when every commandment had been
spoken by Moses unto all the people according to the law, he
took the blood of the calves and the goats, with water and
scarlet wool and hyssop, and sprinkled both the book itself,
and all the people, saying, This is the blood of the covenant
which God commanded to you-ward. Moreover the tabernacle
and all the vessels of the ministry he sprinkled in like manner
with the blood. And according to the law I may almost say,
all things are cleansed with blood, and apart from shedding
of blood there is no remission.*
—Hebrews 9:18–22

The writer returned here to the idea of the covenant as expressed
in verse 15. He had there said that a death was needed for
the redemption of the transgressions under the first covenant
before Christ, as Mediator of the new, could put the heirs in possession of the promise. In confirmation of this necessity, he reminded
us how *"even the first covenant hath not been dedicated without blood."*

Andrew Murray

God has made more than one covenant with man, but ever, *"not...without blood"*! And why? We know the answer: *"The life of the flesh is in the blood: and I have given it to you upon the altar to make atonement for your souls: for it is the blood that maketh atonement by reason of the life"* (Leviticus 17:11). The life is in the blood. The blood shed is the token of death, life taken away. Death is always and everywhere God's judgment on sin: The sting of death is sin. The shed blood sprinkled upon the altar, or the person, is the proof that death has been endured, that the penalty of the transgressions, for which atonement is being made, has been borne. In some cases the hands were laid upon the head of the sacrifice, confessing over it and laying upon it the sin to be atoned for. The shed blood upon the altar was the pledge that God accepted the death of the substitute: The sins were covered by the blood and the guilty one restored to God's favor. *"Apart from shedding of blood there is no remission."* In the bloodshed there is remission, full and everlasting.

Not without blood! This is the wondrous note that rings through all Scripture, from Abel's sacrifice at the gate of Paradise to the song of the ransomed in Revelation. God is willing to receive fallen man back again to His fellowship, to admit him to His heart and His love, to make a covenant with him, to give full assurance of all this— but not without blood. Even His own Son—the almighty and all-perfect One, the gift of His eternal love—even He could only redeem us and enter the Father's presence in submission to the words, *"not without...blood."* But, blessed be God, the blood of the Son of God, in which there was the life of the Eternal Spirit, has been given and has now wrought an eternal redemption! He did, indeed, bear our sins, and take them away. He put away sin by the sacrifice of Himself. The life He poured out in His bloodshedding was a life that had conquered sin and rendered a perfect obedience. The bloodshedding as the completion of that life, in its surrender to God and man, has made a complete atonement, a covering up, a putting away of sin. And so the blood of the new covenant, in which God remembers our sins no more, cleanses our hearts to receive

His law so into it that the spirit of His law is the spirit of our lives and takes us into full and direct fellowship with Himself. It was in this blood of the eternal covenant that God brought again from the dead our Lord Jesus: The blood had so atoned for sin and made an end of it that, in its power, Christ was raised again. It became the power of a new life to Him and to us. With it, He opened the way into the Holiest for us; the way into our hearts for Himself.

Not without blood! In earth and heaven, in each moment of our lives, in each thought and act of worship, these words reign supreme. There can be no fellowship with God but in the blood, in the death, of His blessed Son.

But, praised be His name, in that blood there is an access and a fellowship, a life and a blessedness, a nearness and a love that passes understanding! Let us seek to cultivate large thoughts of what the blood has effected and can effect. Men have sometimes rejected the word, *blood*: Its associations are so coarse and at variance with a finer culture. Others do not reject it and yet have not been able to sympathize with or approve the large place it sometimes takes in theology and devotion. The strange fascination, the irresistible attraction, that the word has is not without reason. There is not a word in Scripture in which all theology is so easily summed up. All that Scripture teaches of sin and death, of the Incarnation and the love of Christ, of redemption and salvation, of sin and death conquered, of heaven opened and the Spirit poured out, of the new covenant blessings, of a perfect conscience and a clean heart and access to God and power to serve Him, of personal attachment to Jesus, and of the joy of eternity—all that Scripture teaches on these has its root and its fruit in this alone: the precious blood of Christ, the blood of the eternal covenant.

Chapter Note...

1. Hear what Steinhofer says: "One drop of that blood, sprinkled out of the sanctuary on the heart, changes the whole heart, perfects the conscience, sanctifies the soul, makes the

garments clean and white, so that we are meet for fellowship with God, ready and able to live in His love. Such a heart, sprinkled and cleansed with the blood of Jesus, is now fitted for all the grace of the now covenant, all the heavenly gifts, all the holy operations of divine love, all the spiritual blessings of the heavenly places. The blood of the Lamb does indeed make the sinner pure and holy, worthy and fit to partake of all that the inner sanctuary contains, and to live in God. Therefore, the apostle said, 'Let us, as those whose hearts are sprinkled from an evil conscience, boldly draw near before the face of God.' (See Hebrews 10:22.) To be sprinkled with the blood, to have the living, cleansing, all-pervading power of the blood of Jesus in the heart—this fits us for serving God, not in the oldness of the letter, but in the newness of the Spirit."

Seventy-Three

Heaven Itself Cleansed by the Blood

It was necessary therefore that the copies of the things in the heavens should be cleansed with these; but the heavenly things themselves with better sacrifices than these. For Christ entered not into a holy place made with hands, like in pattern to the true; but into heaven itself, now to appear before the face of God for us.
—Hebrews 9:23–24

In the previous verses we saw how, at the dedication of the first covenant with blood, both the book and the people and, later on, the tabernacle and all the vessels of the ministry, were sprinkled with blood. Even so, the writer told us, the bloodshed on earth was not enough, but there was a need for *"the heavenly things themselves"* to be cleansed with the blood of the better sacrifice before heaven could be opened to us and we could obtain access to a life in the presence of God. There must not be a vestige or sign of sin left there to rise up against us. Such is the power of this better sacrifice and its blood, that *"the heavenly things themselves"* were cleansed by it and that Christ, our Surety with His own

Andrew Murray

blood, *"entered...into heaven itself,"* now to appear before the face of God for us. *"The heavenly things themselves"* cleansed, and Christ *"entered...into heaven itself"* for us—these are the two aspects of the eternal redemption here put before us.

"The heavenly things themselves" cleansed. What can this mean? We speak of the heavens being dark, black with clouds. The light of the sun is there, but clouded. When the clouds are gone, the heavens are bright and clear. God's Word speaks of our sins rising up as a cloud, as a smoke before Him. Our sins are come up before Him, are in His presence, written in His book of remembrance, calling for vengeance. God says to Israel: *"I have blotted out, as a thick cloud, thy transgressions, and, as a cloud, thy sins"* (Isaiah 44:22). Just as the tabernacle had to be sprinkled and cleansed and hallowed from all the uncleanness of the children of Israel, so too the heavenly things themselves had to be cleansed by the blood of Christ. As the blood was brought in, every vestige of a thought of sin was removed out of God's presence; the heavens were cleansed; the heavens are now clear and bright, and the love of God can shine out in noonday glory.

And this because Christ is not entered into the Holiest made with hands but *"into heaven itself, now to appear before the face of God for us."* This is the great consummation to which all the teaching of the heavenly priesthood of Christ and the true sanctuary and the blood of the covenant leads up. Heaven itself is now opened up to us. Christ has entered, not simply on His own behalf, but entirely to *"appear before the face of God for us."* Yes, for us; His entering in has obtained for us boldness to enter in. His entering in was through the rent veil; there is no veil now between God and us. We are called to draw near in the fullness of faith. We are taught, "Ye are come to the heavenly Jerusalem and to God." (See Hebrews 12:22.) *"Before the face of God,"* in the presence of God, is now the home of the soul. Heaven is not only a locality, with its limitations, but a state of life, that condition of spiritual existence in the full enjoyment of God's love and fellowship into which Christ entered. Christ passed through the heavens, was made higher than the heavens. *"He...ascended far above all the heavens, that he might fill all things"* (Ephesians 4:10).

Heaven itself—the Holiest of All, into which He entered, the presence of God—is now the sphere in which He exercises His heavenly ministry, into which He brings us in as an actual life and experience, in which we alone can truly serve the living God.

And, we may well ask, what is the reason that so few of God's children can testify to the joy of entering in and having their abode here in the very presence of God? There can be but one answer: There is such a difference between being the heir of a promise and actually inheriting it. Each of the great words of our epistle, as God's gift to each one of His children, has an infinitude of meaning and blessing and power in it. Christ, a *"priest for ever"* (Hebrews 5:6; 6:20; 7:17, 21); *"the power of an endless life"* (7:16); He is able to sympathize, *"able to succour"* (2:18), *"able to save* [completely]" (7:25); the true sanctuary, the new covenant, the blood-cleansing of the heavens, the cleansing of the conscience—all these are divine realities with a power and a glory that the heart of man cannot conceive. It is only by faith and longsuffering that we inherit the promises. It is as we give up our whole hearts and lives to be just one act of faith—looking up and longing, praising and expecting, believing and receiving what God gives and works in Christ—that this life in the Holiest will be ours. It is as our faith sees the divine unity of the *"once for all"* and the *"for ever"* that we will be bold to believe that the *"for ever,"* the abiding continually, has in Christ been made ours *"once for all"* and can be made ours in an entering within the veil as clear as that of Christ's. This faith will prove itself in longsuffering. First, as we diligently and perseveringly hold fast, and gaze and draw near and wait on God to take us within the veil; and then, as within the veil, in deepest humility and meekness and patience and resignation to God, we wait upon Him in service to perfect us in the work for which we were admitted into His very presence.

Andrew Murray

But remember where all this begins and of what it all consists—not without blood! With His own blood! How much more will the blood of Christ!—these words are the key to this blessed chapter of the opening of the Holiest to us. As we yield to the Holy Spirit, the Eternal Spirit, to testify to us how the way into the Holiest has been made manifest—and what the blood is by which it was done, and what the cleansing of our consciences in that blood to enter in and serve the living God is—we will in fullness of faith be bold to draw near and enter in and abide.

Chapter Notes...

1. Think not that it will be too difficult for you to dwell always with your heart up yonder in heaven. When the sun shines on you, you do not think of the distance; you rejoice in its warmth. It is so near to you; you enter into it, and it enters into you. Even so, with Jesus and the heavenly life. Heaven comes down. The kingdom of heaven is come with power; the Holy Spirit gives and maintains it in you. The veil is rent, and the light and life of heaven is come down here where we serve in the Holy Place.

2. To open the way to heaven and to God, Jesus died to sin. He who hates and loses his life will find the way to the life of God.

3. Just as the cleansing of the tabernacle was part of the dedicating of the first covenant, so too the sprinkling the heavenly sanctuary, the cleansing of the heavens with the blood of the new covenant, is our assurance that the sanctuary is open to us and that the covenant is sure and will be fulfilled to us.

Seventy-Four

Sin Put Away by the Sacrifice of Himself

Nor yet that he should offer himself often, as the high priest entereth into the holy place year by year with blood, not his own; else must he often have suffered since the foundation of the world: but now once at the end of the ages hath he been manifested to put away sin by the sacrifice of himself. And inasmuch as it is appointed unto men once to die, and after this cometh judgement; so Christ also, having been once offered to bear the sins of many, shall appear a second time, apart from sin, to them that wait for him, unto salvation.
—Hebrews 9:25–28

In the previous verses, the spiritual and heavenly character of Christ's work was contrasted with the material and earthly figures of the old worship. Here the contrast will be between the unceasing repetition of the old and the *"once"* and *"for ever"* of the new. Repetition is the proof of imperfection; what needs doing only once is finished, is perfect, is forever. *"Now once at the end of the ages hath he been manifested to put away sin by the sacrifice of himself. And inasmuch as it is appointed unto men once to die, and after this*

Andrew Murray

cometh judgement"—with death, life is finished and complete, and ripe for judgment. After that comes the full revelation of what that death was—*"So Christ also, having been once offered to bear the sins of many, shall appear a second time"*—in the full manifestation of what that death accomplished—*"apart from sin, to them that wait for him, unto salvation."* What is done *"once"* is done *"for ever"*; all it waits for is the everlasting manifestation of what is already perfect and complete.

"Now once at the end of the ages hath he been manifested to put away sin by the sacrifice of himself." This is the great lesson of our passage. What Christ effected by His dying once is forever. And what He did effect was this—He *"put away sin by the sacrifice of himself."* He was manifested to put it away out of God's presence, out of His book and His remembrance—to put it away from us so that it has no more power over us and we enter upon an entirely new state of life with sin removed and God's law written in our hearts.

The question comes up, Is not the expression too strong? Is not the experience of the church a proof that it cannot be meant so literally? The solution of the difficulty will be found in a truth that leads us into one of the deepest mysteries of the spiritual life. As we saw in our last meditation, the words of God have a divine, an infinite, fullness of meaning. They set before us what is an actual fact, a divine reality, a spiritual truth in *"the power of the endless life"* (Hebrews 7:16). But this truth is seldom fully understood or accepted by believers. And as their knowledge limits their faith, and their faith their experience, the human exposition and witness of what God means seldom, if ever, reaches to the fullness of what the Word contains. We limit the Holy One of Israel perhaps most when we think we honor Him, by thinking that we know and hold in our formulas all His Word means. With its divine contents, the Word infinitely exceeds our comprehension and ever invites us to press on to perfection and prove the deeper and higher truths that are still hidden in the old familiar words. As we yield ourselves to the Holy Spirit, whose purpose it is to reveal the power of the blood and the opening of the way into the Holiest, we will be led to inherit this promise, too, in all its divine significance—sin put away *"by the sacrifice of himself."*

"By the sacrifice of himself." The words reveal the inmost meaning of the death of Christ: It was self-sacrifice. Sin, in its deepest root, is a turning from God to self, rejecting God to please self. From the wilderness to the garden, this was the one temptation with which Satan sought to lead Him astray. By doing not His own will but the will of His Father, by the sacrifice of Himself to God and His will, He conquered sin in His own person and gained a victory over it whereby it was forever vanquished and brought to nought. He gave Himself up to death, as His submission to it to do its utmost, rather than yield to temptation. He gave Himself up to death, as His submission to God's righteous judgment upon sin. It was in this that His death to sin, as the obedient One, and His death for as our Substitute, had its power, and His atonement, its efficacy. To Him, our Head, death was a personal spiritual victory, and thereby a vicarious propitiation. In both aspects, He made an end of sin, and of both we are made partakers.

And how? Did He put away sin* by the sacrifice of Himself? And now He offers us Himself to take the place of sin. He gives Himself, the sacrificed One, who has finished redemption, to us to put away sin within us, too. It is as the Son, the living One, that He is High Priest; it is in eternal life power, by a life working in us, that He brings us to God. And so, by His Spirit, He, in His self-sacrifice, lives in us and makes it true in the experience of each true disciple—sin put away by the sacrifice of self. The law for the Head is the law for every member.

And now the alternative is put before us: Which will it be: sin and myself, or Christ and His Self? Christ has opened for us

---

* *"The putting away of sin.* The thought goes beyond the redemption from transgressions (verse 15). It is literally for the disannulling of sin (compare with 7:18). Sin is vanquished, shown in its weakness, set at nought (Mark 7:9; Galatians 3:15)." —Westcott

a heavenly life-sphere, out of which sin has been put away—the sanctuary of God's presence. Which will it be: self-pleasing or self-sacrifice? A life in self or a life in Christ? Though we may not always be able to see fully all that Christ's work means, or realize all the riches of blessing it brings, there is one word, not difficult to carry, in which all is centered. That word is *Himself.* He gave *Himself,* a sacrifice for sin; He gives *Himself,* the putter-away, the conqueror of sin; He is *Himself* all we can desire or need. Blessed the soul that rests in nothing less than Himself.

Chapter Notes...

1. Sin is the refusal to sacrifice one's self to God. Self-sacrifice in the fellowship and Spirit of Jesus is the way out of sin to God.

2. Christ as our Head is our Substitute. The value of His work as Substitute rests in His personal character and obedience. The two aspects are inseparable, both in Him and in us. We draw near to Him and accept Him and are saved at once by Him as our Substitute. But then we are at once implanted into Him, and the Spirit in which He worked our salvation is imparted to us. And so salvation by sacrifice, putting away sin by the sacrifice of self, rules our whole being.

THE NEW WAY INTO THE HOLIEST

Seventy-Five

The Sacrifices of the Law Cannot Make Perfect

For the law having a shadow of the good things to come, not the very image of the things, they can never with the same sacrifices year by year, which they offer continually, make perfect them that draw nigh. Else would they not have ceased to be offered, because the worshippers, having been once cleansed, would have had no more conscience of sins? But in those sacrifices there is a remembrance made of sins year by year. For it is impossible that the blood of bulls and goats should take away sins.
—Hebrews 10:1–4

We have now seen the *"priest for ever,"* able to save completely (chapter 7); *"the true tabernacle"* in which He ministers (chapter 8); and *"the blood"* through which the sanctuary was opened and we are cleansed to enter in (chapter 9). There is still a fourth truth of which mention has been made in passing but that has not yet been expounded: What is the way into the Holiest by which Christ entered in? What is the path in which He walked when He went to shed His blood and pass through the veil to enter in and appear before God? In other words, what was it that gave His sacrifice its worth; and what was the disposition, the inner essential nature of that mediation, that secured His acceptance as our High Priest? The answer to be given in the first eighteen verses of this chapter will form the conclusion of the doctrinal half of the epistle, and especially of the higher teaching it has for the perfect.

To prepare the way for the answer, the chapter begins with once again reminding us of the ineffectiveness of the law. *"The law having a shadow of the good things to come, not the very image of the things."* The law had only the shadow, not the substance. The Gospel gives us *"the very image."* The image of God in which man was created was an actual spiritual reality. The Son Himself, as the image of the Father, was His true likeness—ever in possession of His Father's life and glory.

When man makes an image, it is but a dead thing. When God gives an image, it is a living reality, sharing in the life and the attributes of the original. And so, the Gospel brings us not a shadow, a picture, a mental concept, but the very image of the heavenly things so that we know and have them, really taste and possess them. A shadow is first of all a picture, an external figure, giving a dim apprehension of good things to come. Then, as the external passes away and sight is changed into faith, there comes a clearer concept of divine and heavenly blessings. And then faith is changed into possession and experience, and the Holy Spirit makes the power of Christ's redemption and the heavenly life a reality within us. Some Christians never get beyond the figures and shadows; some advance to faith in the spiritual good set forth; blessed are they who go on to full possession of what faith had embraced.

In expounding what the law is not able to do, the writer used four remarkable expressions that, while they speak of the weakness of the law with its shadows, indicate at the same time what the good things to come are, of which Christ is to bring us the *"very image,"* the divine experience.

The priests *"can never...make perfect them that draw nigh."* This is what Christ can do. He makes the conscience perfect. He has perfected us forever. These words suggest the infinite difference between what the law could do and what Christ has truly brought. What they mean in the mind of God, and what Christ our High Priest in *"the power of an endless life"* (Hebrews 7:16) can make them to be to us—this the Holy Spirit will reveal. Let us be content with no easy human exposition, by which we are content to count the ordinary low experience of the slothful Christian—the hope of being pardoned—as an adequate fulfillment of what God means by the promises of the perfect conscience. Let us seek to know the blessing in its heavenly power.

"The worshippers, having been once cleansed, would have had no more conscience of sins." This is the perfect conscience—when there is *"no more conscience of sins"*—a conscience that, once cleansed in the same power in which the blood was once shed, knows how completely sin has been put away out of that sphere of spiritual fellowship with God to which it has found access.

"In those sacrifices there is a remembrance made of sins year by year." The cleansing of the heavens and the putting away of sin is so complete that with God our sins are no more remembered. And it is meant that the soul that enters fully into the Holiest of All, and is kept there by the power of the eternal High Priest, should have such an experience of His eternal, always lasting, always acting redemption—that there will be no remembrance of anything but of what He is and does and will do. As we live in the heavenly places, in the Holiest of All, we live where there is no more remembrance of sins.

"It is impossible that the blood of bulls and goats should take away sins." What is impossible for the law is what Christ has done. He takes away not only guilt but also sins; and He does this in such *"power of an endless life"* (7:16) that those who draw near are made perfect, that there is *"no more conscience of sins"* and no more remembrance of sins.

Andrew Murray

To how many Christians the Cross and the death of Christ are nothing so much as a remembrance of sins. Let us believe that, by God's power, through the Holy Spirit revealing to us the way into the Holiest, it may become the power of a life with *"no more conscience of sins"* and a walk with a perfect conscience before God.

Chapter Notes...

1. Here we have again the contrast between the two systems. In the one, God spoke by the prophets, giving thoughts and concepts—shadows of the good things to come. But now, He speaks to us in His Son, the likeness of God, who gives us the very image, the actual likeness, in our experience of the heavenly things. It is the deep contrast between the outward and the inward—the created and the divine.

2. A perfect conscience. *"No more conscience of sins."* Let me not fear and say, "Yes, this is the conscience Christ gives, but it is impossible for me to keep it or enjoy its blessing permanently." Let me believe in Him who is my Priest, after the power of an endless life, who ever lives to pray, and is able to save completely, because every moment His blood and love and power are in full operation—the perfect conscience in me because He is for me, in heaven, a Priest perfected forevermore.

Seventy-Six

A Body Didst Thou Prepare for Me

*Wherefore when he cometh into the world, he saith, Sacrifice
and offering thou wouldest not, but a body didst thou
prepare for me; in whole burnt offerings and sacrifices for
sin thou hadst no pleasure: then said I, Lo, I am come (in
the roll of the book it is written of me) to do thy will, O God.*
—Hebrews 10:5–7

The writer reminded us of the utter insufficiency of the sacrifices of the law to do what was needed to take sin away
or to perfect the worshiper. In contrast to these, he next
unfolded to us the inner meaning, the real nature and worth of the
sacrifice of Christ. In speaking of the blood in chapter 9, he taught
us what its infinite power and efficacy is. But what we need still to
know is this: What gave it that infinite efficacy? What is its spiritual
character and its essential nature that it has availed so mightily
to open for us the way to God? Even when we believe in Christ's
death, we are in danger of resting content with what is not much
better than its shadow, the mere doctrinal conception of what it

has effected, without entering so into its divine significance, that *"the very image"* (10:1), the real likeness of what it means, enters into us in power.

Our writer here again found what he wanted to expound in the Old Testament. He quotes from Psalm 40, where the psalmist used words that, though true of himself, could only have their full meaning revealed when the Messiah came. Our author made special use of two significant expressions, *"A body didst thou prepare for me,"* and, *"Lo, I am come...to do thy will, O God."* Speaking of the sacrifices of the Old Testament, the psalmist had shown that he understood that they never were what God really willed: They were but the shadows pointing to something better, to a spiritual reality, a life in the body given up to the will of God, as a divine prophecy of what has now been revealed in Christ.

"A body didst thou prepare for me." Instead of the sacrifices, God prepared a body for Christ, which He so offered up or sacrificed that we have now been sanctified by the offering of the body of Jesus Christ once for all. Christ's body was to Him just what any man's is to him—the dwelling and organ of the soul; the channel for communion with the outer world, susceptible to impressions of pleasure and of pain and, therefore, one of the first occasions of temptation. His body was a part of His human personality and life. He was in danger, just as we are, of using the body for His own service or pleasure, a means of gratifying self. But He never did this. He was filled with one thought—"God prepared this body for Me; I have it for His disposal, for His service and glory; I hold it ready every moment to be a sacrifice to Him. The body comes from God; it belongs to Him; it has no object of existence but to please Him. The one value My body has is that I can give it as a sacrifice to God."

The purpose of the Old Testament sacrifices was to waken this disposition in the worshiper. There was to be not only the thought—as especially in the sin offering—that "This sacrifice dies in my stead, so that I need not die"; but the further thought was to be—this, the burnt offering especially symbolized—"The giving up of this lamb and its life in sacrifice to God is the image and the pledge of my giving up my life to Him. I offer the sacrifice to God, in token of my offering myself to Him." Substitution and consecration were equally symbolized in the altar.

This was David's feeling when writing the Psalms. What he could only partly understand and fulfill has since been realized in Christ. And we become full partakers of what Christ accomplished for us as it is worked out in us, in a life of fellowship with Him. The Word comes to us, *"Present your bodies a living sacrifice, holy, acceptable to God"* (Romans 12:1). The real essential nature of the sacrifice of Christ, which gives it its worth and efficacy, is this: The body that God prepared for Him, He offered up to God. And just as David, before Christ and through the Spirit of Christ, said these words of himself, so every believer after Christ, in the Spirit and power of Christ, says them, too: *"A body didst thou prepare for me."* This is the new and living way that Christ has opened up. David walked in it by anticipation; Christ, the Leader and Forerunner, walked in it and fully opened it up; it is only as we, too, by participation with Him, walk in it, that we can find access into the Holiest.

Every believer who would be fully delivered from the Old Testament religion—the trust in something done outside of us that leaves us unchanged—and would fully know what it means that we are sanctified and perfected by the one offering of the body of Christ, must study to appropriate fully this word as true of Christ and of himself as a member of His body—*"A body didst thou prepare for me."* In Paradise, it was through the body that sin entered; in the body, it took up its abode and showed its power. In the lust for forbidden fruit, in the sense of nakedness and shame, in the turning to dust again, sin proved its triumph. In the body, grace will reign and triumph. The body has been redeemed; it becomes a temple of the Spirit and a member of Christ's body; it will be made like His glorious body. *"A body didst thou prepare*

Andrew Murray

for me." For Christ and all who are sanctified in Him, the path to perfection lies through the body.

And yet how many believers there are to whom the body is the greatest hindrance in their Christian life. Simply because they have not learned from Christ what the highest use of the body is—to offer it up to God. Instead of presenting their members unto God, of mortifying the deeds of the body through the Spirit, of keeping under the body, they allow it to have its way and are brought into bondage. Oh, for an insight into the real nature of our actual redemption, through a body received from God, prepared by Him, and offered up to Him. *Amen!*

Chapter Notes...

1. The soul dwells in the body. The body has been well compared to the walls of a city. In time of war, not only the city and its indwellers must be under the rule of the king, but especially the walls. Jesus, for whom God prepared a body, and who offered His body, knows how to keep the body, too.

2. The mystery of the Incarnation is that Godhead dwelt in a body. The mystery of atonement is the one offering of the body of Christ. The mystery of full redemption is that the Holy Spirit dwells in and sanctifies wholly the body, too.

3. *"Know ye not that your body is a temple of the Holy Ghost which is in you, which ye have from God?...glorify God therefore in your body"* (1 Corinthians 6:19–20). Did you ever know that the Holy Spirit is especially given for the body to regulate its functions and sanctify it wholly?

Seventy-Seven

Lo, I Am Come to Do Thy Will

Saying above, Sacrifices and offerings and whole burnt offerings and sacrifices for sin thou wouldest not, neither hadst pleasure therein (the which are offered according to the law), then hath he said, Lo, I am come to do thy will. He taketh away the first, that he may establish the second. By which will we have been sanctified through the offering of the body of Jesus Christ once for all.
—Hebrews 10:8–10

O n the word, *"A body didst thou prepare for me"* (Hebrews 10:5), as the expression of God's claim, there follows now in the psalm that other, concerning surrender to that claim—*"Lo, I am come to do thy will."* In this, the doing of God's will, we have the destiny of the creature, the blessedness of heaven, the inmost secret of redemption. In this consists the worth of Christ's sacrifice, and this alone is the reason why His blood prevails. The path He opened up to God, the path He walked in and that we walk in to enter the Holiest is—*"I am come to do thy will."* It is through God's will alone that we enter in to God Himself.

Andrew Murray

The central blessing that Jesus, the Mediator of the new covenant, gives us when He gives us Himself is a heart in which the will of God lives.

We have more than once spoken of the two aspects of Christ's death—substitution with the atonement it wrought, and fellowship with the conformity it brings. The two are inseparably connected. As long as we look to the substitution simply as an act accomplished outside of us, without seeking to know its inner nature and meaning, the fellowship and conformity of Christ's death will be an impossibility. But as we enter into the real meaning of the death for us and in our stead, to what constituted its divine life and power, we will find that death and the life out of death becomes ours in truth, laying ahold of us and bringing us into the true life-fellowship with our blessed Leader and Forerunner; we will see and experience that what was to Him the way into the Holiest will be to us the only, but the certain, the living way there.

"Lo, I am come to do thy will." "He humbled himself, becoming obedient....Wherefore also God highly exalted him" (Philippians 2:8–9). Because God is the all-perfect Fountain of life and goodness and blessing, there can be no life or goodness or blessing but in His will. The whole evil and ruin of sin is that man turned from God's will to do his own. The redemption of Christ had no reason, no object, and no possibility of success except in restoring man to do God's will. It was for this that Jesus died. He gave up His own will; He gave His life, rather than do His own will. It was this that gave value to His bearing our sins, with their curse and consequences, to His tasting death for every man. It was this that gave such infinite worth to His blood. It was this that made Him a real propitiation for the sins of the world. And it is this that we are made partakers of—first, as an obedience for the sake of which we are made righteous; but, further also, in the fellowship of the very spirit of the death and the life in which He entered the presence of God. *"I am come to do thy will,"* is the way into the Holiest, for Him and for us.

"By which will we have been sanctified." "By which will," as willed by God, as done and fulfilled by Christ in His one offering, as accepted by us in faith. When we accept Christ, the will of God worked out in Christ on our behalf is accepted by us, too; it becomes the power that rules in our lives by the Holy Spirit. *"By which will"*—not as a dead past transaction or as the mere performance of a certain work to be done, but as a living eternal reality restoring man into God's will in living power—this it is in which we have the new and living way to God.

"By which will we have been sanctified." Sanctification in this epistle is a word of larger meaning than what is meant by that title in ordinary church doctrine. It includes all that is implied in bringing us into living fellowship with God. He is the Holy One. His life is His holiness. The inner sanctuary to which we enter in is the Holiness of Holinesses. In chapter 2, we read, *"Both he that sanctifieth and they that are sanctified are all of one"* (verse 11). Our sanctification is rooted in our oneness with Jesus. *"By which will we have been sanctified"*—delivered from the power of sin and this evil world, brought into fellowship with the Holy One, and fitted for entering the Holiest of All.

"By which will we have been sanctified through the offering of the body of Jesus Christ." His offering has such power because it was the doing of the will of God—the entering into the will of God and, through it, into the holiness of God, into the very Holiest of All. And now, as no one but Christ had power of Himself to say, *"Lo, I am come to do thy will,"* so too no one can speak thus, or live thus, unless the divine nature of Christ is truly born and formed within him and is become the Life of his life and the Spirit of his spirit. It is thus that His priesthood manifests His power to bring us near to God.

Fellow Christian! Have you learned to believe and to regard yourself as sanctified in the will of God as done by Jesus, admitted to the fellowship of the Holy One? Is not this possibly the reason that you have not yet entered the rest of God within the veil, because you have never, in accepting Christ, accepted what really constitutes Him, the Christ? He is the Christ who came to do the will of God—this constitutes Him as a Savior. Oh, come and believe that this is what He did for you and on your behalf, that you might be able to do it, too. The new and living way into the Holiest, which Jesus as Leader and Forerunner has opened up, is the way of a body prepared for me by God, a body offered to Him, and a life given to do His will. As I say with Jesus, "I am come to do Thy will," I have no other object in life; for this alone, I live and will abide with Him in God's presence.

Chapter Notes...

1. The only way to God is through the will of God. A truth so simple and self-evident! And yet so deep and spiritual that but few fully comprehend it. Yes, this is the way, the only way, the new and living way into the Holiest that Jesus opened up. Let me follow Him, our Leader and Forerunner, walking in His footsteps, in the will of God.

2. Do not be afraid to say, "Yes, O my God, here am I, absolutely given up in everything to do the will of God; by Thy grace and Holy Spirit, to make every part of my being a work of the will of God! So help me, God!"

3. For the penitent convert, it is enough to know the beginning of the doctrine of Christ; His obedience has atoned and makes me righteous. The believer who seeks to grow and become conformed to the image of the Son seeks and finds more. The obedience that gave the sacrifice its power in heaven exercises that power in his heart. The praiseworthy Substitute becomes the beloved Leader and Brother, the High Priest in the power of the heavenly life, bringing us near to God by leading us and keeping us in His will.

Seventy-Eight

Once and Forever

*And every priest indeed standeth day by day ministering
and offering oftentimes the same sacrifices, the which can
never take away sins: but he, when he had offered one
sacrifice for sins for ever, sat down on the right hand of
God; from henceforth expecting till his enemies be made the
footstool of his feet. For by one offering he hath perfected
for ever them that are sanctified.*
—Hebrews 10:11–14

In the last verses of chapter 7, where the eternal priesthood of
Jesus had been set forth, He was spoken of as One who does not
need to offer daily, for this He did once for all when He offered
up Himself—a Son, perfected forevermore. And so, in chapter 9,
with its teaching on the efficacy of His blood, we had the thought
repeated—Christ entered in once for all:

> *Nor yet that he should offer himself **often**...else must he **often**
> have suffered.* (verses 25–26, emphasis added)

> *But now **once** at the end of the ages hath he been manifested.*
> (verse 26, emphasis added)

> *So Christ also, having been **once** offered to bear the sins of many,
> shall appear a second time.* (verse 28, emphasis added)

Andrew Murray

The contrast is put as strongly as possible between the sacrifices ever repeated and the offering of Christ once for all. So, too, in the beginning of chapter 10, the ineffectiveness of the sacrifices year by year continually is proved from the fact that the conscience once cleansed would need no new sacrifice (verse 2); as a fact, they only renewed the remembrance of sins. And now, in the concluding verses of the argument, the thought is summed up and pressed home anew: *"And every priest indeed standeth **day by day** ministering and offering **oftentimes** the same sacrifices....*[Christ] *offered **one** sacrifice for sins **for ever**....By **one** offering he hath perfected **for ever** them that are sanctified"* (emphasis added). The *"once"* of Christ's work is the secret of its being *"for ever"*: the more clear the acceptance of that divine *"once for all,"* the more sure the experience of that divine *"for ever,"* and the continually abiding working of *"the power of an endless life"* (7:16).

"Once" and *"for ever"*: See how the two go together in the work of Christ in its two principal manifestations. In His death, His sacrifice, His bloodshed—it is *"once for all."* The propitiation for sin, the bearing and the putting away of it, was so complete that there never can be any thought of His suffering again or offering Himself again. God now remembers the sin no more forever. He has offered *"one sacrifice for sins for ever"*; *"he hath perfected* [us] *for ever."* No less is it so in His resurrection and ascension into heaven. He entered *"once for all"* through His blood into the Holiest. When He had offered *"one sacrifice for sins for ever,* [he] *sat down on the right hand of God"* (10:12). The *"once for all"* of His death is the secret of the *"for ever"* of the power of His sacrifice. The *"once for all"* of His entering through the blood is the power of the *"for ever"* of His sitting on the throne.

What is true of Christ is true of His people. The law of His life is the law of theirs. Of the *"once for all"* and the *"for ever"* of His work on earth and in heaven, their lives and spiritual experience will feel the power and bear the mark. See it in conversion. How many have struggled for years in doubt and fear, simply because they did not apprehend the *"once for all"* of Christ's atonement. They could not understand how it was possible for a sinner *"once for all"* to believe and be saved. No sooner was it made plain to those who the punishment was borne and that the debt was paid *"once for all,"* that all became clear and they counted it their duty and joy at once to accept what was so finished and so sure. And they could see, too, how the *"once"* was *"for ever"*—the power of the endless life bearing them on into the *"for ever"* of God's presence.

And it is not otherwise with the believers entering within the veil, into a life of unclouded and unbroken fellowship. We saw in Christ's work the two manifestations of the *"once"* and the *"for ever."* It was not only in the death and bloodshed but also in the entering into the Holiest and the blood sprinkling in heaven. To many, it appears at variance with all the laws of growth and development that there should be a *"once for all"* of an entrance within the veil. And yet there are witnesses, not a few, who can testify that when the *"once"* of Christ's entering in was revealed in its infinite power as theirs, all doubt vanished; and not only boldness but also power of access was given, which brought them into an experience of the eternal and unchanging power of the heavenly priesthood, and of the kingdom within as set up and kept by the Holy Spirit, that they never had thought of. And that *"once"* was followed by the *"for ever"* of the continually abiding, which the priesthood of Jesus was meant to secure.

"But he, when he had offered one sacrifice for sins for ever, sat down on the right hand of God; from henceforth expecting till his enemies be made the footstool of his feet." We have said before that the epistle would fill us with the thought of a heavenly Christ; nothing less than the knowledge of that can enable us to live as the partakers of a heavenly calling. Let us fix our eyes here again upon Christ as King. The *"once"* of sacrifice and death issues in the *"for ever"* of the nearness and the power of God. The *"once"* of our entrance into the death of Christ and His life brings us back to the fellowship with Christ in the love and power of the Father in heaven. His

"for ever" is one of victory and of the blessed expectation of its full manifestation in the subjugation of every enemy. Our life within the veil may be one, too, of possession and expectation combined—the enjoyment of the overcoming life with the going on from strength to strength in the victory over every foe. Between these two pillars—on the one hand, this *"once for all,"* on the other this *"for ever"*—the way into the Holiest passes and brings us to the throne of God and of the Lamb. *Yes!*

Chapter Notes...

1. The time when the long and patient preparation was perfected in this *"once for all"* was in God's hands. Christ waited on the Father. Even so, our full participation in it is not something we can count a thing to be grasped; in the faith of it, we bide God's time, seeking each day to live in a redemption that is perfected and eternal. Through faith and longsuffering, we inherit the promises.

2. *"Once for all."* That covers my past completely—my past not only of guilt but also of sin with all its consequences. *"For ever."* That covers my future, with all its possible needs. Between these two, in the present moment, the *"now"* of daily life, I am saved with an everlasting salvation. The *"to-day"* of the Eternal Spirit—*"even as the Holy Ghost saith, To-day"* (3:7)—makes the *"once"* and the *"for ever"* a daily present reality.

Seventy-Nine

The Sanctified Perfected Forever

*For by one offering he hath perfected for ever
them that are sanctified.*
—Hebrews 10:14

This verse is, in reality, the conclusion of the doctrinal part of the epistle. The four following verses are simply the citation of the words of the new covenant to confirm its teaching with the witness of the Holy Spirit. The writer, having in the context expounded the nature of Christ's sacrifice as showing what the way into the Holiest is, summed up his proof of its worth and efficacy in the words: *"By one offering he hath perfected for ever them that are sanctified."* We find here five of the most important words that occur in the epistle.

"Sanctified." That looks back to the great purpose of Christ's coming, as we had it in chapter 2. *"Sanctified"* is cleansed from sin, taken out of the sphere and power of the world and sin, and brought to live in the sphere and power of God's holiness in the Holiest of All. This word looks back, too, to Hebrews 10:10: *"By*

Andrew Murray

which will we have been sanctified through the offering of the body of Jesus Christ once for all."

"*He hath perfected...them that are sanctified.*" It not only says that He has finished and completed for them all they need. The word points back to what was said of His own being made perfect. All that He became was for us. In His one sacrifice, He was not only perfected Himself but He also perfected us; He took us into the fellowship of His own perfectness, implanted His own perfect life in us, and gave His perfected human nature to us that we were to put on and to live in.

"*For ever.*" He has perfected us once for all and forever. His perfection is ours; our whole lives are prepared for us, to be received out of His hand.

"*By...offering.*" The death, the blood, the offering, the sacrifice of Christ, is the power by which we have been alike sanctified and perfected. It is the way that He opened up, in which He leads us with Himself into what He is and does as the One who is perfected forevermore, and into the Holiest of All.

"*By one offering.*" "*One*" because there is none other needed, either by others or Himself; one divine—and, therefore, sufficient and forever.

The chief thought of the passage is, "*He hath perfected for ever them that are sanctified.*" The words in verse 10, "*By which will we have been sanctified,*" speak of our sanctification as an accomplished fact: We are saints, holy in Christ, in virtue of our real union with Him and His holy life planted in the center of our being. Here we are spoken of as being sanctified. There is a process by which our new life in Christ has to master and to perfect holiness through our whole outer being. But the progressive sanctification has its rest and its assurance in the "*once*" and "*for ever*" of Christ's work. "*He hath perfected for ever them that are sanctified.*"

In 9:9 and 10:2, we read that the sacrifices could never, "*as touching the conscience, make the worshipper perfect,*" never make perfect

those who draw nigh, so that they have *"no more conscience of sins."*
Our conscience is what defines what our consciousness of ourselves
before God should be: Christ makes the worshiper perfect, concerning
the conscience, so that there is no more conscience of sins. *"He hath
perfected for ever them that are sanctified."* At the close of the chapter
on Christ's priesthood, we read of Himself that He is a High Priest, *"a
Son, perfected for evermore"* (7:28). Here, at the close of the unfolding
of His work, it is said of His saints: *"He hath perfected for ever them."*
The perfection in both cases is one and the same. As the Son of Man,
as the Second Adam who lives in all who are His, He perfected Himself for them, and them in Himself. His perfection and theirs are one.

And we know, too, of what His perfection consists. A Leader
in the way of glory, God made Him *"perfect through sufferings"*
(2:10); perfected in Him was that humility and meekness and
patience that mark Him as the Lamb—which is what God asks of
man and is man's only fitness for dwelling with God.

> *Having offered up prayers...and having been heard for his
> godly fear, though he was a Son, yet learned obedience by the
> things which he suffered; and having been made perfect, he
> became unto all them that obey him the author of eternal sal-
> vation.* (5:7–9)

His godly fear, His waiting on God in the absolute surrender of His will, His submitting to learn obedience, His spirit of
self-sacrifice even unto death—it was by this that, as man, He was
perfected; it was in this that He perfected human nature and perfected His people, too. In His death, He accomplished a threefold
work: He perfected Himself, His own human nature and character;
He perfected our redemption, perfectly putting away sin from the
place it had in heaven (9:23) and in our hearts; and He perfected
us, taking us up into His own perfection and making us partakers
of that perfect human nature that, in suffering and obedience in
the body prepared for Him, and the will of God done in it, He had
wrought out for us. Christ Himself is our perfection; in Him it is
complete; abiding in Him continually is perfection.

Andrew Murray

"Let us...press on unto perfection" (6:1) was the call with which we were led into the higher life teaching of the epistle. Here is our goal: Christ, by one offering, has perfected us forever. We know Him as the Priest forever, the Minister of the new sanctuary, and the Mediator of the new covenant, who by His blood entered into the Holiest. There He lives forever, in the power of an endless life, to impart to us and maintain within us His perfect life. It is the walk in this path of perfection, which as our Leader He opened up in doing the will of God, which is the new and living way into the Holiest.

Chapter Notes...

1. The work of Christ is a perfect and perfected work. Everything is finished and complete forever. And we have just, by faith, to behold and enter in and seek and rejoice and receive all of His fullness, grace for grace. Let every difficulty you feel in understanding or claiming the different blessings set before you, or in connecting them, find its solution in this one thought—Christ has perfected us forever; trust Him, cling to Him. He will do all.

2. *"One offering...for ever."* We, perfected forever. And He who did it all, He is forever seated on the throne. Our blessed Priest-King, He lives to make it all ours. In the power of an endless life, in which He offered Himself unto God, in which He entered the Holiest, He now lives to give and be in our hearts all He has accomplished. What more can we need? *"Wherefore, holy brethren, partakers of a heavenly calling, consider...Jesus"* (3:1).

Eighty

The Witness of the Holy Spirit

And the Holy Ghost also beareth witness to us: for after he hath said, This is the covenant that I will make with them after those days, saith the Lord; I will put my laws on their heart, and upon their mind also will I write them; then saith he, And their sins and their iniquities will I remember no more. Now where remission of these is, there is no more offering for sin.
—Hebrews 10:15–18

The writer has concluded his argument. He has made clear that the sacrifice of Christ, as the offering up of His body to the will of God, had opened for us a new way into the Holiest. *"We have been sanctified through the offering of the body of Jesus Christ once for all"* (Hebrews 10:10). *"When he had offered one sacrifice for sins for ever, sat down on the right hand of God"* (verse 12). *"For by one offering he hath perfected for ever them that are sanctified"* (verse 14). His sacrifice is over and has everlasting power; in virtue of it, He sits on the throne, expecting His final triumph; those He has sanctified are perfected forever. The sacrifice is of infinite worth; it has opened the entrance to a state of perfect and everlasting holiness and glory; nothing is now needed but to rejoice and wait and see the King on the throne applying and revealing the power of His finished work.

The writer appealed to the words of the institution of the new covenant in support of what he has said. (See 8:6–13.) He did so with the words, *"And the Holy Ghost also beareth witness to us."* The words of Jeremiah are to him the words of the Holy Spirit. He believes in a direct inspiration. It was the God who knows the end from the beginning who had planned all, from the least to the greatest, in the preparation of redemption, who had revealed to Jeremiah the new covenant that would be made centuries later. It was the same Holy Spirit who had inspired the first record of Melchizedek and the psalm with the oath of God; who had ordered the tabernacle and the veil to signify that the way into the Holiest was not yet open; who had watched over the first covenant and its dedication "not without blood"; and through whom the promise of the new covenant was spoken and recorded. Our writer appealed to Him and to His witness.

He did so as one who himself has the teaching of that Spirit. Anyone might read the words of the covenant and of the death of Jesus; no one could connect and expound them in their divine harmony and their everlasting significance but one taught by the same Spirit. These men *"preached the gospel unto you by the Holy Ghost sent forth from heaven"* (1 Peter 1:12); the Spirit, from the King sitting upon the throne, revealed in and to them the will of God, and the eternal power of the one sacrifice, to open the way into the Holiest.

And what is now the witness of the Holy Spirit in the new covenant? It is the witness to the two blessings of the covenant in their divine inseparable unity. *"I will put my laws on their heart... and their sins and their iniquities will I remember no more."* The complete remission of sins, the removal of sin out of God's sight and remembrance forever, was promised. Now, our writer argued, *"where remission of these is, there is no more offering for sin."* The one offering has perfected forever those that are sanctified. The death of Christ has opened up and introduced us into a relationship to God, a state of life before Him in which sin has been finally put away and God receives us into His fellowship as those who have been sanctified in Christ. He receives us into the Holiest of All through the blood. The blood that sprinkles the mercy seat also sprinkles and cleanses our conscience; bringing the full remission, the full deliverance, from sin and its power into our inmost being; and fitting our hearts to receive that Spirit of heaven, which witnesses with the blood, as a Spirit of life that puts the law within us, as the law of our life.

And so we enter into the finished work of Christ and the rest of God in it. Enter the perfection with which He Himself was perfected forevermore and has perfected us forever; into that Holiest of All, into which God fulfills the promise, *"And I will be to them a God, and they shall be to me a people"* (Hebrews 8:10). And the offering of the body of Christ once for all, the one sacrifice forever, becomes, in ever-growing blessedness, the one thought, the one trust, the one joy, the one life of the believer. His salvation and redemption are finished and eternal realities, as are His perfection and sanctification. Our one need is to believe and abide in and receive what our Priest-King on the throne imparts through His Spirit: a full entrance into the *"no more offering for sin,"* with all that flows from it, in the person and throne and work of our Priest forever. This is the entrance into the Holiest.

"And the Holy Ghost also beareth witness to us." It is easy to understand the truth of the forgiveness of sins as one of the elementary foundational truths, of which we read in 6:1. But if we seek to press on to perfection and to know what the fullness of salvation is into which it leads, we may count upon the Holy Spirit to reveal it, to witness to it, in our inner lives. He does not reveal

Andrew Murray

it to the mind, or as the reward of earthly study, but to the poor in spirit and those who are of a lowly heart. It is in the heart that God sends forth the Spirit of His Son; the heart that longs for and chooses and loves and waits for this life of perfect fellowship with God more than its chief joy will have it witnessed by God's Spirit that the *"no more offering for sin"* is indeed the opening up of the Holiest of All. The Holy Spirit who comes from heaven bears witness of what is in heaven. We can know nothing really of what takes place in heaven except by the Holy Spirit in our hearts. Dwelling in us, He gives, in our inmost life, the full witness to all the efficacy of Christ's atonement and His enthronement in the presence of God.

Chapter Notes...

1. The one central truth to which the Holy Spirit testifies is this: that the old way of living and serving God is now completely and forever come to an end. Death and the devil are brought to nothing; the veil is rent; sin is put away; the old covenant is disannulled, vanished away, taken away. A new system, a new way, a new and eternal life has been opened up in the power of Christ Jesus. Oh, to have our eyes and hearts opened to see that this is not merely a thought, a truth for the mind, but rather a spiritual state of existence into which the Holy Spirit can bring me.

2. *"The Holy Ghost also beareth witness."* For this He came down on the day of Pentecost, out of the heavenly sanctuary and from our exalted Priest-King—to bring down the heavenly life, the kingdom of heaven to the disciples, and to make it real to them as a thing found and felt in their hearts. Each one of us needs and may claim the Holy Spirit in the same Pentecostal power; and the new, the eternal, the heavenly life will fill us, too.

The Call to a Life in Harmony with the Glory of God's Revelation of Himself in the Son

Ninth Section—Hebrews 10:19–25
OF LIFE IN THE
HOLIEST OF ALL

It may help us the better to master the rich contents of this central passage, containing a summary of the whole epistle, if we here give the chief thoughts it contains.

A. The four great blessings of the new worship:
   1. The Holiest opened up.
   2. Boldness in the blood.
   3. A new and living way.
   4. The great High Priest.

B. The four chief marks of the true worshiper:
   1. A true heart.
   2. Fullness of faith.
   3. A heart sprinkled from an evil conscience.
   4. The body washed with clean water.

C. The four great duties to which the opened sanctuary calls:
   1. Let us draw nigh (in fullness of faith).
   2. Let us hold fast the profession of our hope.
   3. Let us consider one another to provoke onto love.
   4. Let us not forsake the assembling of ourselves together.

Eighty-One

The Entrance into the Holiest

Having therefore, brethren, boldness to enter into the holy
place* by the blood of Jesus,...let us draw near.
—Hebrews 10:19, 22

Enter into the [holiest]." With these words, the second half of the epistle begins. Hitherto the teaching has been mainly doctrinal. The glory of Christ's person and priesthood; of the heavenly sanctuary that He, through His own blood, has opened and cleansed and taken possession of for us; of the way of obedience and self-sacrifice that led Him even to the throne—all of this has been unfolded. Now comes the practical part, and our duty to appropriate the great salvation that has been provided is summed up in the one thought: *"Having...boldness to enter into the* [holiest]...*let us draw nigh."* Access to God's presence and fellowship, the right and the power to make that our abiding dwelling place and to live our lives there, has been provided in Christ: *"Let us draw near."* Here let us abide.

___
* Holiest.

"*Enter into the* [holiest]." It is a call to the Hebrews to come out of the life of unbelief and sloth that leads to a departing from the living God and to enter into the Promised Land, the rest of God, a life in His fellowship and favor. It is a call to all lukewarm, halfhearted Christians to remain no longer in the outer court of the tabernacle, content with the hope that their sins are pardoned; nor even to be satisfied with having entered the Holy Place and there doing the service of the tabernacle while the veil still hinders full fellowship with the living God and His love. It calls to enter in through the rent veil, into the place where the blood has been brought and where the High Priest lives, there to live and walk and work always in the presence of the Father. It is a call to all doubting, thirsting believers, who long for a better life than they have yet known, to cast aside their doubts and to believe that this is what Christ has indeed done and brought within the reach of each one of us: He has opened the way into the Holiest! This is the salvation that He has accomplished and that He lives to apply in each of us so that we will indeed dwell in the full light of God's countenance.

"*Enter into the* [holiest]." This is, in one short phrase, the fruit of Christ's work, the chief lesson of the epistle, the one great need of our Christian life, the complete and perfect salvation that God gives us to enjoy in Christ.

"*Enter into the* [holiest]." What Holiest? To the reader who has gone with us through the epistle thus far, it is hardly necessary to say. It is none other than that very same Holiest into which Christ, when He had rent the veil in His death, entered through His own blood, to appear before the face of God for us. That Holiest of All is the heavenly place. But not heaven, as it is ordinarily understood, as a locality, distinct and separate from this earth. The heaven of God is not limited in space in the same way as a place on earth. There is a heaven above us, the place of God's special manifestation, but there is also a spiritual heaven, as omnipresent as God Himself. Where God is, heaven is; the heaven of His presence includes this earth, too. The Holiest into which Christ entered and into which

Andrew Murray

He opened the way for us is the inaccessible (to nature) light of God's holy presence and love; it is full union and communion with Him. Into that Holiest the soul can enter by the faith that makes us one with Christ. The Holy Spirit, who first signified that the way of the Holiest was not yet open; through whom Jesus shed the blood that opened the way; who, on the day of Pentecost, witnessed in the hearts of the disciples that it was now indeed open—this Holy Spirit waits to testify to us what it means to enter in and to bring us in. He lifts the soul up into the Holiest; He brings the Holiest down into the soul.

"*Enter into the* [holiest]." Oh, the glory of the message. For fifteen centuries, Israel had a sanctuary with a Holiest of All into which, under pain of death, no one might enter. Its one message was this: Man cannot dwell in God's presence, cannot abide in His fellowship. And now, it is all changed! Just as the warning sounded then, "Enter not!" so now the call goes forth, "Enter in! The veil is rent; the Holiest is open; God waits to welcome you to His bosom. Henceforth, you are to live with Him." This is the message of the epistle: "Child, I, your Father, long for you to enter, to dwell, and to go out no more forever."

Oh the blessedness of a life in the Holiest! Here the Father's face is seen and His love tasted. Here His holiness is revealed and the soul made partaker of it. Here the sacrifice of love and worship and adoration, the incense of prayer and supplication, is offered in power. Here the outpouring of the Spirit is known as an ever-streaming, overflowing river from under the throne of God and the Lamb. Here the soul, in God's presence, grows into more complete oneness with Christ and more entire conformity to His likeness. Here, in union with Christ, in His unceasing intercession, we are emboldened to take our place as intercessors, who can have power with God and prevail. Here the soul mounts up as on eagle's wings, the strength is renewed, and the blessing and the power and the love are imparted with which God's priests can go out to bless a dying world. Here each day we may experience the fresh anointing, in virtue of which we can go out to be the bearers and witnesses and channels of God's salvation to men, the living instruments through whom our blessed King works out His full and final triumph.

O Jesus, our great High Priest, let this be our life!

Chapter Notes...

1. *"One thing have I asked of the* LORD, *that will I seek after; that I may dwell in the house of the* LORD *all the days of my life, to behold the beauty of the* LORD, *and to inquire in his temple"* (Psalm 27:4). Here the prayer is fulfilled.

2. "Did not Jesus say, 'I am the door of the sheepfold' (John 10:1)? What to us is the sheepfold, dear children? It is the heart of the Father, whereunto Christ is the gate that is called Beautiful. O children, how sweetly and how gladly has He opened that door into the Father's heart, into the treasure chamber of God! And there within He unfolds to us the hidden riches, the nearness and the sweetness of companionship with Himself." —Tauler

3. We have read of a man's father or friends purchasing and furnishing a house for a birthday or a wedding gift. They bring him there and, handing him the keys, say to him, "This is now your house." Child of God, the Father opens unto you the Holiest of All and says, "Let this now be your home." What will your answer be?

Eighty-Two

Boldness in the Blood of Jesus

Having therefore, brethren, boldness to enter into the holy
place by the blood of Jesus,...let us draw near.
—Hebrews 10:19, 22

nter into the [holiest]." These words brought us the message
of the epistle. Christ has, in very deed, opened the Holiest of
All for us to enter in and to dwell there. The Father would
have His children with Him in His holy home of love and fellowship, abiding continually all the time. The epistle seeks to gather all
in. *"Having...boldness to enter...let us draw near."*

It may be that some—who in their study in the epistle of the
wondrous mystery of the way the Holiest is now opened—have
entered in; they have said, in faith, "Lord, my God, I come. Henceforth I would live in Thy secret place, in the Holiest of All." And
yet, they fear. They are not sure whether the great High Priest has
indeed taken them in. They do not know for certain whether they
will be faithful, always abiding within the veil. They have not yet
grasped what it means—*"having...boldness to enter in."*

And there may be others who have, with longing, wistful hearts, heard the call to enter in and yet have not the courage to do so. The thought that a sinful worm can every day and all the day dwell in the Holiest of All is altogether too high. The consciousness of feebleness and failure is so strong; the sense of personal unfaithfulness so keen; the experience of the power of the world and circumstances and of the weakness of the flesh and its efforts are so fresh that, for them, there is no hope of such a life. Others may rejoice in it; they must even be content without it. And yet, the heart is not content.

To both—those who have entered but still are full of fears and those who in fear do not enter—the Holy Spirit speaks, *"To-day if ye shall hear his voice, harden not your hearts....Having therefore, brethren, boldness to enter into the holy place by the blood of Jesus,... let us draw near"* (Hebrews 3:7–8; 10:19, 22). The boldness with which we are to enter is not, first of all, a conscious feeling of confidence; it is the objective God-given right and liberty of entrance of which the blood assures us. The measure of our boldness is the worth God attaches to the blood of Jesus. As our hearts repose their confidence on that truth in simple faith, the feeling of confidence and joy on our parts will come, too, and our entrance will be amid songs of praise and gladness.

"Boldness...by the blood of Jesus." Everything depends upon our comprehension of what that means. If the blood is to be to us what it is to God, then the boldness that God means it to give will fill our hearts. As we saw in chapter 9, what the blood has effected in rending the veil and in cleansing the heavens and in giving Jesus, the Son of Man, access to God will be the measure of what it will effect within us, making our hearts God's sanctuary and fitting us for perfect fellowship with the Holy One. The more we honor the blood in its infinite worth, the more it will prove its mighty energy and efficacy—opening heaven to us and in us and giving us, in divine power, the real living experience of what the entrance into the Holiest is.

Andrew Murray

"The blood of Jesus." The life is the blood. As the value of this
life, so the value of the blood. In Christ there was the life of God;
infinite as God is the worth and the power of that blood. In Christ
there was the life of man in its perfection; in His humility and obedience to the Father and self-sacrifice, there was what made Him
unspeakably well-pleasing to the Father. That blood of Jesus, as
God and as the Man, poured out in a death that was a perfect
fulfillment of God's will and a perfect victory over all the temptations of sin and self, effected an everlasting atonement for sin and
put it forever out of the way, destroying death and him who had
the power of it. Therefore it was that in the blood of the everlasting
covenant, Jesus was raised from the dead; that in His own blood,
as our Head and Surety, He entered heaven; and that His blood is
now forever in heaven, in the same place of honor as *"God the Judge
of all, and...Jesus the mediator"* (12:23–24). It is this blood, now in
heaven before God for us, that is our boldness to enter in, even into
the very Holiest of All.

Beloved Christian! The blood of Jesus! The blood of the Lamb!
Oh, think what it means. God gave it for your redemption. God
accepted it when His Son entered heaven and presented it on your
behalf. God has it forever in His sight as the fruit, the infinitely well-
pleasing proof, of His Son's obedience unto death. God points you
to it and asks you to believe in the divine satisfaction it gives to Him,
in its omnipotent energy, in its everlasting sufficiency. Oh, will you
not this day believe that the blood gives you, sinful and feeble as you
are, liberty, confidence, boldness to draw nigh—to enter the very
Holiest? Yes, believe it, that the blood and the blood alone brings
you into the very presence, into the living and abiding fellowship, of
the everlasting God. And let your response to God's message concerning the blood and the boldness it gives you be nothing less than
this—that this very moment you go with the utmost confidence and
take your place in the most intimate fellowship with God. And if
your heart condemns you, if coldness or unbelief appear to make a
real entrance impossible, do not rest until you believe and prove to

the full the power of the blood indeed to bring you near. *"Having... boldness...by the blood of Jesus,...let us draw near"*!

Chapter Notes...

1. Which is now greater in your sight: your sin or the blood of Jesus? There can be but one answer. Then draw near and enter in, into the Holiest of All. As your sin has thus far kept you back, let the blood now bring you near. And the blood will give you the boldness and the power to abide.

2. "One drop of that blood, coming out of the Holiest on the soul, perfects the conscience, makes that there is no more conscience of sin, and enables us to live in the fellowship of God and His Son. Such a soul, sprinkled with the blood, is able to enjoy the heavenly treasures and to accomplish the heavenly service of the living God."*

3. And that blood, such is its heavenly cleansing power, can keep the soul clean. *"If we walk in the light, as he is in the light,"* if we live in the Holiest, in the light of His countenance, *"we have fellowship one with another, and the blood of Jesus his Son cleanseth us from all sin"* (1 John 1:7) so that no sin touches us whereby we lose fellowship with the Father.

4. Understand how the Father's heart longs for His children to draw near to Him boldly. He gave the blood of His Son to secure it. Let us honor God and honor the blood by entering the Holiest with great boldness.

---

* Author unknown.

Eighty-Three
The New and Living Way

*Having therefore, brethren, boldness to enter into the holy
place by the blood of Jesus, by the way which he dedicated* (inaugurated)
*for us, a new and living way, through the veil,
that is to say, his flesh...let us draw near.*
—Hebrews 10:19–20, 22

The Holiest of All is opened for us to enter in and appear before God, to dwell and to serve in His very presence. The blood of the one Sacrifice forever, taken into heaven to cleanse away all sin forever, is our title and our boldness to enter in. Now comes the question, "What is the way that leads up and through the opened gate and in which we have to walk if we are to enter in?" This way—the only way, the one infallible way—is *"a new and living way, [which he dedicated for us] through the veil, that is to say, his flesh."* The boldness we have through the blood is the right, or liberty of access, that Jesus won for us when we regard His death as that of our Substitute, who did what we can never do—made redemption of transgressions and put away sin forever. The *"new and living way, through the veil, that is to say, his flesh,"* has reference to His death, regarded as that of our Leader and Forerunner, who opened up a path to God, in which He first walked

375

Himself and then draws us to follow Him. The death of Jesus was not only the dedication, or inauguration, of the new sanctuary and of the new covenant but also of the new way into the holy presence and fellowship of God. Whoever in faith accepts the blood He shed as His boldness of entrance must accept, too, the way He opened up as that in which he walks.

And what was that way? The way *"through the veil, that is to say, his flesh."* The veil is the flesh. The veil that separated man from God was the flesh, human nature under the power of sin. Christ came in the likeness of sinful flesh and dwelt with us here outside the veil. *"And the Word became flesh"* (John 1:14). *"Since then the children are sharers in flesh and blood, he also himself in like manner partook of the same"* (Hebrews 2:14). *"In the days of his flesh"* (5:7), He was tempted like as we are; He offered prayer and supplication with strong crying and tears. He learned obedience even to the death. Through the rent veil of His flesh, His will, His life, as yielded up to God in death, He entered into the Holiest. *"Being made in likeness of men; and being found in fashion as a man, he humbled himself, becoming obedient even unto death, yea, the death of the cross. Wherefore also God highly exalted him"* (Philippians 2:7–9). Through the rent veil, He rose to the throne of God. And this is the way He dedicated for us. The very path in which, as our Substitute, He accomplished redemption is the path that He opened for us to walk in, the path of obedience unto death. *"Christ also suffered for you, leaving you an example, that ye should follow his steps"* (1 Peter 2:21). Christ our High Priest is as literally and fully Leader and Forerunner as He is Substitute and Redeemer.

His way is our way. As little as He could open and enter the Holiest for us, except in His path of suffering and obedience and self-sacrifice, as little can we enter in unless we walk in the same path. Jesus said as much of His disciples as of Himself, *"Except a grain of wheat fall into the earth and die, it abideth by itself alone.... He that hateth his life in this world shall keep it unto life eternal"* (John 12:24–25). Paul's law of life is the law of life for every believer:

Andrew Murray

"Bearing about in the body the dying of Jesus, that the life also of Jesus may be manifested in our body" (2 Corinthians 4:10). The way into the Holiest is the way of the rent veil, the way of sacrifice and of death. There is no way to put away sin from us but the way of Jesus; whoever accepts His finished work accepts what constitutes its Spirit and its power; it is for every man as for the Master—to put away sin by the sacrifice of self. Christ's death was something entirely and essentially new and so also was His resurrection life, a life out of death such as never had been known before. This new death and new life constitute the new and living way, the new way of living in which we draw near to God.

Even as when Christ spoke of taking His flesh as daily food (see John 6:56), so here, where the Holy Spirit speaks of taking the rent veil of His flesh as our daily lives, many may say, *"This is a hard saying; who can hear it?"* (John 6:60). *"Who then can be saved?"* (Matthew 19:25). To those who are willing and obedient and believe, all things are possible, because it is *"a new and living way." "A new...way."* The word *"new"* means "ever fresh," a way that never decays or waxes old (see Hebrews 8:13) but always retains its first perfection and freshness. *"A...living way."* A way always needs a living man to move upon it; it does not impart either life or strength. This way, the way of obedience and suffering and self-sacrifice and death—however hard it appears and, to nature, utterly impossible—is a living way. It not only opens a track but also supplies the strength to carry the traveller along. It acts in the power of the endless life, in which Christ was made a High Priest. We saw how the Holy Spirit watches over the way into the Holiest and how He, as the Eternal Spirit, enabled Christ, in opening the way, to offer Himself without spot unto God; it is He whose mighty energy pervades this way and inspires it with divine life. As we are made partakers of Christ and as we come to God through Him, His life, the law of the Spirit of life in Christ Jesus, takes possession of us; and, in His strength, we follow in the footsteps of Christ

Jesus. The way into the Holiest is the living way of perfect conformity to Jesus, wrought in us by His Spirit.

The *"new and living way, through the veil"* into the Holiest—we now know what it is: It is the way of death. Yes, the way of death is the way of life. The only way to be set free from our fallen nature, with the curse and power of sin resting on it, is to die to it. Jesus denied Himself and would do nothing to please that nature He had taken, sinless though it was in Him. He denied it; He died to it. This was to Him the path of life. And this is, to us, the living way. As we know Him in the power of His resurrection, He leads us into conformity to His death. He does it in the power of the Holy Spirit. So His death and His life—the new death and the new life of deliverance from sin and fellowship with God, which He inaugurated—work in us, and we are borne along, as He was, to where He is. *"Having therefore...boldness to enter into the...new and living way...let us draw near."*

Chapter Notes...

1. When first a believer avails himself of the boldness he has in the blood, and enters into the Holiest, he does not understand all that is meant by the *"new and living way."* It is enough if his heart is right and he is ready to deny himself and take up his cross. In due time, it will be revealed what the full fellowship is with His Lord in the way He opened up, of obedience unto death.

2. The *"new and living way"* is not only the way for once entering in, but the way for a daily walk, entering ever deeper into God's love and will.

3. The way of life is the way of death. This fallen life, this self, is so sinful and so strong that there is no way of deliverance but by death. But, praise God, the way of death is the way of life; in the power of Christ's resurrection and indwelling, we dare to walk in it.

Eighty-Four

A Great Priest over the House of God

*And having a great priest over the
house of God...let us draw near.*
—Hebrews 10:21–22

We said before that in the symbols of Mosaic worship, there were especially four things that, as types of the mystery of the coming redemption, demand attention. These are—the Sanctuary, the blood, the Way into the Holiest, and the priest. The first three, all heavenly things, we have already discussed; we now come to the fourth, the chief and the best of all—a living Person, Jesus, a great High Priest over the house of God. The knowledge of what He has won for me, the entrance into the Holiest; of the work He did to win it, the shedding of His blood; of the way in which I am to enter into the enjoyment of it all—all this is very precious. But there is something better still, and it is this: that the living, loving Son of God is there, personally to receive me and make me partaker of all the blessedness that God has for me. *"Now in the things which we are saying the chief point is this: We have such a high priest, who sat down on the right hand of the throne of the Majesty in the heavens"* (Hebrews 8:1). *"And having a great priest over the house of God...let us draw near."*

And what is now the work we need Jesus to do for us? Has it not all been done? The Holiest is opened. Boldness through the blood has been secured. The living way has been dedicated to carry us in. What more is there that Jesus has to do for us? Nothing more; it has all been finished, once and forever. And why is it then that we are pointed to Him as the great Priest over the house of God? And what is it that we may expect of Him? What we need, and what we must look to Him for, is this: that He will work in us so that the work He has done for us may be made real within us, as a personal experience of *"the power of an endless life"* (7:16) in which He was constituted Priest. *"Because he abideth for ever,"* we read, *"he is able to save to the uttermost"* (7:24–25). Salvation is a subjective, experimental thing, manifested in the peace and holiness of the heart that He gives. We—our lives, our inner selves, our hearts, our wills and affections—are to be delivered from the power of sin and to taste and enjoy the putting away of sin as a blessed experience. In our very hearts, we are to find and feel the power of His redemption. As deep and strong as sin proved itself in its actual power and its mastery within us is Jesus to prove the triumph of redeeming grace.

His one work as Priest over the house of God is to bring us into it and to enable us to live there. He does this by bringing God and the soul into actual harmony, sympathy, and fellowship with each other. As Minister of the sanctuary, He does all that is to be done in heaven with God; as Mediator of the new covenant, He does all that is to be done here on earth in our hearts—the one as effectually as the other. The two offices are united in the one great Priest; in each act of His, He unites both functions to the soul that knows what to expect and that trusts Him. Every movement in the presence of God can have its corresponding movement in the heart of man.

Andrew Murray

And how is this effected? In virtue of His union with us and our union with Him, Jesus is the Second Adam, the new Head of the race. He is the Head in virtue of His real humanity, having in it the power of true divinity that filleth all. Just as Adam was our forerunner into death, and we have all the power of his sin and death working in us and drawing us on, so we have Jesus as our Forerunner into God's presence, with all the power of His death and His resurrection-life working in us and drawing and lifting us in with divine energy into the Father's presence. Yes, Jesus with His divine and heavenly life, in the power of the throne on which He is seated, has entered into the deepest ground of our beings, where Adam and sin do their work; He is there unceasingly carrying out His work of lifting us heavenward into God's presence, of making God's heavenly presence here on earth our portion.

And why is it that we enjoy this so little? And what is needed so that we come to its full enjoyment? And how can Jesus truly be to us a great High Priest, giving us our actual life in the Holiest of All? One great reason for failure is what the epistle so insists on: our ignorance of the spiritual perfection-truth it seeks to teach, and especially of what the Holy Spirit witnesses of the way into the Holiest. And what we need is just this: that the Holy Spirit Himself—that Jesus in the Holy Spirit—be waited on and accepted and trusted to do the work in power. Do keep a firm hold of this truth: that when our great High Priest once for all entered the Holiest and sat down on the throne, it was the Holy Spirit sent down in power into the hearts of His disciples through whom the heavenly High Priest became a present and an indwelling Savior, bringing down with Him into their hearts the presence and the love of God. That Pentecostal gift, in the power of the glorified Christ, is the one indispensable channel of the power of Jesus' priesthood. Nothing but the fullness of the Spirit in daily life, making Jesus present within us, abiding continually, can keep us in the presence of God as full experience. Jesus is no outward High Priest, who can save us as from a distance. No, as the Second Adam, He is nowhere if He is not in us. The one reason why the truth of His heavenly priest-hood is so often powerless is because we look upon it as an external distant thing, a work going on in heaven above us. The one cure for this evil is to know that our great Priest over the house of God is the glorified Jesus who, in the Holy Spirit, is present in us and makes all that is done in heaven above for us to be done within us, too, by the Holy Spirit.

He is Priest over the house of God, the place where God dwells; we are His house, too. And as surely as Jesus ministers in the sanctuary above, He moment by moment ministers in the sanctuary within. *"Having therefore, brethren"* (10:19)—not only in gift, not only in the possession of right and thought, but in our hearts—*"And having a great priest over the house of God...let us draw near."*

Chapter Notes...

1. *"Having a great priest"*! You know a great deal of Jesus, but do you know that His chief, His all-comprehensive work, is to bring you near, oh so near, to God? Has He done this for you? If not, ask Him; trust Him for it.

2. It is Jesus Himself I want. He alone can satisfy me. It is in the holy faith of Jesus, the compassionate Sympathizer, in the holy love of Jesus who calls us brethren, that we can draw near to God. It is in a heart given up, with its trust and love and devotion to Jesus, that the presence of God will be felt.

3. We have such a High Priest! Yes, say, "I have Him; in all His power and love, He is mine." And yield to Him to do His work.

Eighty-Five

With a True Heart

Let us draw near with a true heart.
—Hebrews 10:22

We have been looking at the four great blessings of the new worship by which God encourages us to draw near to Him. We will now see what the four chief things are that God seeks for in us as we come to Him. Of these, the first is a true heart.

In man's nature, the heart is the central power. As the heart is, so is the man. The desire and the choice, the love and the hatred of the heart, prove what a man is already and decide what he is to become. Just as we judge a man's physical character—his size and strength and age and habits—by his outward appearance, so the heart gives the real inward man his character, and *"the hidden man of the heart"* (1 Peter 3:4) is what God looks to. God has, in Christ, given us access to the secret place of His dwelling, to the inner sanctuary of His presence and His heart; no wonder that the first thing He asks, as He calls us unto Him, is the heart—a true heart; our inmost being must, in truth, be yielded to Him, true to Him.

True religion is a thing of the heart, an inward life. It is only as the desire of the heart is fixed upon God—with the whole heart seeking for God and giving its love and finding its joy in God—that a man can draw near to God. The heart of man was expressly planned and created and endowed with all its powers that it might be capable of receiving and enjoying God and His love. God's great quarrel with His people is that their hearts have turned from Him. In chapter 3, we heard Him complain of the hardening of the heart, the wandering heart, the unbelieving heart. No wonder that the first requisite for entering the Holiest of All should be a true heart. It is only with the heart that religion, holiness, and the love and will of God can be known. God can ask for nothing else and nothing less than the heart—a true heart.

What the word *"true,"* means we see from the use of it made previously—*"the true tabernacle"* (Hebrews 8:2), and, *"a holy place made with hands, like in pattern to the true"* (9:24). The first tabernacle was only a figure and a shadow of the true. There was, indeed, a religious service and worship, but it had no real abiding power; it could not make the worshiper perfect. *"The very image"* (10:1), the substance and reality, of the heavenly things themselves were only brought by Christ. And God now asks that, to correspond with the true sanctuary, there will be *"a true heart."* The old covenant, with its tabernacle and its worship, which were but a shadow, could not put the heart of Israel right. In the new covenant, God's first promise is, *"I will put my laws on their heart"* (10:16); *"a new heart also will I give you"* (Ezekiel 36:26). As He has given His Son, full of grace and truth, in *"the power of an endless life"* (Hebrews 7:16), to work all in us as the Mediator of a new covenant, to write His law in our hearts, He calls us to draw near with *"a true heart."*

God asks for the heart. Alas, how many Christians serve Him still with the service of the old covenant. Religion is a thing of times and duties. There are seasons for Bible-reading and praying and churchgoing. But when one notices how speedily and naturally and happily—as soon as it is freed from restraint—the heart turns to worldly things, one feels how little there is of the heart in it: It is not the worship of *"a true heart,"* of the whole heart. The heart, with its life and love and joy, has not yet found in God its highest good. Religion is much more a thing of the head and its activities than of the heart and its life, of the human will and its power than of that Spirit that God gives within us.

The invitation comes: *"Let us draw near with a true heart."* Let no one hold back for fear that his heart is not true. There is no way for obtaining the true heart but by acting it. God has given you, as his child, a new heart—a wonderful gift, if you but knew it. Through ignorance or unbelief or disobedience, it has grown feeble and withered; its beating can, nevertheless, still be felt. The epistle, with its solemn warnings and its blessed teaching, has come to bring awakening and healing. Even as Christ said to the man with the withered hand, *"Stand forth"* (Mark 3:3), He calls to you from His throne in heaven, "Rise and come and enter in with a true heart." As you hesitate and look within to feel and to find out if the heart is true and, in vain, to do what is needed to make it true, He calls again, *"Stretch forth thy hand"* (Luke 6:10). When He spoke this to the man with the withered arm, whom He had called to rise up and stand before Him, the man felt the power of Jesus' eye and voice, and he stretched it forth. You, do the same. Stretch forth, lift up, and reach out that withered heart of yours that has so been cherishing its own helplessness—stretch forth, and it will be made whole. Yes, in the very act of obeying the call to enter in, it will prove itself a true heart—a heart ready to obey and to trust its blessed Lord, a heart ready to give up all and find its life in the secret of His presence. Yes, Jesus, the great Priest over the house of God, the Mediator of the new covenant, with the new heart secured for you, calls, "Draw near with a true heart."

During these last years, God has been rousing His people to the pursuit of holiness—that is, to seek the entrance into the Holiest, a life in full fellowship with Himself, the Holy One. In the teaching that He has been using to this end, two words have been very much in the foreground: *consecration* and *faith*. These are precisely what are here put first—a true heart and the fullness of faith. The true heart is nothing but true consecration, the spirit that longs to live wholly for God, that gladly gives up everything so that it may live wholly for Him and that, above all, yields up the heart, as the key of the life, into His keeping and rule. True religion is an inward life in the power of the Holy Spirit. Let us enter into the inner sanctuary of God's love, and the Spirit will enter into the inner sanctuary of our love, into our hearts. *"Let us draw near with a true heart"*—longing, ready, utterly given up to desire and receive the blessing.

Chapter Notes...

1. If you look at your own constitution, you see how the head and the heart are the two great centers of life and action. Much thought and study make the head weary; strong emotion or excitement affects the heart. It is the heart for which God asks—the power of desire and affection and will. The head and the heart are in partnership. God tells us that the heart must rule and lead, that it is the heart He wants. Our religion has been too much that of the head—hearing and reading and thinking. Let us beware of allowing these to lead us astray. Let them stand aside at times. Let us give the heart time to assert its supremacy. *"Let us draw near with a true heart."*

2. *"A true heart"*—true in what it says that it thinks of itself; true in what it says that it believes of God; true in what it professes to take from God and to give to Him.

3. It is the heart God wants to dwell in. It is in the state of the heart God wants to prove His power to bless. It is in the heart that the love and the joy of God are to be known. *"Let us draw near with a true heart."*

Eighty-Six
In the Fullness of Faith

Let us draw near with a true heart in fulness of faith.
—Hebrews 10:22

This translation, *"fulness of faith,"* is not only more correct than that of *"full assurance of faith"* (KJV), but also much more significant. *"Full assurance of faith"* refers only to the strength and confidence with which we believe. The truth we accept may be very limited and defective, and our assurance of it may be more an undoubting conviction of the mind than the living apprehension of the heart. In both respects, the *"fulness of faith"* expresses what we need—a faith that takes in objectively all that God offers it in its fullness and subjectively all the powers of our hearts and lives in their fullness. *"Let us draw near...in fulness of faith."*

Here, if anywhere, there is indeed need of *"fulness of faith,"* that we may take in all the fullness of the provision God has made and of the promises that are waiting for us to inherit them. The message comes to a sinful man that he may have his continual abode in the Most Holy; that, more real and near than with his nearest earthly friend, he may live in unbroken fellowship with the Most High God. He is assured that the blood of Christ can cleanse his conscience in such power that he can draw near to God with a perfect conscience and with undoubting confidence, and that he can ask and expect to live always in the unclouded light of God's face. He receives the assurance that the power of the Holy Spirit, coming from out of the Holiest, can enable him to walk exactly in the same path in which Christ walked on His way to God, and make that way to him *"a new and living way"* (Hebrews 10:20), with nothing of decay or weariness in his progress. This is the *"fulness of faith"* we are called to. But, above all, we are to look to Jesus in all the glory in which He has been revealed in the epistle—as God and as the Man; as Leader and Forerunner; as Melchizedek; as the Minister of the sanctuary and Mediator of the new covenant— in one word, as our *"great priest over the house of God"* (verse 21). And, looking to Him, we are to claim that He will do for us this one thing: to bring us near and, even on earth, allow us to dwell forever in the presence of God.

Faith ever deals with impossibilities. Its only rule or measure is what God has said to be possible to Him. When we look at our lives and their failures, at our sinfulness and weakness, at those around us, the thought will come up, "Is it for me? Dare I expect it? Is it not wearying myself in vain to think of it or to seek for it?" Soul, God who redeemed you, when yet an enemy, with the blood of His Son: What do you think? Would He not be willing thus to take you to His heart? He who raised Jesus, when He had died under the curse of your sins, from the death of the grave to the throne of His glory, would He not be able to take you, too, and give you a place within the veil? Do believe that He longs to do it; He is able to do it. His home and His heart have room for you even now. *"Let us draw near...in fulness of faith."*

"In fulness of faith." The word also has reference to that full measure of faith that is found when the whole heart is filled and possessed by it. We have very little idea of how the weakness of our faith is owing to its being more of a confident persuasion of the

Andrew Murray

mind with regard to the truth of what God says, than the living apprehension and possession of the eternal spiritual realities of the truth with the heart. The Holy Spirit asks us first for *"a true heart,"* and then at once, as its first exercise, for *"fulness of faith."* There is a faith of insight, a faith of desire, a faith of trust in the truth of the Word, and a faith of personal acceptance. There is a faith of love that embraces, a faith of will that holds fast, a faith of sacrifice that gives up everything, a faith of despair that abandons all hope in self, and a faith of rest that waits on God alone. This is all included in the faith of the true heart, the *"fulness of faith,"* in which the whole being surrenders, lets go of all, and yields itself to God to do His work. *"Let us draw near with a true heart in fulness of faith."*

"In fulness of faith," not of thought. What God is about to do to you is supernatural, above what you can think. A love that passes knowledge is going to take possession. God is the incomprehensible, the hidden One. The Holy Spirit is the secret, incomprehensible working and presence of God. Do not seek to understand everything. *"Draw near"*—it never says with a clear head, but *"with a true heart."* Rest upon God to do for you far more than you understand.

"In fulness of faith," and not in fullness of feeling. When you come and, gazing into the opened Holiest of All, hear the voice of Him who dwells between the cherubim call you to come in; and, as you gaze, you long indeed to enter and to dwell there, the word comes again, *"Draw near with a true heart"*! Your answer is, "Yes, Lord; with my whole heart—with that new heart Thou Thyself has given me." You make the surrender of yourself, to live only and always in His presence and for His service. The voice speaks again, "Let it be today—now, *'in fulness of faith.'*" You have accepted what He offers. You have given what he asks. You believe that He accepts the surrender. You believe that the *"great priest over the house"* (verse 21) takes possession of your inner life and brings you before God. And yet, you wonder why you feel so little changed. You feel just like the old self you were. Now is the time to listen to the voice—

"in fulness of faith," not of feeling! Look to God, who is able to do above what we ask or think. Trust His power. Look to Jesus on the throne, living there to bring you in. Claim the Spirit of the exalted One as His Pentecostal gift. Remember these are all divine, spiritual mysteries of grace, to be revealed in you. Apart from feeling, without feeling—*"in fulness of faith,"* in bare, naked faith that honors God—enter in. Reckon yourself to be indeed alive to God in Christ Jesus, taken into His presence, His love, His very heart.

Chapter Notes...

1. Be followers of those who, through faith and longsuffering, inherited the promises. Faith accepts and rejoices in the gift; longsuffering waits for the full enjoyment; and so faith, in due time, inherits; and the promise becomes an experience. By faith take your place in the Holiest at once; wait on the Holy Spirit in your inner life to reveal it in the power of God; your High Priest will see to your inheriting the blessing.

2. The fullness of the whole heart to accept the whole fullness of God's salvation—this is what God asks.

3. *"As in heaven, so on earth"* (Matthew 6:10). The more I look at the fullness of grace in Christ, the more the *"fulness of faith"* will grow in me. Of His fullness we have received, and grace for grace.

4. A whole chapter is to be devoted to the exhibiting of what this *"fulness of faith"* implies. Let us go on to study it with the one object for which it is given—our entering into that life, in the will and love of God, that Jesus has secured for us.

Eighty-Seven
Our Hearts Sprinkled

*Let us draw near...our hearts sprinkled from
an evil conscience.*
—Hebrews 10:22

In Hebrews 10:19 we had *"boldness...by the blood of Jesus"* as one of the four precious things prepared for us by God. It is that actual liberty, or right, that the blood of Jesus gives, apart from any use we make of it. Along with the opened sanctuary and the living way and the great Priest, the blood and our boldness in it is a heavenly reality waiting for our faith and acceptance. Here, the blood is mentioned a second time, and our being sprinkled with it is one of the things God asks of us. It is in the personal application and experience of the power of the blood that we are to draw near.

This second mention of the blood is in accord with what we had in chapter 9 of its twofold sprinkling. First, Christ entered with it into heaven, to cleanse the heavenly things and fulfill the type of the sprinkling on the mercy seat. It proved its power with God in putting away sins. And then we read of its cleansing our conscience. The blood, which has had its mighty operation in heaven itself, has as mighty of a power in our hearts. It makes us partakers of a divine and eternal cleansing. In heaven, the power of the blood is proved to be infinite and immeasurable, never-ceasing and eternal, giving boldness to enter even as Christ did. As the soul learns to believe and rejoice in this heavenly power of the blood, it will claim and receive the very same power in the heart; as Jesus washes us in His blood, we know by faith what it is to have, in a heavenly reality, a heart *"sprinkled from an evil conscience."*

There will ever be harmony between a home and those who dwell in it, between an environment and the life that is sustained by it. There must be harmony between the Holiest of All and the soul that is to enter in. That harmony begins with—and has its everlasting security in—the blood of sprinkling. The ever-living and never-ceasing energy of the blood, always speaking better things than the blood of Abel and keeping heaven open for me (see 12:24), has a similar effect on my heart. The blood has put away the thought of sin from God; He remembers it no more, forever. The blood puts away the thought of sin in me, too, taking away the evil conscience that condemns me. The better things that the blood speaks in heaven, it speaks in my heart, too; it lifts me into that heavenly sphere, that new state of life and communion with God, in which an end has been made of sin and the soul is taken in to the full and perfect enjoyment of the love of God.

The action of the blood in heaven is unceasing—there is never a moment when the blood is not the delight of the Father and the song of the ransomed. Draw near when you will; the blood is there, abiding continually, with not a moment's interval. And even so, it will be in the soul that enters in. The difficulty that staggers the faith of many lies just here: They cannot understand how one who has to live amid the cares and engagements and companionships of this daily life can every moment maintain a heart *"sprinkled from an evil conscience."* They do not know that, if once they enter in with their hearts sprinkled, they are in an inner sanctuary where everything acts in the power of the upper world, in *"the power of*

Andrew Murray

an endless life" (7:16). They breathe the inspiring, invigorating air of the Holiest of All; they breathe the Holy Spirit and enjoy the power of the resurrection life. The Minister of the heavenly sanctuary is also the Mediator of the new covenant in our hearts. All that He does in heaven, He does each moment on earth in our hearts if faith will trust Him, for the blood of sprinkling is the blood of the covenant.

And what may be the reason that so few Christians can testify of the joy and the power of a heart at all times *"sprinkled from an evil conscience"*? The answer is that, in the apprehension of this, as of every other truth, there are stages according to the measure of faith and faithfulness. See it in Israel; there you have three stages. The Israelite who entered the outer court saw the altar, and the blood sprinkled there, and received such assurance of pardon as that sight could give him. The priest who was admitted to the Holy Place not only saw the blood sprinkled on the brazen altar; he had it sprinkled upon himself, too, and might see it sprinkled on the golden altar in the Holy Place. His contact with the blood was closer, and he was admitted to a nearer access. And the access of the high priest was still more complete; he might, with the blood for the mercy seat, once a year enter within the veil. Even so, there are outer-court Christians, who trust in Christ who died on Calvary but know very little of His heavenly life, or nearer access to God, or service for others. Beyond these, there are Christians who know that they are called to be priests and to live in the service of God and their fellowmen. They know more of the power of the blood as setting apart for service, but yet their lives are still outside the veil. But then come those who know what Christ's entering with His blood implies and procures; these Christians experience the Holy Spirit applying the blood in such power so that it indeed brings to them life in the inner sanctuary, in the full and abiding joy of God's presence.

"Let us draw near with a true heart in fulness of faith, having our hearts sprinkled from an evil conscience." Oh, let us not bring a

reproach upon the blood of the Lamb by not believing in its power to give us perfect access to God. Let us listen and hear them sing without ceasing the praise of the blood of the Lamb in heaven; as we trust and honor and rejoice in it, we will enter the heaven of God's presence.

Chapter Notes...

1. "Wherein is the blood of Jesus better than the blood of goats and bulls, if it cannot free us from the spirit of bondage and the evil conscience, if it cannot give us a full glad confidence before God? What Jesus hath perfected, we can experience and enjoy as perfect in our heart and conscience. You dishonor your Savior when you do not seek to experience that He has perfected you as touching the conscience, and when you do not live with a heart entirely cleansed from the evil conscience." —Steinhoffer

2. A true heart—a heart sprinkled: You see everything depends upon the heart. God can do nothing for us from without, only by what He can put into the heart. Of all that Jesus is and does as High Priest in heaven, I cannot have the least experience but as it is revealed in the heart. The whole work of the Holy Spirit is in the heart. Let us draw nigh with a true heart, a sprinkled heart, our inmost being entirely and unceasingly under the heavenly power of the blood.

3. "The blood contains life (see John 6:53). The blood not only removes death (judicial and spiritual), but it gives and preserves life (judicial and spiritual). It quickens. We are not only to be sprinkled with it outwardly, but we are to receive it inwardly, to drink it. As with the water, so with the blood; they are for inward as well as outward application." —H. Bonar

Eighty-Eight
Our Bodies Washed

Let us draw near...our body washed with pure water.
—Hebrews 10:22

Man belongs to two worlds, the visible and the invisible. In his constitution, the material and the spiritual—the body and the soul—are wonderfully united. In the Fall, both came under the power of sin and death; in redemption, deliverance has been provided for both. It is not only in the interior life of the soul, but in that of the body, too, that the power of redemption can be manifested.

In the Old Testament worship, the external was the more prominent. It consisted mostly in carnal ordinances, imposed until a time of reformation. They taught a measure of truth, they exercised a certain influence on the heart, but they could not make the worshiper perfect. It was only with the New Testament that the religion of the inner life, the worship of God in spirit and truth, was revealed. And yet we need to be on the watch lest the pursuit of the inner life lead us to neglect the external. It is in the body, as much as in the spirit, that the saving power of Christ Jesus must be felt. It was with this view that our Lord adopted one of the Jewish washings and instituted the baptism with water. He who believed with his heart came with his body to be baptized. It was a token that the whole exterior physical life, with all its functions and powers, was to be His, too. In was in this connection that John wrote, *"There are three who bear witness, the Spirit, and the water, and the blood"* (1 John 5:8). The same Spirit who applies the blood in power to the heart takes possession and mastery of the body washed with water. And where, in Scripture, the Word and water are joined together (see Ephesians 5:26; John 13:10; 15:3), it is because the Word is the external manifestation of what must rule our whole outer lives, too.

It is in this connection that the two expressions are used here: *"Our hearts sprinkled from an evil conscience"* (Hebrews 10:22), and *"our body washed with pure water."* The thought was suggested to our author by the service of the tabernacle. In the court, there were only two things to be seen—the brazen altar and the laver. At the one, the priest received and sprinkled the blood; at the other, he found the water in which he washed before he entered the Holy Place. At the installation of the priests in their office, they were first washed and then sprinkled with blood. (See Exodus 29:4, 20.) On the great Day of Atonement, the high priest, too, had first to wash before he entered into the Holiest with the blood. (See Leviticus 16:4.)

And so, the lesson comes to us that if we draw near with *"hearts sprinkled from an evil conscience"* (Hebrews 10:22), we must also have the *"body washed with pure water."* The liberty of access, the cleansing that the blood gives, can only be enjoyed in a life in which every action is cleansed by the Word. Not only in the heart and the disposition but also in the body, the outer visible life, everything must be clean. *"Who shall ascend into the hill of the LORD? And who shall stand in his holy place? He that hath clean hands, and a pure heart"* (Psalm 24:3–4). A heart sprinkled with the blood, a *"body washed with pure water"* from every stain—these God has joined together; let no man separate them. There have been some who have sought very earnestly to enter into the Holiest of All and have failed. The reason was that they had not clean hands, they were not ready to have everything that is not perfectly holy discovered and put away. *"Cleanse your hands, ye sinners; and purify your hearts, ye double-minded"* (James 4:8)—is a word that always holds. The blood of Christ has unspeakable and everlasting power for the soul that, with a true heart, is ready to put away every sin. Where this is not the case, and where the body is not washed with pure water, the perfect conscience that the blood gives cannot be enjoyed.

"Our body washed with pure water." It is not only in spirit, but with the body, too, that we enter into the Holiest of All. It is on us here, where we are in the body, that the presence of God descends. Our whole lives in the flesh are to be in that presence; the body is very specifically the temple and in charge of the Holy Spirit; in the body, the Father is to be glorified. Our whole beings—body, soul, and spirit—are in the power of the Holy Spirit, a holy sacrifice upon the altar, a living sacrifice for service before God. With the body, too, we live and walk in the Holiest. Our eating and drinking, our sleeping, our clothing, our labor and relaxation—all these things have more influence on our spiritual lives than we know. They often interrupt and break the fellowship we seek to maintain. The heart and the body are inseparably joined—a heart *"sprinkled from an evil conscience"* (verse 22) needs a *"body washed with pure water."*

"Wherefore when he cometh into the world, he saith, Sacrifice and offering thou wouldest not, but a body didst thou prepare for me" (10:5). This word of Christ must be adopted by each of His followers. Nothing will help us to live in this world and keep ourselves unspotted but the Spirit who was in Christ, who looked upon His body as prepared by God for His service; who looks upon our bodies as prepared by Him, too, so that we might offer them to Him. Like Christ, we, too, each have a body in which the Holy Spirit dwells. Like Christ, we, too, must yield our bodies—with every member, every power, every action—to fulfill His will and to be offered up to Him, to glorify Him. Like Christ, we must prove in our bodies that we are holy to the Lord.

The blood that is sprinkled on your heart came from the body of Jesus—prepared by God and, in His whole life, even to His one offering, given up to God. The object of that blood sprinkling is that your body—of which the heart sprinkled with the blood is the life—should, like His, be wholly given up to God. Oh, seek to take in this blessed truth and to accept it fully. The heart sprinkled from the evil conscience will then become an unbroken experience, and the blood of the Lamb will be the ever-living motive and power for a life in the body like Christ's, a sacrifice holy and acceptable to God.

Chapter Notes...

1. I am deeply persuaded that in the self-pleasing that we allow in gratifying the claims of the body, we will find one of the most frequent causes of the gradual decline of our fellowship with God. Do remember, it was through the body that Satan conquered in Paradise; it was in the body that he tempted Christ and had to be resisted. It was in suffering of the body, as when He hungered, that Christ was perfected. It is only when the law of self-denial is strictly applied to the body that we can dwell in the Holiest.

2. He was *"in all points tempted like as we are"* (4:15)—in His body especially—and is able to succor us. Let the commitment of our bodies into the keeping and the rule of Jesus be very definite and entire.

3. "If Miranda was to run a race for her life, she would submit to a diet that was proper for it. As the race that is set before her is a race for holiness and heavenly affection, so her everyday diet has only this one end—to make her body fitter for this spiritual life."*

---

* Author unknown.

Eighty-Nine
Let Us Draw Near

Having therefore, brethren...let us draw near.
—Hebrews 10:19, 22

We have studied the four great blessings of the new worship as the motives and encouragements for us to draw nigh. They are: the Holiest opened up; *"boldness...by the blood"* (Hebrews 10:19); the *"new and living way"* (verse 20); and the *"great priest over the house of God"* (verse 21). And we have considered the four great marks of the true worshiper—*"a true heart"*; *"fulness of faith"*; the heart *"sprinkled"*; and the *"body washed"* (verse 22). We now come to the four injunctions that come to us out of the opened sanctuary— and specifically to the first—*"Let us draw near."* Both in speaking of the entering in of Christ and the power of His blood in chapter 9, and in the exposition of our context, we have had abundant occasion to point out what is meant by this entering in and what is needed for it. And yet, it may be well to gather up all we have said and, in the very simplest way possible, once again, by the grace of God, throw open the door and help each honest-hearted child of God to enter in and take his place for life in the home the Father has prepared for him.

And first of all, I would say this: Believe that a life in the Holiest of All, a life of continual abiding in God's presence, is most

certainly your duty and within your power. As long as this appears
a vague uncertainty, the study of our epistle must be in vain. Its
whole teaching has been to prove that the wonderful priesthood
of Christ, in which He does everything in *"the power of an endless
life"* (7:16) and is therefore *"able to save* [completely]*"* (7:25); that
His having opened a way through the rent veil into the Holiest
and entered in with His blood; that His sitting on the throne in
heavenly power, as Minister of the sanctuary and Mediator of the
covenant—that all this means nothing if it does not mean that the
Holiest is open for us. We may, we must, and we can live there.
What is the meaning of this summing up of all, *"Having therefore, brethren, boldness to enter...let us draw near,"* if a real entrance
into and abode in the Holiest is not for us? No, beloved Christian,
do believe that it can be. Let no thought of your weakness and
unfaithfulness hold you back. Begin to look at God, who has set
the door open and calls you in; at the blood that has prevailed over
sin and death, and given you a boldness that nothing can hinder; at
Christ the Almighty, and most loving High Priest, who is to bring
you in and keep you in—begin to look at these and believe that,
"Yes, such a life is meant for me; it is possible; it is my duty; God
calls me to it." And say, then, whether your heart would not desire
and long to enter into this blessed rest, the home of God's love.

The second step is the surrender to Christ, so as to be brought
by Him into the life of abiding fellowship with God. This surrender implies an entire giving up of the life of nature and of self; an
entire separation from the world and its spirit; an entire acceptance
of God's will to command your life, in all things, down to the very
least. To some, this surrender comes as the being convicted of a
number of things that they thought harmless and that they now
see to have been in the will of the flesh and of man. To others, it
comes as a call to part with some single doubtful thing, or some
sin against which they have hopelessly struggled. The "surrender
of all" only becomes possible when the soul sees how truly and
entirely Jesus, the Mediator of the new covenant, has undertaken

for all and how He engages to put His own delight in God's law into the heart to give the will and the strength to live in all God's will. Such a faith gives the courage to place oneself before Christ and to say, "Lord, here am I, ready to be led by Thee in the new and living way of death to my will, and a life in God's will alone: I give up all to Thee."

Then comes, accompanying this surrender, the faith that Jesus does now accept and undertake for all. The more general faith in His power, which led to the surrender, now becomes a personal appropriation. I know that I cannot lift or force myself into the Holiest. I trust Jesus, as my almighty and ever-living Priest on the throne, even now, at this moment, to take me in within the veil, to take charge of me there, and to enable me to walk up and down before the face of the living God and serve Him. However high and impossible such a life appears, I cannot doubt but that He, who with His blood opened the Holiest for me, will take me in; and that He, who sits on the throne as my great High Priest, is able and faithful to keep me in God's presence. Apart from any feeling or experience of a change, I believe that He takes me in, and I say, "Thank God, I am in the Holiest." *"Let us draw near...in fulness of faith."*

And then follows the life of faith in the Holiest, which is "holding fast my confidence and the glorying of hope, firm to the end" (3:6). I believe that Jesus takes me in to the fulfillment and the experience of all the new covenant blessings and makes me inherit all the promises. I look to Him day by day to seal my faith with the Holy Spirit sent down from heaven in my heart. The disciples, when their Lord ascended the throne, kept waiting, praising, and praying until the Spirit came as the Witness and the Revealer within their hearts of the glory of Jesus at the right hand of God. It was on the day of Pentecost that they truly entered within the veil, to which the Forerunner had drawn their longing hearts. The soul that gives itself over to a life within the veil, in full surrender and in simple faith, can count upon this most surely— that, in the power of the eternal, Pentecostal Spirit in the heart, faith will become experience, and the joy unspeakable will be its abiding portion. *"Therefore, brethren...let us draw near."*

Chapter Notes...

1. *"Having...boldness to enter into the holy place"* is the summary of the doctrinal teaching of the first half of the epistle; *"let us draw near"* is the summary of the life and practice that the second half expounds.

2. The faith that appropriates the blessing—Jesus now takes me in and gives me my place and my life in the Father's presence—is but a beginning. Faith must now count upon the Holy Spirit, in His Pentecostal power bringing down the kingdom of heaven to us, to make it a personal experience. Until this comes, faith must in patience wait until it obtains the promise, in accordance with the teaching we had, *"Cast not away therefore your boldness, which hath great recompense of reward. For ye have need of patience, that, having done the will of God, ye may receive the promise"* (10:35–36).

Ninety

The Confession of Our Hope

*Let us hold fast the confession of our hope that it waver
not; for he is faithful that promised.*
—Hebrews 10:23

The three chief words of this injunction we have had before—
"hold fast," "confession," and *"hope." "If we hold fast our boldness and the glorying of our hope firm unto the end"* (Hebrews
3:6). *"Shew the same diligence unto the fulness of hope even to the end"*
(6:11). Christ, the *"High Priest of our confession"* (3:1). *"Let us hold
fast our confession"* (4:14). *"A better hope, through which we draw nigh
unto God"* (7:19). We have now been brought to see what Christian
perfection is, in that perfect life in God's presence to which Jesus
brings us in; here, more than ever, we will need to hold fast our hope.

Faith and hope ever go together. *"Faith is the assurance of
things hoped for"* (11:1). Faith accepts the promise in its divine reality; hope goes forward to examine and picture and rejoice in the
treasures that faith has accepted. And so here, on the words *"Let us
draw near...in fulness of faith"* (10:22), there follows immediately,

"Let us hold fast the confession of our hope." Life in the Holiest, in the nearness of God, must be characterized by an infinite hopefulness.

It is not difficult to see the reason for this. Entering into the Holiest is only the beginning of the true Christian life. As we tarry there, God can begin to do His work of grace in power. There, the holiness of God can overshadow us and can be assimilated into our life and character. There, we can learn to worship in that true humility and meekness and resignation to God's will, which does not come at once but in which we may grow up, even as Jesus did. There, we have to learn the holy art of intercession, so as to pray the prayer that prevails. There, we wait to receive in larger measure, in ever-fresh communication, that fullness of the Spirit that comes and is maintained only by close and living contact with Jesus on the throne. The entrance into the Holiest is only a beginning. It is to be a life in which we, every hour, receive everything from God; in which God's working is to be all in all. Here, if anywhere, we have need for an infinite hopefulness. After we have entered in, we will very probably not find what we expected. The light and the joy and the power may not come at once. Within the veil it is still—nay, rather, it is eminently—a life of faith; not looking to ourselves but to God and hoping in Him. Faith will still be tried, will perhaps most be tried when God wants most to bless. Hope is the daughter of faith, the messenger it sends out to see what is to come; it is hope that becomes the strength and support of faith.

"Let us hold fast the confession of our hope." Men always speak out of the abundance of the heart of that for which they hope. We, too, must confess and give expression to our hope. The confession strengthens the hope; what we utter becomes clearer and more real to us. It glorifies God. It helps and encourages those around us. It makes God and men and ourselves see that we are committed to it. *"Let us hold fast the confession of our hope,"* so that it does not waver. Let the better hope, by which we draw near to God and by which we enter within the veil, be the one thing to which we hold fast and confess with a confidence that never wavers.

Andrew Murray

"For he is faithful that promised." Study the references on the word *"promise"* in this epistle, and see what a large place they take in God's dealings with His people; learn how much your life depends on your relation to the promises. Connect the promises, as is here done, with the Promiser; connect the Promiser with His unchanging faithfulness as God; and your hope will become a glorying in God, through Jesus Christ our Lord. Faithful is He who promised; that word lies at the root of the life within the veil. Just as it is God who speaks in Christ—who sent Him, who appointed Him Priest, who perfected Him—so it is God to whom Christ brings us into the Holiest for Him now to work directly and continually in us that life in which, as His redeemed creatures, we are to live. This is the blessedness of being brought into the Holiest: Christ has brought us to God. And we are now in the right place and spirit for honoring Him as God—that is, for allowing Him to work freely, immediately, unceasingly in us such a life as He wrought in Christ. *"He is faithful that promised."* God is going to fulfill His promises of life and love, of blessing and fruitfulness, in a way we have no concept of. *"Let us hold fast the confession of our hope that it waver not; for he is faithful that promised."*

My reader, you have heard the call, *"Let us draw near...in fullness of faith"* (verse 22). And have you obeyed? Have you believed that Jesus takes you into a life of abiding in God's presence? And are you, even amid the absence of feeling or experience, even amid the doubts and fears that threaten to press in, holding fast the confession of your hope? Listen, look up—*"He is faithful that promised"*! Let this be your rock. Say continually, "O my soul, put your hope in God, for I will yet praise Him. Thou are my hope, O God. I will hope continually and praise Thee yet more and more." This is the blessing of the inner sanctuary, that you have found your true place at God's feet, there to wait in absolute dependence and helplessness on His working. Look up in the boldness that the blood gives you. Look up with a true heart, in which the Holy Spirit dwells and works. Look up with a heart sprinkled by your blessed High Priest with the blood. And hope—yes hope!—in God to do His divine work in you soul. Let Him be to your more than ever the God of hope. Claim the fulfillment of the promise of His word: *"The God of hope fill you with all joy and peace in believing, that ye may abound in hope, in the power of the Holy Ghost"* (Romans 15:13). The infinite faithful God, as the God of our hope, filling us with joy and peace in believing; and we, learning to abound in hope through the power of the Holy Spirit: Be this our life in the secret of God's presence!

Chapter Notes...

1. Fullness of faith and fullness of hope are two dispositions that mark the true heart. It is because we are to have nothing in ourselves, and because God is to be all and to do all, that our whole attitude is to be looking up to Him, expecting and receiving what He is to do.

2. *"That ye may abound in hope, in the power of the Holy Ghost"* (verse 13). See how the life of hope in the Holiest depends entirely upon the Holy Spirit dwelling within us. To live this life, we need to be filled with the Spirit. Not a moment can we dwell in the Holiest but by the Holy Spirit. Let us abound in hope, through the power of the Holy Spirit.

Ninety-One

Love and Good Works

And let us consider one another to provoke
unto love and good works.
—Hebrews 10:24

We have had the *"fulness of faith"* (Hebrews 10:22) in which we are to draw near and the *"confession of our hope"* (verse 23) that we are to hold fast; now follows the third of the sister graces: *"Let us consider one another"*—let us prove our love and care for each other in the effort—*"to provoke unto love and good works."* These three thoughts form the subdivision of the practical part of the epistle. Chapter 11 may well be headed, "The Fullness of Faith"; chapter 12:1–14, "The Patience of Hope"; and chapter 13, "Love and Good Works."

"And let us consider one another." He that enters into the Holiest enters into the home of eternal love; the air he breathes there is love; the highest blessing he can receive there is a heart in which the love of God is shed abroad in power by the Holy Spirit and that is on the path to be made perfect in love. *"That thou mayest know how men ought to behave themselves in the house of God"* (1 Timothy 3:15)—remember this, *"But now abideth faith, hope, love, these three; and the greatest of these is love"* (1 Corinthians 13:13).

"Let us consider one another." When first we seek the entrance into the Holiest, the thought is mostly of ourselves. And when we have entered in in faith, it is as if all we can do is stand before God and wait on Him for what He has promised to do for us. But it is not long before we perceive that the Holiest and the Lamb are not for us alone; that there are others with whom it is blessed to have fellowship in praising God; that there are some outside who need our help to be brought in. It is into the love of God that we have had access given us; that love enters our hearts, and we see ourselves called to live like Christ in entire devotion to those around us.

"Let us consider one another." All the redeemed form one body. Each one is dependent on the other; each one is for the welfare of the other. Let us beware of the self-deception that thinks it possible to enter the Holiest, into the nearest communion with God, in the spirit of selfishness. It cannot be. The *"new and living way"* (Hebrews 10:20) that Jesus opened up is the way of self-sacrificing love. The entrance into the Holiest is given to us as priests, there to be filled with the Spirit and the love of Christ and then to go out and bring God's blessing to others.

"Let us consider one another." The same Spirit that said, "Consider Christ Jesus"—take time, and give attention to know Him well—says to us, *"Consider one another."* Take time and give attention to know the needs of your brethren around you. How many are there whose circumstances are so unfavorable, whose knowledge is so limited, whose whole life is so hopeless, that there is but little prospect of their ever attaining the better life? For them, there is but one thing to be done: *"We that are strong ought to bear the infirmities of the weak, and not to please ourselves"* (Romans 15:1). Each one who begins to see what the blessedness is of a life in the full surrender to Christ should offer himself to Christ, to be made His messenger to the feeble and the weary.

"Consider one another to provoke unto love and good works." *"Love and good works"*—these are to be the aim of the church in the exercise of its fellowship. Everything that can hinder love is to

be sacrificed and set aside. Everything that can promote, prove, and provoke others to love is to be studied and performed.

And with love, good works, too. The church has been redeemed by Christ, to prove to the world what power He has to cleanse from sin, to conquer evil, to restore to holiness and to goodness. *"Let us consider one another,"* in every possible way, *"to provoke"*—to stir up, to help—*"unto love and good works."*

The chief thought is this: Life in the Holiest must be a life of love. As earnest as the injunction, *"Let us draw near...in fulness of faith"* (Hebrews 10:22), and *"Let us hold fast the confession of our hope"* (verse 23), is this: *"Let us consider one another to provoke unto love and good works."* God is love. All He has done for us in His Son, as revealed in this epistle, is love. And Christ is love. There can be no real access to God as a union with Him in His holy will, no real communion with Him, but in the Spirit of love. Our entering into the Holiest is mere imagination if we do not yield ourselves to the love of God in Christ, to be filled and used for the welfare and joy of our fellowmen.

O Christian, study what love is! Study it in the Word, in Christ, in God. As you see Him to be an ever-flowing Fountain of all goodness—who has His very being and glory in this: that He lives in all that exists and communicates to all His own blessedness and perfection as far as they are capable of it—you will learn to acknowledge that he who loves not has not known God. And you will learn, too, to admit more deeply and truly than ever before that no effort of your will can bring forth love; it must be given to you from above. This will become to you one of the chief joys and beauties of the Holiest of All, that there you can wait on the God of love to fill you with His love. God has the power to shed abroad His love in our hearts, by the Holy Spirit given unto us. He has promised to give Christ, so dwelling in our hearts by faith, that we will be rooted and grounded in love, and know and have in us something of a love that passes knowledge. The very atmosphere of the Holiest is love. Just as I breathe in the air in which

I live, so the soul that abides in the presence of God breathes the air of the upper world. The promise held out to us, and the hour of its fulfillment, will come, when the love of God will be perfected in us and we are made perfect in love. Nowhere can this be but in the Holiest; but there, most surely. Let us draw near in the fullness of faith and consider one another. While we are only thinking of others to bring God's love to them, we will find God thinking of us and filling us with it.

Chapter Notes...

1. It is the very essence, the beauty, and the glory of the salvation of Christ, that it is for all. He that truly receives it, as the Holy Spirit gives it, receives it as a salvation for all and feels himself impelled to communicate it to others. The baptism of fire is a baptism of redeeming love, but that not as a mere emotion but as a power at once to consider and to care for others.

2. How impossible to love others and give all for them in our strength! This is one of the real gifts to be waited for in the Holiest of All, to be received in the power of the Pentecostal Spirit—the love of God so shed abroad in the heart that we—spontaneously, unceasingly, and joyfully—love because it is our very nature.

Ninety-Two
The Assembling Together

*Not forsaking the assembling of ourselves together, as the
custom of some is, but exhorting one another; and so much
the more, as ye see the day drawing nigh.*
—Hebrews 10:25

The inward and the outward must ever go together. As there is in every man a hidden inner life of the soul, along with the outer life of the body, so, too, in the church of Christ. All its members are one body; the inward unity must be proved in active exercise; it must be seen in the assembling together. The assembling of His saints has its ground in a divine appointment as well as in the very nature of things; all who have entered into the Holiest to meet their God must turn to the meeting of His people. The tabernacle of old was the tent of meeting; to meet God and to meet our fellowmen are equally necessary. Among the Hebrews, it was already the custom with some to forsake the assembling together; it was one of the dangerous symptoms of backsliding. They are reminded not only of the personal duty of each to be faithful but also to care for others and to exhort one another. For exercise and strengthening of the faith and hope and love, to which we have just been urged; for the full development of the life in the Holiest of

All; for the helping and comforting of all who are feeble; for the cultivation of the fellowship of the Spirit and the Word—for all of these, the assembling of ourselves together has unspeakable value. Let us listen to the exhortation, in connection with our entrance into the Holiest. *"Not forsaking the assembling of ourselves together, as the custom of some is."*

If we would rightly understand the importance of this word, let us not forget the link to its context. Our section has been teaching us what life in the Holiest is to be. As those who have drawn near to God, we are to draw near to our fellowmen. Meeting God is a thing of infinite blessedness and peace and power. Meeting our fellowmen is often accompanied with so much of weakness, distraction, and failure that some have thought it indeed better to forsake the assembling together. Let us see how life in the Holiest of All points to both the duty and the power of our assemblies.

It suggests duty. The Holiest of All is the home of eternal love. Love dwells there. Love came forth from there to seek me and bring me in. I have been welcomed and taken into everlasting love. Love has been shed abroad in my heart. My entrance in was only in the path of self-sacrifice; my abiding there can only be as one dead to self and filled with love. And love seeks not its own; it gives itself away, and only lives to make others partakers of its happiness. And it loves the assembly of God's people, not only for what it needs and hopes to receive but also for the communion of saints and the help it can give in helping and encouraging others.

It not only does this, but it obeys the added injunction— *"Exhorting one another."* It seeks to watch over those who are in danger of becoming unfaithful. It cares for those who have grown careless in their neglect. True love is quick of invention; it devises means for making smaller or nearer or more attractive assemblies for those who have become estranged. It counts nothing too humble or too difficult if it may but win back to the gathering of God's children those who may there be blessed and

Andrew Murray

saved. It lives in the Holiest of God's love; it gives itself up to the one work of winning others to know that love.

The life in the Holiest is thus not only the motive but also the power for doing the work aright. Yes, it is as those who profess to have entered the Holiest of All truly draw near to God and prove the power of fellowship with Him that they will have power in prayer and speech and service among their fellow Christians. The Holiest of All is the place for daily worship and consecration and intercession; even a little band in the assembly will have power to make the divine presence felt. The worship in the place of prayer may become so linked to the secret worship of the Holiest of All that its blessing may come to those who have never known of it. God is willing so to bless the fellowship of His redeemed that the assembly will be crowned with a fuller sense of His love and presence than ever can be found in the solitary approach to Him. *"Having therefore, brethren, boldness to enter into the holy place by the blood of Jesus,...let us draw near,...not forsaking the assembling of ourselves together, as the custom of some is, but exhorting one another"* (Hebrews 10:19, 22, 25).

"And so much the more, as ye see the day drawing nigh." The writer doubtless had in view the then approaching day of judgment on Jerusalem. We do not know how far in advance the perspective of prophecy was clearly revealed; additionally, that day was connected with the coming of the Lord Himself, as well. It is enough for us to know, however, that the fear of an approaching day of judgment was the motive to which appeal is made and that this call was made not only to move the indifferent but especially to urge the earnest to exhort others. Christians need to be reminded of the terrible doom hanging over the world and of all the solemn eternal realities connected with our Lord's coming in their bearing upon our daily lives. So will our efforts for helping and saving others all be under the power of the thought of how short the time is, how terrible the fate of those who perish, and how urgent the call for everyone who knows redeeming love to do its work with all his might. In the Holiest of All, we hear the voice of warning, and we come out to save before it is too late.

Chapter Notes...

1. Note the intensely practical character of the Gospel. Our section (19–25) is only one sentence. It begins with spiritual, heavenly mysteries; it ends in the plainest rules for our conduct to our fellowmen. Let us be sure that the deeper we enter into the perfection-teachings of chapters 7–10, the fitter we will be to be a blessing in the world.

2. When Christ spoke His farewell discourse to His disciples, one of the things He pressed most urgently was that they should love one another. He loves all His redeemed ones, however feeble or perverse they are, so intently that He tells us that we cannot prove our real love to Him in any other way than by loving them; the proof of a real entrance into the Holiest of All is the humility and gentleness and self-sacrifice with which we speak and think and prove our care for one another.

3. Study carefully the connection between these last twelve meditations, and see to get a clear hold of the unity of thought in this portion, the living center of the epistle.

pg 367-414

ch 81-92
12 chapters
meditations

The Fourth Warning—Hebrews 10:26–39
OF THOSE WHO SIN
WILLFULLY AND DRAW BACK

Ninety-Three
Of Willful Sin

*For if we sin wilfully after that we have received the
knowledge of the truth, there remaineth no more a sacrifice
for sins, but a certain fearful expectation of judgement,
and a fierceness of fire which shall devour the adversaries.*
—Hebrews 10:26–27

In mentioning those who forsake the assembling together of
God's people, the writer has touched one of those sore places
that, to him, were the symptoms of imminent danger. This
neglect of Christian fellowship is at once an indication of that indifference that is so dangerous and is the cause of further backsliding.
All this leads him once again to sound the alarm and to point out
how neglect of outward and apparently secondary duties opens the
way to active sin and eternal loss. He had scarcely finished his wondrous exposition of the glory of the heavenly Priest and the heavenly sanctuary and the way into it—he had only just begun to speak
of the life and walk to which that opened sanctuary calls us—when,
thinking of the state of the Hebrews, he sounded a trumpet-blast of
warning more terrible than any we have heard yet. In the three previous warnings, he had spoken first of neglect (see Hebrews 2:1–4);
then of unbelief and disobedience (see 3:1–4:13); then of sloth,

leading to hopeless falling away (see 5:13–6:19); here he spoke of willful sinning, with the awful rejection of God's mercy it implies and the sore and certain punishment it will inevitably bring. John Bunyan, in his dream, saw a way leading from the very gate of heaven down to the pit. It is not only the Holiest of All that is set wide open for us; the gate of hell is opened wide, too, to receive all who neglect or refuse to enter the gate of mercy and of heaven. Let all who believe that it is indeed God who, by His Spirit, speaks in this Word, listen with holy fear.

"For if we sin wilfully after that we have received the knowledge of the truth, there remaineth no more a sacrifice for sins." As we had, in chapter 6, mention of *"those who were once enlightened and tasted of the heavenly gift,…and tasted the good word of God"* (verses 4–5) and who yet fell away, so here he spoke of those who, after having *"received the knowledge of the truth,"* yet *"sin wilfully."* The expressions used show us that, in the case of these, the enlightening and the acceptance of the truth had been more with the mind than with the heart. Their judgment had been convinced; through the mind, their desire and will had been affected and worked upon; and yet, the heart, the whole inner life, had never been truly regenerate, had never received that eternal life that cannot be taken away. And so, there was a possibility of their still sinning *"wilfully"* and being shut out forever from the one sacrifice for sin. As we saw before, the true assurance of salvation, the assuring of our hearts before God, can only be enjoyed in a life under the teaching of the Spirit and a walk in obedience to God's will. (See 1 John 3:19–24.) True assurance of faith is the witness of the Holy Spirit that is given in living fellowship with and obedience to Christ as Leader.

"If we sin wilfully." The question will be asked, "But what is willful sin? How are we to know when we are guilty of it?" No answer can be given; no one on earth can draw the line between what is and what is not willful sin. Only He who sits on the throne, and who knows the heart, can judge. But how will this warning

profit if we cannot see what wilful sin is? The warning will just thus profit us most—it will make us fearful of committing any sin, lest it might be, or might lead us into, willful sin. He that would know what willful sin is—with the thought that he is safe as long as he keeps from that extreme—deceives himself. The only sure way of being kept from willful sin is to keep far from all sin.

A captain of a ship, sailing between two harbors on a rocky coast, was once asked by an anxious passenger if the coast was not very dangerous. The answer was, "Very." And was he not afraid? "No; our way is perfectly safe; you can be at ease." But how, if the rocks are so dangerous? "Oh, very simply—I put out to sea and keep far from the rocks." O Christian, here is your only safety: Launch out into the deep of full obedience to all the will of God; keep far from all sin, and you will be kept from willful sinning.

*"For if we sin wilfully after that we have received the knowledge of the truth, there remaineth **no more a sacrifice** for sins"* (emphasis added). What a terrible contrast to the same expression as we had it before (Hebrews 10:18): *"No more offering for sin."* There, it was the blessed secret of the glory of the Gospel and redemption, the joy of Christian faith and life—*"no more offering for sin"*: Salvation is finished and perfected forever. Here, it is the awful revelation of the highest sin and its terrible doom: The one sacrifice has been rejected, and now *"no more a sacrifice for sins"* is ever to be found. How awful to sin willfully!

"There remaineth no more a sacrifice for sins, but a certain fearful expectation of judgement, and a fierceness of fire which shall devour the adversaries." Fearful judgment, fierceness of fire, devouring the adversaries—these words are in God's Gospel; they follow closely on its highest teaching; they are words He speaks to us in His Son. In the religion of the world—alas, in a great deal of the Christian teaching and the religious literature of our day professing to honor the God of love whom the Bible reveals—these words are set aside and rejected. And yet, there they stand, and behind them

stand the divine realities they express. God help us to believe them with our whole hearts, and to exhort one another. If so, we may save some, snatching them out of the fire!

Chapter Notes...

1. Let all who have entered the Holiest of All turn around and look to the hole of the pit—the horrible pit—whence they have been drawn up. And as they see the multitudes going down to the pit, oh, let them remember that the highest glory of life in the Holiest is, even as it is of Him who opened it with His blood and sits on the throne, to go out and bring others in.

2. Even though you know, through grace, that you escaped the judgment and the fire, take time to gaze upon them. Take upon you the burden of those who are asleep, and plead with Christ to use you to warn and to save them.

Ninety-Four

The Sin Against the Triune God

*A man that hath set at nought Moses' law dieth without
compassion on the word of two or three witnesses: of how much
sorer punishment, think ye, shall he be judged worthy, who
hath trodden under foot the Son of God, and hath counted
the blood of the covenant, wherewith he was sanctified, an
unholy thing, and hath done despite unto the Spirit of grace?
For we know him that said, Vengeance belongeth unto me, I
will recompense. And again, The Lord shall judge his people.
It is a fearful thing to fall into the hands of the living God.*
—Hebrews 10:28–31

The epistle has set before us the more excellent glory of the New
Testament. We can draw near to God as Israel never could;
God hath indeed made His grace to abound more exceedingly. But let no one think that greater grace means less stringency
with sin or less fierceness of the fire of judgment. Nay, the very opposite. Greater privilege brings greater responsibility and, in the case of
failure, greater judgment. As elsewhere (Hebrews 2:2–3; 12:25) we
are reminded that the New Testament exceeds the Old, not only in

its blessing but also in its curse. As he had asked, *"How much more will the blood of Christ...cleanse?"* (9:14), so here he asked, *"How much sorer* [will] *punishment* [be]?" Oh, that men would believe it; the New Testament, with its revelation of God as love, brings on its rejectors a far more fearful judgment than the Old. May God in His mercy show us what it means, for our own sakes and that of others.

"A man that hath set at nought Moses' law dieth without compassion"—note this terrible word, *"without compassion" "Of how much sorer punishment, think ye, shall he be judged worthy,"* who sins against New Testament grace? The measure of the superior greatness of the New Testament will be the only measure of the greater fearfullness of the punishment sent; as in the first warning, the greatness of salvation was connected with the part each person in the Holy Trinity had taken in it; so here, too. The Father gave His Son: *"Of how much sorer punishment, think ye, shall he be judged worthy, who hath trodden under foot the Son of God."* The Son gave His blood: Here is one who *"hath counted the blood of the covenant, wherewith he was sanctified, an unholy thing."* The Father and the Son gave the Spirit: He *"hath done despite unto the Spirit of grace."* Under Moses' law a man died *"without compassion"*: How much sorer punishment, without compassion, will be the fate of those who reject Christ? Hear what all this means.

"Who hath trodden under foot the Son of God"! There was once an aged father who had often pleaded in vain with a dissipated son to forsake his evil ways. One night, as the son was preparing again to go out, the father, after renewing his entreaties, went and stood in the door, saying, "My son, I cannot let you go; if you do, it will be over my body." The son tried to push the father aside. The old man fell, and in rushing out, the son trod on the father! Jesus Christ, God's Son, comes and stands in the sinner's path, pleading with him to turn from his evil way. He casts Himself in the way, with His wounded, bleeding body. And the sinner, not heeding what he does, passes over it; he *"hath trodden under foot the Son of God"*! What a sin against the Father and the love that gave the Son!

Andrew Murray

And *"hath counted the blood of the covenant, wherewith he was sanctified, an unholy thing."* The Father gave the Son, and the Son gave His blood—the blood of the covenant, securing and conveying to us all its wondrous privileges—the blood with which he was sanctified, admitted to the Holiest of All; and, yet, the Holy One, he *"hath counted...an unholy thing."* When I come to water in which I wish to wash and find it impure, I reject it; I throw it out. Christ calls the sinner to wash in His blood and be clean, but he rejects it as an unclean thing. Yes, the blood that speaks of the love of Jesus and remission of sins and the opened heaven is rejected and cast aside! Oh, what sin! If the rejectors of the blood of bulls and goats died *"without compassion,"* how much more the despisers of the blood of the Son of God!

And *"hath done despite unto the Spirit of grace"*! I can put no greater affront on my king, or my father, than by shutting my door in his face. If they come to me with a message or a gift of love in my wretchedness, to turn them away is to do them despite. The Spirit comes as the Spirit of grace, to convince of sin and stir to prayer and lead to Jesus. To close the door, to refuse surrender, and to open the heart to the spirit of the world instead of Him is to do *"despite unto the Spirit of grace"*! The Son trodden under foot, the blood counted unclean, the Spirit of grace despised and rejected—alas, what terrible sin!

For such *"there remaineth no more a sacrifice for sins"* (10:26)! And such are they among us and around us who reject the Christ of God! And such their fate! *"For we know him that said, Vengeance belongeth unto me, I will recompense. And again, The Lord shall judge his people."* For we know Him! How many there are who profess to believe in Scripture and to worship God but who do not know this God. They have framed to themselves a God after their own instincts and imaginations; they believe not in the Holy One in whom righteousness and love meet in perfect harmony. They refuse to say, *"We know him that said, Vengeance belongeth unto me, I will recompense."* Oh, let us seek to know Him so that our hearts may be filled with compassion for all who are still exposed to this fearful vengeance. *"It is a fearful thing to fall into the hands of the living God."* Let us think in love on all who are still exposed to this judgment until it stirs us to thanksgiving for our own redemption, to an infinite compassion for all who are in danger, to new fervency of prayer for their salvation, and to a consecration of ourselves to the one work of warning them of their danger and leading them to Christ.

Chapter Notes...

1. In accepting God's Word, let us remember that as little as we could have devised or understood the glorious redemption in Christ—such as God's love has provided—without a divine revelation, can we arrange for or understand a judgment day such as God's righteousness requires. The one is a mystery of love and the other a mystery of wrath, beyond all we can think or know.

2. It was to meet the judgment and the wrath of God that Christ's blood was needed. The blood stands midway between the judgment threatened and the judgment yet to be poured out. As we believe in the judgment, we will honor the blood; as we believe in the blood, we will fear the judgment.

Ninety-Five

The Former Days

But call to remembrance the former days, in which,
after ye were enlightened, ye endured a great conflict
of sufferings; partly, being made a gazingstock both by
reproaches and afflictions; and partly, becoming partakers
with them that were so used. For ye both had compassion on
them that were in bonds, and took joyfully the spoiling of
your possessions, knowing that ye yourselves have a better
possession and an abiding one.
—Hebrews 10:32–34

T he solemn warning now, just as was the case in Hebrews 6:9, turns to encouragement and exhortation. As there, the Hebrews are reminded of the former days, when they were first enlightened—the time of their first love. But, in the previous instance, they were told that God was not unrighteous to forget their work and love; here, they themselves are urged not to forget what had taken place. *"Call to remembrance the former days."* The retrospect would call up the joy with which they once had sacrificed all for the name of Jesus; would humble them in view of past backsliding and present coldness; would stir within them the desire and the hope of regaining the place they once had occupied. *"Call to* remembrance," he said, *"the former days, in which...ye endured a great conflict of sufferings,"* in not only bearing *"reproaches"* and taking *"joyfully the spoiling of your possessions,"* but also in *"compassion"* toward and *"becoming partakers"* with others *"that were in bonds."*

It is a sad thought that a community that had so remarkably proved its faithfulness to the Lord in the midst of persecution and suffering should, in a few years, have gone so far back as to need the warnings that have just been given. And yet, it has often been so. In some cases, it happened that the persecution ceased and the spirit of ease and of sloth, or of worldly prosperity, obtained the mastery. In others, the persecution lasted too long, and those who had appeared to forsake all succumbed to the severity and length of the trial. The Hebrews were not only an instance of such defection but also of so many other cases in which Christians, after having begun well, *"wax...weary, fainting in* [their] *souls"* (12:3). They stand out as beacons to warn us of the danger the epistle so strongly urges— that the best beginning will not avail unless we endure to the end. (See 3:14; 4:11.) They call us to remember that we need a faith and a religion that stands fast and lasts because it has its steadfastness, as the epistle teaches, in the promise and the oath of God; in the hope within the veil; in Him, the Surety of the covenant, who is seated on the right hand of God, the Priest after the power of an endless life, the Surety of an everlasting covenant.

In reminding them of the past, a very remarkable expression is used to indicate what the power was that enabled them at first to endure so bravely. You *"took joyfully the spoiling of your possessions, knowing that ye yourselves have a better possession and an abiding one"* (10:34). The Christian stands between two worlds; each offers him its goods as possessions. In unceasing conflict the two compete for mastery. The one has the advantage of being infinitely more worthy than the other, giving infinite satisfaction and lasting forever. The other is in no wise to be compared with it; it cannot satisfy, and it does not last. But, in the conflict, it has two immense,

Andrew Murray

two terrible advantages. The one advantage is that it is nearer; it is visible; it has access to us by every sense; its influence on us is natural and easy and unceasing. The other advantage is that our hearts are prepossessed; the spirit of the world is in them. And so it comes that, for most people, the possessions of this world actually win the day, even against the better and abiding possession.

"Ye...took joyfully the spoiling of your possessions, knowing that ye yourselves have a better possession and an abiding one." What is this better and abiding possession? It is the love and grace of God. It is the eternal life within. It is Christ as our heart's treasure. It is a life and a character in the likeness of Christ. The old heathen moralists teach us most striking lessons as to the nobility of a man who knows that all earthly possessions are as nothing compared with being master of himself. How much more reason the Christian has to rejoice in the good things, in the eternal realities that Christ bestows, both in the heaven above and the heart within. Though the world may rob you of personal liberty or earthly goods, it cannot compel you to commit sin or separate you from the living God in Christ Jesus. Heaven and its blessing in your heart can fill you with a joy that counts every sacrifice a privilege, that makes every loss a gain, and that turns all suffering into an exceeding weight of glory.

Alas, that the Hebrews—after knowing this better and abiding possession and after having, for its sake, joyfully taken the spoiling of their possessions—should yet, many of them, have waxed weary and fainted and turned back! Alas for the terrible possibility of making sacrifices and enduring reproach for Christ and then falling away! No wonder that our author at once followed up his appeal to the former days with the exhortation, *"Cast not away therefore your boldness,...for ye have need of patience"* (verse 35–36).

Let us learn the solemn lesson: The lawful possessions and pleasures and occupations of this world—its literature and its culture—are unceasingly and most insidiously seeking to undermine the influence of the better and abiding possession. This influence is greater than we know because they are seen and near and ever active. Nothing can secure us against their power but a life of faith, a life in the Holiest, a life in the power of Christ, the Priest forever who works all in the power of the endless life. Alone, through Him who abides continually, can we abide continually, too, and can we endure unto the end.

Chapter Notes...

1. If there is any reader who has to look back with shame and regret on his first love and his leaving it, let him listen to the call, "[Remember] *the former days.*" Think of them. Face the fact of your having gone back. Confess it to God. And take courage in the assurance that there is restoration and deliverance. Trust Jesus.

2. *"A better possession and an abiding one."* A rich man counts his money. He spends time and thought on preserving it safe and making it more. Our power to resist the world, so that its possessions will not tempt us nor its threats terrify us, lies in the full consciousness and enjoyment of our heavenly treasures. Take time to know your possessions; draw out an inventory of what you have and what you expect; and all the world offers will have no power.

Ninety-Six

Boldness and Patience

Cast not away therefore your boldness, which hath great
recompense of reward. For ye have need of patience, that,
having done the will of God, ye may receive the promise.
—Hebrews 10:35–36

We know how often we have had the word *"boldness"* in our epistle. *"If we hold fast our boldness"* (3:6); *"Let us therefore draw near with boldness unto the throne of grace"* (4:16); *"Having therefore, brethren, boldness to enter into the holy place by the blood of Jesus"* (10:19). The boldness and confidence toward God is one of the strongest roots of the Christian life. Without it, there is no strength to persevere, no power to draw near to the throne of grace in prayer, no liberty to enter into the full fellowship of God in the Holiest. And so the Hebrews were urged not to cast away their boldness because it has *"great recompense of reward."* In the vigor and joy of the Christian life, in the bright and joyous fellowship with God, and in the courage for meeting the battle with the world and sin, the reward of boldness is great.

"Cast not away...your boldness." When I have my hands filled and something more tempting is offered, I may either directly cast away what I have or, by trying to take the new object into hands

427

already full, may gradually lose hold of what I first held fast. Casting away our boldness always has its cause in something else that we allow to take its place in the heart. It may be sin, whether only rising in the heart or breaking out into act, if it be not immediately confessed and cleansed away. It may be something in itself lawful but which is allowed too large a share in our interest or affections. It may be something doubtful, so insignificant that it hardly appears worth considering, and yet, something that somehow robs us of perfect liberty in looking up into God's face. It may be care or fear; it may be self-effort, self-seeking, or self-trust; anything that is not in the perfect will of God loosens our hold on the boldness before God, and, before we know, we have cast it away; it is lost.

But we must not only know how we lose it; we want as much to know how to keep and increase it. The texts we quoted tell us. Among the foundational truths we had this: "Since we have a High Priest able to sympathize, let us come with boldness." (See Hebrews 4:15–16.) And in the fuller teaching, it came again: *"Having therefore, brethren, boldness to enter into the holy place by the blood of Jesus"* (10:19). The High Priest and the blood—these are the everlasting and unchanging ground of our confidence. As we consider Christ Jesus and follow Him, and as we grow in the knowledge and the faith of His blood and enter through it into God's presence, we will hold fast our boldness with an ever firmer grasp. As we draw near with true hearts, and as we, in the consciousness of our integrity that in holiness and sincerity of God we are walking in the world, place ourselves in the light of God, we will receive, even in this life, something of the great *"recompense of reward"* that boldness of faith ever brings.

"Cast not away therefore your boldness,...for ye have need of patience." You cannot dispense with your boldness for a single moment; to the end of life, it is your only strength. Cast it not away; remember that, without patience in the persevering exercise and daily renewal of faith, you cannot inherit the promise. Between the faith that accepts a promise and the experience that fully inherits

or receives it, there often lie years of discipline and training needed to fit and perfect you for the inward possession of what God has to give. Whether it is a promise to be realized in this world or the coming world, you *"have need of patience."* Therefore cast not away your boldness; never for a moment lose hold of it; hold your boldness fast firm to the end—*"ye have need of patience."* In chapter 6, it was said to be *"imitators of them who through faith and patience inherit the promises"* (verse 12). This is one of the great practical lessons of the epistle. Without perseverance, endurance, and steadfastness, faith is vain; the only proof that it is a living, saving faith is that it holds fast its boldness firm unto the end.

"For ye have need of patience, that, having done the will of God, ye may receive the promise." Doing the will is the way to receive the promise. Doing the will is to be the one thing that is to occupy us while we patiently wait. Between God's giving the promise to Abraham and his receiving its fulfillment, there lie years of the obedience of faith. And each new act of obedience was crowned with new and larger blessing. Doing the will was the proof of his faith, the occupation of his patience, the way to his blessing. It was even so with our blessed Lord. Between the promise given to Him from the Father and His inheriting it, in the resurrection and ascension, lay what? His life of obedience: *"Lo, I am come to do thy will"* (10:9). With every Christian who puts his trust in the living Christ and who enters the Holiest of All to live there, doing the will of God must be the link that unites the end to the beginning. Between the faith that accepts the promise and the experience that fully inherits it, there may for us, too, be years of waiting and trial. These must be marked by the obedience of faith, by patient continuance in well-doing, or we can never reach the promised end. If we see to the doing of God's will, He will see to our inheriting the promise. The sure mark of true faith, the blessed exercise of life within the veil, the proof of the power of Christ, the obedient One within us, the blessedness of fellowship with God—all these will come with this: doing His will. To do the will of God is the only

way to God and His presence. Therefore, day by day, hour by hour, let this be our motto: *"Patience, that, having done the will of God, ye may receive the promise."*

Chapter Notes...

1. We have been so little accustomed in our Christian lives to give the doing of God's will its right place, and there is so much misconception about it, as if it is not actually expected of us, that it will take time and trouble to get the heart under the complete mastery of the thought, "I am every moment to be doing nothing but the will of God." Jesus Christ lived so. He, our Leader, will teach it to us. He, our Life, will live it in us. He, our High Priest, will by His Spirit, in this new and living way, bring us in very deed near to God.

2. Boldness, courage, bravery: the chief of the manly virtues. Patience: one of the loveliest of the gentler sisterhood of passive graces. In each full Christian character, the two must be combined. *"Cast not away therefore your boldness,...for ye have need of patience."* Boldness to undertake, and patience to carry out, the doing of God's will.

3. O believer, let the truth enter deep into you—boldly, patiently doing the will is the way to inherit the promise.

NLT (web) Pg 427

318 (37) For in just a little while, THE COMING ONE will come & not delay 38 And my righteous ones will live by faith (or their faithfulness) BUT I WILL TAKE NO PLEASURE IN ANYONE WHO TURNS AWAY. But we are not like those who turn away from God to their own destruction. we are the faithful ones, whose souls WILL BE SAVED!!!!!

Ninety-Seven

Believing or Drawing Back

*For ye have need of patience, that, having done the will of
God, ye may receive the promise. For yet a very little while, He
that cometh shall come, and shall not tarry. But my righteous
one shall live by faith: and if he shrink back,* my soul hath no
pleasure in him. But we are not of them that shrink
back unto perdition; but of them that have
faith unto the saving of the soul.*
—Hebrews 10:36–39

I n the summary we had of what life in the Holiest means
(Hebrews 10:19–25), the last word, after we had been urged
to exhort one another, was, *"and so much the more, as ye see
the day drawing nigh."* And then came the warning of the fearful
expectation of judgment and the terror of falling into the hands of
the living God. Here, the warning closes with once again pointing
to the Lord's coming as not far off. Christian faith lives not only
in the unseen present but also in the future; more especially, in

---

* Draw back.

the future coming of Him who will appear a second time to them who wait for Him, who is now seated on the throne, waiting until all His enemies are made His footstool. Let our faith so live in the future that all our lives may be in the power of eternity and of Him in whom eternity has its glory.

The passage quoted is from Habakkuk, the same that forms the text of the epistles to the Galatians and the Romans. The prophet is told by God, in the midst of the oppression of Israel by the Chaldæans, that the vision will surely come. Two classes among the people are spoken of. Of one it is said, *"His soul is puffed up, it is not upright in him."* Of the other, *"But the just shall live by his faith"* (Habakkuk 2:4). Our writer used the words to contrast the two classes among the Hebrews. On the one side, those who are not upright; on the other, the righteous who live by faith. The righteous man will—in the midst of trouble and while the vision is delayed—put his trust in God and live in that trust. He will live by it, too; the God whom He trusts will not fail him but will send deliverance.

Our writer introduced the passage of set purpose, to serve as the text of the following chapter. He had in chapters 3 and 4 spoken of unbelief as the great sin through which Israel had perished in the wilderness, of faith as the one necessary thing if we are to enter into the rest of God. In chapter 6, he spoke of the faith by which the fathers inherited the promises. He had in this chapter, in his summing up of the epistle, said, *"Let us draw near with a true heart in fulness of faith"* (Hebrews 10:22). He wished, after his exposition of what the purpose and the work of Jesus can be to us, to show us the way to a full personal experience and enjoyment of it all, through faith alone. He proposed to do so by proving how all the Old Testament saints had lived and conquered through faith, and how it is the one thing God asks if we are to experience His mighty saving power and the blessedness of His good pleasure. He is going to point out all the variety of circumstances and difficulties in which faith will give us God's help and sure deliverance, as well as all the various tempers and dispositions with which it will

Andrew Murray

be accompanied. For all this, he finds a most suggestive text in the words, *"My righteous one shall live by faith."*

That means a great deal more than what many think—the sinner will be counted righteous by faith; more, too, than the righteousness, he will also have eternal life by faith. It means that the righteous man will live—his whole life will be—by faith. This is just the lesson we need. The righteous man who lives by faith is contrasted with him who draws back, of whom God says, *"My soul hath no pleasure in him"* (verse 38). The one cause of backsliding is the want of faith in the unseen; a yielding of the heart to the visible; and, in the battle against it, a trusting in our own strength and not in Christ. We see here again that there is no other alternative—either believing or drawing back. In the Christian life, nothing will avail to keep us from backsliding but the fullness of faith—always and in everything, to live the life of faith. It is only when faith gives itself up entirely to Christ for Him to do all in us—to keep us standing, too—and when faith so dominates our lives that every moment and every engagement will all be under its influence, that we can hope to be safe from drawing back. If I am to be sure of salvation, if I am to be strong against every temptation, if I am to live daily as one in whom God's soul has pleasure, I must see to one thing—to be a man of faith.

Let us prepare ourselves for the wonderful chapter that is coming, and all its blessed teaching, by looking back on what has been set before us of Christ and His redemption as the object of our faith. He is the Priest forever, the Priest of God's oath, able to save completely—will we not throw our whole beings wide open to Him in trust? We have Him, a Priest-King upon the throne, the Minister of the sanctuary He has opened for us and where He presides, to bring us in—oh, will we not be strong in faith, giving glory to God? We have Him, the Mediator of the new covenant, who with one sacrifice hath perfected Himself and us forevermore, and whose work it is to write and put God's law within us as the power of a living obedience—again, I say, will we not believe, and allow this mighty Savior to do His perfect work in us? We have entered the Holiest of All; we have in faith claimed God's presence, and the life of abiding continually in it as our portion; and we have the great Priest over the house of God to make it all true and sure to us; surely it needs no words to urge us to make faith—faith alone, the faith of the heart—the unceasing sacrifice we bring our God so that we, too, may say, *"We are not of them that draw back,... but of them that have faith unto the saving of the soul."*

Chapter Notes...

1. The only cure for all the coldness and backsliding in the church is the preaching of faith. Holiness by faith, standing by faith, being kept by the power of God through faith, having Christ dwell in our hearts by faith—this must be the daily food of the Christian. A preaching that insists solely upon salvation by faith as pardon and acceptance must produce feeble Christians. The fullness of faith is indispensable to the full Christian life.

2. Believing or drawing back—there is no other alternative. Look back over the warning of which these words form the conclusion, and let us fear at the terrible possibility for ourselves and others. And look forward to the coming chapter, with the one prayer that our whole lives may be in the fullness of faith, in the very presence and power of God.

Tenth Section—Hebrews 11:1–40
THE FULLNESS OF FAITH

Ninety-Eight
Faith—The Sense of the Unseen

Now faith is the assurance of things hoped for, the proving of things not seen. For therein the elders had witness borne to them. By faith we understand that the worlds have been framed by the word of God, so that what is seen hath not been made out of things which do appear.
—Hebrews 11:1–3

The previous chapter closed with the solemn lesson: There is no alternative, either believing or drawing back; there is no safety or strength for the Christian but to be strong in faith; there is no way of pleasing God, of abiding in His presence and favor, except by faith. *"And if he shrink back, my soul hath no pleasure in him"* (Hebrews 10:38). And so, after the teaching of the epistle as to what God has done, we are now to see that for our enjoyment of its power and blessing, only one thing is needed—the fullness of faith. It will be shown to us how this is the key to the life of all God's saints and to all that God did for them.

The writer began with a general statement of what faith really is in its nature and action. *"Now faith is the assurance of things hoped for, the proving of things not seen."* Faith is the spiritual faculty of the soul that deals with the spiritual realities of the future and the unseen. Just as we have our senses, through which we hold communication with the physical universe, so faith is the spiritual sense organ through which the soul comes into contact with and is affected by the spiritual world. Just as the sense of seeing or hearing is a dormant power until the objective reality—light or sound—strikes it, so, too, faith in itself is a sense with no power beyond the possibility or capacity of receiving the impressions of the eternal. It is as an empty vessel that wants to be filled with its unseen contents. Only when the eternal realities draw near and exercise their power does faith become the substance of things hoped for, the foundation that they lay in the soul, the proof or conviction of things unseen, the convincing power with which these eternal realities give evidence and proof of their own supernatural existence.* Faith as a dormant faculty is the capacity for receiving this communication; faith as an active power is what it is in virtue of the overshadowing of the invisible. The invisible takes the initiative and wakens faith; faith receives the impression and seeks forever fuller union with it.

Faith is thus much more than trust in the word of another. That trust is of extreme importance as its initial exercise, but the word must only be the servant leading in to the divine truth it contains, the living person from whom it comes. To deal too exclusively with the word as the ground of faith will lead to a faith that is more intellectual than spiritual, a faith that, as the church so universally shows, rests more in the wisdom of men, in the power of reason, than in the power

---

* The two words *substance* and *proof* are used both in the objective and subjective sense. The word for *substance* properly means "the foundation," and is used of the real nature of a thing as opposed to its appearance (as in Hebrews 1:3, of the *"substance"* of God; the divine essence). It is also used of the confidence that knows it rests on a sure foundation (as in 3:14, *"the beginning of our confidence"*). It is of importance to hold fast the connection between the two meanings. The word *proof,* or conviction—from the verb used in passages such as, "[The Spirit] *will convict...of sin"* (John 16:8), and often used elsewhere to mean "reproof," or "chiding"—means both the conviction of guilt or the conviction of a truth that is brought from without, and the subjective conviction that comes when one submits and allows himself to be convicted. It thus means both the means of proof and the proof itself. See 2 Timothy 3:16: *"Scripture...profitable for...reproof."*

Andrew Murray

of God. We need to be persuaded very deeply that faith is not only a dealing with certain promises but an unceasing spiritual communion with the unseen world around us. Just as in breathing, our lungs (or in seeing, our eyes) hold themselves open to receive unceasingly, from the air (or the light), what they without ceasing in the literal sense press upon us, so faith is the unceasing reaching out heavenward of that spiritual sense to which things future and unseen reveal themselves as near and present, as living and powerful. Faith must in the spiritual life be as natural, as unceasing, as our breathing and seeing when we are doing our ordinary work.

"For therein the elders had witness borne to them." Of Abel we read, *"He had witness borne to him that he was righteous, God bearing witness in respect of his gifts"* (11:4). And Enoch, *"He hath had witness borne to him that he had been well-pleasing unto God"* (verse 5). And so it is said of all, in verse 39, *"These all...had witness borne to them through their faith."* Faith does not depend on the intensity of its effort for its blessing. The unseen world, the eternity that surrounds us, is all filled by the living God; and to the faith that opens itself heavenward, He bears witness. Let us be sure of this: Faith can grow into firm and full assurance; it finds its confidence not in itself but in God. Let us count upon it: The faith that seeks for the eternal will be met by God and have the witness borne by Himself that God counts us righteous, that we are well-pleasing in His sight.

"By faith we understand that the worlds have been framed by the word of God, so that what is seen hath not been made out of things which do appear." This visible world is, to man, his great temptation to forget God. Faith is the eye with which he can see God in all, which makes every part of it the transparent revelation of the nearness and goodness of God. By faith, we understand that all was framed by God; by faith, we see divinity and omnipotence in all so that what is seen is known to be made out of things that do not appear. The invisible things of Him from the Creation of the world are clearly seen, even His eternal power and Godhead. Faith sees His superscription on every part of His handiwork, sees it all pervaded by the living God; surrounded by the things that perish

and pass away, faith yet stands in the midst of eternity; it knows itself allied to the unchangeable One. The world, instead of being a hindrance, becomes a help in revealing the everlasting God. And faith finds its life and its delight and its ever-increasing strength in meeting everywhere the God who delights to bear witness of Himself to them who seek after Him.

Chapter Notes...

1. Faith is mostly thought of as a power by which we grasp the heavenly things, and we weary ourselves in vain attempts to do so. No, faith is the substance, the substructure, that the divine things lay in me, the proof they give in me of their actual reality. Just as the light of the sun is its own evidence and proof, so, too, with the light of God. The more we see this, the more confident will our hope be that they will prove themselves to us, and the more meek and patient and humble will be the spirit in which we wait for their self-revelation.

2. The rules for the strengthening of faith are thus very simple. Regard the unseen world as an actually existing kingdom of divine truth and power, which seeks to conquer and get possession of and bless you. Accept the measure of faith there is within you as the proof of its existence and operation, the pledge of a fuller revelation. Accept all that is revealed of it in the Word as a fingerpost to wake the longing and to show the way to the full possession. Set the heart open, in holy separation from the world; in meditation and adoration and expectation, the unseen world can become more real and more near than the seen.

3. Nothing can be a proof of anything but what partakes of the nature of the thing proved. Thus it is with faith and the spiritual world.

THE POWER OF BOLD FAITH TPT

Faith moved Abel to choose a more Heb 11
acceptible sacrifice to offer God than
his brother Cain, & God declared him
righteous because of his offering by
faith. By his faith, Abel still speaks
instruction to us today, even though
he is long dead.

Ninety-Nine

Abel—The Sacrifice of Faith

*By faith Abel offered unto God a more excellent sacrifice
than Cain, through which he had witness borne to him
that he was righteous, God bearing witness in respect of his
gifts: and through it he being dead yet speaketh.*
—Hebrews 11:4

One of the chief words of the epistle is *offering*, or *sacrifice*. Christ *"offered* [himself] *unto God."* He *"put away sin by the sacrifice of himself"* (Hebrews 9:26). *"By one offering he hath perfected for ever them that are sanctified"* (10:14). The inner spirit and power of that life by which Christ pleased His Father and put away sin and gained His seat on the throne of the Majesty on high, was the offering of His body. As the Leader of our salvation, He guides His people in the same, the new and living way—that of self-sacrifice.

It is a most remarkable and deeply suggestive fact that among those who have preceded us in the way of faith, we should find that with the very first one, Abel, the first fruit of faith was to sacrifice.

The disposition, of which sacrifice is the expression, lies at the very root of the life of faith. If I would in this chapter learn what faith is, and how I can grow strong in faith, I must mark well what the very first step is: *"By faith Abel offered...a more excellent sacrifice."*

We know what the double meaning was of Abel's sacrifice. It was, on the one hand, his offering to God of a life to be given up to death, and so in his stead, to bear the death that is in its very nature the punishment of sin. It was an acknowledgment of the righteous judgment of God against sin—the confession that, without blood-shed, there could be no remission of sins. It was an act of faith; he counted that the sacrifice would be acceptable and that, with it, he would be accepted, too. On the other hand, the sacrifice was the offering and yielding up of himself to God and His service. He knew it was something that lay in the very nature and spirit of a true sacrifice, that it could not be pleasing to God if he offered the lamb and yet kept back himself. No, the sacrifice was the double confession—that he was unworthy to offer himself to God without atonement but also that, believing he was accepted in the sacrifice, he gave himself to God's worship and service, to the very death, to die to self and to live to God. And it was as if his own death had to confirm and seal the truth; the man who had offered the sacrifice of faith, had founded his worship in the death of a lamb, had to die himself to find the way to God. The atoning sacrifice has ever two sides; the lamb was at once both a substitute and a symbol, its death an atonement and a consecration.

Faith draws near to God through sacrifice; in Christ this truth finds its full realization. *"For by one offering he hath perfected for ever them that are sanctified"* (verse 14). Our access to God and our fellowship with Him can only be in Christ's finished work. We have boldness through His blood. His blood cleanses and perfects the conscience. The first great work of faith is to appropriate the sacrifice and obedience and righteousness of Christ as accepted for us to hold it up before God; and, by the Holy Spirit, to have the witness given and to experience how acceptable we are. But faith cannot fully do this without, at the same time, entering into the inner spiritual significance of the sacrifice and becoming partaker of the spirit and disposition it breathes and in which alone it has its value. Faith sees that the law of self-sacrifice, under which the Head went in to God, is the law for each of the members. There is no way out of sin and sinful flesh but through death to life. And as faith sees the beauty and the power of the truth in Christ, it hungers for conformity to Him in this His highest moral glory and becomes itself the root of an inward self-sacrifice, a continual offering of itself to God and His holiness—because it is nothing less than a real, living union with Christ the High Priest Himself. Christ became our Substitute because He was our Head; faith begins with the knowledge of him as Substitute but grows up into Him, the Head of all things, and especially in the fellowship of His death. We find this truth throughout Scripture. All that is said in Romans 6 and Colossians 3 of our being dead to sin in Christ and alive to God; in 2 Corinthians 4 of bearing about in the body the dying of Jesus that His life may be manifested in us; in Galatians 2 and 6 of our being crucified with Christ and being crucified to the world; in Philippians 3 of our being made conformable to His death—all that is said in these Scriptures points to this: The inward spirit and disposition of selfsacrifice is born within us by His Spirit, is breathed in us every day where there is true communion with Him. The blessing of Christ's death as atonement is only surpassed because it is only fulfilled in that of His death as fellowship.

Beloved Christian, we know what the great lesson of the epistle is: The way into the Holiest is opened up; we can live and abide continually in the presence of God. And now the chapter is to teach us how the power to come thus near and abide near to God, to enjoy the full salvation provided for us, is given to faith alone. And the story of Abel, the first of the men of faith, teaches us just what the epistle and what Christ our High Priest has taught—that the way to God, the way of faith, is the way of sacrifice and of death. Christ entered in to God in the way of self-sacrifice; in faith, I accept of Him, and His entrance into God's presence is mine; in union with Him, it is once and forever mine. His self-sacrifice becomes the spirit and the power of my life, and the life of faith in me becomes the union of the two—His and my self-sacrifice.

God said, *"Man shall not see me and live"* (Exodus 33:20). Through death, the death of Christ, our death in and with Him is the way to God. This is the new and living way, the way into the Holiest. Let us walk in it, in the power of the Holy Spirit. Let us yield ourselves in great simplicity and humility to die to self, as we confess our helplessness and look to God to quicken us in Christ. Let us tarry in childlike dependence and patience, with one desire: to please the Father as Jesus pleased Him. And as we wait and patiently do the will of God, He may show us, in the *"once"* and *"for ever"* of His death and resurrection, how there is for us a perfect entrance into the perfect life that has been offered to our faith.

Chapter Notes...

1. *"Abel...had witness borne to him that he was righteous."* As he bowed to God's righteous judgment on sin and trusted in God's righteous deliverance from it through sacrifice, he was righteous in God's sight. As he worshiped with his eye on the dying lamb, he had witness borne to him. How, I know not. But it is the same as when, with my eye on the dying Lamb, I worship, and the witness comes to me by the Holy Spirit that I am righteous.

2. Let me believe in the immeasurable power of the blood of the Lamb, until my whole being is filled with the witness of the Holy Spirit.

3. The more I gaze, in confession and trust, on the dying Lamb, the more may I claim the spirit of His sacrifice to enter into me and make me conformed to His likeness.

4. A more excellent sacrifice. Cain brings his offering without death, without blood—the spirit and religion of the world. With Abel and the hosts of heaven, it is all—the blood of the Lamb.

One Hundred

Enoch—The Walk of Faith

*By faith Enoch was translated that he should not see death;
and he was not found, because God translated him: for
before his translation he hath had witness borne to him
that he had been well-pleasing unto God: and without
faith it is impossible to be well-pleasing unto him: for he
that cometh to God must believe that he is, and that he is a
rewarder of them that seek after him.*
—Hebrews 11:5–6

The sacrifice of faith is the entrance to the life of faith and ever remains its chief characteristic. After the sacrifice of faith there follows the walk of faith—abiding, continuous fellowship is the fruit of Christ's self-sacrifice and ours. After Abel follows Enoch. Abel showed how death is the entrance to life; he triumphs over death by submitting to it. In Enoch, we see how life triumphed over death; he did not see death. Through faith, Abel, being dead, yet speaks; Enoch speaks as one who ever lives. In Abel, we see how death leads to life. In Enoch, we see the life that never dies. In Abel, we see Christ the crucified, and the boldness we have through the blood to enter in in the new and living way that goes through the rent veil. In

Enoch, we see Christ glorified and have life in the Holiest—the walk with God, the living One.

In connection with Enoch, there are three things taught us in regard to faith. The first is as to its nature. *"He that cometh to God must believe that he is, and that he is a rewarder of them that seek after him."* Faith is the spiritual sense by which we recognize the presence and character of the unseen God—both that He *is* and that He *rewards* the seeker. Desire is the root of faith; without a hunger for God, His existence is a matter of indifference; the knowledge of His being does not affect the soul. Faith seeks for God; it believes that He is; it keeps the heart open toward Him; it bows in humility and hope for Him to make Himself known. To know God, to see God in everything and everywhere, in our daily lives to be conscious of His presence so that we always walk with Him—this is the true nobility of man; this is the life that faith lives; this is the blessedness that Jesus has now fully revealed in the rending of the veil. Faith can walk with God. *"He that cometh to God must believe that he is, and that he is a rewarder of them that seek after him."* Faith believes that God can be found; that He can and will make Himself known; that He cares for everyone who truly longs for Him; that He has a divine reward for he who seeks after Him. In seeking Him, the way may at times be dark and long, and the progress slow; faith honors God with its confidence that He is the God of love and truth. He will reward and bless. Let the deep restfulness of this assured conviction be the root of all your seeking after God.

The second lesson we have is as to what the reward of faith will be. *"Before his translation he hath had witness borne to him that he had been well-pleasing unto God: and without faith it is impossible to be well-pleasing unto him."* God created us for Himself; it is our destiny; we were made with the one object of pleasing Him and being His delight. God is perfect goodness, and a state of life in which we please God must be one of goodness and perfect blessedness. In our fallen state, we are well-pleasing by faith. Faith is the surrender to God. Faith honors God by acknowledging and seeking His presence, by expecting everything from Him alone, by resting on Him. Faith gives God His place and His glory; faith wills what God wills; faith lets God have His own way and makes Him All in All. No wonder that faith is infinitely well-pleasing to Him. If Christians only believed this and only made it their one study to draw near and enter in and walk before Him in the fullness of faith!

3. Then comes the third lesson—faith knows that it pleases God. *"Enoch...had witness borne to him that he had been well-pleasing unto God."* It was by faith that this witness came. (See Hebrews 11:2, 4, 39.) It is of the very essence of a healthy faith. God does not leave Himself without a witness to the soul that trusts in Him, least of all in the New Testament. The Lord Jesus promised to send from the Father in heaven the Holy Spirit, as a Witness of all that took place in heaven after His ascension. All that the epistle has taught us of the rent veil and the opened sanctuary and the entrance into God's presence—of Christ's perfect work and complete salvation as the Priest in the power of an endless life—has its seal and its worth and its power and its reality in our hearts from the Pentecostal gift. The Holy Spirit brought down, out of that Holiest of All within the veil, as an actual reality, the kingdom of heaven into men's hearts, so that the presence of God and the Father's delight in His Son and the Father's love now shed abroad in their hearts became their everyday experience and consciousness. And even so now, still to them who seek and receive and yield to the Holy Spirit in His full indwelling and witness, faith receives and gives the witness that we are well-pleasing.

By faith, Enoch walked with God. My friend, who with Abel has drawn near to God in the infinite self-sacrifice of Jesus, learn with Enoch to walk with God the walk of faith. Let the presence of God be your one desire; the will of God your one choice; the help of God your one trust; the likeness to God your one hope. Let every day—the most ordinary one or the most difficult one—be a day with God, as one of the days of heaven upon earth, a day of which faith is the beginning and the end. Let all the teaching of the epistle, as to the wonderful, the perfect, the everlasting redemption in the Son of God, have this one result—that it makes you full of faith in God and guides you to draw near to God, to walk with God. And you, too, will know what it is not to see death; by faith to be translated, and have it written—*"He was not; for God took him"* (Genesis 5:24).

Chapter Notes...

1. Jesus said that John the Baptist was the greatest of all the prophets, greater than Enoch, too. And yet, the least in the kingdom was greater than John. And must it then be counted impossible for men even now to walk with God and to have the witness that they are well-pleasing to Him? Alas, for the church that scarce believes it.

2. The one great work of Jesus is to bring us near to God, in the nearness of unity of will and heart. And what He does is in the power of an endless life; He abides continually. And what He gives abides continually, too. We can ever abide in God's presence and walk with Him.

3. By faith, that lives in the unseen; that allows Christ to do His mighty work; that believes that the presence of God is now its home—by this faith, we enter into its rest.

One Hundred One

Noah—The Work of Faith

By faith Noah, being warned of God concerning things
not seen as yet, moved with godly fear, prepared an ark to
the saving of his house; through which he condemned the
world, and became heir of the righteousness
which is according to faith.
—Hebrews 11:7

In Abel, we see how faith makes death the path to life; in Enoch, how faith conquers death; in Noah, how faith saves others from death by the work it does for them. The moment the entrance into the Holiest through the blood had been set open to us, we were called to the work of love. (See Hebrews 10:19, 24–25.) If with Abel we have drawn nigh to God, in the death of Christ and the death to self (this is the root of the tree), if with Enoch we have given ourselves to a walk with God, in His presence and good pleasure (this is the tree growing from the root); then let us, with Noah, do the work of faith that can bless and save those around us (this is the fruit of the tree). In his story, we find all the essential elements of faith combined.

"*By faith Noah, being warned of God concerning things not seen as yet.*" Faith has ever to do with the future and the unseen. It lives in God's Word and thoughts; it sees what the world cannot see; it sees all, the future, too, in the light of God. When God reveals His terrible, almost incredible, judgment, it simply believes. It does not trust to its own experience or instinct, its thoughts or wishes. It believes in the inconceivable fearfulness of a judgment to come. O believer! if you would live and save men, believe what God has said of the impending doom that is coming on the world.

"Moved with godly fear." When Jesus prayed in Gethsemane under the sense of what sin and death are, it was with godly fear. We are exhorted to offer service that is well-pleasing to God with godly fear (see 12:28), because our God is a consuming Fire. *"It is a fearful thing to fall into the hands of the living God"* (10:31). How awfully and repeatedly our epistle speaks of the fate of the disobedient. Surely it becomes us, whose eyes have been opened with godly fear, to listen to God's warnings and then, under the mighty impulse of that motive, moved with godly fear, on some to have mercy with fear, snatching them out of the fire. Jude 23

"By faith Noah...prepared an ark." Faith brought fear, and fear worked diligence, and faith guided heart and hand for the work of deliverance. No one had ever heard of a coming flood, and the destruction of a world by water. No one could ever have thought, if the world were drowned, of an ark escaping alone. But faith lives in fellowship with God; it knows His secrets of judgment and of salvation; it so possesses a man that he gives up his life to act it out. In the face of the mockery of men, and the long delay of the day, and all the difficulties of the work, Noah held fast to God's promise. Simply to listen to what God says, and in the obedience of faith to give up our whole hearts and lives to carry it out: This is faith.

"To the saving of his house." The believer is blessed by God to be made a blessing. The faith of Noah, made perfect by works, saved his family; and with the family, he saved the race and became the father of us all. His preaching appeared to have little fruit, and yet the whole church of God, since his day, owes its life to his faith, too. Man was created in God's likeness in this, too, that he has power over other lives. The power begins with the family

wow.

but reaches further. The man of faith who, with Abel, in the one sacrifice, has passed through death to life, and with Enoch walks with God, has power with God, the power of life and of blessing.

"Through which [faith] *he condemned the world."* The difference between the unbeliever and the believer is this: The one is a man of the world and lives here; the other is a man of God and lives in heaven. His whole life is a protest and a condemnation of the world. Abel, Enoch, Noah—all three were equally rejected and despised by the world because they condemned its works. God grant that the life of his believing children may be so clear and bright that the world may feel itself condemned by them.

"And became heir of the righteousness which is according to faith"—the righteousness of standing in right relation to God, of a life of which faith is the root and power. Righteousness has been defined as the giving each his due. This is the worth of faith in the sight of God; it gives Him His place as God. In it, the soul confesses that it is nothing and that God is all. This faith God counts for righteousness.

The faith that Noah manifested with regard to the ark and the salvation it was to bring—we must show this same faith in relation to Christ and His salvation. The opened sanctuary is an ark of refuge: Christ has completed and perfected all. But what work there is for us to do, gathering into it all that can be saved! Let us, like Noah, give our lives to this. Let us listen to God's awful threatenings on a sinful world and be moved with fear. Let us believe in the infinite power of the great salvation provided, with the love that waits to dispense and apply it. Let us believe in the call of God that invites and enjoins each one of His redeemed children to be a messenger of mercy to the perishing and that assures us that He will abundantly use everyone who trusts Him. *"By faith Noah,... prepared an ark to the saving of his house."* Does this not give faith a new attractiveness and value? By the prayer of faith and the labor of faith, by the death to self in Christ, and by the walk in the presence of God, our hearts can be filled with a love and a power that cannot be fruitless. The Holy Spirit that came from our beloved Priest-King on the throne in the Holiest, as a witness to God's pleasure in us and to the indwelling of our Lord, came specially as an enduement of power, to make us in our turn witnesses for Him. O all who, by faith, have entered into the Holiest and its blessings—go forth and work the work of faith; by faith, bring in those who are still outside. This is the faith that makes you an heir of the righteousness that is according to faith.

Chapter Notes.

1. Abel, Enoch, Noah: all types of Jesus. Abel: the righteous one, hated and slain by his brethren, coming to God with sacrifice. Enoch: the beloved son, in whom God is well pleased, walking with Him on earth, and taken up into heaven. Noah: preparing salvation, saving His people, condemning the world.

2. The one thing God gives me is Jesus: the dying One, the living One, the redeeming One. The one thing He asks of me is faith. Faith will make me like Him. Beginning with the Abel-blessing by drawing near to God through death, I come to the Enoch-blessing, the life of unbroken fellowship; and so I learn the secret of the Noah-blessing and become a savior of others. And all of this, by faith.

One Hundred Two
Abraham—The Obedience of Faith

By faith Abraham, when he was called, obeyed to go out
unto a place which he was to receive for an inheritance;
and he went out, not knowing whither he went. By faith he
became a sojourner in the land of promise, as in a land not
his own, dwelling in tents, with Isaac and Jacob, the heirs
with him of the same promise: for he looked for the city which
hath the foundations, whose builder and maker is God.
—Hebrews 11:8–10

There is no child of Adam who is held in honor by such a large portion of the human race as Abraham. Jews, Christians, Mohammedans*—all look up to him as the father of the faithful. And God honors him as His friend! If anyone can tell us the secret of a life of faith, this hero of the obedience of faith can. Our epistle has called us to be *"imitators of them who through faith and patience inherit the promises"* (Hebrews 6:12), with special mention of Abraham as one who, *"having patiently endured,...*

---

* Muslims.

451

obtained the promise" (verse 15). Paul, too, spoke of those *"who also walk in the steps of that faith of our father Abraham which he had"* (Romans 4:12). Let all who have with purpose of heart determined, like Abraham, to be strong in faith, giving glory to God, listen to the lesson of his life. God expects from us—we do indeed need, and it is within our reach—the very same faith that he had.

"By faith Abraham, when he was called, obeyed to go out unto a place which he was to receive for an inheritance; and he went out, not knowing whither he went." What was the object of God's thus dealing with Abraham? And what, in real truth, was the worth and the blessing of his obedience? The call of God was no arbitrary one; as we see into its divine meaning, we will understand what God asks of us and what our faith must lay hold of. Man stands between the visible and the invisible. His sin and Fall consisted in his having turned from God to the world. His redemption from the power of sin could only be found in his giving up the world and setting his whole heart upon God. It was to train him to this, to teach him to find his life and his happiness in God Himself, that the call came: *"Get thee out of thy country, and from thy kindred, and from thy father's house, unto the land that I will shew thee"* (Genesis 12:1). God wanted to have him alone with Himself, separated from all he could cling to or trust in, that He might teach him to find his all in Himself. And it was by faith—faith that not only saw the land and the promise connected with it afar off, but faith that also saw the living God near to fulfill the promise—that Abraham obeyed. The call of God is ever accompanied by the promise; true faith in the promise is ever joined to obedience to the call. Obedience is of the very essence of faith. Faith is always the power by which a man gives himself up to an unseen object and receives it into his heart and being. It is in the very nature of things impossible to receive God without receiving His will.

"By faith Abraham,...obeyed." We have seen how it was by obedience, by the doing of God's will, that the Son Himself was perfected and that He perfected us, becoming the Author of salvation

to those who obey Him. Let us learn that obedience is the very life of faith and the only way into the Holiest. Let immediate, unreserved, joyful obedience be the one thing our hearts are set upon. And let it especially manifest itself in this, one of the root principles of God's will—His call to come out and be separate—and let us give ourselves to walk with Him wherever He leads.

"He went out, not knowing whither he went." Do not say that you cannot understand what it is to come out and forsake all. You do not need to know. You need to know something else—that you have a God who is watching and guiding you and working out in you a character fit for heaven and eternity. The one great mark of that character—of likeness to the Son and fitness for heaven—is very absolute surrender to God to let Him be all. Of that surrender, deep humility that only wants to obey and to trust is the first essential. Therefore, say to God that, at every cost and in every way, you are ready to obey. He will never disappoint the trust of a soul fully committed to Him and His will.

"By faith he became a sojourner in the land of promise." He not only went out from Haran but also into Canaan. And not even this alone—but he sojourned, he abode, he lived there. He not only began well, but in faith and longsuffering, he inherited the promise. It is the great lesson of perseverance again. Every day, over again, it must just be obedience and faith until God has brought us into closer communion with Himself and can speak to men of us or through us as those who are His tested and trusted friends—men who live only to honor Him.

"For he looked for the city...whose builder and maker is God." By faith, He saw the unseen; in hope, he lived in the future. He had his heart as little in Canaan as in Haran. His heart was truly in heaven; it was with God. And we, who have been called to enter into the true tabernacle, which God has pitched—oh, will we not obey and go out, even though it means not knowing where we go? Let us separate ourselves entirely from the world and its spirit; let us, like the Son, die to the creature that we may live to God.

A worldly spirit in the church or the Christian is a deadly disease; it makes the life of faith impossible. Let us count it our worst enemy and live as foreigners, who seek the city that is to come. Let us hear the voice calling us out to Himself, to close fellowship, to obedience as of the angels in heaven, to be a testimony and a blessing for the world. And let it be said of us too: *"By faith* [he],... *obeyed...and he went out,* [and]*...he became a sojourner in the land of promise.*

Chapter Notes...

1. See in Abraham how the whole life of faith is supernatural. His call—the promise of a country, of a son, of a seed—all is distinctly divine, above all sense and reason. It is only when the soul looks steadily at the really supernatural things God is to do for us and in us and through us that its faith will rest entirely on the power of God and obey at any cost.

2. God will hold personal conversation with you as with Abraham. God will be all to you as to him. Let your life be supernatural; perfect surrender under the operation of divine omnipotence. God, by His Spirit, working out in you His own life.

3. Be a sojourner in the land of promise—in the life opened up to us by the promises of God—the life in the Holiest of All, through the Holy Spirit. Live in the promises.

4. *"He went out, not knowing whither he went."* Christ is not only Priest but Prophet, Teacher, and Leader. Trust Him to bring you within the veil and to guide you all through life in the new and living way. It is a peace that passes all understanding, a love that passes knowledge, a power that is able to do exceeding abundantly above all we can think—this marks the life of faith in the land of promise. Let us go out, not knowing whither we go.

One Hundred Three

Sarah—Faith in the Faithfulness of God

By faith even Sarah herself received power to conceive seed when she was past age, since she counted him faithful who had promised: wherefore also there sprang of one, and him as good as dead, so many as the stars of heaven in multitude, and as the sand, which is by the sea shore, innumerable.
—Hebrews 11:11–12

y faith Sarah received power to give birth to Isaac. To judge by nature and its possibilities, there was no hope of a son. But the birth of Isaac was to be a work of God's power: He had promised and He would perform. Sarah believed the promise because she believed God the Promiser; by faith she received power to become Isaac's mother; and of one who was *"as good as dead,"* there sprang up as *"many as the stars of heaven in multitude."*

We are told that, in sight of what was impossible with man, her faith found its strength: *"She counted him faithful who had promised."* She looked to the promise; she considered Him who had given it; she rested on His faithfulness. The faithfulness of God was the rest of her heart and her faith.

What is the lesson Sarah taught us in regard to the life of faith and the work that God would work in us through faith? From one who was as good as dead, there sprang as the stars in multitude. God is the living God who delights to give life in death. When Adam sinned, he and the whole race died; they lost the life of Paradise and of God. God's great work is to restore that life. In the Old Testament, He showed this in a case like that of Isaac, by proving that the new race He was going to prepare must have a life from Himself, a life born of one *"as good as dead."* Isaac's life was to be, in a special sense, a God-given life. In the New Testament, He showed it by the miraculous birth of Jesus Christ: God's mighty power revealing the divine life in the babe of Bethlehem. What God would teach us is that the new life must come from God; His mighty power must alone and directly work it or else all is vain. It is for this that our faith must trust Him.

Just as truly as the life of Adam, the life of Isaac, and the life of Christ was the immediate work of God's almighty power, so is His work the divine life in our souls. And it is not only His work in its beginning, as if He bestowed upon us a life that we had to keep in safety and to nourish and bring to perfection. No, as the tree grows every day on that root from which it sprang, so our spiritual lives must every day stand and grow in God and Christ. One great cause of the weakness of the spiritual life of earnest Christians, notwithstanding their prayers and efforts, is that they seek to do the work that God alone can do. They know not that God, whose Spirit dwells in us, will maintain our lives in a divine power, working in us what is pleasing in His sight. If they knew this aright, they would see that their one duty was in utter helplessness, in deep humility and dependence, to wait upon God and to trust and count upon Him to do His blessed work.

It is this that Sarah teaches us. She knew what God had promised. For twenty-five long years her heart yearned for the son of

Andrew Murray

whom God had spoken. At times, her faith was sorely tried, but she ever came back to this one thing: He who promised is faithful! And in due time, God did His omnipotent quickening work, and Sarah received power to become the mother of Isaac and of Jesus. And down the ages, her voice of witness is heard: "Trust God; He is faithful; He is the living God; He gives life from the dead."

The teaching of the epistle speaks to us of the living God and the city of the living God to which we are come; of a High Priest who lives forever; of a work that He does within us, the power of an endless life; of a new and living way in which we are borne into God's presence; of the law of life written in the heart; and of a life within the veil, in the Holiest of All. This new and wondrous life it has revealed is nothing less than the life and work of God in the soul. To the question that is so often asked, "Why we do not experience that life more mightily?" there can be but one answer: "We do not allow God in Christ to work it in us; we do not believe in the continual indwelling and working of the Holy Spirit." Even as Sarah failed when she sought for the promised son by giving Hagar to Abraham, we fail because we seek by our effort to do what God will not allow any but Himself to do. Let us, like Sarah, come back from our self-devised ways and enter by the new and living way— the way of death to nature and to self and the way of life through the Holy Spirit into the life that God alone can maintain.

Faith is the power by which we take up into our beings and yield ourselves up to and become one with the Object our heart clings to and reposes on. God has spoken to us in His Son. His Son is the great Promise to us, the Token and the Pledge of what God will make us. Let us look to the promise; let us look to the Son; let us look to the faithful One who has promised and with whom it is impossible to lie; and we will receive power to receive and bring forth the new life that is of God. Let us, above all, take the place before God that Sarah did, as of one dead—hopelessly, helplessly dead—as far as the prospect of bringing forth a new life was concerned, and we may count upon it: God will do His work! Helplessness is ever

Helplessness is even [handwritten marginal note]

one of the conditions of true faith. Sink down before God in utter emptiness; bow before Him and wait upon Him and walk with Him in deep humility and meekness of soul, as having nothing and being nothing; fall down as dead at His feet, and He will say, "Fear not; I am He who lives and who makes alive."

Chapter Notes...

1. Now, bow down; say to God that you trust Him for the wonderful new life the epistle has revealed Christ. Trust Him to reveal Christ, in the power of an endless life, within you.

2. Let every doubt and fear be met by looking afresh to the promise; to God the Promiser; to the faithfulness of Him who, by an oath, has confirmed His promise of blessing; and to the power of the eternal priesthood of Christ to you.

3. In this trust, take your place of deep helplessness and dependence and humility. Be nothing that God may be all. Just yield yourself for the living God through His Son and Spirit to do His mighty work in you.

4. The full blessing of Sarah's faith was not only Isaac, but *"so many as the stars of heaven in multitude."* So with you. As you give yourself wholly to be filled directly from God Himself with the divine life, it will break forth in blessing around. *"Blessing I will bless thee, and multiplying I will multiply thee"* (Hebrews 6:14).

Wow! [handwritten marginal note]

One Hundred Four

Faith and Its Pilgrim Spirit

These all died in faith, not having received the promises, but having seen them and greeted* them from afar, and having confessed that they were strangers and pilgrims on the earth. For they that say such things make it manifest that they are seeking after a country of their own. And if indeed they had been mindful of that country from which they went out, they would have had opportunity to return. But now they desire a better country, that is, a heavenly: wherefore God is not ashamed of them, to be called their God: for he hath prepared for them a city.
—Hebrews 11:13–16

Most instructive is the description given us here of the way in which faith prepared the saints of old for the fulfillment of God's promises. First comes—*"having seen them... from afar"*; faith was to them the revelation of unseen things. Then follows—"having embraced them, they gladly greeted, welcomed,

---

* Embraced.

accepted, and appropriated them, and lived as those to whom they belonged." Then follows the receiving. Of the Old Testament saints, it is here said, *"Not having received the promises."* Some of the promises they did indeed receive, as we have seen in the birth of Isaac. But the promises, in their full meaning, they did not receive; this is our privilege. Seeing, embracing, and receiving are the three great steps in the life of faith.

On this follows a description of the life in which their faith was made manifest: *"Having confessed that they were strangers and pilgrims on the earth."* Faith is such a power that it rules the whole life. The faith of a man makes him forsake his home for our gold-fields. If he sees his way to make a fortune and return to some great center of attraction, this faith maintains in him the spirit of a stranger and a pilgrim, whose heart is in the homeland. So these saints proved that they were *"seeking after a country of their own,"* that they had no mind to return to that from which they went out that *"now they desire a better country, that is, a heavenly."* Faith made them pilgrims and strangers and secured them the divine blessing. *"Wherefore God is not ashamed of them, to be called their God: for he hath prepared for them a city."*

Our great lesson is this: Faith makes us pilgrims and strangers here on earth. Such was Christ, and such are we to be. The moment we begin to press home the message to our own hearts, many questions arise. Will it not unfit us for daily life? What if all men were to live in this pilgrim spirit, as strangers and sojourners? What would become of the development of the world? Do we not see that in science and politics and literature, the men who give themselves wholly to these things accomplish the most? Those who come to a colony, and then return home to spend their money there, never take the interest of those who give themselves to settle in the colony. Is the true, intense pilgrim spirit really a duty for all? There is no more subtle temptation than to wait with what God calls us to do until we are first informed what others are to do, or what God is to do with the rest of the world. We may safely leave to

Him, who is Ruler of all, the All-wise, what will come of obedience to His commands. To every question, *"And what shall this man do?"* (John 21:21), Christ's answer is, *"What is that to thee? follow thou me"* (verse 22). If we are disciples of Christ, each one of us must seek to have as much of His Spirit as can be. If we are to be led by Him in the new and living way, to live with Him in the Holiest of All, we must, like Him, live here as pilgrims and strangers.

Faith makes us heavenly minded. As partakers of a heavenly calling, we look to Jesus, who endured the cross and despised the shame. Separation from the world is essential to a life of faith. Adam's fall was a fall under the power and spirit of this visible world. Christ gave Himself that He might deliver us from this present evil world. The world we live in—the so-called "Christian" world—is still the same that rejected Christ. While professing His name, its spirit of devotion to the things that are seen; its pursuit of pleasure and riches and honor; its delight and its boasting of culture and prosperity—each of these shows a spirit that is utterly at variance with the Christlike and heavenly minded spirit. This is the reason why so many seek to grow in faith but fail. They would desire to live in the Holiest, but they would do so without forsaking the world. Abraham and his seed lived as men *"seeking after a country of their own,"* as those who *"desire a better country, that is, a heavenly."* Until the kingdom of heaven in its power, as it came down from the throne of God in heaven, becomes our one desire, and until we leave all and sell all for this pearl of great price, our faith cannot stand in the power of God or overcome the world. If it be not our one desire to live as those who are partakers of a heavenly calling—yea, partakers of Christ—as those who are pilgrims and strangers, and make it manifest that they are seeking after a country of their own, as those who desire a heavenly country, no wonder if God is ashamed to be called our God and our souls cannot taste the joy of a walk in His presence.

There is nothing so heart-searching as faith. If we profess to believe all that this epistle has revealed, let us prove it by following our Leader in the new and living way and by living with Him in the Holiest of All. As we give ourselves wholly to this, our faith will grow; we will become men and women of faith, marked by this one thing—a faith that lifts us into the heavenly world and makes us pilgrims and strangers here.

The eye of faith will become ever clearer, seeing, perhaps at first afar off, what so many cannot see—the promise and the reality and the possibility of abiding continually in the Holiest of All, in the power of an endless life, separated and made free from the world and its spirit. The boldness of faith will become ever stronger—we will greet and embrace, we will claim and hold fast, all that God hath spoken in Christ of a life in the city of the living God here below as our very own. And we will, in patience, persevere in doing the will of God, knowing that the power of God Himself and the Son of God is Surety that we will receive the promise. True faith begins with counting upon what God has promised, but it does not end there—it leads into the actual possession and enjoyment, in the power of God, of all it had embraced in His Word. What God hath spoken to faith, His hand will perform.

Chapter Notes...

1. Note well the three steps of faith. I must first see what God has promised. I must believe in the blessed life Christ can give and maintain within me. Let us pray for the Spirit's enlightening. (See Ephesians 1:14–20.) Then I embrace, greet, welcome, and claim as my own the promise—and expect its fulfillment. This in due time I receive, in heart and experience. Whatever God has promised me, I must expect to experience.

2. The promise is over the expression of what God's omnipotence is going to work; our faith must ever be the expression of what we expect that omnipotence to work.

One Hundred Five

Faith Counting on the Power of God

*By faith Abraham, being tried, offered up Isaac: yea, he
that had gladly received the promises was offering up his
only begotten son; even he to whom it was said, In Isaac
shall thy seed be called: accounting that God is able to raise
up, even from the dead; from whence he did also in
a parable receive him back.*
—Hebrews 11:17–19

As the characteristic of Abraham's faith, we have here again
the great word, *offering.* Abel offered; Christ offered Himself; Abraham offered his only begotten, and, in doing so,
himself, too. In some shape or other, communion with God and
the life of faith always means sacrifice. In a sinful world, there is no
way of drawing near to God, of coming out of the sinful nature,
but by dying to it and receiving a new life from God Himself—or
rather by God giving His own life into the dead one to raise it
again. There is no way to God but by giving up our own lives, and
what is as dear as life, unto death.

This sacrifice is only possible by faith. The faith that has seen and embraced the promise, that knows God as the living and life-giving God, and that dares claim and count upon His Power to do to me what He has spoken is the faith that has the courage for the altar and the knife and the fire. God's great object in leading His people in the path of faith is to train them for ever larger sacrifice. It was a sacrifice of all he held dear when Abraham left his kindred and his father's home. It was a sacrifice of all his own thoughts and wishes when he was kept waiting for Isaac twenty-five years. But all this was only to prepare him for the crowning sacrifice—the giving up of his only son, the son of the promise, to the death.

And what was it that gave faith its strength and its victory here in this his severest trial? It was faith in God as the almighty One, *"able to raise up, even from the dead."* In the birth of Isaac he had learned to know God as the Giver of life, even when he was as good as dead. He knew and trusted his God, as God *"who quickeneth the dead, and calleth the things that are not, as though they were"* (Romans 4:17). And what is it that will give our faith the same all-victorious strength and prepare us for the same mighty exhibition of God's quickening power on our behalf? If we are to have the same faith and the same experience of God, we must be prepared to make the same sacrifice. Our lesson of today leads us to the very deepest roots of the life of faith. The deeper we are willing to enter into the death to self, the more will we know of the mighty power of God and the perfect blessedness of a perfect trust.

In the faith of Sarah, we saw what the meaning and the power was of faith in the living and life-giving God. But Abraham on Moriah carries us much further. Sarah trusted God to supply a power that was wanting in nature; Abraham trusted God to restore a life that had been taken away. Sarah is the type of a soul that waits on God for His quickening power, as an act of grace and faithfulness, before it thinks much of the death of self. With her, the quickening came to meet a deadness that appears simply the result of the weakness of nature. With Abraham, all is different.

Isaac, the God-given life, must be sacrificed before this new display of power can be expected. That sacrifice was to teach that even the God-given life is still subject to the power of fallen nature; that only through death can it be delivered from the power of sin and death; that only so can it become a life wholly possessed of God. The first time quickened by Him, and yet under the power of sin; the second time, dead to sin, and alive to God in the perfect life of eternity. It was the symbol of what was to take place in Christ Jesus and everyone who is made like Him in the fellowship of His death.

We see where this leads us in the Christian life. Even as Christ in His birth received His life from the Father, so we, too, in our new birth. But that life had to be sacrificed before He could enter the full life in the glory of the Father. Even so with us. The life God gives us in the new birth is only to prepare us for understanding and deserving and accepting and entering into a perfect voluntary conformity to Christ's death. As we see how much there still is of self, we begin to learn and long for what is implied in death to self. It means a deeper insight into our own entire and complete inability to do any good. It means a willing and a hearty consent to be and to do nothing and to let God be and do all. It means a real ceasing from our own works and an entire surrender to the immediate and unceasing operations of God by His Holy Spirit, for Him to work both to will and to do what is pleasing in His sight. It means such a hating of one's own life, such a denial of one's self, that one is content with nothing less than death to it.

The soul that seeks to follow its Lord in this new and living way, and feels the need of the faith in the living God who raises the dead, will be fitted to exercise it. The trial of faith calls out its power; the need of faith calls down the power of God. Oh, if we did but hear the call of God to bring the life He has Himself given us, with all its blessed experience, and yield it up to the death, how we would learn to know Him in His mighty quickening power. Instead of the life with something of God but far more of man, He who led Abraham would bring us to the place of death where He would give us the assurance that, henceforth, His almighty power would do all and we would find our blessedness in being nothing and allowing God to be our life.

Christian, Abraham offered up Isaac, accounting that God is able to raise him up, even from the dead. Take the place of death; trust God who raises the dead and gives life in death; believe and you will see the glory of God.

Chapter Notes...

1. The highest manifestation of God's power is the raising of Christ from the dead. The highest exercise of faith by Christ was in death—He committed His Spirit into the Father's hands. The highest exercise of faith in a believer is the daily surrender of the life God has given us to death, in the faith that He will quicken it each moment by His indwelling Spirit.

2. Before Isaac's birth, Abraham had nothing to lean upon but the promise. After it, he was in danger of leaning on Isaac. Therefore, Isaac had to be given up. All gifts of God received in faith may become our trust, and must be given up to Him in a higher faith.

3. Our whole lives every day, every moment, are to be the work of almighty God within us by His Holy Spirit.

One Hundred Six
Faith Blessing the Children

*By faith Isaac blessed Jacob and Esau, even concerning
things to come. By faith Jacob, when he was a dying, blessed
each of the sons of Joseph; and worshipped, leaning upon
the top of his staff. By faith Joseph, when his end was nigh,
made mention of the departure of the children of Israel;
and gave commandment concerning his bones. By faith
Moses, when he was born, was hid three months by his
parents, because they saw he was a goodly child; and they
were not afraid of the king's commandment.*
—Hebrews 11:20–23

It is remarkable how much, both in this chapter and through all
Scripture, faith has to do with the relationship of parents and
children. In nature, the life of the parents is imparted to the
children. In the spiritual world, it may be so, too; the communion
of faith with God reaches the children, too; the man of strong faith
is a blessing to his children. We have seen in Noah and Abraham
and Sarah how largely their faith in God had to do with their children. And here we find four more examples.

"By faith Isaac blessed Jacob and Esau." His blessing on his children was the manifestation of his faith in the promise of God to his

father and himself, and the transmission of the blessing to them. *"By faith Jacob,...blessed each of the sons of Joseph,"* giving each of them their place in the future that was coming. *"By faith Joseph,...made mention of the departure of the children of Israel,"* saying, *"I die: but God will surely visit you, and bring you up out of this land"* (Genesis 50:24). *"By faith Moses, when he was born, was hid three months by his parents, because they saw he was a goodly child."* Their faith in the destiny that they knew was waiting for the children of Israel, and in the mercy of God watching over His people, gave them the courage not to fear the king's commandment. In all these cases, faith was the secret inspiration of their treatment of their children and the source of blessing. Faith never confines itself to the person of the believer himself but also takes in his home and children.

And how is it that the Christian parent can secure this longed-for blessing for his children? There is but one answer: by faith. Our lives must be all faith—that is, the unseen things must be our life; yea, rather, the unseen God must be our life. The blessing and the power are His, and it is as we have more of God in our lives and in our home that there will be the hidden power resting on our children. Faith does not only mean a knowing that there is a covenant promise for our children and a pleading of it in prayer. This is an exercise of faith and has great value, but the chief thing is the life; faith is the making way for God and giving Him place in our lives. And when at times the vision tarries and the promise appears to fail, faith understands this as only a call to trust God more completely and more confidently. As we hold fast our confidence firm to the end, as in patience and longsuffering we are strong in faith, giving glory to God, we will know for certain that we will inherit this promise, too: "I will be thy God and the God of thy seed" (Genesis 17:8–9).

From the patriarchs, we learn what the atmosphere and what the soil is in which there grows such a faith that blesses the children. They were living in the Land of Promise as strangers and pilgrims,

Andrew Murray

or in Egypt as strangers and pilgrims, too, longing for the return to the land. Their whole life was hope in God and what He would do. They were men whom God had taken hold of, to prove in their history how gloriously He would fulfill His promise. And they had nothing to live on but God. It is a law of nature that no body can be in two places at the same time. This is just as true of the heart. When God took Abraham and his seed out of their country, it was so that the Land of Promise—the land of separation from men, of separation unto God—might be to them the training school of faith. They went out from the fellowship of home and family to live in the fellowship of God. It was there that they learned by faith to bless the children.

Separation from the world; a being set apart unto God; the denial of self and its life; the imitation of Abraham in his going out and of Christ in His self-sacrifice—this is the only way to the Land of Promise where the faith-life flourishes. To live wholly for God; to hope alone in God; to always to walk with God; in all things to hearken to God—this is the new and living way into the inner sanctuary, in which Jesus our High Priest leads us. What the Land of Promise was to the patriarchs, as a place for the life of separation and obedience and faith, so the Holiest of All is to us. That is the place of which God has said to us, *"Get thee out of thy country, and from thy kindred, and from thy father's house, unto the land that I will shew thee...and I will bless thee"* (Genesis 12:1–2); that is the only place where our faith can grow freely and God can prove all His power in us so that we, like they, can be a display of what God can do. And that is the place where our faith will, in full measure, be a blessing to our children.

It is only by faith that we can bless. God is willing to bless us to larger circles than our own house. He is calling for vessels, empty vessels—and not just a few—in which He can multiply his blessing. He is the only Fountain of blessing; as our faith yields to God and allows Him to be all, His blessing will flow. Let the Christian who would be a blessing be a man of faith—that is, a man who has nothing and is nothing, in himself, and in whom God has free scope to work; and the blessing will not be wanting. Oh, that God might have the place that belongs to Him in this His own world. And if that may not yet be—oh, that He might have that place in the hearts of His people. And if it is as if even that will not yet be—oh, let Him have that place, my reader, in your heart and in mine. Let faith see and consent and prove that God is all, and He will prove that He is a God of blessing for you and all around you.

Chapter Notes...

1. Parent, teacher, worker—the secret of blessing in the work, the power to influence, is faith. Not simply the faith in some promise at times, but the habit of a holy faith that makes God the all of our lives. Have faith in God as the God of your life, the God who maintains His life and presence within you. He will work through you.

2. How blessed to be an instrument in the hands of God, with which He works out His purpose; to be a vessel He fills with His love.

3. Learn to regard yourself as set to be a blessing, and let faith and love mark your whole life.

One Hundred Seven
Moses and the Decision of Faith

*By faith Moses, when he was grown up, refused to be called
the son of Pharaoh's daughter; choosing rather to be evil
entreated with the people of God, than to enjoy the pleasures
of sin for a season; accounting the reproach of Christ
greater riches than the treasures of Egypt: for he looked
unto the recompense of reward.*
—Hebrews 11:24–26

We all live by faith. What we love and live in, we believe in. He who trusts and yields himself to the visible and the temporal lives an earthly, fleshly life. He who looks to the unseen and the eternal, and joins himself to it, lives a divine and heavenly life. Between these two, faith ever has to make its choice. The clearer and more deliberate and more conscious the decision is for the unseen, the more will faith in God be strengthened and rewarded. The great difficulty in making the right choice lies in the fact that, by the victory that earthly things gained over us in Paradise, our eyes have been blinded; and the things of time, even where we acknowledge them to be of less value, have acquired, in virtue of their continual presence and their pressing claims, superior power. The great work faith has to do, and the best school for its growth and strength, is the choice of the unseen.

Of this choice, Moses was a striking illustration. Just see what there was on the one side. The lust of the flesh: *"the pleasures of sin for a season."* The lust of the eye: *"the treasures of Egypt."* The pride of life: *"to be called the son of Pharaoh's daughter."* On the other side, to be *"evil entreated"* and to bear *"reproach."* And what was it that enabled him to make a wise choice? He saw that to be *"evil entreated"* with the people of God is to have God as his portion and defense. He bore the *"reproach of Christ,"* in the power of the Spirit of Christ from heaven, lifting his heart above earth. Even as Christ, for the joy set before Him, endured the cross, so Moses looked *"unto the recompense of reward."* Faith in the blessing of God on the people of God; union in spirit with the Christ of God; the assurance of a coming world, with its reversal of the judgments of earth—no wonder that all this guided and strengthened him to the choice he made, the good part never to be taken away.

We are studying this chapter in its connection with the epistle and its teaching as to a life under the leadership of Christ—a life in the new and living way of conformity to Him, leading into the Holiest of God's presence. We long to know how we can grow strong and live in the full exercise of a faith that inherits the promise and enters into the rest of God. Moses' witness is clear: Let faith prove itself in choosing, once for all and for always, at any cost, the unseen—the reward will be sure and large. In Abraham, we saw this choice when there was no special opposition or persecution. This is the feature in Moses' choice we must notice: With the danger threatening us of being evil entreated and bearing reproach and having to face the loss of all, faith must not hesitate or halt. To be evil entreated with God's people, to bear the reproach of Christ, and to count these greater riches than all the treasures of Egypt—this is what faith enables a man to do. This is the spiritual discipline that makes faith strong. Faith looks at everything in the light of eternity, judging of it as one will do when the Judgment Day is past and the glory begun; everything is seen in its true value, and sacrifice and suffering and loss and trial are welcomed as the training in which the glad decision, firm will, strong character, and the victory of faith are attained.

We have here the great cause of the weakness of faith in our days: There is no separation from the world. So many Christians seek to have as much of its pleasure and honor and riches as they possibly can, consistently with their profession of religion. In such an atmosphere, faith is stifled. Many hardly believe, or never remember, that the world, with its arts and culture and prosperity, amid all its religious professions, is still the same world that rejected Christ. The disciple who would be as his Lord, not of the world, even as He was not of the world (see John 17:14–16), seeks to say with Paul, *"Far be it from me to glory, save in the cross of our Lord Jesus Christ, through which the world hath been crucified unto me, and I unto the world"* (Galatians 6:14).

How wonderful is the place Moses occupies in the kingdom of God. A pattern of Jesus as a prophet, as a mediator, as an intercessor, in his meekness and his faithfulness, there are few of God's servants who stand higher. And what fitted him to take this place? Just this—the choice to give up everything for the reproach of Christ. Christian, would you live in the favor of God and enter into His tent to meet Him as Moses did? Would you be an instrument and a power of blessing, a person strong in faith? Then seek to be perfectly separate from the spirit of the world; refuse its pleasure and honor and riches; count the contempt of God's people and the reproach of Christ as your treasures. Ask for the enlightening of the Holy Spirit to teach you what true conformity to Christ is in your relation to the world, its culture, its possessions, and its friendship. Beware of judging what is lawful by any human standard: Christ alone can teach you what it means to forsake all, to sell all, to deny yourself, and to take up your cross and follow Him. Count all things loss to be conformed to Him. It was in bearing the reproach of Christ that a character like that of Moses was formed. This is the sure path of faith to power and to blessing.

Follow Moses, accounting the reproach of Christ as your riches, and you will share with him the recompense of the reward. Let us therefore go forth unto Him, bearing His reproach.

Chapter Notes...

1. Examine very carefully where your danger lies. Is it the friendship and honor of men? Is it pleasure? Is it the cares of the world? Whatever it is, give it up. It is only an unworldly spirit that can be strong in faith.

2. What is the faith that enables a man to bear all and to sacrifice all? Nothing but an eye that sees into the true nature and value of things, that judges of them as God does. Yea, rather that we see God to be all, and the creature nothing, except as it leads to Him.

3. Exercise yourself in this faith by retirement into solitude and fellowship with the invisible. Beware of too free communion with the literature of this world: Its spirit enters into you. The world does not know God; make your choice and maintain it.

One Hundred Eight

Israel and Redemption by Faith

By faith he forsook Egypt, not fearing the wrath of the king: for he endured, as seeing him who is invisible. By faith he kept the passover, and the sprinkling of the blood, that the destroyer of the firstborn should not touch them. By faith they passed through the Red sea as by dry land: which the Egyptians assaying to do were swallowed up. By faith the walls of Jericho fell down, after they had been compassed about for seven days. By faith Rahab the harlot perished not with them that were disobedient, having received the spies with peace.
—Hebrews 11:27–31

In these verses we have, in five examples from the history of Israel on its way from Egypt to Canaan, the truth confirmed anew that in all God does in redemption, faith is the beginning and ending when it comes to man's part. Whether we look at His revelation as a whole or at its individual parts, the one thing He always asks, the one thing that pleases Him, and the one thing that secures His blessing is faith. In the five times that *"by faith"* is repeated, we see that in the greatest variety of circumstances and duties the first of all duties is always faith in the invisible One. Oh, that we might at length learn the lesson: As there is one God, and one redemption, so there is but one way to Him and to it—faith in Him. As absolute, and universal, and undisputed as the sole supremacy of God is, so is the supremacy of faith in our hearts to be. Why? Because when faith reigns supreme, it makes way for God, and God can become within us what He is in the universe, what He is in His very nature—the All in All.

The history of Israel, under the guidance of the Holy Spirit of God, is a real type and figure of the life of Christ in the soul. In the illustrations taken from the beginning of that history, we have some of the chief steps of the Christian life strikingly illustrated. By faith Moses, with Israel, left Egypt, *"not fearing the wrath of the king"* who would pursue them. That is ever the first step—coming out; being separate; parting with sin; bidding farewell to Egypt, the land of our birth; and not fearing the wrath of Satan or the world. It is by nothing but faith that this can be done, definitely and perseveringly. But faith can enable us to do it, as it did Moses. *"For he endured, as seeing him who is invisible."* Here is the mighty power of faith: It sees what others cannot see. It sees, amid the thousand things others see and are guided by, something infinitely greater—it sees God. No wonder it leads a man to act differently from other men. On everything it looks at, the bright light of eternity, of God, is shining. No wonder that, under the inspiration of that vision, it can do mighty deeds, for it sees God its Helper and Strength.

Let me here say to every believer that just as, in any pursuit, the eye by practice can be trained to see what others cannot see, so the eye of faith can be trained to see God everywhere. Abide in His presence until the heart is filled with it. Recognize Him in everything that happens. Seek to walk in the light of His countenance. Seeing the invisible will make it easy to forsake the world and to do the will of God.

"By faith he kept," with Israel, *"the passover, and the sprinkling of the blood, that the destroyer of the firstborn should not touch them."*

Andrew Murray

When faith is ready for the first step, the forsaking of Egypt, God meets it with His divine provision, and faith finds perfect safety and rest under the shelter of the blood. And if Israel thus honored God's word and trusted in the blood of a lamb—oh, will we not ten thousand times more honor the blood of the Lamb and believe and claim the eternal salvation that it brings us? We have been taught its wonderful power in conquering sin and death, in opening heaven, in cleansing and perfecting our consciences and hearts, and in bringing us nigh to God; let us open our whole beings to the power of the blood that cleanses from all sin. Let our faith rejoice in the invisible God and the precious blood of the Lamb of God.

"By faith they passed through the Red sea as by dry land." After the sprinkling of the blood there follows the entrance into a new life; the surrender is to be led by God in a way that we know not, through difficulties that are, to us, insurmountable. *"By faith they passed through"* between the waters in a way man had never trod, in a way that their pursuers in vain sought to follow. Where nature fails, faith triumphs, for it follows in a way where God leads.

"By faith the walls of Jericho fell down." The strength in which the enemy trusted, in view of the helplessness of God's people, availed nothing when faced with the power of faith. When will we learn, in quiet patience and perseverance, to wait upon God our seven days, too, the circle of a completed time, until He gives the possession of the promised rest? Let our faith claim it; we are the children of a God who does impossibilities; we are called to a life of faith that expects and receives them. Let our life be faith in God.

"By faith Rahab...perished not." Salvation by faith was not for Israel only but for the heathen, too. By faith, Rahab was not only saved but also became one of the ancestors of Jesus, and one of the cloud of witnesses that tell of the blessedness of faith. With one accord, they call to us, "Have faith in God; all things are possible to him who believes." Let faith be all with us, and God will be all. Let God be all, and He will do all.

"By faith." Let this be the motto of our lives. In every need and perplexity, with every desire and prayer, with every work and trial, with every thought of ourselves and of God, let this be the one thing we seek—ever to breathe a living faith in a living God. Once again I say this: As absolute and universal and undisputed as the supremacy of God is, so is the supremacy of faith in our hearts and lives to be. We can only have as much of God in our hearts as we have of faith. And because God is all, and must be all to us, faith in us must be all, too.

Chapter Notes...

1. The old saints had less light than we—how is it they had more faith than so many? It is because we trust in the light we have, as we hold it in our minds and reason. They were thrown upon God and trusted Him. Let us but give ourselves over to the perfect life Jesus has revealed—what power faith would give us.

2. But notice everywhere how it was only in obedience that faith could act. In leaving Egypt and sprinkling the blood and passing through the Red Sea and going around Jericho and in Rahab's deliverance—it was all, wholly and entirely, in obedience that faith acted and triumphed.

3. Faith is the power of the will choosing God's will, entering into it and yielding to it. If you would desire to be strong in faith, stand perfect in all the will of God.

One Hundred Nine
Faith and Its Power of Achievement

*And what shall I more say? for the time will fail me if I tell
of Gideon, Barak, Samson, Jephthah; of David and Samuel
and the prophets: who through faith subdued kingdoms,
wrought righteousness, obtained promises, stopped the
mouths of lions, quenched the power of fire, escaped the
edge of the sword, from weakness were made strong, waxed
mighty in war, turned to flight armies of aliens. Women
received their dead by a resurrection: and others were
tortured, not accepting their deliverance; that they might
obtain a better resurrection.*
—Hebrews 11:32–35

With the entrance into Canaan and the fall of Jericho, the
first period of Israel's history closes. It would take too
much time for the writer to proceed as he had done; he
now mentions a few of the most prominent names from among the
judges, the kings, and the prophets, and then passes on to a general
view of the very wonderful proofs that faith had given of what it
could do or suffer. His desire is to take the veil from the hearts of

the Hebrews and to show them what so many who know Scripture history will never see—that under and behind and within all the outward events recorded, there lives, as the vital principle, faith in God. The history is, on the one hand, the record of what God has done through and for those who have trusted Him; on the other hand, it is the proof that in God's leading of His people, the one token of His presence and working was always the spirit of faith that He gave. Faith in exercise is the breaking out of the divine life within, the very substance of things hoped for, the proof of the presence of things not seen.

In mentioning the great achievements of faith, our writer gave three separate trios. In the first, we find mentioned what the heroes of faith had accomplished. In combat with their enemies, they *"subdued kingdoms"*; in ruling the people and opposing evil, they *"wrought righteousness"*; in dealing with God, they *"obtained promises."* In the second, personal deliverance from wild beasts, from the powers of nature, and from the violence of men is in the foreground. They *"stopped the mouths of lions," "quenched the power of fire," "escaped the edge of the sword."* In the third, we have the experience of the power of faith for personal strengthening: *"From weakness were made strong, waxed mighty in war, turned to flight armies of aliens."* And then there is added one thing more: *"Women received their dead by a resurrection."* By faith, women conquered the power of death. There is no power on earth that can stand before the power of faith, because the power of faith is the power of God working in us.

The memory of the heroes and heroisms of the olden time may be most instructive if we regard them in their true light. One thing that impresses us is how little God has promised that faith will be free of difficulty and danger. It would be as easy for God to prevent the enemy from coming as to give the victory over him. To do this would be infinite loss; faith would never be called into exercise; man would never learn to know either his God or himself as His child. Every trial accomplishes a double purpose. It gives us the opportunity of honoring God by the trust with which we wait on Him. And it gives God the opportunity of showing how faithful He is in watching over His child, and how truly He is working for him and in him. It is in trial that the entire heart of the child is drawn out toward the father, in dependence and humility and trust. It is in trial that God can reveal in the opened heart of His child all the tenderness and all the saving power of His love. Without trial, there could be no school of faith, no growth of spiritual character, no strength of will given up to God and clinging to Him. Let us bless God for every trial, small or great; it gives us a grand opportunity for putting the crown upon the head of God and of being made fit so that He may crown us, too.

Another thought of no less importance, that comes as we think of the achievements of faith in the history of Israel, is how closely they were all identified with the public welfare, with lives devoted to the cause of God and the people. Selfishness is the death of faith. *"How can ye believe, which receive glory one of another?"* (John 5:44). As long as we seek to be strong in faith, for the sake of our own comfort and goodness and the possession of power, even if we dream of using it all for others, when once we obtain it, we will fail. It is the soul that at once, in its weakness, gives itself up for the sake of God and others, that will find in that self-sacrifice the need and the right to claim God's mighty help. Gideon and Barak, David and Samuel—they were all men whose names and whose faith would never have been known except that they lived for their nation and God's cause in it, that they were God's chosen instruments for doing His redeeming work in His people.

The sphere of God's special revelation is now no longer Israel but the world. What a work there is to be done in it! Among Christians and heathen, in church and mission and school, in temperance and purity work, in the great fight against iniquity and worldliness in every shape, in larger and smaller circles—what room, what need for the heroes of faith to subdue kingdoms, to work righteousness, to obtain promises! Let each of us offer himself to God for the struggle. And as we do so, let us remember well the double lesson: No faith without difficulties for it to conquer, and no difficulty but faith can surely conquer. In this connection let us cease seeking faith in our own interest; let us lose ourselves in the work for God and souls. We will lose ourselves to find ourselves back in God and His love.

Chapter Notes...

1. *"Having therefore, brethren, boldness to enter into the holy place by the blood of Jesus,...let us draw near with a true heart in fulness of faith"* (Hebrews 10:19, 22). Live the life of faith in the Holiest with God; then your whole life on earth will be one of faith.

2. Give yourself wholly to God—your faith will have the confidence to ask that God give Himself wholly to you.

3. In the little things of daily life we need faith as much as in larger interests. Faith counts nothing insignificant because nothing is good in which God is not. Faith yields itself to God for Him most literally and completely to be all.

4. Remember the real value of strong faith is to gain victories for God, to live for the salvation of souls and the extension of His kingdom.

One Hundred Ten
Faith and Its Power of Endurance

And others were tortured, not accepting their deliverance;
that they might obtain a better resurrection: and others had
trial of mockings and scourgings, yea, moreover of bonds and
imprisonment: they were stoned, they were sawn asunder, they
were tempted, they were slain with the sword: they went about
in sheepskins, in goatskins; being destitute, afflicted, evil
entreated (of whom the world was not worthy), wandering in
deserts and mountains and caves, and the holes of the earth.
—Hebrews 11:35–38

Faith has a twofold victory. In one case, it conquers the enemy, or the difficulty, by securing its removal or destruction. In the other, there is no deliverance from the trouble, and yet faith conquers in the power it receives to endure and to prove that its spirit is superior to all that men or devils can do. The triumphs of faith are often seen as remarkably in those who obtain no deliverance from the threatened evil as in those who do. After the mention of the heroes whose faith was rewarded with success, we have here the mention of those who, in the midst of suffering that was not removed, proved that their faith lifted them up above all the pains with which earth could threaten them. They *"were tortured, not accepting their deliverance"* when offered them at the price of their faithfulness, *"that they might obtain a better resurrection."* Spiritual and eternal realities were by faith so clear and near that they did not reckon the sufferings of this present time worthy to be compared with the glory that will be revealed. The triumph of faith is seen as much in bearing a temporary defeat as in securing a victory. The victory of the vanquished is often the highest achievement.

In these men and women, leaders in the noble army of the martyrs who were rejected and despised by the world, God sees the heavenly beauty of a faith that honors Him and that counts His will, His favor, and His righteousness as more than all earthly happiness. By faith, they had such a sight of God and His good pleasure that they could, with joy, sacrifice everything to secure it. By faith, they could, for the joy set before them, in the assurance of a heavenly recompense, count all the pleasures of earth as less than nothing. It is one of the highest and noblest exercises of faith to suffer aright. And the blessing that comes through suffering is one of the richest rewards that faith can win.

God has given us these examples of those who, by faith, triumphed over the extremities of suffering, so that we might learn from them how to bear our lesser trials. Their faith in extraordinary suffering must strengthen our faith in ordinary suffering. It is in the little common trials of daily life that every believer can follow in the footsteps of these saints and in the footsteps of the great Leader of our salvation. By faith alone are we able to bear suffering, great or small, aright, to God's glory or our own welfare.

Yes, by faith alone. Faith sees suffering in the light of God and eternity; its short pain, its everlasting gain; its helplessness to hurt the soul, its power to purify and to bless it. Faith sees Him who allows it, with us in the fire, as a Refiner watching our purging and perfecting, as a Helper of our strength and comfort. It sees that the

Andrew Murray

forming of a character like that of the Son of God, maintaining at every cost the Father's will and honor, is more than all the world can give. It sees that to be made partaker of His holiness, to have the humility and weakness and gentleness of the Lamb of God worked out in us, and, like Him, to be made perfect in suffering is the spirit of heaven, and it counts nothing too great to gain this treasure. By faith alone, but by faith most surely, we can, in the midst of the deepest suffering, be more than conquerors.

We live in a world of suffering. What a privilege that suffering, instead of unfitting or excluding us, is God's special invitation to trust and glorify Him. As we read of all that these men of faith did, more than one has thought of his own unfavorable circumstances and his feeble strength; never could his faith reach to the achievements of the men who are set before him as an example, such a one might think. What a privilege, however, that there is no suffering so great and depressing, or so little and harassing, but can be a school of faith, a heavenly instruction in the blessed art of making God all; of proving that, for God's will and submission to it, we are willing to bear all. Faith transfigures suffering and makes it transparent with the love of God, the presence of Jesus, the beauty of holiness, and the blessing of heaven.

As long as we live under the influence of the world and the flesh, all this appears as only a beautiful thought, without reality or possibility. Our epistle speaks to those whom it has led into the Holiest of All, who are walking in the new and living way of the will of God, of the obedience and the self-sacrifice and the death of Jesus. It is as we tarry in God's presence and seek, above everything, His holiness and His will that we will look at things as God does and regard suffering in His light. Let this be our aim. Our passage gives new confirmation to the one lesson: By faith alone! Would you please God, would you conquer sin and the world, would you be holy and perfect, would you live as the heir of heaven and eternity? Then live as a man of faith, meet every trial in the spirit of a joyful faith in God; every trial will make you more meet for, and bring you nearer to, God's blessed presence.

Chapter Notes...

1. In the Old Testament, prosperity was promised. And yet faith could endure adversity. In the now, we are taught to expect adversity: The cross is the symbol of our faith; the Man of Sorrows is our Leader—how much more ought we to be able to endure!

2. Let every suffering one, everyone who is bound to a sickbed or bowed down under some cross, learn to believe that, in the affliction, we can greatly glorify God by faith; and that, by faith, we can become teachers and helpers of others, fulfilling, by example and intercession, in our measure, a very blessed part of the work of the body of Christ.

One Hundred Eleven

Some Better Thing for Us

And these all, having had witness borne to them through their faith, received not the promise, God having provided some better thing concerning us, that apart from us they should not be made perfect.
—Hebrews 11:39–40

In these closing verses, we have the summing up of the chapter. The superior excellence of the New Testament is stated to be this: that we have some better thing, something perfect, which the saints had waited for but had never seen. We are told of them what it was that they had and what they had not. *"These all, having had witness borne to them through their faith, received not the promise."* They received not the promise. There were indeed certain promises of which they received the fulfillment. (See Hebrews 6:15; 9:15.) But the great promise of Jesus Christ and His redemption and the outpouring of the Holy Spirit, the better promises of the better covenant (see 8:6), these they received not. *"These all died in faith, not having received the promises, but having seen them and greeted them from afar"* (11:13). They saw and rejoiced in the promises, into the full possession of which it is our privilege to enter.

They received them not, but they *"had witness borne to them through their faith."* (See also 11:2, 4, 5.) The living God, who had given them the promise and was waiting in His own time for the fulfillment, gave them witness through faith that they were pleasing to Him. The witness borne to Abel that he was righteous, and to Enoch that he pleased God, was given to them all. God was not ashamed to be called their God and to let them know it. With all the difference between their faith and ours, in regard to the clearness of the revelation and the actual possession of the promise, in this their faith was one with ours: The unseen God revealed Himself to them and was their God.

They *"received not the promise, God having provided some better thing concerning us, that apart from us they should not be made perfect."* The two words here, *"better"* and *"perfect,"* are the words that characterize the new dispensation, the time of the fulfillment of the promise. We said before that the word *"better"* occurs thirteen times. Christ has inherited a better name; He has brought us a better hope; He is the Surety of a better covenant enacted in better promises; in Him, we have the better country and the better substance. To them, God spake in the prophets; but to us, in the Son. To them, was offered the rest of Canaan; to us, the rest of God. Their high priest was a man who died; ours is a Priest forever, in the power of an endless life. Their sanctuary was on earth, and even that had its veil; ours is the true sanctuary, with the veil taken away. Theirs was the old covenant, in which there was no power to continue; ours is the new, with the heart made new by the Spirit. Theirs was the blood of bulls and of goats; ours is the blood of Jesus. Theirs was a sanctifying cleanness of the flesh; ours is the cleansing of the heart from the evil conscience. Theirs a worship that made nothing perfect; in ours, we are perfected forevermore. Their worship was a witness that the way into the Holiest was not yet open; ours is the blessed experience that, in the new and living way, we have living access into the very presence and love of the Father. God has indeed provided some better thing for us.

Andrew Murray

"That apart from us they should not be made perfect." The better thing God has provided is perfection. The word *"perfect,"* or forms of it, is used fourteen times in the epistle. The law made nothing perfect. Jesus Himself was, in His obedience and suffering, made perfect in His human nature, in His will and life and character, that He might have a true, new, perfect human life to communicate to us. As the Son, perfected forevermore, He is our High Priest; having perfected us forever in His sacrifice, He now brings us, in the communication of that perfection, into real, inner, living contact with God. And so, He is the Perfecter of our faith, and He makes us His perfect ones, who press on unto Perfection. And our life on earth is meant to be the blessed experience that God perfects us in every good thing to do His will, working in us what is pleasing in His sight. Apart from us, they might not be made perfect; to us, the blessing of some better thing, of being made perfect, has come.

My fellow Christians, the old saints had only the promise; we have the thing promised, the divine reality, the full inheritance of what were to them only the good things to come! The promise was sufficient to make them live a wonderful life of faith. What would the effect be in our lives of having obtained the promises, of having entered into the possession of that of which the mere promise stirred them so? As much as deliverance is greater than the hope of it, as a divine possession is than the promise of it, so much greater is the better and perfect thing that God has provided for us—and so much greater ought to be the joy and the holiness and the nearness to God and the power of our lives. Is it so?

If not, the reason must be plain. We do not accept the possession with the intensity with which they accepted the promise. Our whole epistle was written to expose this evil, and to set before us the glory of the better, the perfect, thing that God has provided for us in Christ. Will we not listen to the witness of the heroes of our faith in the days when the sun had not yet risen, and let ourselves be ashamed out of our worldliness and sloth? If we will but yield ourselves to the glorious perfection-truths of our epistle—the perfection of our High Priest and His work—and press on unto it, then He to whom it has been given to work His work in us in the power of an endless life, and so to save completely, will reveal in us that better and perfect thing as we have never yet known it. By faith, they obtained the promises. By faith, the fulfillment of every promise will be made true to us in the power of the Pentecostal Spirit, who comes from the throne of our great High Priest.

Chapter Notes...

1. *"Wherefore, holy brethren, partakers of a heavenly calling, consider the Apostle and High Priest of our confession, even Jesus"* (3:1). It is He who has done all; it is He who, as much, must do all now. It is He who makes the Holiest of All, and the entrance into it, and the life there to serve the living God, a living and continual reality. If, until now, you have been living outside the veil, do believe that God has provided some better thing for you, too.

2. He does this in the power of the Holy Spirit, dwelling within us. Christ redeemed us so that we might receive the promise of the Spirit through faith. The Holy Spirit is the all-inclusive blessing of the better covenant. It is His to bring Jesus and heaven and the power of an endless life into us—and to keep us in it.

3. May God reveal to us what Abraham's going out from his country, what Moses' choice of suffering and reproach, and what Israel's leaving Egypt means. If we are ready to forsake all, we will inherit all.

Eleventh Section—Hebrews 12:1–13
THE PATIENCE OF HOPE

One Hundred Twelve
Let Us Run with Patience the Race

Therefore let us also, seeing we are compassed about with so great a cloud of witnesses, lay aside every weight, and the sin which doth so easily beset us, and let us run with patience the race that is set before us.
—Hebrews 12:1

The epistle has taught us that one of the greatest dangers in the Christian life is that of remaining stationary and not advancing beyond the beginnings of Christ. It leads almost inevitably to backsliding and sin. The great virtue the epistle has sought to impart, next to faith, is patience—the perseverance and longsuffering that holds fast from the beginning firm unto the end and diligently presses on to perfection. After having shown us, in his wonderful picture gallery, what the fullness of faith is, the author now calls us—in view of all the trials life may bring and, with them, the temptation to grow disheartened and faint—to patience as the virtue by which faith is to prove its persistence and secure its reward. True religion is not only drawing near to God once in the Holiest but also a life to be renewed there every day; it is not only the entrance upon the new and living way but also a continually abiding life and walk in it. It is running a race with patience. We have seen what life in the Holiest is, in the place where the power of the eternal life enters and possesses us. Let us now look at that life in its visible manifestation as a race we run, and let us learn what is needed to run well and win the crown.

"Therefore let us also, seeing we are compassed about with so great a cloud of witnesses,...run with patience the race that is set before us." The first encouragement to run the race with patience is to yield ourselves to the influence of the cloud of witnesses that encompass us and to follow their example of faith and patience. We had the word *"witness"* five times in the previous chapter. Through faith, they received witness. And so, they become witnesses to its power and the good pleasure of God it brings to the soul. They all, with one accord—Abel and Enoch and Noah, Abraham and Sarah, Moses and the prophets—as with one heart and mouth, witness to us, *"Be strong and of a good courage, fear not, nor be afrighted at them: for the LORD thy God, he it is that doth go with thee; he will not fail thee, nor forsake thee"* (Deuteronomy 31:6). The victory and the reward are sure and glorious. We are one with them and they with us. They could not be perfected without us; what they began is to be perfected in us. They held fast the promise when all was dark, and they plead with us now that the full light has come, to hold fast the faith firm unto the end.

"Therefore let us also," even as they, *"lay aside every weight, and the sin which doth so easily beset us."* Here is our second lesson. One of the first thoughts connected with a race is the laying aside of everything that can hinder. In the food he eats and the clothing he wears, how resolutely the runner puts aside everything, the most lawful and pleasant, that is not absolutely necessary to his success. Sacrifice, self-denial, giving up, and laying aside is the very first requisite on the course. Alas, it is this that has made the Christian life of our days the very opposite of running a race. The great study

Andrew Murray

is, both in our religious teaching and practical life, to find out how to make the best of both worlds, how to enjoy as much as possible of the wealth and the pleasure and the honor that the world offers. With many Christians, if their conversions ever were an entering through a staight gate, their lives since never were, in any sense, a laying aside of everything that might hinder their spiritual growth. They never heeded the word, *"Whosoever he be of you that forsaketh not all that he hath, he cannot be my disciple"* (Luke 14:33 KJV). But this is what we are called to as indispensable: *"lay*[ing] *aside every weight, and the sin which doth so easily beset us."* Yes, laying aside every sin however little it seems, however much it be our special weakness; it may not be spared. Sin must be laid aside if we are to run the race. It is a race for holiness and perfection, for the will of God and His favor; how could we dream of running the race without laying aside the sin that so easily besets us?

"Let us run...the race that is set before us." A race means—this is our third lesson—"concentration of purpose and will" or "strenuous and determined effort." It means that a man, while he is on the course, gives himself wholly to one thing—running, with all his might. It means that, for the time being, he forgets everything for the all-absorbing desire—to gain the prize. The Christian course means this all through life: a wholehearted surrender of oneself, to put aside everything for the sake of God and His favor. The men who enter the course are separated from the crowd of idle spectators: They each of them can say, *"One thing I do"* (Philippians 3:13)—they run.

"Let us run with patience the race." *"Ye were running well; who did hinder you?"* (Galatians 5:7). This was as true of the Hebrews as of the Galatians; many had gone back. Alas, is this not true of multitudes of Christians in our days, as well? They began well and everything was so hopeful; but it would be utterly untrue to say of them today that they are running a race for eternal life. And there is no way for us, and those for whom we labor, to be saved this terrible fate but for us to learn the lesson that this word *"patience"*

(endurance,* perseverance) is meant to teach us. Under the inspiring influence of the cloud of witnesses, to lay aside every weight and sin and then to enter and begin the race is not enough—we must run with patience. Day by day, our separation from the world and sin, our giving up of every weight and every sin, must be renewed. Day by day, our desire and our will to live wholly for God must be reaffirmed. Day by day, we must wait on God afresh, to receive grace with all our hearts and all our strength; with undivided purpose and in the boldness of faith, we must still run in the race for God. Therefore, let us also run the race with patience.

Chapter Notes...

1. Get clear hold of the three elements of success in a race: self-denial, that gives up everything that hinders; decision, that puts the whole heart into the work and runs; and patience, that, day by day, enters the course afresh.

2. It is the heart of him who runs that is the power that urges him on. Whether it be for a prize or a pleasure, his heart is the driving power. The Holy Spirit is the only power that can keep our hearts daily fresh and bright in the race.

3. The *"new and living way"* (Hebrews 10:20). The race is but another aspect of it, to bring out the thought of devotion and earnestness and energy.

---

* The word is the same as *endured,* in verses 2, 3, and 7.

One Hundred Thirteen
Looking unto Jesus

Let us run with patience the race that is set before us, looking
unto Jesus the author* and perfecter of our faith, who for the
joy that was set before him endured the cross, despising shame,
and hath sat down at the right hand of the throne of God.
—Hebrews 12:1–2

The practical and the contemplative Christian life are often spoken of as if they were at variance. Here we see them in their perfect harmony. *"Let us run"*—there we have intense exertion, claiming body and soul; *"looking unto Jesus"*—there we have the inner life of the spirit, a heart always fixed on Jesus in faith and worship, drawing inspiration and strength from His example and His love. *"Let us run...looking unto Jesus."* Let all that we have learned of Him in the epistle, all the faith and joy with which we have seen and considered Him, bear this fruit: Let us with patience, and perseverance, run the race.

"Looking unto Jesus the [leader] *and perfecter of our faith."* Jesus is the Leader of our salvation (see Hebrews 2:10), the Forerunner who has entered within the veil for us, leaving behind His

---
* Leader.

track and footsteps for us to walk in. This is the new and living way that, through obedience and death, leads to life and to God. And so, He is the Leader of our faith, too. He leads in the way of faith; He walked in it Himself, He opened it for us, and He draws and helps us in it. The old saints had given us examples of faith; but Jesus is the Leader of our faith—the faith that, through death, enters into resurrection life and the Holiest of All, that better and perfect thing that God has provided for us.

"The [leader] *and perfecter of our faith."* Jesus is the Perfecter of our faith. He perfected it in His own person, by acting it out to its fullest possibility, when, in the darkness of death, He entrusted His Spirit into His Father's hands. He perfected it when He was Himself perfected by it and proved that faith is the highest perfection because it gives God room to be all. He perfected it when, having perfected us in Himself, He became the perfect Object for our faith. He perfects it in us because He who is the perfect Object of our faith is the living One, who lives and works in us in the power of our endless life. He is the Perfecter of faith—the faith that looks away to Him, the perfect One and the Perfecter, is the secret of Christian perfection. He has not only perfected Himself and us; He perfects our faith, too. Let us entrust our faith to Him above everything; He will make it His care, the chief and most blessed work of His Spirit. Let us run, looking to Jesus—in His life on earth, He is the Leader of our faith; in His glory on the throne, He is the Perfecter of our faith. Let us look to Jesus. There is life in a look, and power, too—the life and the power of a divine transformation in which, as we behold, we are changed into the same image from glory to glory.

"Let us run...looking unto Jesus...who for the joy that was set before him." Like Moses, He had respect unto *"the recompense of reward"* (11:26). He triumphed over suffering and death by the faith that lived in the future and the unseen. It was in faith that He lived and endured and conquered. *"Who for the joy that was set before him endured the cross, despising shame, and hath sat down at*

Andrew Murray

the right hand of the throne of God." Let us look to Jesus in His path on earth, and on His throne in glory. In His path on earth, as He endured the cross, He is the Leader of our faith, only in the path in which He walked Himself. In His life of self-denial and humility, of obedience and death, He showed us that there is no way to God but that of sacrifice, resisting the world and self unto death; no way of deliverance from fallen nature but by dying to it. He is the Perfecter of our faith as He sits on the throne. Looking to Him, we see what the sure reward is of dying with Him, what the divine power and glory are to which He invites our trust and the committal of our souls, what the heavenly life is that His Spirit will bring down into our hearts. Let every thought of Him on the throne remind us of the path that brought Him there and brings us too; and let every thought of Him in that path of trial lift our hearts in loving, steady gaze to the throne, where He reigns to communicate to us, in unbroken continuity, the power of His glorified life, His complete and eternal salvation.

Yes, let us run, looking to Jesus. Looking, not to ourselves or our sins, but only to Him who hath put away sin forever. Not to ourselves or our faith, whether in its weakness or its strength, but only to Him whose presence is the life of our faith. Not to the world or its temptations, but only to Him who hath said, *"Be of good cheer; I have overcome the world"* (John 16:33). Not to Satan or his threats, but to Him who hath brought him to nothing. Not to men—their fear or their favor—but to Jesus, the God-Man, Immanuel, God with us, our Brother, and our King. Looking to Jesus and Jesus alone.

Looking to Him always and in all. In trial and trouble, as in joy and prosperity; in solitude and repose, as in company and busyness; in religious worship, as in daily life—always, only, looking to Jesus. Looking to Him, to see what He is, to hear what He speaks, to do what He says, to follow where He leads, to trust for all He waits to give. Looking to Him and His love, until my heart burns with that love. Looking to Him, until His eye meets mine and I know that He watches over me. Looking to Him in the power of His love and Spirit, knowing that He Himself is drawing me to Himself, leading and perfecting my faith. Looking to Him, to be changed into His likeness from glory to glory. Let us run the race with patience, looking to Jesus.

Chapter Notes...

1. "'Looking to Jesus,' with the look of faith, because our salvation is in Him alone; with the look of love, because He alone can satisfy our hearts; with the look of strong desire, longing to know Him better; with the look of soul devotion, waiting only to know His will; with the look of gladness, because we know He loves us; with the look of wonder and admiration, because He is the brightness of the Father's glory, our Lord and our God."*

2. Let us say it once again: The whole secret of the Christian life consists in the personal relationship to Jesus. What Jesus has done or does for me cannot be my salvation, except as He Himself has my heart and binds me to Himself in dependence and attachment and trust and love.

3. *"Let us run."* The Gospel is intensely practical. It means, for every day, "Let us live like men who are running a race for life and laying aside everything that can in the least hinder them." We judge everything by this one standard: Can it help me in the race?

---

* Author unknown.

One Hundred Fourteen

Faint Not

*For consider him that hath endured such gainsaying of
sinners against themselves, that ye wax not weary, fainting
in your souls. Ye have not yet resisted unto blood, striving
against sin: and ye have forgotten the exhortation, which
reasoneth with you as with sons, My son, regard not lightly
the chastening of the Lord, nor faint when thou art reproved
of him; for whom the Lord loveth he chasteneth, and
scourgeth every son whom he receiveth.*
—Hebrews 12:3–6

It is ever still the danger of discouragement and backsliding that
the writer sought to avert. In these verses, we find the message,
"faint not," used twice. And twice, the way to be kept from
fainting is pointed out. The first time, the word is used in connection with the considering of Jesus, our Example and Leader; the
second time, with the teaching that it is God from whom all affliction comes. In affliction, look to Jesus as our Forerunner, who was
Himself so tried, and to God as our Father, who has appointed the
trial, as the safeguard against fainting.

"*For consider him that hath endured such gainsaying of sinners
against themselves, that ye wax not weary, fainting in your souls.*" We

have previously had the injunction, *"Consider the Apostle and High Priest of our confession, even Jesus"* (Hebrews 3:1), which pointed to the work He did for us. Here it is: Consider Him in His suffering and patient endurance. The thought that He suffered like you, that you are suffering like Him, will give courage and patience.

"Consider him." It will remind you how necessary suffering is. If He could not be perfected without it, how much more for us. If suffering effected such blessing in Him, how surely it will in us, too, for whose sake He was made perfect and to whom God has given Him as a Leader in the path that leads through suffering to glory. We may be sure of it: All that is most precious in a Christlike character—the virtues that were perfected in Him through suffering, the meekness and lowliness of heart, the gentleness and patience and submission of the Lamb of God—will come to us, too, if we will but consider Him. Looking to Jesus, the suffering One, will bring us the comfort of His sympathy, the courage of His victory, the blessed consciousness of conformity to Him. *"Ye have not yet resisted unto blood, striving against sin."* The thought of His blood in Gethsemane and on Calvary, and the insignificance of our own suffering, will urge us to endure and resist. And we will neither wax weary nor faint.

"And ye have forgotten the exhortation, which reasoneth with you as with sons, My son, regard not lightly the chastening of the Lord." The words from Proverbs warn against a double danger. On the one hand, we may regard lightly the chastening of the Lord and think too little of it. We may seek to bear up against it with human wisdom, looking upon it as the lot of all, counting ourselves too manly to bow before it, trusting to time and fortune to bring a change. We may fail to recognize the hand of God in it; we do not accept it as indeed God's chastening, and we lose all the teaching and the blessing it was meant to bring. *"My son, regard not lightly the chastening of the Lord."*

"Nor"—here is the other danger—*"faint when thou art reproved of him."* Be not discouraged or downcast as if the chastening was too heavy, more than you deserved or are able to bear. In your Christian

life, beware above everything of casting away your boldness, of becoming impatient, of losing courage. It is trial and vexation, care and anxiety, persecution or reproach that often causes this. Learn today the secret of never suffering loss in the soul by the sufferings of life—yea, rather, of always making them your greatest gain. Link them to God and to Jesus. It is God who sends them. He sent them to Jesus and perfected Him through them. He sends them to you in the same love and will make them your highest gain. "Receive every inward and outward trouble...every disappointment, pain, uneasiness, temptation, darkness, and desolation, with both your hands as a true opportunity and blessed occasion of dying to self and entering into a fuller fellowship with your self-denying, suffering Savior."*

"For whom the Lord loveth he chasteneth, and scourgeth every son whom he receiveth." Sufferings are for chastening. And chastening is from love, a token of God's fatherly care. We live in a world full of trial and suffering. Thousands of God's children have complained that their circumstances were too unfavorable for a life of full devotion, of close communion with God, of pressing on to perfection. The duties and difficulties, the cares and troubles of life, render it impossible, they say, to live a fully consecrated life. O Lord, that they might learn the lesson of Thy Word! Every trial comes from God as a call to come away from the world to Him, to trust Him, to believe in His love. In every trial, He will give strength and blessing. Let this truth be accepted in every trial, small or great: First of all and at once, recognize God's hand in it. Say at once, "My Father has allowed this to come; I welcome it from Him; my first care is to glorify Him in it; He will make it a blessing." We may be sure of this; let us by faith rejoice in it. The salvation God has provided for us, the blessed life in the new and living way into the Holiest, through Jesus Christ, has such power that it can enable us, amid every trial, to be *"more than conquerors through him that loved us"* (Romans 8:37). "Give up yourself absolutely and entirely to God

---

* William Law, quoted in *Daily Strength for Daily Needs*, by Mary Tileston (New Kensington, PA: Whitaker House, 1997), 19.

in Christ Jesus, as into the hands of infinite love; firmly believing this great and infallible truth, that God has no will toward you, but that of infinite love, and infinite desire to make you a partaker of his divine nature; and that it is as absolutely impossible for the Father of our Lord Jesus Christ, to refuse all that good and life and salvation that you want, as it is for you to take it by your own power."*

Chapter Notes...

1. *"Consider him."* If Christians would only understand that God's Word says that it is impossible for them to live the true Christian life unless they keep their eyes daily and unceasingly fixed on Jesus! Not a step in the race is safe if they are not looking to Jesus.

2. *"Consider him."* But is it possible? Is it not too great a strain, an unnatural life—to be always looking to Jesus? *"With men this is impossible; but with God all things are possible"* (Matthew 19:26). *"All things are possible to him that believeth"* (Mark 9:23). By faith.

3. Yes, but is such a faith possible? Bless God! it is indeed. This is the open secret of the higher Christian life—Jesus revealing Himself so that the soul can as little forget Him as it forgets to breathe or to see; Jesus so taking possession of the soul by the Holy Spirit and so dwelling within it that faith never ceases going out to Him who is above. Lord, reveal Thyself to us! The soul that, amid effort and failure, begins and gives itself to consider Jesus, in separate acts of faith, will be led on and, in due time, receive this deeper blessing—a heart in which, by the Holy Spirit, looking to Jesus is its spontaneous and most natural exercise.

---

* William Law, *A Collection of Letters on the Most Interesting and Important Subjects, and on Several Occasions,* (London: Pater-Noster Row, 1760). <http://www.ccel.org/l/law/letters/let.htm>

One Hundred Fifteen
Chastening and Holiness

It is for chastening that ye endure; God dealeth with you as with sons; for what son is there whom his father chasteneth not? But if ye are without chastening, whereof all have been made partakers, then are ye bastards, and not sons. Furthermore, we had the fathers of our flesh to chasten us, and we gave them reverence: shall we not much rather be in subjection unto the Father of spirits, and live? For they verily for a few days chastened us as seemed good to them; but he for our profit, that we may be partakers of his holiness.
—Hebrews 12:7–10

We live in a world full of suffering. A great part of the daily life of many is made up of little trials and vexations. A sharp word; an unkind judgment; neglect or ingratitude from someone from whom we did not expect it; the carelessness of a servant; the temper of a husband or wife; the loss accruing through the neglect or unfaithfulness of others; the disappointment of our wishes; the accidents that vex us—all these things in daily life often come to us with far greater temptation and danger than the times of persecution for faith that the martyrs experienced. By their littleness and their frequency and their suddenness, these vexations surprise and conquer us before we know. If Christianity is to be a success, if Christ is to save completely, there must be a provision, sufficient and effective, to prevent suffering from causing discouragement or defeat, transforming it into blessing and help.

If it can enable us to rejoice in tribulation, to glory in infirmities, and to pass unharmed through trial, it will indeed be the religion man needs in a world of suffering. He who has this secret— whereby what have been hindrances become helps, and his very enemies are made to serve him—is on the way to becoming the Christian God would have him be.

God has made such a provision. First of all, He gives His own Son, as the Chief of sufferers, to show us how close the relation is between suffering and His love, suffering and the victory over sin, suffering and perfection of character, suffering and glory. Yea more, to provide us with One who can sympathize, who can teach us how to suffer, and who, as the Conqueror of sin through suffering, can breathe His own life and strength into us. And thus, He comes as our Father, to shed His heavenly light on our afflictions and to teach us the lessons our portion contains. They are these. Chastening is part of a father's training and one of the marks of sonship. Submission to chastening forms and proves the truly childlike character. God's chastening makes us partakers of God's holiness. See how these three thoughts are brought out here.

Chastening is a needful part of a father's training. *"It is for chastening that ye endure;"* all suffering is a divine chastening. *"God dealeth with you as with sons; for what son is there whom his father chasteneth not?"* Our own childhood and fatherhood teach it to us; discipline, chastening, and reproof, in whatever form, are indispensable parts of education; where a child needs discipline, a father may not withhold it. In the will of God, and in the very nature of things, sin and suffering go together; and even love can cause suffering for the greater good of casting out the sin. Let the child of God learn the lesson—suffering is chastening, the chastening of love. We ought to spare no pains to learn this lesson well; we ought to repeat and repeat it, until we can say, "Now, I know it perfectly: Every trial, small or great, I will look upon at once as a messenger of God's love." If you thus meet it as God's appointment, whether it comes through men or yourself or more directly from above, you are in the right attitude for bearing and being blessed by it.

Submission to chastening forms and proves the truly childlike spirit. *"Furthermore, we had the fathers of our flesh to chasten us, and we gave them reverence: shall we not much rather be in subjection unto the Father of spirits, and live?"* When the Lamb of God came to this earth to suffer God's will, it was that He might teach us the place that becomes the creature and the child—absolute subjection to the perfect will of love. He came to show that the thing that makes life worth having is to have it to give up to God; to prove that humility and resignation are the sacrifices God delights in, the sure and only path to God. No religion or worship of God can be acceptable to Him except as He sees in it conformity to the life and Spirit of His Son. We can only please Him as we are like-minded to Christ. Learn, O child of God, the unspeakable privilege in suffering, of giving up your will to God, even as Jesus did; of adoring His wisdom and goodness; and of entering deeper into the child's spirit and the child's place—to reverence and submission. Chastening is one of the marks of sonship. *"If ye are without chastening, whereof all have been made partakers, then are ye bastards, and not sons."* Suffering is not, in itself, a sign of sonship. An enemy or a criminal may be scourged; even a slave may be chastened as well as a son. But to him who is a son, chastening reminds him of his place and calls him to meet this part of a son's heritage in the spirit and with the hope of a son—with the assurance that it will draw him nearer and lock him closer to the Father.

Chastening makes us partakers of God's holiness. He chastens us *"for our profit, that we may be partakers of his holiness."* What a new light on suffering and chastening! He who maketh holy, and they who are made holy, *"are all of one"* (Hebrews 2:11). We have entrance into the Holiest of All, where we will have been made holy. He has made the people holy by His blood. And now comes suffering—will we not welcome it when He sends it with such a message?—to break open our inner beings, or waken our desires, and make us partakers in our inmost lives of that holiness that Jesus gives, of that holiness into which we enter in God's presence. Yes, welcome suffering, if it leads us, through subjection to God's will and love, into His holiness as our portion.

Chapter Notes...

1. What can teach us to welcome suffering? A heart set upon holiness. Suffering is meant by God to make us holy. No one can welcome suffering except as he welcomes the holiness it brings.

2. "That state is best which exercises the highest faith in, and fullest resignation to, God."*

3. "Receive every inward and outward trouble...with both your hands as a true opportunity...of dying to self and entering into a fuller fellowship with your self-denying, suffering Savior."†

---

* William Law, quoted in *Daily Strength for Daily Needs,* by Mary Tileston (New Kensington, PA: Whitaker House, 1997), 19.

† Ibid.

One Hundred Sixteen
Yet Afterward

*All chastening seemeth for the present to be not joyous, but
greivous: yet afterward it yieldeth peaceable fruit unto
them that have been exercised thereby, even the fruit of
righteousness. Wherefore lift up the hands that hang down,
and the palsied knees; and make straight paths for your
feet, that that which is lame be not turned out of the
way, but rather be healed.*
—Hebrews 12:11–13

He chastens us *"for our profit, that we may be partakers of his
holiness"* (Hebrews 12:10). That word was the summing
up of all that there was to say of affliction. Suffering was to
be God's messenger to lead us into a life and an experience—not
a place or a position—into fitness for and inner union with the
Holiest of All and the Most Holy One who dwells there. Higher
honor have none of God's servants than this one, unwelcome and
rejected though it so often may be. By all that is sacred and worthy
of desire, the Word would have us know and believe that affliction
is a blessing. And yet, it does not ignore the fact that chastisement
causes pain. As an old believer said, when speaking of one of the
promises, "Yes, it is blessedly true; but still it hurts." Therefore, our

writer continued, *"All chastening seemeth for the present to be not joyous, but greivous: yet afterward it yieldeth peaceable fruit unto them that have been exercised thereby, even the fruit of righteousness."* To the flesh that judges by what is present and by sense, it is distinctly—often terribly—grievous. Faith that lives in the future and unseen, however, rejoices in the assurance not only of deliverance but also of the heavenly blessing it brings.

"For the present...yet afterward." These two expressions contain the great contrast between time and eternity, of the visible and the invisible, of sorrow and of joy, of sense and of faith, of backsliding and of progress to perfection. *"For the present"*—to be guided by the present and to sacrifice all for its gratification is the sin and the folly and death in which we live by nature. *"Yet afterward"*—to throw eternity into the balance and to judge everything by that, this is what even the patriarchs did; this is what Christ taught us when, for the joy set before Him, He endured the cross; this is what faith can teach us in every trial. With that *"yet afterward"* of the peaceable fruit of righteousness, the light of eternity and its reward shines on the least of our trials as on the greatest and makes each one the seed of an everlasting harvest, of which we pluck the fruits even here. And so light arises upon the command, *"Count it all joy, my brethren, when ye fall into manifold temptations"* (James 1:2). We read it in the light of what Paul said of himself, *"As sorrowful, yet alway rejoicing"* (2 Corinthians 6:10). When the hurricane is sweeping the ocean into mountain-high waves, down in the deep waters all is serene and quiet; the disturbance is only on the surface. And even so, the joy of eternity can keep a soul in perfect peace amid abounding afflictions. *"For the present"* is swallowed up in the *"yet afterward"* of a living faith.

Now there follows, on the strength of what has been said of God's love and His blessing, the call to the Hebrews to rise up out of their dejection and despair and gird themselves for the race in the way in which Jesus leads us to God. *"Wherefore lift up the hands that hang down, and the palsied knees; and make straight paths for your*

Andrew Murray

feet." "Take courage," he said, "and gird yourselves for the race—without it the prize can never be won." *"Lift up the hands that hang down, and the palsied knees; and make straight paths for your feet."* Rouse your whole being; and, with your eye once more on Jesus and in the faith He inspires, follow Him in the path of endurance. See the mistake you made when you thought your trials were an excuse for despondency; accept God's message that they are the very proof of His love, the very means of His grace, the very mark of His own Son. Accept them as a part of your Christian maturity and perfection. Rise up and stand forth as runners ready for the race.

"That that which is lame be not turned out of the way, but rather be healed." What is lame would, if they continued in their desponding state, go from worse to worse and be put entirely out of joint—instead, let it be healed. As they lifted up their hands and knees and roused themselves to enter the straight path, the lame would be healed—the courage of faith would give new strength, and faith in Jesus would give perfect soundness. Yes, to faith in Jesus the blessing still comes as to the man of old: *"Immediately his feet and his ankle-bones received strength. And leaping up, he stood, and began to walk; and he entered into the temple, walking, and leaping, and praising God"* (Acts 3:7–8).

"But rather be healed." Is there anyone among my readers who feels that his life is not what it should be, whom the cares and troubles of this life have hindered, and who feels half-hopeless as to the possibility of running the race as Jesus the Leader would have? Let him learn from this word what he needs. Let him take courage and rouse himself. Lift up the feeble hands and knees and make straight paths; turn at once boldly to the course, the way Jesus has marked. Yield, surrender, consecrate yourself to be His, wholly and forever. This is the first step. And then as—in the name of Jesus, in the faith of all God has spoken in His Son in this blessed epistle of a complete salvation and a perfect Savior—you rise up and step onto the course, you, too, will know what healing is. Leaping and praising God, you too can enter into the temple, the Holiest of

All, to praise your God and abide with Him, your mighty Keeper. Desponding Christian, there is healing—choose it; take it. Looking to Jesus, rise and run the race.

Chapter Notes...

1. *"Yet afterward"*—the great word that hope is ever using as it points to what is still hidden, but surely coming. The section concerning patience of hope began with patience and ends here with this note of abounding hopefulness—*"Yet afterward."*

2. The state of absolute resignation to the will of God, and of a naked faith in His infinite love, is the highest perfection of which the soul is capable. Seek for this with the simplicity of a little child, judging everything by the heavenly standard of value, as it helps to bring us nearer to God.

3. *"Be healed."* Let all who complain of hands that hang down and palsied knees, of limbs that are lame or out of joint, hear the voice of Jesus: *"I say unto thee, Arise,* [and walk]" (Mark 2:11).

The Fifth Warning—Hebrews 12:14–29
AGAINST THE REJECTION OF GOD'S SON

One Hundred Seventeen
Follow After Sanctification

Follow after peace with all men, and the sanctification
without which no man shall see the Lord.
—Hebrews 12:14

The section on patience in tribulation (the patience of hope), is concluded, and there now remains the subject of love and good works. It is as if the writer began here what he gave in chapter 13, but is led into this last warning by the thought of so many who fail in the pursuit of holiness and fall back. When the warning is concluded, he returned to his subject in chapter 13.

"Follow after peace with all men, and the sanctification." My relation to my fellowmen is most intimately one with my relation to God. In the Beatitudes, we have mercy and purity following each other: *"Blessed are the merciful....Blessed are the pure in heart"* (Matthew 5:7–8). *"The wisdom that is from above is first pure, then peaceable."* (James 3:17). Where there is no peace with men, peace with God cannot be enjoyed. Paul wrote, *"Be at peace among yourselves"* (1 Thessalonians 5:13). In our summons to dwell in the Holiest,

we remember how the call to faith, *"Let us draw near"* (Hebrews 10:22), was at once followed by that to love: *"Let us consider one another to provoke unto love and good works"* (verse 24).

"Follow after...sanctification," literally, "holy-making." We know this word. Holiness is the highest glory of God, and so holy-making is being taken up into His fellowship and being made partakers of His holiness. It is receiving into our natures and characters the spirit of that heavenliness and holiness in which He dwells. *"Follow after...*[holy-making] *without which no man shall see the Lord."* Holy-making is the spiritual preparation, the inner capacity, for meeting the Lord and being at home with Him. The passages in the epistle in which we have already had the word will be our best instruction as to the way in which we are to follow after holiness.

"For both he that sanctifieth and they that are sanctified are all of one" (2:11). It is Jesus who makes holy. *"Of him are ye in Christ Jesus, who was made unto us...from God...sanctification"* (1 Corinthians 1:30). It is the living Christ who is our sanctification; the more deeply we enter into His life on earth, His obedience, His doing God's will, His giving Himself up to God alone, the more we have His life abiding in us, then the holier will we be. Holiness is the losing of self and being clothed with the spirit and likeness of Jesus.

"Then hath he said, Lo, I am come to do thy will. He taketh away the first, that he may establish the second. By which will we have been sanctified through the offering of the body of Jesus Christ once for all" (10:9–10). The more deeply I enter into the truth—or rather, the truth enters into my life—that the sacrifice of Jesus is the crowning act of His perfect surrender to God's will and giving up everything to be one with it, and that it is in His doing of that will that I have been sanctified, then the clearer will my insight grow that holiness is the actual living in the will of God with my will, having the will of God as the moving power of my life. Jesus, doing the will of God and sanctifying me in it, has taken me up into it and planted me forever in it. As I live in living union with God's will—doing

it and rejoicing in it—that holy will becomes my holiness. It was in the doing of God's will and glorifying God thereby that Christ was prepared for the glory. The heavenly life, which He sends down by His Spirit into my heart, is a life in which God's will is always and perfectly done. To live in God's will is the true following after sanctification.

"Having therefore, brethren, boldness to enter into the holy place"—the Holiness of Holinesses—*"...let us draw near"* (10:19, 22). The Holiest into which we have been taken to dwell, and the holiness that is to be our characteristic, are closely linked. There, where God dwells in His holiness, even there, is the dwelling of the sanctified one who enters in by faith. There is the place where we are made holy. The Son who sanctifies, the will in which we are sanctified, and the presence of the Holy One—there is the place where all these meet and are known in power. He who does not know what it is to enter in and tarry and worship in the Holiest, to separate himself from the world and its fellowship, to hold communion with the Holy One, will seek in vain by his prayers or efforts to become holy. Holiness is found nowhere but with God in the Holiest of All. Union with Jesus the Son who sanctifies us, union with the will in which we have been sanctified by loving and doing it, union with God Himself in the Holiest—in these is the power of sanctification.

Then comes a fourth thought. We have had the Son, the will, and the presence—now we have the rod of God. He chastens us *"for our profit, that we may be partakers of his holiness"* (12:10). Blessed be God that it is not only in spiritual things that we are to seek our help in the pursuit of holiness, but that everything that meets us in providence can help it, too. There is not a trial or difficulty, not a disappointment or vexation, that is not God's chosen instrument for making us holy. Our lives in Jesus, in the will of God, in the Holiest, is all one with our lives in the body and in the world. It became God to perfect His Son through suffering; the very least of our daily crosses, God will use to free us of our self-will, to draw us from the world, to point us to the example and spirit of Jesus. *"Follow after...sanctification"*; everything in heaven and earth can help you in the pursuit.

"Follow after peace with all men, and the sanctification without which no man shall see the Lord." Seeing the Lord! What blessedness and what glory to the soul that has once learned to love Him! As the bride puts on her beautiful garments to meet the man she loves and to whom she is to be united, the call comes to us to put on our holy garments, to array ourselves in the beauty of holiness to meet our Lord. Let our whole hearts respond in the prayer: "Lord, make us holy, that we may be found ready to meet Thee when Thou come."

Chapter Notes...

1. This sanctification is as much by faith as justification. Both are received in union with Christ: The peace of the one and the power of the other are found in the abiding union through an abiding habit of faith.

2. *"Follow after"*—the same words as in Philippians 3:12, 14: *"I press on, if so be that I may apprehend that for which I was apprehended by Christ Jesus....I press on toward the goal."* It is the thought of the race—pressing on after holiness and fellowship with God, with Jesus, and with God's will.

One Hundred Eighteen

Of Falling Short of the Grace of God

*Looking carefully lest there be any man that falleth short
of the grace of God; lest any root of bitterness springing
up trouble you, and thereby the many be defiled; lest there
be any fornicator, or profane person, as Esau, who for one
mess of meat sold his own birthright. For ye know that even
when he afterward desired to inherit the blessing, he was
rejected (for he found no place of repentance), though he
sought it diligently with tears.*
—Hebrews 12:15–17

"*Take heed, brethren, lest haply there shall be in any one of you an
evil heart of unbelief*," was the warning in Hebrews 3:12. And
in chapter 4, "*Let us fear therefore, lest haply, a promise being
left of entering into his rest, any one of you should seem to have come
short of it*" (verse 1). And in chapter 10, "*Let us consider one another,...
exhorting one another*" (verses 24–25). Here, it is the same thought—
"*Looking carefully*"—the word really means "taking oversight." "*Lest
there be any man*"—each is not only to care for himself, but for his
brother too. "*Lest there be any man*"—there must not, through our

lack of faithfulness, be one—*"that falleth short of the grace of God."* Here, we have again the great danger against which the epistle warns us earnestly. It is the terrible complaint from which every congregation suffers. There are so many who, just as Israel left Egypt but came short of the promised rest, for a time make an earnest Christian profession and yet come short of the grace of God; they receive the grace of God in its beginnings in vain and never truly become possessed of it and by it. As it was true of the Galatians, with all their zeal for religion and its forms, so of these, too: *"Ye are fallen away from grace"* (Galatians 5:4). The running of the race with patience; holiness, or even the earnest pursuit of it; the joy and the power and the fruit of the Christian life—all of these are wanting. Let us look carefully lest anyone fall short of the grace of God.

Three things are mentioned as causes and marks of this falling short of grace. *"Lest any root of bitterness springing up trouble you, and thereby the many be defiled."* The root of bitterness may refer to a person, who by wrong conduct or doctrine, causes trouble and leads others astray. Or it may refer to the error itself, some mode of thought or behavior by which many are defiled. The spirit of the world; too great interest in temporal things; bitterness in religious differences; being led by the carnal reason more than by God's Word or Spirit; giving way to sin—any of these things may be the root of bitterness in regard to which the call sounds: "Be careful, look around, and watch."

"Lest there be any fornicator." Here a special sin is mentioned. Each church as a whole must watch against this sin, not waiting until it is found but rather looking carefully and doing everything to prevent it, lest there be any. Christians must maintain in society the high moral tone that refuses to condone sin, in either the high or the low. In all its members, and among its young people, it must be a witness for purity of life and lips and heart. And to all who are fallen, it must seek, in the power of the Gospel, to offer the helping hand of love. *"Lest there be any fornicator."*

Andrew Murray

"Or profane person, as Esau, who for one mess of meat sold his own birthright." We have seen that faith is ever the separation from the visible. Abraham and Isaac and Jacob sacrificed all to become heirs of the heavenly city of the future and the heavenly blessing. Esau lived in the present; for a momentary satisfaction, he parted with his blessing, the promise of God, and his inheritance in the future. And even so, there are numbers who are called Christians and yet are profane. There is nothing sacred or holy in their spirits or lives. They are absorbed in the present of the possessions and pleasures of the world. To speak of their pursuit of holiness would be a mockery. Let us think of such and mourn and pray and labor for them. *"Looking carefully lest there be any...profane person, as Esau."*

"For ye know that even when he afterward desired to inherit the blessing, he was rejected (for he found no place of repentance), though he sought it diligently with tears." We remember the *"yet afterward"* (Hebrews 2:11) of faith. What a contrast here, the afterward of the worldling. For the present with its pleasures, the divine birthright, the promise of God, and the future inheritance is neglected. And when it is too late—when the heart is shrivelled up and the power of the will and the power of faith is lost—the thought of something better is awakened. But alas, it is found to be too late! Many will seek to enter in and will not be able when once the Master of the house is risen up and has shut the door! Esau *"afterward"* desired to inherit, but was rejected!

"Looking carefully lest there be any man that falleth short of the grace of God." What a solemn thing the Christian life is, the race for life we have to run! With what dangers we are surrounded! Our daily needs and our daily food may be our destruction. It was eating that lost Esau his birthright. It was eating that lost Adam and his seed the kingdom of God. It was in refusing to eat, when Satan tempted Him in the wilderness, that Jesus won back heaven for us. In our homes, in our bodies, and in our daily needs, the temptations to ease and enjoyment, to sloth and standing still, are

ever around us and in us; let us take heed lest we fall short. Let us look carefully and see if there are not others around us who are fainting and turning back, and let us count it our duty and privilege to care for them. Let us beseech grace of God to give us power in faith and love to be the deliverers of our people and our brethren. If we feel powerless to speak to others or to influence them, let us lay ourselves before God with the cry that He would use us to save some; He can fill us with His Spirit and His love.

Chapter Notes...

1. *"Looking carefully"*—the word is the same as "bishop," or "overseer." *"Lest there be any man"*—we are all to watch over each other. Do we really take the state of Christians to heart? Do we indeed look round carefully and lovingly to consider what can be done? Consider Jesus! Consider one another!— the two commands are inseparable.

2. *"Afterward...he was rejected."* O my friend, if you have escaped this danger, I beseech you, by the mercy of God, think of those who are in it, and say to God that you will do anything He wishes you to do to save them from that terrible fate.

One Hundred Nineteen
Not Sinai, but Zion

For ye are not come unto a mount that might be touched,
and that burned with fire, and unto blackness, and
darkness, and tempest, and the sound of a trumpet, and the
voice of words; which voice they that heard intreated that
no word more should be spoken unto them: for they could
not endure that which was enjoined, If even a beast touch
the mountain, it shall be stoned; and so fearful was the
appearance, that Moses said, I exceedingly fear and quake.
—Hebrews 12:18–21

In confirmation of the call to follow after sanctification and the warning against falling short of the grace of God, or despising the birthright blessing, we are now reminded of what our true position is as believers, and of the fullness of blessing of which we have been made partakers. This is set before us first by way of contrast. We are not come to Mount Sinai (Hebrews 12:18–21), the place and state of Israel at the giving of the law. We are told (verses 22–24) what the wonderful life is to which we now have access; we are come to Mount Zion. It is only the living faith that realizes our true position and privileges that will nerve us in the pursuit of holiness and keep us from falling short.

Our whole epistle has taught us that all God's dealing with man is founded on the principle of two dispensations—the one of preparation and promise, of weakness and failure; the other of fulfillment and perfection, of life and power, the power of the endless life. The epistle has taught us, too, that though we now have our place in the new dispensation, we, just as the Hebrews, may be living in the old, through ignorance and unbelief, experiencing nothing of the power and the life of the better covenant. As a consequence, all the weakness and sin of Israel of old still continues in the Christian; he does not know what the eternal redemption is and cannot live in it. We have the difference between these two dispensations in the suggestive *"Ye are not come unto a mount that might be touched,...but ye are come unto Mount Zion"* (verses 18, 22).

> *Which things contain an allegory: for these women are two covenants; one from mount Sinai, bearing children unto bondage... and answering to the Jerusalem that now is....But the Jerusalem that is above is free, which is our mother.* (Galatians 4:24–26)

The whole secret of the Christian life lies in the right apprehension of the difference between the two systems—the one with the spirit of bondage and fear, the other with its boldness and liberty.

*"Ye are not come unto a mount that might be touched."** This caused alarm with its fear and terror; with its command not to draw nigh under pain of death; with its words that only made those who heard entreat that no word more should be spoken to them; and with the mediator of the covenant himself saying, *"I exceedingly fear and quake."* All this is a symbol of what the law does; it works wrath and fear and death. It comes with demands we cannot fulfill; with its threats, it rouses to effort and performance but gives neither the love of God's will nor the power to do it. It only discovers

---

* "The apostle reminds us of seven things in connection with the giving of the law—(1) the mount touched by God; (2) fire; (3) blackness of cloud ; (4) darkness ; (5) thunder; (6) the sound of a trumpet; (7) the voice of God." —Saphir (Notice in the next passage the sevenfold glory of Mount Zion.)

and condemns sin; the sense of self-reproach and self-condemnation is all it can bring. Read Romans 7 and see there where the law alone, and not the Spirit, is mentioned—the helplessness and the wretchedness that it reveals. Read Romans 8 and see there what the liberty and the peace—the life and the love, the joy and the strength—is that comes with the Spirit of life in Christ Jesus.

"Ye are not come unto a mount that might be touched." Why should it be necessary to tell the Christian this? If Sinai is so terrible, who could wish to live there? Who would not gladly accept the first message that God calls him away from there? Strange to say, the awakened soul is ever in danger of thinking that there is no way to pacify Sinai but by fulfilling its demands. God's grace is so wonderful—the way in which He has met the claims of Sinai is so divine and beyond man's comprehension—that the human heart, when it begins to seek salvation, ever does so in the way of effort. And even after we have believed in Jesus, we are always inclined to look for what we can do to satisfy the demands of God. We do not know that, in calling us away from Sinai to Mount Zion, God not only gives us a free and full pardon for sin but the law is also written in the heart, the power for a new obedience by the Holy Spirit, and the fitness for entering into His presence and dwelling in unbroken fellowship with Him.

You are not come to Mount Sinai. This is just the word every Christian needs who is in danger of being discouraged and fainting in the race. You are not under the law. Your complaints that when you would do good, evil is present with you, prove that you are still under the law, trying to fulfill it. It is all in vain. You must ask for the Holy Spirit's teaching to show you how entirely you are taken from under the shadow of Sinai and placed on Mount Zion. Oh, try to understand what God is speaking to you in His Son. Christ is to be your life. In the power of an endless life, He is your High Priest, bringing you near to God; He is your covenant Mediator, putting in divine reality the law into your inmost parts; your Priest-

King, sending from His throne the Holy Spirit to reveal Himself as the Law of your life. You are not come to Mount Sinai; its fear and terror are exchanged for faith and trust. Come and live by faith, and Christ will be your Life.

Chapter Notes...

1. In studying the meaning of a word or truth, it is often most helpful, in cases where we are in danger of confounding things that differ (owing to apparent resemblances), to find out what it is not. There is so much in salvation by the law that looks like true salvation that many are led astray all their lives. It is, therefore, of infinite consequence to know well what this means: *"Ye are not come unto."* The place to which Christ brings you is, not in the least, Mount Sinai. Say now, "I have nothing to do with Mount Sinai."

2. Mount Sinai means, as man takes it, life by self-effort, by our own goodness, with God helping us; a religion of self, with God's grace to fill out what self cannot do. Mount Sinai, as God means it, is sin and wrath and condemnation; the death and the end of self, to prepare the way for Christ. Mount Sinai points away to Mount Zion and to Christ. There, He does all.

One Hundred Twenty
Ye Are Come unto Mount Zion

*But ye are come unto mount Zion, and unto the city of the
living God, the heavenly Jerusalem, and to innumerable
hosts of angels, to the general assembly and church of the
firstborn who are enrolled in heaven, and to God the Judge
of all, and to the spirits of just men made perfect, and to
Jesus the mediator of a new covenant, and to the blood of
sprinkling that speaketh better than that of Abel.*
—Hebrews 12:22

"*Y*e *are come unto mount Zion.*" A traveller by train has often
reached a place without his knowing that he is there. The
guard or a friend has to tell him. Often, it is because he had
expected the journey to last longer. So deep is there in us the spirit
of salvation by effort and attainment, by what we are and feel, that
the rousing call is needed continually. Here you are, sooner than
you thought, in very deed, come to Mount Zion! Come, let us walk
about Zion and go around about her. Beautiful in elevation, the joy
of the whole earth is Mount Zion. God has made Himself known
in her palaces; she is a refuge! Let us consider its sevenfold glory

as here set before us. And may God, in the power of His Holy Spirit within us, reveal to us what it means that we *"are come unto mount Zion,"* that we have been made meet for dwelling there, that Mount Zion is, in actual spiritual reality, our dwelling place where the powers of the heavenly world rest upon us and work in us.

1. *"Ye are come unto mount Zion, and unto the city of the living God, the heavenly Jerusalem."* Read the description of the heavenly Jerusalem in Revelation, and listen to the voice: *"Behold, the tabernacle of God is with men, and he shall dwell with them, and they shall be his peoples, and God himself shall be with them, and be their God"* (21:3). *"And the throne of God and of the Lamb shall be therein: and his servants shall do him service; and they shall see his face; and his name shall be on their foreheads"* (22:3–4). This is the glory to which Jesus brought you when He took away the veil. In the power and experience of that opened way, the Holy Spirit enables you to live. This is the city that Abraham looked for, which has the foundations. You are come to it. Of this city, you are now a citizen. In it, you can live, for you have been brought into the Holiest, the very center of the city, the very presence of God. *"Ye are come unto mount Zion."*

2. *"And to innumerable hosts of angels."* These are they who stand around the throne of God and who fulfill His will. These are they through whom the power of God works in all nature. These are they who are sent out to minister to the heirs of salvation. With these, with their worship and obedience, we are now in fellowship, doing the will of our Father as it is done in heaven.

3. *"To the general assembly and church of the firstborn who are enrolled in heaven,"* that is, the church on earth, enrolled in heaven but not yet gathered in. They are the firstborn—destined, as having the image of the firstborn One, to take the first place in creation among

all the creatures of God. (See Colossians 1:15; James 1:18.) God keep us from despising this, our birthright; let us live as God's firstborn, in living union with all His saints on earth.

4. *"And to God the Judge of all."* It is not only to the living God, dwelling in the city of God, that we are come, but to Him who is Judge of all. Our redemption gives us such deliverance from sin that we have already been admitted into the home of our Judge.

5. *"And to the spirits of just men made perfect."* These are the saints in heaven. There are those on earth who are called perfect, but these are they who, like Christ, have been wholly perfected. These spirits, too, waiting for the redemption of the body, belong to the blessed fellowship to which we have been admitted.

6. *"And to Jesus the mediator of a new covenant."* Moses was the mediator of the covenant on Sinai; Jesus is the mediator of the better covenant, enacted upon better promises. As we saw in Hebrews 8:6–13, the covenant has especially to do with our hearts, with our fitness for holding fellowship with God, with a will and a life in perfect unison with God's will. In Mount Zion, we are come to Jesus, who, in the power of the Holy Spirit, lives and does all His saving work within us.

7. *"And to the blood of sprinkling that speaketh better than that of Abel."* What a heavenly mystery! It is not enough that, for our lives in the city of God, we have Jesus, the living One, as our Life; we find there, too, the token of His death—the blood of sprinkling, speaking and pleading for us each moment. Speaking, not as Abel's, of wrath, but of atonement and eternal redemption. We are come to the blood, not only as shed on earth, but as sprinkled in heaven—our boldness, our cleansing, our sanctification; speaking to

God for us and speaking for God to us, of peace and
love; speaking in divine and heavenly power within us.

Christian, to all this, you are come. Just as sure as you are
come to God in the Holiest, to dwell with Him, you are *"come"**
to all this and dwell in the midst of it. God has brought you to
it by the Holy Spirit, and He will, by the Holy Spirit, reveal it in
your heart so that you know the things that are freely given to
you from God. Can it be that any are content to sleep while the
call is heard: "You are come to the heavenly Jerusalem—enter in
and dwell here"? There is no other choice—can it be that any will
prefer to live under Sinai and its bondage? Can it be that any will
count the price too great and, because they love the world, refuse
to go out and live by faith, with Abraham and Moses, in this city
of God? God forbid that it should be so with us. Let Zion, the
city of God, with its heavenly joy and its beauty of holiness and its
eternal life power, be the place of our abode. The Holy Spirit, sent
down when Jesus had entered and opened the gates for us, brings
down into our hearts the very life and light of heaven, brings us
into the experience of it all.

Chapter Notes...

1. Salvation brings us to the city of God, to a fellowship of the
saints, to a social life of mutual connection and help. To find
our happiness in the welfare of others, for the sake of Jesus
Christ, is of the essence of religion and a condition of dwelling
in Mount Zion.

2. *"And I saw the holy city, new Jerusalem, coming down out of
heaven"* (Revelation 21:2)—that took place in part on the day
of Pentecost. The kingdom of heaven descended upon earth,
in the power of the Holy Spirit, into the hearts of those praying disciples. It is only in the power of the Holy Spirit that
this, *"Ye are come unto mount Zion"* can be more than a beautiful imagination.

* The word *"come"* is the same as in 4:16, 7:25, and 10:1, 22. It means *"draw
near."*

Andrew Murray

3. The Holy Spirit makes all the work and glory of Jesus an inward life in our hearts. Let every word that is too high for us, like this, *"Ye are come,"* make us believe more firmly in His hidden inward teaching. He will work in our hearts more than our minds can understand.

One Hundred Twenty-One
Our God Is a Consuming Fire

See that ye refuse not him that speaketh. For if they escaped not, when they refused him that warned them on earth, much more shall not we escape, who turn away from him that warneth from heaven: whose voice then shook the earth: but now he hath promised, saying, Yet once more will I make to tremble not the earth only, but also the heaven. And this word, Yet once more, signifieth the removing of those things that are shaken, as of things that have been made, that those things which are not shaken may remain. Wherefore, receiving a kingdom that cannot be shaken, let us have grace, whereby we may offer service well-pleasing to God with reverence and awe: for our God is a consuming fire.
—Hebrews 12:25–29

"S *ee that ye refuse not him that speaketh.*" The writer was fully aware of the danger of their falling short, tarrying under Sinai and then perishing there. For the third time, he urged the Hebrews to remember how much more terrible the punishment of sin will be under the new covenant than under the old. (See

Andrew Murray

Hebrews 2:2–3 and 10:26.) The certainty and the sureness of the punishment under the law give us terrible warning of the danger we incur. Greater privileges bring greater responsibility; the neglect of these brings greater punishment. *"For if they escaped not, when they refused him that warned them on earth, much more shall not we escape, who turn away from him that warneth from heaven."* The terrors of Sinai will be far surpassed by the awful judgment on those who refuse Him who speaks from Mount Zion. Mount Zion has its terrors, too; let these, far more terrible than Mount Sinai, rouse us to accept its wonderful blessing. He

> *whose voice then shook the earth...hath promised, saying, Yet once more will I make to tremble not the earth only, but also the heaven. And this word, Yet once more, signifieth the removing of those things that are shaken, as of things that have been made, that those things which are not shaken may remain.*

In that final shaking, all created things will be removed so that only the things that cannot be shaken, the city that has foundations, may remain. In that day, nothing will stand but Mount Zion, which will never be moved, and they who dwell there.

"Wherefore, receiving a kingdom that cannot be shaken." There is only one thing that cannot be shaken: the kingdom of God, that spiritual world in which His will is done and His love is revealed. That kingdom we receive by faith into our hearts. The kingdom of God is within you. And the more our faith knows and owns the unmovable kingdom, amid the things that are shaken and that will not remain, the more our faith will become firm and steadfast and enable us to stand unshaken and immovable, too.

"Wherefore, receiving a kingdom that cannot be shaken, let us have grace, whereby we may offer service well-pleasing to God with reverence and awe." Let us have grace—let us accept and realize and always hold fast the grace promised at the throne of grace for every time of need. (See 4:16.) *"Whereby we may offer service well-pleasing to God."* We have been cleansed by the blood from dead works to

serve the living God. Our entrance into the Holiest and our draw-ing near was so that we might serve Him day and night in His temple—serve Him so that we obtain the witness that our service is well-pleasing. Nothing less can satisfy our hearts or His heart. But this is what grace will indeed effect. It will not only pardon and accept and cover what is defective, but it will also enable us to offer service well-pleasing to God. Let us have grace and faith for this; without faith, it is impossible to please God.

"Whereby we may offer service well-pleasing to God with rever-ence and awe: for our God is a consuming fire." Jesus was heard for His godly fear. Noah was moved with godly fear. The Father of Jesus, the God of Noah, is our God; surely it becomes us to serve Him with godly fear. It will be one of the sure fruits of grace in us. The awful realities of sin and judgment that Noah and Christ had to deal with still exist and surround us. The holiness and the glory of God, the power and the curse of sin, our own utter weak-ness and the terrible danger of the multitudes around us—all of these call every Christian to offer his service to God with godly fear and awe.

"For our God is a consuming fire." The fire and blackness and darkness of Sinai were but shadows—the reality will be seen when God breaks forth in His judgment on those who reject His Son. His holiness is a fire that, by the eternal law of His nature, must consume all that is evil. His love is a fire that must burn up and destroy all that hinders or refuses the triumph of love.

Fire may be either a blessing or a curse. All depends upon my relation to it, whether it meets me as a friend or an enemy. The fire of God as it comes to purify, to consume the sacrifice and convert it into its own heavenly light-nature, to baptize with the Holy Spirit and with fire, to transform our beings into flames of love—blessed the man who knows His God as a consuming Fire. But woe to him on whom the fire of God descends, as on Sodom and Gomorrah, in wrath and judgment. Oh, that in the fullness of

Andrew Murray

faith all believers might see and fear this impending judgment and, moved with the compassion of Christ, give themselves to warn men and snatch them from the fire. *"For our God is a consuming fire."*

Chapter Notes...

1. I know almost nothing that makes one feel his own help-lessness more than when a sight is given of the approaching fate of so many around us, and it is as if nothing avails to awaken or save them. Our only hope is to place ourselves per-sistently at His feet who is mighty to save and to wait on Him for the fire of His zeal and love to burn within us.

2. *"Reverence and awe."* "And as good as God is, so great He is; and as much as it belongs to His goodness to be loved, so much it belongs to His greatness to be dreaded. For this rev-erent dread is the fair courtesy that is in heavenbefore God's face. And as much as He will then be known and loved over-passing that He is now, in so much He will be dreaded over-passing that He is now....But well I know our Lord shewed me no souls but those that dread Him."*

---

* Julian of Norwich, *Revelations of Divine Love.* <http://www.ccel.org/j/julian/revelations/htm/xviii.ix.htm#xviii.ix> and <http://www.ccel.org/j/julian/revelations/htm/xviii.x.htm>

Twelfth Section—Hebrews 13:1–25
LOVE AND GOOD WORKS

One Hundred Twenty-Two
Of Love

Let love of the brethren continue. Forget not to shew love
unto strangers: for thereby some have entertained angels
unawares. Remember them that are in bonds, as bound
with them; them that are evil entreated, as being yourselves
also in the body. Let marriage be had in honour among
all, and let the bed be undefiled: for fornicators and
adulterers God will judge.
—Hebrews 13:1–4

At the door of the Holiest, coupled with the invitation to enter in (Hebrews 10:19–25), we heard the name of the three sisters—Faith, Hope, and Love. The life into which faith leads us has been set before us in chapter 11; that of hope and its patience in chapter 12:1–13. We now have the life of love and good works. Our author began with pointing out four of the chief characteristics of the life of love. These are: the love of the brethren, hospitality, sympathy with those who are in bonds or persecuted, and the love of the married state.

"*Let love of the brethren continue.*" The word "*love*" used by God or Christ is not found in the epistle. It was not needed, for the letter's whole teaching is the revelation of that love. Of the love and loving care of the saints for each other, mention has more than once been made. He who enters the Holiest finds there the God of love. The life and the blessing he receives is nothing but the nature of God, the love of God shed abroad in his heart. He cannot truly enter the presence of God or enter His love without finding his brethren there; he cannot but prove his love to God and his joy in God in love to his brethren. On Mount Zion is the city of God, where God makes the solitary to dwell in families; we cannot share its blessings in any way but as we share them with our fellow citizens.

The command of our text reminds us of how love may wax cold and how it may be sadly wanting in the church. In divisions and separations, in indifference and neglect, in harsh judgments and unloving thoughts—alas, how little has Christ's church proved that it has its birth from the God of love; that it owes its all to Him who loved us, gave us the new commandment of love, and asked us to prove our love to Him by bestowing it on our brethren. If our study of the epistle has not been in vain, if we have seen or tasted anything of the power of the eternal redemption it reveals, let us yield ourselves to live lives of love. Let every child of God, be he ever so feeble or erring or unlovable, be to us the object of a deep, Christlike love. Let us show it in the humility and gentleness, the kindness and helpfulness, with which we give ourselves to care for them and to comfort them. The life in the city of the living God is a life of love: The more we love, the more the mists will roll away and our souls will see it in sunshine and beauty. The greatest of all is love: He who dwells in love dwells in God, and God in him.

"Forget not to shew love unto strangers: for thereby some have entertained angels unawares." Love must prove itself in deeds. Our Lord's words, *"I was a stranger, and ye took me in"* (Matthew 25:35), teach us the sacredness and the blessedness of hospitality, shown not only to friends but also to those whose only claim is that they are Christ's. It is too sadly true that, with the increase of riches and luxury, the simplicity that loves to entertain strangers is often

lost. Scripture lays down no rules; it only points us to the law of love. It addresses us as those who have entered the Holiest, who are come to Mount Zion, and asks us—who, apart from all worthiness or merit, have been so freely and wonderfully loved and received into the home of God—that we in turn should open our homes to the stranger and the needy. The Holiest is the abode of perfect love; let him who enters live in love. Let us remember the deep spiritual mystery that our actions often mean more than we know; we may be entertaining angels, or even their Lord. *"Whosoever shall receive this little child in my name receiveth me"* (Luke 9:48).

"Remember them that are in bonds, as bound with them; them that are evil entreated, as being yourselves also in the body." We know so well in our own bodies that when one member suffers, all the members suffer with it. The Word points to loving union with Jesus and His body on earth as close and real. This feeling of sympathy may and must be as quick and as real in the spiritual as in the natural body. We are to feel toward the prisoners and the persecuted as if we ourselves were suffering. We have been admitted to a life in the home and the love of God; they who abide there will learn thus to love.

"Let marriage be had in honour among all, and let the bed be undefiled: for fornicators and adulterers God will judge." From the broader, we are now led to the inner circle. Marriage is the God-ordained type of the love of Christ to His church. Alas, how its holy union has been abused and defiled! Christianity raised marriage out of the deepest degradation and made it, with the home that gathers around it, what it has been in the Christian church. Love, the love of God in Christ alone, can keep it pure and holy.

"Ye are come...unto the city of the living God" (Hebrews 12:22). Let your life be one of love. Its claims appear too high and exacting; they appear impossible to one who stands outside the gate. They become the joy of him who knows what it is to have entered the rest of God, where He works all. They become the very nature of him who has, in fullness of faith, accepted Jesus as His High

Andrew Murray

Priest, in the power of the endless life, bringing him near, giving him entrance into the life of God. The covenant, of which Christ is the Mediator, has written on the new heart the one law of love and has given us the spirit of love.

Chapter Notes...

1. The first half of the epistle opened our eyes to the heavenly glory of Jesus and of that heavenly sanctuary into which He lifts us. The second shows us how we are to live that heavenly life on earth. The more a man lives in heaven, the better fitted he is to live on earth.

2. Love is the new nature we receive from heaven and is renewed from heaven day by day. *"The fruit of the Spirit is love"* (Galatians 5:22). When the Spirit was poured out from heaven, love filled the hearts. Let us beware of attempting to fulfill these commands of love by our own will. It is only a love given from God that can love all, at all times and in all circumstances.

3. *"Ye are not come unto"* (Hebrews 12:18) Mount Sinai, the life of law and effort, of strain and failure. But *"ye are come unto mount Zion"* (verse 22), a life in the Holy Spirit, in the power of Jesus, in joy and strength and perfect love.

One Hundred Twenty-Three
False and True Riches

*Be ye free from the love of money; content with such things
as ye have: for himself hath said, I will in no wise fail thee,
neither will I in any wise forsake thee. So that with good
courage we say, The Lord is my helper; I will not fear:
what shall man do unto me?*
—Hebrews 13:5–6

The first duty that the Christian, who has drawn near to God in Christ, has to learn is what his relation is to his fellowmen and how his life is to be one of love. The second duty concerns his relation to the world and its goods. The outer world surrounds him on every side; he is in contact with it every moment. With a never-ceasing solicitation, it asks his care, his interest, his affections. It tempts him with its offer of pleasure and its threat of pain; it comes to him holding life and death in its hand. The world, which was meant to be transparent with the light of God's presence and goodness, has, since sin blinded man's eyes, become the veil that hides God from him. One of the first things that the Christian who is running the race must watch most carefully is the power that the world has, with its lawful needs and interests and pleasures, to become the weight that keeps him back—and too often causes the loss of the prize.

Andrew Murray

In money, we have the concrete embodiment of all that the possessions of the world can offer. And so, in the love of money we have the very spirit of the world. Our text says, *"Be ye free from the love of money."* The temptation comes so unobservedly, both to the rich man who has money and to him who is still seeking for it. The tempter comes like a very angel of light. In money itself, there is no sin. Is it not one of God's good gifts? May not the possession of it be the proof of honest labor and diligence and forethought, of self-denial and wise economy; a token of God's blessing on our work; a power to help others and benefit society? Is not poverty frequently a sign of sloth and sin? Is not money one great means for attaining God's purpose, that man should bring the whole world into subjection to Himself?

Scripture knows and teaches all this. And yet, it raises its voice aloud and cries, *"Beware of covetousness"* (Luke 12:15). *"The love of money is a root of all kinds of evil"* (1 Timothy 6:9; see also verses 10, 16–18). So insidious is the approach and entrance of this sin, so many and specious are the arguments by which it can be cloaked and made to wear the garments of the truest virtue, that the Christian to whom prosperity comes needs ever to be on his guard. It is only the man who truly seeks first the kingdom of God; who longs after the utmost conformity to the Master and seeks to be taught by Himself what and how to own; who holds all He has, not in name but in actual practice, at the disposal of Jesus—it is only he who will escape the snare. *"Be...content with such things as ye have."* Here is the safety of the Christian. Study well the Master's teaching in the Sermon on the Mount; learn from His Spirit in you. Let the treasure in heaven, the being rich in God and in good works; let the blessedness of living in the love and the will of God, in the heavenly riches of a holy character, and a life of Christlike beneficence—let these fill the heart, and we will be content in any lot and will, in contentment, find our safeguard against anxious care or love of money.

"For himself hath said, I will in no wise fail thee, neither will I in any wise forsake thee." Yes, when God is the portion of the soul, it may well be content with what it has of earth. It is the consciousness of the favor and nearness of God that makes the soul rise above all that the world can offer. To lead the truly Christian life, the life of faith amid daily duties and daily cares, we need the presence of God as our better and abiding possession. Our earthly and our heavenly life are more closely linked than we know. Too much interest in or attachment to earthly things inevitably weakens our hold on God. True fellowship with God at once brings us into the right relation to earthly things. Let our faith study and feed on the promise: *"Himself hath said, I will in no wise fail thee, neither will I in any wise forsake thee."* The faith that clings to its fulfillment will overcome the world.

"So that with good courage we say, The Lord is my helper; I will not fear: what shall man do unto me?" God's promise ever claims an answer. Here, the answer is given us with which our hearts ought to respond to His, *"I will in no wise fail thee."* *"With good courage we say, The Lord is my helper; I will not fear."* Let us speak the words out loud and repeat them until we feel that they are ours. Whether it be in temporal need or in our many spiritual requirements, we are often tempted to faint and fear. A promise of God, such as we have here, is meant for the hour of trial. Everything may at times appear very dark; we cry and no answer comes; it almost looks as if God had forgotten us. In the fullness of faith, let the voice of the cloud of witnesses, all bidding us to be of good courage and to wait patiently, enter our hearts; and let us say, *"Himself hath said, I will in no wise fail thee."* *"Let us hold fast the confession of our hope that it waver not; for he is faithful that promised"* (10:23), and let us boldly say, *"The Lord is my helper; I will not fear."*

Free from the love of money; content with what he has; holding fast what God Himself has said; and, with good courage, answering, *"The Lord is my helper"*—such is the life that the man who has entered the Holiest is able to live amid the cares and needs of daily life.

Chapter Notes...

1. The promise, *"I will in no wise fail thee"* was first given to Jacob, then to Joshua, and again to Solomon, and afterward to Israel. It teaches us how every promise of the Old Testament may be appropriated by us. We, in our daily lives, are to God of as deep interest as those on whom, of old, the working out of His purpose depended. The abiding, uninterrupted presence of God is our one great need in daily life. It is the one great blessing that, in Christ, is made doubly clear and sure.

2. *"Himself hath said...so that...we say."* As we listen to and repeat what God, the everlasting One, has said, we will know what to say in response and will say it with good courage.

3. *"Be...content"*: This is the power that conquers the love of money and opens the heart for the faith in God's promise and abiding presence.

One Hundred Twenty-Four
Jesus Christ, the Same Forever

Remember them that had the rule over you, which spake unto you the word of God; and considering the issue of their life, imitate their faith. Jesus Christ is the same yesterday and to-day, yea and for ever.
—Hebrews 13:7–8

R*emember them that had the rule over you,...*[and] *imitate their faith.*" The reference may be to teachers who had been with them for a time and then had gone elsewhere, or to those who had been called away by death. The Hebrews were called to consider what the issue, the result, of their lives had been—the impression they had left—and to imitate their faith as the power that brought forth their lives. Happy is the church where the holy life and manifest faith of the leaders can be pointed to even more than their teaching. Happy is the church that imitates and emulates the faith of its leaders.

We remember the contrast we had in Hebrews 7 between the priests who die and are succeeded by others and the unchanging priesthood of Jesus. The thought here of the loss of those who had taught them, but had now left them, appears to suggest the words that follow: *"Jesus Christ is the same yesterday and to-day, yea and for ever."* There may be loss and change of men who are beloved and of great worth as teachers. Jesus, however, we can never lose—in Him, there is no change. *"Jesus Christ is the same yesterday and to-day, yea and for ever."* Through all the changes in the church around us, through all the changes in the spiritual life within us, He does not change—He is ever the same. As our faith sees and seizes hold upon this, and rests upon Him as the same forever, it will participate in His unchangeableness; like Him, it will know no change but will always be the same.

Throughout the epistle, we have now so often seen that the great defect in Christians is that there is no steadfast, certain progress, no holding fast firm to the end—they abide not continually. As with Israel in the old covenant, *"they continued not in* [it]" (8:9). And the great difference of the new covenant, the wonderful perfection of Christ's redemption and eternal priesthood, is to be that now there is to be an end to backsliding. The new life is no longer to be fitful and changing and intermittent; its measure and its power—its anchor within the veil—is to be the unceasing action of Jesus the High Priest after the power of an endless life, maintaining for us in heaven, and within us in the heart, the free, undisturbed, abiding fellowship with God. And, as we have more than once said, the only reason why so many young or earnest Christians never attain this unchanging life is that they do not know Jesus. They do not know Him by faith, as the epistle has set Him before those who are pressing on to perfection—as a Priest forever, who always lives to pray and, therefore, every moment will watch over and keep the soul that trusts Him for it. They do not know that what He has done for one day, or one hour, He will do every day and every hour, because *"yesterday and to-day, yea and for ever,"* He always is the same.

All that He was yesterday, He is today. All that He was yesterday—in the past of the great eternity, as the Object of the Father's delight, and the Bearer and Dispenser of the Father's life and love—He is today. All that He was yesterday—in His life upon earth, with His meek and gentle and sympathizing heart—He is today. All that He has been on His throne—in sending down His Spirit, in working mighty things in and on behalf of His church, in revealing Himself in joy unspeakable to trusting souls, in meeting and blessing you who read this—He is today. All that He is, He can be to you today. And the only reason that you ever had to look back to a "yesterday" that was better than "today" was that you did not know, or that you failed to trust, this Jesus, who was waiting to make each today a new revelation and a larger experience of the grace of yesterday.

"The same yesterday and to-day, yea and for ever." Yea, all that He has been, He will be forever, even from henceforth, from the present moment, and forevermore. And all that He will be forever, He is at this moment for you. Think of Him in the fullest revelation of His glory, in the inconceivable closeness of the union with Him and His love that will be yours hereafter, and let faith say, "All that He ever will be, He is today." In the external revelation, there may be change and advance; in Jesus Christ Himself, none. All that He can in eternity be, He is to you today—the same today and forever. Amid all the changes in the church and the circumstances around us or in our hearts within us, in this one message is a strength and a joy that nothing can take away: *Jesus Christ is the same yesterday and to-day, yea and for ever."*

Today!—*"Even as the Holy Ghost saith, To-day"* (3:7)! Yes, today, claim and trust this unchanging Jesus as your life. His unchangeableness enters into the faith that feeds upon it and communicates itself to it—yea, imparts itself to the soul that clings to Him as such. Look not at yourself, your feelings or attainments, but at Him who changes not. In the power of the Holy Spirit strengthening us with might in the inner man, He, this unchanging Christ, dwells in the heart by faith. Let the faith that worships Him on the throne, the same forever, rejoice in Him as the indwelling Savior who abides continually and who changeth not. According to your faith, be it unto you. *"Even as the Holy Ghost saith, To-day"* (verse 7).

Chapter Notes...

1. Jesus Christ, forever the same. The power in which He gave His blood and rose again and entered heaven is the power in which He is working each moment in us. The reason we do not experience it is simply because of our unbelief. Let us open our hearts, the hidden depths of our inner lives, to worship and receive and experience.

2. Jesus Christ ever the same; then my life, too, is ever the same, for Christ is my life.

3. Let us pray for the Holy Spirit's teaching; let us turn inward in stillness of soul, that He may reveal in us this unchanging Savior as our life. There is no true knowledge of Christ but through the life of Christ in us.

4. As the Holy Jesus is but One—the same yesterday, today, and forever—so too His quickening, sanctifying Spirit in fallen man is but One, always working in one and the same power.

One Hundred Twenty-Five
Let Us Go Forth, Without the Camp

Be not carried away by divers and strange teachings: for it is good that the heart be stablished by grace; not by meats, wherin they that occupied themselves were not profited. We have an altar, wherof they have no right to eat which serve the tabernacle. For the bodies of those beasts, whose blood is brought into the holy place by the high priest as an offering for sin, are burned without the camp. Wherefore Jesus also, that he might sanctify the people through his own blood, suffered without the gate. Let us therefore go forth unto him without the camp, bearing his reproach. For we have not here an abiding city, but we seek after the city which is to come.
—Hebrews 13:9–14

Among the Hebrew Christians, many still clung to the temple and its ritual. And there were among them teachers who taught obedience to the laws in regard to food and to eating of the sacrifices as necessary. The writer warned against these strange teachings. *"For it is good that the heart be stablished by grace; not by meats."* No outward observances can sustain the inner life: It is by grace alone, grace that comes from the throne of grace, that the heart must be established. *"Let us have grace,"* we read, *"whereby we may offer service well-pleasing to God"* (Hebrews 12:28). All that Christ has and gives and works in us by the Holy Spirit—this is the grace by which the heart can be confirmed and kept from falling.

The Hebrew Christian might not think of returning to fellowship with the old sacrifices. *"We have an altar, wherof they have no right to eat which serve the tabernacle."* Our altar is the cross: The Levitical priesthood does not share in what it gives. The old and the new worship are utterly different. The old priesthood has no part in the sacrifice of the cross; the new worship, no part in the old sacrifices. What is more, even *"the bodies of those beasts, whose blood is brought into the holy place by the high priest as an offering for sin, are burned"*—not eaten—*"without the camp."* It is not a question of eating, but of understanding what it means—the burning of the body without the camp. This we will see in Jesus. The sin offering, if you understand it aright, leads you to separation and rejection. *"Wherefore Jesus also, that he might sanctify the people through his own blood, suffered without the gate."* He was cast out of the city, as one who was indeed made sin for us. *"Let us therefore go forth unto him without the camp, bearing his reproach."* We now belong to Jesus and do not fear the rejection of those who rejected Him. *"For we have not here an abiding city, but we seek after the city which is to come."*

"Without the camp." This expression, which occurs twice and is accompanied by *"without the gate,"* gives us the chief thought. We are ever inclined to seek our religion and its enjoyment in something external. And it is only to be found in fellowship with Jesus. His death is not only an atonement for our sins—it is that, praise God!—but it is also as an entrance into what is a great deal more and better. It is the way and the power—a living way of fellowship with Him—so that, like Him, we come to God in the path of self-sacrifice and separation from the world and death to sin. His death and life work in us as the power that makes us ready and able, even

like Him, to go *"without the gate,"* to be crucified to the world, bearing His reproach.

To understand this aright, let us look at the two distinguishing features of the sin offering on the Day of Atonement. The blood was brought into the Holy Place; the body was burned outside the camp. Even so, Christ's blood was brought into heaven and is the power of our entrance and our abode there, the sign that that is our place. And the call comes, "Let us draw near; let us enter." But Christ's body was brought without the camp, the sign that that is our place, too. Heaven has received Him and us in Him; we belong there. The world has cast Him without the camp, and us with Him: We belong there. In heaven, we share His honor; on earth, His reproach. *"Let us therefore go forth unto him without the camp, bearing his reproach."*

The camp was not Rome with its heathenism but Jerusalem with its religion and its revelation from God. There, Jesus was rejected by the Jews because He condemned their self-righteousness and formality. It is not the irreligious but rather the religious world from which we must go out—that is, from everything that is not in harmony with His Cross and its spirit of self-sacrifice. Let us go forth, not from one religious connection to another, which in time proves to have as much of the spirit of the camp. No, let us go forth unto Him! to closer fellowship, to more entire conformity to Him, the Cross-bearer, to His meek and patient and loving spirit. Let us not cast our reproach on those we leave behind, but let us bear His reproach.

"Let us therefore go forth." In the summing up of the epistle, it was, "Let us draw nigh; let us enter in." (See 10:19–22.) Here, it is, *"Let us therefore go forth."* The two messages gather up all the teaching of the epistle, all the need of the Christian life. There are two places appointed for the believer in the power of Christ's redemption—within the veil, to worship, and without the gate, to witness. In both places, he can count upon Christ to keep him. The

deeper he enters into the spirit of the one, the more will he realize of the other. The deeper he enters within the veil, the more will he feel withdrawn from the spirit of the camp and the party. And the more he goes forth unto Him, bearing His reproach, the more will he find access through Him to enter in into His glory. In both places, the boldness of which the epistle has spoken so much will be found: the boldness in God's presence to claim Christ and be one with Him and the boldness in presence of the world to witness for Christ as one with Him. *"Let us therefore go forth unto him."*

Chapter Notes...

1. Separated from the world and separated unto God—the negative and the positive side of the Christian life, inseparably and most blessedly joined to each other. If we die with Him, we will also live with Him.

2. There is perhaps no greater need in our day than that God should open the eyes of His people to the solemn truth that the so-called Christian world is the very same world that rejected Christ. We are to bear to it the same relation He did.

3. Christ the rejected One, Christ the glorified One—the disciples were not fit to testify of Him until the Holy Spirit from heaven had revealed Him in their hearts. Much less can we, who have never seen Him, know Him in truth and power without the Holy Spirit, in the same Pentecostal fullness of life, revealing Him within us.

One Hundred Twenty-Six
Well-Pleasing Sacrifices

*Through him then let us offer up a sacrifice of praise to God
continually, that is, the fruit of lips which make confession
to his name. But to do good and to communicate forget not:
for with such sacrifices God is well pleased. Obey them that
have the rule over you, and submit to them: for they watch
in behalf of your souls, as they that shall give account; that
they may do this with joy, and not with grief: for this were
unprofitable for you. Pray for us: for we are persuaded that
we have a good conscience, desiring to live honestly in all
things. And I exhort you the more exceedingly to do this,
that I may be restored to you the sooner.*
—Hebrews 13:15–19

The Hebrews were in danger—we saw this in the previous
verses—of being led to seek the strengthening of their religious life in returning to the old sacrifices. They had been
reminded that of the sin offering of old, the type of Christ, nothing was eaten; it was burned outside the camp. The fellowship of
Christ must be sought in another way. By His blood, He sanctifies us and leads us into the Holiest; by His example and His life,
He leads us outside the camp. This is the true fellowship of the
offering of Christ. The writer next told us what the sacrifices are

in which we may still take part. In the fellowship of Jesus and His one sacrifice, we may bring the sacrifices of praise, of deeds of love and kindness, of humility and of prayer.

"Through him then let us offer up a sacrifice of praise to God continually, that is, the fruit of lips which make confession to his name." In Hosea, we find Israel saying that when God puts away their iniquities, they will render Him the offering of the fruit of their lips. (See Hosea 14:2.) These are the sacrifices God asks and is well-pleased with. These we may bring continually—the fruit of lips that make confession of His name. Speech is one of man's most wonderful endowments, the power of revealing and committing himself. Christ has redeemed us wholly for Himself; our lips belong to Him, and He claims that we will speak of Him and praise Him continually. For our own sake, for His sake, and for the sake of those who hear us, it is an indispensable element of a vigorous Christian life. There can be no continuous joyful life within the veil if we do not, as priests, continually bring these sacrifices.

"But to do good and to communicate forget not." In our Christian fellowship and in the world around us, Christ has given us the poor and needy that we may show in them what we would like to do for Him if He were on earth. Let the Christian study to combine a life with God in the Holiest with lips that praise and confess Him. And this, again, with deeds of love and kindness and Christian help that prove that the Spirit of Jesus is in us, that we are walking in practical fellowship with His self-sacrifice. And let every act of love and kindness be laid at God's feet as a sacrifice to Him. For with such sacrifices, God is well pleased. They are to Him a sweeter savor than the sweetest incense. And as we offer them, in deed, to Him in faith, they will bring our hearts the assurance that we are well pleasing.

"Obey them that have the rule over you, and submit to them." Obedience and submission, even to men, for the Lord's sake: These, too, are elements of the self-sacrifice that is well pleasing to God. In the New Testament, we no longer have a priestly caste to intervene

between God and men; all God's saints are priests. But we have a God-ordained ministry with the gifts and the setting apart, and the duties and the authority, of which Acts and the epistles teach us so fully. This is no mere human arrangement but rather an appointment of Christ by the Holy Spirit, through which He carries out His work as the great Priest over the house of God. Such rulers are no lords over God's heritage and yet have a claim to the honor due to them. The relation between the teacher and the taught is of such importance in the church; the power of the teaching and the watching depends so much on the spirit of harmony and love that this element of the Christian life must be carefully cultivated if we are to suffer no harm. Obey and submit: These are words that may not be forgotten, *"for they watch in behalf of your souls, as they that shall give account."*

"Pray for us....And I exhort you the more exceedingly to do this, that I may be restored to you the sooner." Prayer, too, is one of the sacrifices we may offer; Jesus Himself, in the Garden, offered prayers and supplications. The writer, in the very spirit in which Paul wrote, not only asked for prayer but also believed that the intercession of the church would hasten his restoration to them. Our lives in the Holiest are indeed to be no selfish luxury; there is work there for us—work that calls for self-denial and self-sacrifice. Let us pray much for God's servants and all His saints, and let us be sure that greater wonders are wrought nowhere except where God is sought, by faith, in prayer.

Christian, you are a priest! You have access into the Holiest! Christ went in with the blood of His sacrifice. Enter continually with your sacrifice—the praise of God and the confession of His name; deeds of charity and beneficence; obedience and submission to those over you in the Lord; prayer and intercession. Through Him, let us continually offer.

Chapter Notes...

1. *"Through him"*! God can have no communication with the creature but through Him, that is, as He is in His Son. And we can have no access to God with our service but through

Andrew Murray

Him, that is, as we are in the Son and He, too, in us. God can delight in nothing but the perfect image of His Son. Let us, by faith, abide in Him and so, through Him, offer continually sacrifices that are well pleasing. As the great High Priest, He works it in us through His Spirit.

2. *"Through him...a sacrifice of praise"*—that is, in the joy that He gives, we praise God continually,

3. Self-sacrifice—the power and the glory of Christ's life upon earth. What a privilege that our whole lives, like His, may be ones of sacrifice, too: the sacrifice of praise and confession, of love and beneficence, of humility and submission, of prayer and intercession.

One Hundred Twenty-Seven
The God of Peace—
What He Has Done for Us

*Now the God of peace, who brought (again) from the dead
the great Shepherd of the sheep with the blood of the eternal
covenant, even our Lord Jesus, make you perfect.)*
—Hebrews 13:20–21

The epistle began by telling us that in all that Christ is and does, it is God speaking in us. The great work of Christ is to bring us to God. His death and His blood, His ascension and sitting on the throne—all mean one thing: our being brought near to dwell in God's presence. And with what object? That God may have us, to perfect us, and to work in us what is well pleasing in His sight. Let no one think that the entrance into the Holiest is the end; it is only the beginning of the true Christian life. It brings us into the right place and the right position, in which God now, in His divine power, can work out His own power in us, can make us in full truth one with Christ, can work the likeness of Christ into us.

We have reached the close of the epistle. The writer gathered up all his teaching in the two verses of this beautiful closing prayer.

Andrew Murray

As in it he commited his readers to God, the mention of God's name calls up all that he has said of God's work, and the first of the two verses sums up of all that God has done for us to bring us to Himself. Then follows, in the second verse, the prayer, with its promise of all that we can count upon this God to do in us, that we may live worthy of Him. He pointed to the work God has done for us as the ground and pledge of what He will do in us. The epistle has revealed to us God in Christ; it seeks to send us out into life with the assurance that as wonderful and mighty and perfect as was the work of God in Christ for us, will be His work through Christ, by the Spirit, in us. Let each one who has listened to the call, *"Let us draw near"* (10:22), remember that he has been brought to God; that God may now reveal Christ in Him; and that, as completely as He perfected Christ, He may perfect each one of us to do His will. The more we look to what God has done in Christ, as the pledge of what He will do in us, with the more confidence will accompany our faith's acceptance and expectation of it. And the more our desire is set upon the wonderful work God is yet to do in us, the more our hearts will be fixed in adoration on God Himself as our hope and our joy.

"The God of peace." This is the name by which we are invited to call upon and trust our God. Peace is the opposite of enmity, of war, of care, of unrest. Where everything is finished and perfect, there is peace and rest. God has set the Holiest open for us, in token that we may enter into His rest and trust Him to perfect His work in us. The peace of God, which passes all understanding, can now keep our hearts and minds by Christ Jesus. Peace, an end of all care and fear and separation, has been proclaimed; the God of peace is now waiting to do His work in us.

"Who brought again from the dead the great shepherd of the sheep with the blood of the eternal covenant." The epistle has nowhere directly made mention of the resurrection of Christ. But this was not needed: All its teaching was based upon the fact that He who died and shed His blood is now living in heaven. We have studied

the epistle in vain, and we will in vain attempt to live the true Christian life, if we have not learned that our salvation is not in the death of Jesus but in His life; it is in His death only as the gate to the risen life. And so, the God of peace, whom we are now invited to trust in, is spoken of as He who raised Jesus, the Shepherd of the sheep who gave His life for them, from the dead. Scripture ever points to the Resurrection as the mightiest part of God's mighty power; the God of the Resurrection is to be the God in whom we trust for the work to be done in us. He has raised Christ, as the Shepherd, who watches and tends His sheep, through whom He will do His work.

"With the blood of the eternal covenant." We know how the blood has been coupled in the epistle with the redemption of transgressions, the opening of the entrance into heaven, and the cleansing of the heart from all conscience of sin. Were it not for that bloodshed Christ would not have risen from the dead. In that blood, even the blood of the everlasting covenant, which could only be made after there had been a redemption for transgressions, God raised Jesus from the dead. It was the blood that sealed the covenant, by which the covenant blessings of perfect pardon, of the law written in the heart, and of direct fellowship with God were secured to us. It was the blood that had conquered sin and death and hell, that could give the entrance into heaven and cleanse the sinner's heart for the reception and experience of the heavenly life. And as those who are sprinkled with this blood, the secret of resurrection power, we are invited to trust the God of the Resurrection to work in us.

The God of peace, who raised Jesus from the dead in the blood of the covenant, *"make you perfect in every good thing to do his will"* (13:21). The God who perfected His Son through suffering to do His will, until He raised Him in triumph over death to His own right hand—O soul!—this same God is waiting to do this same work in you in the same power. What He did in Christ for you is all for the sake of what He is now day by day to do in you. All that you have learned of the wonders of His redeeming work and His receiving you into the Holiest is so that you might now confidently trust and expect Him to take possession of you and perfect His work within you. Oh, let us draw near and enter in—in the restful, adoring assurance that God will perfect us in every good thing.

Chapter Notes...

1. Peace is rest. To know the God of peace is to enter the rest of God. And until the soul rests in Him in Sabbath peace, God cannot do His higher, His perfect work.

2. The work of the Father and the Son for us find their completion in the work of the Holy Spirit within us. All the objective revelation is for the sake of the subjective experience, the mighty power of God working in the heart of His child what He longs to see. It is in what God makes us that the power of the redemption in Christ is proved.

3. *"By faith."* Here, more than ever, this must be our watchword—faith that sees and accepts and dwells in all God has done for us in Christ, and then counts upon His faithfulness and power to make it all real within us in Christ through the Spirit.

4. As it was through the Spirit that God wrought that perfect work in Christ by which fallen human nature, as He had taken it upon Himself, was redeemed and raised up and glorified, so nothing can make us partakers of that redeeming and quickening power but that same Spirit, truly living and working in our souls and bodies, in the same manner as it did in the humanity of Christ.

One Hundred Twenty-Eight

The God of Peace—What He Will Do in Us

Now the God of peace,...[make you perfect] in every good thing to do his will, working in us that which is well-pleasing in his sight, through Jesus Christ; to whom be the glory for ever and ever. Amen.
—Hebrews 13:20–21

[handwritten: equip you]
[handwritten: pleasing]

In our last meditation, we saw the link between the two verses of this wonderful benediction. All that God has done in the redemption in Christ is for the sake of what He wishes to effect in our hearts. All that He makes known to us of that redemption is to bring us to trust and yield ourselves to Him—to work out the inner, the subjective, redemption in the same power in which the objective, the heavenly, redemption has been effected. The Father longs to have back again the man he lost in Paradise, his image and likeness restored within us. All that Christ has done on earth and in heaven, even to His sitting at God's right hand, cannot satisfy the heart of God until He sees the kingdom set up within our hearts. There, the true power and glory of the Son are manifested.

Andrew Murray

"The God of peace,...make you perfect in every good thing to do his will." This, then, is the object of all that God has done. That the Son, who is God, should be our Redeemer; that the stupendous miracles of the Incarnation and the Atonement, the Resurrection and the seating of a man on the throne of God, should be wrought; that the Holy Spirit of God should be poured out from heaven—all this was with one view, that we should be brought to do the will of God. The whole relation between God and the creature depends on this one thing; without it there can be no true fellowship with God. It was for this that Jesus became man: *"Lo, I am come to do thy will"* (Hebrews 10:9). It was through this that He redeemed us. It is to make us partakers of the power to do this, that, as Mediator of the covenant, He puts the law in our hearts so that we may do the will of God on earth as in heaven. It is for this alone that He lives in heaven. The only proof and measure of the success of His work is that we do the will of God. Without this, all His work and ours is in vain.

"Now the God of peace,...make you perfect in every good thing to do his will." The doing of God's will depends entirely upon God's fitting us for it. As truly as God Himself perfected Christ and wrought out the redemption in Him must God perfect us to do His will. As surely as He did the first, He will do the second. The word *"perfect,"* used here, means to put into the right position or condition, to readjust, to equip, to fit a thing perfectly for its purpose. The prayer, *"God...make you perfect in every good thing,"* teaches that the work of God is not only a general enabling or endowing with power, leaving to us its use and application, but that He must also perfect us in each one of the good things we have to do; in this way alone can we do His will. It calls us to an absolute dependence upon the Father, as Jesus meant when He said, *"The Son can do nothing of himself"* (John 5:19). It seeks to bring us to a helplessness and a humility that just yields itself to God for every moment, and that counts upon Him, even as He wrought out the great salvation in Christ as a

whole, to work it in us in each minutest particular. With God, nothing is small or insignificant. He must be in things, little as great, All in All.

"Working in us that which is well-pleasing in his sight, through Jesus Christ." Here we have the explanation of how He perfects in us every good thing: He works in us through Jesus Christ. The three persons of the Godhead are indivisibly and inseparably one. The Father works through the Son and the Holy Spirit. When Jesus, our Priest-King, ascended the throne, He sent from the Father the Holy Spirit to be within us, the power and life of His redemption in heaven. Then the ministration of the Spirit, of the inner life, began on earth—God working in men what is pleasing in His sight, through Jesus Christ dwelling in the heart. Then the fruit of Christ's work was made manifest—men on earth, in very deed, doing the will of God and working what was pleasing in His sight because He Himself worked it in them, through Jesus Christ.

Let this parting prayer teach us a double lesson. It is a promise of what God will do. He will perfect us—put us in the right position and give us the right condition of heart—*"in every good thing to do His will,"* Himself *"working in us that which is well-pleasing in his sight, through Jesus Christ."* Let us read the words until we know in truth what God is waiting to do. The prayer becomes then a call to us to prayer and faith. Let us fix our hearts in faith on God and what He has wrought through Christ for us. Let us fix them in faith on what He will do in us through Christ, as surely and as mightily. All that God has done in Christ is only a beginning, a promise, a pledge of what He will do in us. Let that faith stir our desire to rest content with nothing less than the actual experience of the truth of this prayer-promise. Let that faith begin in prayer to claim and embrace and own it as our very own, waiting in deep dependence and humility on God to do it. And let every thought of the teaching of the Hebrews just culminate in a blessed act of adoring surrender. O Thou, God of peace, here I am. Thou will do it.

Andrew Murray

Chapter Notes...

1. God *"working in us."* Look upward in wonder and worship. Turn inward in stillness and meekness of heart, taking time to yield to the Spirit's working. And regard your heart as indeed the sphere of the working of the living God.

2. Pray, pray, pray! The blessing of the epistle, the power of redemption, must come from above. It comes certainly to the heart open toward God and thirsting for Him.

3. *"Make you perfect"*: This means fitting you perfectly to be subject to Him, and in dependence and humility and faith, working what He works in you. It is often a misapprehension or a difficulty that hinders. God can restore you in one moment to the right relation or position.

4. A road is only good for that to which it brings as its end. The whole Gospel is nothing but a way to this end, God finding His place in our hearts to dwell and work there what is pleasing in His sight, so that we do His will.

One Hundred Twenty-Nine
Glory Be to God

Working in us that which is well-pleasing in his sight, [pleasing]
through Jesus Christ; to whom be the
glory for ever and ever. Amen.
—Hebrews 13:21

"To whom be the glory for ever and ever." No wonder that the heart of the author bursted out in adoration. In the closing prayer he had summed up all the glory of what God had done in Christ, and was now waiting to work in us. He had pronounced over his readers the blessing of the God who revealed Himself in His Son and who longs to reveal Himself in us for our complete deliverance; the writer's whole soul bowed in wonder, joy, and worship. The sight of the God who has raised Jesus from the dead, drawing nigh to do His mighty work in us, too, brings the song to His lips: "To [Him] *be the glory for ever and ever"!* Oh, that we may ever learn so to study and admire and appropriate the mysteries of redeeming grace that every mention of it leads to the spontaneous outburst, "Glory be to God!"

It is doubtful whether the *"whom"* refers to God or to Christ; It appears more probable that the writer meant God, to whose glorious work the whole prayer refers. But the question will cause us no difficulty. In Scripture, the same adoration is given to the Son as to the Father. (See 1 Timothy 6:13–16; 2 Peter 3:18; Revelation 1:5–6.) The throne is that of God and the Lamb. All the honor that goes up to the Father goes through the Son He shares in it. And all the honor given to the Son goes through Him to the Father. It is ever of God, in Christ, that we say, *"To whom be the glory."*

Without this note of praise, it is as if there would have been something wanting in the epistle. In God's temple, the chief thing is the praise and honor of Him who dwells there. The epistle has opened up to us the way into the Holiest. It has spoken to us of the glory of the Priest-King whom God has set at His own right hand for our sakes; and of His all-prevailing blood; and of the entrance we have into God's presence for Him to reign and work in us and fit us to enjoy and to serve Him. It has spoken of the continual sacrifice of praise we ought to render. And yet, the writer never sounded a note of praise. But here, at last, when he called us to look back to all that God has done for us, and forward to all that He will do in us, the voice of adoration sounds forth: *"To* [Him] *be the glory for ever and ever."* The joy of heaven consists in this: that they do not rest day or night in the worship and praise of God and the Lamb. If we are indeed come to Mount Zion and into the very presence of God Himself, let our lives and walks ever be in the spirit of adoration: *"To* [Him] *be the glory forever"*! The man who has not learned to praise, with whom it never breaks out spontaneously, has not learned to know his God aright, has not yet tasted the joy of a full salvation.

If we would learn the secret of a life-giving glory to God, on earth as in heaven, it must be found in the faith and the experience spoken of in the prayer to which this doxology belongs. The praise was born out of it, in the heart of the writer; it must be so with our hearts, too. The more we gaze upon Christ, our Priest-King; and upon His precious, cleansing, saving blood; and upon the new covenant, sealed in that blood; and upon the new heart with God's Spirit in it as our law; and upon God Himself who hath done it all—the more we gaze upon these, the more we will feel urged to fall down and worship, *"To* [Him] *be the glory for ever and ever."* But especially—as we claim and realize and yield ourselves to the promise that is the outcome of this great redemption, *"Now the God of peace...make you perfect in every good thing to do his will"* (Hebrews 13:20–21), working in you what is pleasing in His sight—our hearts will swell with joy unspeakable and praise unutterable that can only find relief in the cry, "To Him be glory, to Him be glory!"

I know that it is just here a difficulty will come to many. The promise appears so high, and its fulfillment in their experience— God perfecting them in every good thing—so impossible, that even the praise that came when they thought upon what God had done, passes away. Let me speak one word to such: Just look at this great universe. The God who made it all, the sun and moon and stars, the mighty mountains and the great ocean—this God cares for every blade of grass and gives it its life and beauty. The greatest and the least are alike to Him; He cares for the whole and for each minute detail. And, even so, He who wrought out the mighty redemption in Christ is now still working out, in the same power and love, its application in every soul—in every moment and in every circumstance. God has not done part and left the other part dependent on us. God is All and must, in very deed, do all. As the God of peace, who raised Christ from the dead, He must work in you every good thing that can be pleasing in His sight. And He will do it. What He began in Christ, He will finish in you. A great artist attends to the minutest details. God is engaged, as He perfected Christ the Head, in perfecting every member of His body. He does this by Himself working in us. The Spirit of God's Son sent into our hearts as an inward life, Christ dwelling in our hearts, God working in us—oh, it is when this is believed and waited for and, in some measure, experienced, that the whole life becomes a song of praise: *"To* [Him] *be the glory for ever and ever"*!

Friend, having boldness through the blood, let us draw near and dwell in God's presence. Let us worship Him for what He has done. Let us, in tenderness of spirit, adore Him as the God who is working in us through Christ Jesus. Let us, in deep humility, yield ourselves to Him, to be made so fully one with Christ that Christ may be seen to dwell in us. And the flame of God's love will break out and burn and rise heavenward without ceasing: *"To* [Him] *be the glory for ever and ever"*! *"To* [Him] *be the glory for ever and ever"*!

Chapter Notes...

1. *"As in heaven, so on earth"* (Matthew 6:10). What God has wrought in heaven, through Christ, is the pledge of what He will work in my heart. As I receive this into my heart, His will will be done in me, on earth as in heaven, because He does it Himself. And as in heaven, so in my heart—the praise will never end.

2. My heart, the temple where God dwells and reveals His work and His glory; all in the hidden power of the Holy Spirit!

3. *"To* [Him] *be the glory for ever and ever"*! Lord Jesus, the great High Priest beside the altar, the Minister of the sanctuary—it is because of Thy care that the fire ever burns, and the song never ends, to the glory of the Father.

One Hundred Thirty

Parting Words

*But I exhort you, brethren, bear with the word of exhortation:
for I have written unto you in few words. Know ye that our
brother Timothy hath been set at liberty; with whom, if he
come shortly, I will see you. Salute all them that have the rule
over you, and all the saints. They of Italy salute you.
Grace be with you all. Amen.*

—Hebrews 13:22–25

[handwritten annotations: "urge", "briefly", "take notice", "had released", "admonition or reproof encourage-ment", "soon", "Greet leaders", "Those from greet"]

T hese closing verses are so entirely in the spirit of Paul that,
involuntarily, we feel as if we were listening to him. The
mention of Timothy, of his deliverance and of the hope of
accompanying him, the greeting to the rulers in the church and to
all the saints, the greetings from the saints of Italy, and the final
benediction—all remind us of what we find in his epistles.

"I exhort you, brethren, bear with the word of exhortation."
Before the writer closed, one more word of exhortation; and that
is to bear, to submit to, and to accept the exhortation he had sent
them. The word he used means both admonition or reproof (as in
Hebrews 12:5) and encouragement (as in 6:18). The epistle has
combined both elements most remarkably. In the five warnings and
in its exhortatory parts, its tone has been one of faithful reproof,

with a view to convict of sin, to awaken to a sense of danger, and to urge to repentance. At the same time, everything has been done to quicken faith and hope and to urge to steadfastness by pointing to the strong encouragement found in the Word of God and the power of Christ.

To us, the closing message comes, too: *"Bear,"* yield yourselves to, *"the word of exhortation."* Exhortation is indeed the main characteristic of the epistle. It comes to us as an intensely practical, personal appeal, to give ourselves wholly to the Son of God from heaven, and to live the heavenly life He offers to work within us. We may gather up its chief thoughts in four of the words it has used more than once.

"Take heed"! Its tone is one of solemn warning against the danger of negligence and sloth, disobedience and doublemindedness, unbelief and falling away. Let us yield to its discovery of sin and danger. Let us beware lest the contentment with beginnings; a resting short of an entire devotion to God and perfect conformity to Jesus; a selfish desire to have salvation and heaven without the very Spirit of Christ and of heaven—lest any of these deceive us so that, like Israel, we perish halfway between Egypt and Canaan.

"Press on"! Let us accept its teaching of what the true aim of the Christian life is. We are to give due diligence to enter and dwell in the rest of God. We are to press on to perfection, to be like men running a race for life. We are to take Jesus as our Leader and Forerunner, to follow Him in the path of perfect obedience to God's will and entire self-sacrifice. We are to enter with Him into the Holiest, to make God's presence our home, and His fellowship our daily portion and our chief joy. We are to be like the old saints, to go out from our homes, to live in the pilgrim spirit, seeking a heavenly country. Yea, we are to live as those who are come to the heavenly Jerusalem. We are to go forth to Him without the camp, bearing His reproach, wholly identified with Him. Let us press on. Let us run. Let us enter in. Let us go forth. This is what the exhortation means.

"Consider...Jesus." The one sure and effectual remedy the epistle offers for all the prevailing feebleness and danger of the Christian life, we know. It has been said to us, "You do not know Jesus aright." The knowledge that sufficed for conversion does not avail for sanctification and perfection. You must know Jesus better. Consider Jesus! As God! As the Man! In His sympathy! In His obedience! In His suffering! In His blood! In His glory on the throne; opening heaven; bringing you in to God; breathing the law of God and the Spirit of heaven into your heart as your very life! As little as you can reach heaven with your hand can you, of yourself, live such a heavenly life. And yet, it is possible because God has borne witness to the Gospel of His Son with the gift of the Holy Spirit. The Priest-King, on His ascension to the throne, sent down the Holy Spirit into the hearts of His disciples and, with Him, returned Himself to dwell in those who, in the power of His heavenly life, they might live with Him. Consider Jesus, and you will see that you can live in the heavenlies with Him because He lives in you! *Yes + I in Him!*

"By faith"! This word is the key to all. By faith, in fullness of faith, we can inherit every promise! Faith is moved with godly fear and takes heed! Faith obeys and forsakes all and presses on to enter the land! Faith looks to Jesus, holds fast its boldness, draws near to God, and goes forth without the camp! Faith sees how, in Christ, God has worked out His will; sees that this God will just as surely work in us, too, what is pleasing in His sight; and sees that this God conquers every difficulty and every enemy. By faith, we inherit every promise and dare to sing even now, *"To [Him] be the glory for ever and ever"* (13:21)! *Glory be to the Father and to the Son + to the Holy Ghost, as it was in the beginning is now + ever shall be. World without end. Amen. Amen. 10/03/1*

Chapter Notes...

1. You will find it most profitable to look back over the whole epistle and see whether you have grasped its teaching, and then to say whether you are making it the one aim of your life to live up fully to its glorious revelation of the life of God.

Andrew Murray

2. *The Holiest of All* is the title of our book. I think you see how it expresses the central thought of the epistle. It is the spiritual life-state into which Jesus entered and opened the way for you and calls you to enter in. Have you entered? Are you dwelling there? Are you there now daily drinking in the Holy Spirit of Jesus, yielding to the Father to make you perfectly conformed to the humble, obedient, holy Jesus, your Leader and Forerunner? Oh, do not rest without a full experience of the heavenly priesthood of Jesus and of the heavenly sanctuary as your abode.

3. Grace be with you all, beloved readers; all the grace this epistle has so wondrously revealed; all the day and for all and every need. With all of you, not one excepted—Amen.

About the Author
Andrew Murray

A ndrew Murray (1828–1917) was an amazingly prolific Christian writer. He lived and ministered as both a pastor and author in the towns and villages of South Africa. Some of Murray's earliest works were written to provide nurture and guidance to Christians, whether young or old in the faith; they were actually an extension of his pastoral work. Once books such as *Abide in Christ, Like Christ,* and *With Christ in the School of Prayer* were written, Murray became widely known, and new books from his pen were awaited with great eagerness throughout the world.

He wrote to give daily practical help to many of the people in his congregation who lived out in the farming communities and could only come into town for church services on rare occasions. As he wrote these books of instruction, Murray adopted the practice of placing many of his more devotional books into thirty-one separate readings to correspond with the days of the month.

At the age of seventy-eight, Murray resigned from the pastorate and devoted most of his time to his manuscripts. He continued to write profusely, moving from one book to the next with an intensity of purpose and a zeal that few men of God have ever equaled. He often said of himself, rather humorously, that he was like a hen about to hatch an egg; he was restless and unhappy until he got the burden of the message off his mind.

During these later years, after hearing of pocket-sized paper-backs, Andrew Murray immediately began to write books to be published in that fashion. He thought it was a splendid way to have the teachings of the Christian life at your fingertips, where they could be carried around and read at any time of the day.

One source has said of Andrew Murray that his prolific style possesses the strength and eloquence that are born of deep earnestness and a sense of the solemnity of the issues of the Christian life. Nearly every page reveals an intensity of purpose and appeal that stirs men to the depths of their souls. Murray moves the emotions, searches the conscience, and reveals the sins and shortcomings of many of us with a love and hope born out of an intimate knowledge of the mercy and faithfulness of God.

For Andrew Murray, prayer was considered our personal home base from which we live our Christian lives and extend ourselves to others. During his later years, the vital necessity of unceasing prayer in the spiritual life came to the forefront of his teachings. It was then that he revealed the secret treasures of his heart concerning a life of persistent and believing prayer.

Countless people the world over have hailed Andrew Murray as their spiritual father and given credit for much of their Christian growth to the influence of his priceless devotional books.

Ps 104:4 MSG   O my soul, bless God!

God, my God, how great you are
            beautifully, gloriously rob[ed]
Dressed up in sunshine,
      all all heaven stretched out
            for your tent.
      You built your palace on the ocea[n]
made a chariot out of clouds & took off
      on wind-wings.
      You commandeered winds as messenge[rs]
appointed fire & flame as ambassadors.

Heb 1:1-2 Going through a long line of prophe[ts]
God has been addressing our ancestors in
different ways for centuries. Recently He spoke
to us <u>directly</u> through His Son. By His Son, God
created the world in the beginning, + it will all
belong to the Son at the end. This Son perfectly
mirrors God, & is stamped with God's nature.
He holds everything tog. by what He says —
powerful words!